GOOD FAITH IN INTERNATIONAL LAW

There is a great degree of controversy on the proper complexion and role of general principles of law in the international legal order. Opinions range from total rejection of some types of principles to the most enthusiastic endorsement of principles as the necessary oil for the many complex wheels of the legal order.

In this book one of the leading public lawyers of his generation explores the concept of good faith and its role in international law. Rather than offer a detailed, comprehensive examination, Kolb aims to map the true points of gravity of the principle of good faith in the international legal order. In so doing, he illustrates how the various legal institutions who operate in the sphere of public international law allow the principle of good faith to unfold.

Good Faith in International Law

Robert Kolb

·HART·
PUBLISHING
OXFORD AND PORTLAND, OREGON
2017

Hart Publishing
An imprint of Bloomsbury Publishing Plc

Hart Publishing Ltd
Kemp House
Chawley Park
Cumnor Hill
Oxford OX2 9PH
UK

Bloomsbury Publishing Plc
50 Bedford Square
London
WC1B 3DP
UK

www.hartpub.co.uk
www.bloomsbury.com

Published in North America (US and Canada) by
Hart Publishing
c/o International Specialized Book Services
920 NE 58th Avenue, Suite 300
Portland, OR 97213-3786
USA

www.isbs.com

HART PUBLISHING, the Hart/Stag logo, BLOOMSBURY and the Diana logo are trademarks of Bloomsbury Publishing Plc

First published 2017

British Library Cataloguing-in-Publication Data
A catalogue record for this book is available from the British Library.

ISBN: HB: 978-1-50991-409-8
ePDF: 978-1-50991-406-7
ePub: 978-1-50991-407-4

Library of Congress Cataloging-in-Publication Data

Names: Kolb, Robert, author.

Title: Good faith in international law / Robert Kolb.

Description: Oxford [UK] ; Portland, Oregon : Hart Publishing, 2017. | Includes bibliographical references and index.

Identifiers: LCCN 2017006467 (print) | LCCN 2017008743 (ebook) | ISBN 9781509914098 (hardback : alk. paper) | ISBN 9781509914074 (Epub)

Subjects: LCSH: Good faith (Law)

Classification: LCC K579.G6 K65 2017 (print) | LCC K579.G6 (ebook) | DDC 341—dc23

LC record available at https://lccn.loc.gov/2017006467

Typeset by Compuscript Ltd, Shannon
Printed and bound in Great Britain by Lightning Source UK Ltd

PREFACE

After I had transformed my habilitation thesis written in French on the notion of *jus cogens* into a small and apparently elegant little booklet in English,[1] the idea in due course ripened to do the same with my earlier doctoral thesis on good faith in international law,[2] and thereby to make it more widely accessible to the English-speaking public. The original PhD thesis slightly exceeded 750 pages; the present work is a shortened version of the work deposited at the Graduate Institute of International studies, Geneva University as my original PhD. Being now in a wholly different phase of life, I have little sympathy with the idea of reproducing the many detailed informative (or otherwise) reasoned passages of the original. I thought it more expedient and more rewarding—both for me and for the reader—to shorten the text to the gist of the matters, thus better mapping the true points of gravity of the principle of good faith in the international legal order. Better mapping I said—better mapping because a less tortuous and less leafy tree lays more bare the main lines of functioning of a principle, and allows one to understand more at first glimpse. For those who prefer a more detailed argument, there is still be the original published thesis, albeit burdened with the unforgiveable odium of having been written in French. Since I sought to shorten the original text, it may be understood that I dropped the many explanatory passages on the scope and functioning of the legal institutions mentioned in the table of contents, and focused only on their link with good faith and how they allow the latter to function in, and factor itself into, the legal order. In other words, the point is now more essentially than it was in the doctoral thesis to show how the various legal institutions mentioned allow the principle of good faith to unfold in the legal order; and less to show how the various institutions are built up in themselves. This also means that I suppose more knowledge on the part of the reader of this text than was the case with my doctoral thesis. That may be a slight privilege of increasing age.

Cutting down the number of words and areas of exploration was not enough. I had written my PhD in the midst of the 1990s. Since then, the law has developed. In particular, WTO law was still in its infancy at the time of the original draft. Since then, it has developed a robust doctrine of the protection of legitimate expectations, which required an entirely new chapter to be presented in this book.

[1] *Peremptory International Law (Jus Cogens)* (Oxford, 2015).
[2] *La bonne foi en droit international public* (Paris, 2000).

I also added some other chapters (eg the one on the 'critical date' or on international investment law) and reintroduced a chapter (on the law of armed conflicts) that I had written for the original PhD but dropped for its published version, for reasons of space. I chose to omit certain small entries contained in the published PhD, since they are marginal in state practice: eg the doctrine on 'sudden change' or issues linked to instructions of an agent in the negotiation of treaties (article 47 of the VCLT). The interested reader can be referred to the French text on these points—once again apologising for the use of a language nobody decent could think to write in! The overall hope is thereby expressed that I managed to somewhere square the circle with a text that is at once precise enough to be useful, yet lightened enough to be agreeable. I updated the text in each chapter with regard to newer documents, case law, doctrinal writings, and so on; but overall I have been somewhat sparing in the process, considering that I had over 5,000 footnotes replete with materials in the original PhD. I did not want to inflate the already present older materials with many new ones.

There are two further points to be shortly made. First, I refer in the footnotes to developments contained in the published PhD which I have not included into the present version. Second, as the reader will recall, I allowed myself to make some borderline jokes about the French language in the lines above. The point was to some extent to instil in the Anglo-Saxon reader a modest degree of regret for not reading often enough languages other than English. In order to encourage him or her on the road to greater linguistic openness, I shall quote in the present book from the most different European languages, with the only restriction that I ought to be able to understand them. *Inter*national law is certainly a commonplace for many cultures and approaches; it cannot be properly grasped when approached from a unique cultural (and consequently to some extent also linguistic) lens.

One further purely formal remark is in place. When some work is quoted in an abridged form in the footnotes (eg Kolb, *Bonne*), reference is thereby implicitly made to the bibliography appended to the text. The mention op cit points to a work quoted or referred to in the preceding footnote.

CONTENTS

ABBREVIATIONS

AADI: Annuaire africain de droit international
AFDI: Annuaire français de droit international
AJIL: American Journal of International Law
ASDI: Annuaire suisse de droit international
ASIL Proceedings: American Society of International Law Proceedings
ATF: Arrêts du Tribunal fédéral
AVR: Archiv des Völkerrechts
BYIL: British Yearbook of International Law
CJEU: Court of Justice of the European Communities
CYIL: Canadian Yearbook of International Law
ECHR: European Convention on Human Rights
ECtHR: European Court of Human Rights
EJIL: European Journal of International Law
GATT: General Agreement on Tariffs and Trade
GYIL: German Yearbook of International Law
IACHR: Inter-American Convention on Human Rights
IACtHR: Inter-American Court of Human Rights
ICC: International Criminal Court
ICCo: International Chamber of Commerce (Paris)
ICJ: International Court of Justice
ICLQ: International and Comparative Law Quarterly
ICSID: International Center for the Settlement of Investment Disputes
ICTY: International Criminal Tribunal for the Former Yugoslavia
IDI: Institut de droit international
ILC: International Law Commission
ILR: International Law Reports
ITLOS: International Tribunal for the Law of the Sea (Hamburg)

JDI:	Journal du droit international (Clunet)
NAFTA:	North American Free Trade Agreement
NILR:	Netherlands International Law Review
NYIL:	Netherlands Yearbook of International Law
ÖZöR(V):	Österreichische Zeitschrift für öffentliches Recht (und Völkerrecht)
PCA:	Permanent Court of Arbitration
PCIJ:	Permanent Court of International Justice
RBDI:	Revue belge de droit international
RCADI:	Recueil des Cours de l'Académie de droit international de La Haye
RDI:	Rivista di diritto internazionale
REDI:	Revista española de derecho internacional
RGDIP:	Revue générale de droit international public
RHDI:	Revue hellénique de droit international
RSDIE:	Revue suisse de droit international et de droit européen
UN:	United Nations
UNCC:	United Nations Compensation Commission (for Iraq)
UNCIO:	United Nations Conference on International Organization
VCLT:	Vienna Convention on the Law of Treaties, 1969
WTO:	Word Trade Organization
Yb.:	Yearbook
ZaöRV:	Zeitschrift für ausländisches öffentliches Recht und Völkerrecht
ZöR:	Zeitschrift für öffentliches Recht

Part I

The Definition and Scope of Good Faith in Public International Law

1

The Role of Principles in the Body of Public International Law

There is a great degree of controversy on the proper complexion and role of general principles of law in the international legal order. Opinions range from total rejection of some types of principles (in particular municipal law analogies) to the most enthusiastic endorsement of principles as the necessary oil for the many complex wheels of the legal order.[1] Overall, positivistic authors have been more circumspect and hostile,[2] since principles can play a dynamic role and tend to escape to some degree from the all too sharp constraints of a purely consensual international legal order. Conversely, more policy-oriented scholars and natural law jurists were and are in most cases ideologically sympathetic to general principles of law,[3] since they allow the instillation into the law of some moral, political or other content, flexibilising and civilising its application.

We shall not pursue an attempted definition of the general principles. There are many different types of principles,[4] ranging from 'principles of international law' rooted in customary law, to municipal law analogies for closing gaps of international law, to principles inherent in the very idea of law, to legal maxims and rules abstracted from a given set of detailed norms by some induction (e.g. the principle-maxim of the 'proper administration of justice'), and to yet others. What is common to all these principles is that they tend to have a general legal structure, i.e. a normative content which is not limited to a specific set of facts but which can be used in many situations, sometimes throughout the whole legal order, as the basis for legal argument. Legal solutions can then be 'deduced' or 'abstracted' from the principle; or at least the principle can serve as an argumentative basis for upholding a certain legal result. Some of these principles, especially the most powerful of the legal order, are the basis for the development of a series of concretisations, ie subordinate principles, rules, maxims and norms, which will carry

[1] See the detailed developments in R Kolb, *Bonne* 3ff.

[2] See, eg AP Sereni, *Diritto internazionale*, vol I (Milan, 1956) 156. See also L Kopelmanas, 'Quelques réflexions au sujet de l'article 38,3 du Statut de la CPJI' (1936) 43 *RGDIP* 293ff.

[3] See, eg A Verdross, *Die Quellen des universellen Völkerrechts* (Freiburg, 1973) 120ff.

[4] On these several meanings of the concept of principles, see B Vitanyi, 'Les positions doctrinales concernant le sens de la notion de principes généraux de droit reconnus par les nations civilisées' (1982) 86 *RGDIP* 48ff.

the normative content of the principle to concrete applications in the various branches of the legal order where they are operating. Such principles can be likened to the sun, lighting up the most remote corners of the legal order to realise some normative injunction or idea—eg the 'protection of legitimate expectations', linked to the principle of good faith; or the 'less-onerous means' idea, linked to the principle of proportionality. Considering the principles as providers of some general legal ideas (i.e. general normative contents), which can and must operate in various complexions across the legal order, what then are the main functions of the general principles of law?

There are several such functions:

(i) *Logical function*. From the logical point of view, there are some general principles which must be supposed so as to be able to conceive a functioning legal order. Without these principles, the construction of the sources would fall into a vicious circle. Thus, for example, the principle *pacta sunt servanda* is a necessary normative proposition in any developed legal order. Practically speaking, it stands to reason that if the pledged word was not binding, an international legal order would be impossible. Moreover, a derogation to this principle is logically impossible. It is thus a special type of *jus cogens*, albeit the principle has its own legal exceptions when considering it with regard to specific agreements (e.g. the doctrine of fundamental change of circumstances). If some actors agreed not to honour their agreements, they would at least have to honour their agreement not to honour; and this again supposes the rule *pacta sunt servanda*. Finally, from a violation of the principle there could never flow its legal inexistence or desuetude. The principle remains a logical and axiological premise. This aspect brings out the particular legal complexion of such primary principles within the legal order. They are on this account different from ordinary customary rules based on practice and opinion.[5] The main difference lies in the fact that they must always be supposed in practice and that they have in fact been so supposed. In a sense, the principle has thus gained a customary cloth over time, but its legal root lies deeper. It lies in some original legal conviction that the principle ought to rule social relations. The result is that such principles are consequently intensely normative and are not based on induction to be valid. Their number is extremely limited; to the rule *pacta sunt servanda*, good faith may be added.

(ii) *Axiological function*. Some general principles serve to maintain the fundamental unity of the system of international law beyond its almost infinite variety (the function is here one of *unitas in varietate*). They guarantee some minimum common ground of values, functions and concepts, without

[5] D Anzilotti, *Cours de droit international* (Paris, 1929) 44–45. We may also recall Winkler, who was right when he proclaimed that: 'In tota iurisprudentia, nihil est quod minus legaliter tractari possit quam ipsa principia' (B Winkler, *Principiorum juris* (Leipzig, 1615), lib I, cap II, first phrase).

which the legal order would dissolve itself into concurring and unrelated legal blocks. Verdross has aptly insisted on this aspect: 'The positive international law contained in customary and conventional rules is composed of a number of isolated rules and precedents. In order to become a system, these rules and precedents need some directing principles'.[6] He adds this: 'Without these principles … international law would not only be silent on many matters, but also scattered into a mass of detailed rules and precedents which no common link would unite'.[7] This particular form of normativity leads to principles which—as we have seen—can serve as starting points for deductive or concretising reasoning. The legal operator will avoid pure legal conceptualism or usurpation of the legislative function by carefully considering the social necessities, the acceptability of certain deductions for the states and existing international practice. It may thus occur that a principle can be abstracted from the arenas of practice through a meticulous analysis of analogy, deduction and induction.[8] The principle will then not be simply subjectively postulated; it will have its roots in some complexion of international practice. Once shaped, the principle will develop some autonomy and be able to format further legal arguments. It may serve to develop the law, to fill gaps within the law, to elaborate new rules or to sustain a deductive conclusion. Thus, for example, the principle *pacta sunt servanda* can be extracted (apart from its logical necessity) from the practice with respect to agreements, contracts and treaties, and later serve as normative pillar to deduce or to accompany—together with the principle of good faith—the binding character of unilateral acts such as promises (*promissio vel pollicitatio est servanda*).[9] Through such a course, the value of faithfulness and legitimate expectation is being transported throughout the legal system.

(iii) *Normative function*. The principles reinforce the reach and the density of international law. As has been aptly noted: 'By introducing general principles of law recognised by civilised nations into the sources of applicable law, the drafters of the Court's Statute purported to develop to its utmost degree the domain of judicially applicable law, and, as has been claimed, to push to apogee the productivity of the sources'.[10] There are several functions here.

[6] A Verdross, 'Les principes généraux du droit applicables aux rapports internationaux' (1938) 45 *RGDIP* 50 (our translation).

[7] ibid, 52.

[8] See the interesting developments described in K Engisch, *Einführung in das juristische Denken*, 3rd edn (Stuttgart, 1956) 134ff. According to one famous definition, the principle is: 'Principes de droit: Propositions premières dégagées de l'ensemble du système juridique par voie de synthèse, considérées comme exactes et susceptibles, en conséquence, de justifier des déductions dans l'ordre juridique' (J Basdevant (ed)), *Dictionnaire de la terminologie du droit international* (Paris, 1960) 472. See also M Virally, 'Le rôle des « principes » dans le développement du droit international', in M Virally (ed), *Le droit international en deveni* (Paris, 1990) 201–02, 204, 212.

[9] See the reasoning of the ICJ in the *Nuclear Test* cases: (1974) *ICJ Reports* 267–68, §§ 43ff and 472–73, §§ 45ff.

[10] C de Visscher, *Théories et réalités en droit international public*, 4th edn (Paris, 1970) 419 (our translation).

First, the general principles complement the customary and conventional rules by filling potential gaps. It is open to debate, indeed controversial, as to whether true gaps exist in the legal order.[11] For the present purposes, it suffices to note that through the principles, the normative content of international law is increased to the detriment of the residual domain of state freedom.[12] Thus, if any rule in one of the other recognised sources of international law is lacking, the general principles can serve as the last possible pillar on which to erect a legal reasoning so as to 'discover' some auxiliary rule. When the conduct of one state infringes on a legitimate interest of another state, or creates some damage to that other state, but no norm of international law expressly prohibits this course, there is the possibility of looking at the matter through the lens of some principle, e.g. good faith, abuse of rights, proportionality, or the principle that a state may not allow the use of its territory in a way that breaches the rights of other states ('principle not to allow use of territory injurious to other states').[13] *Second*, principles provide a tool for the interpretation of customary or conventional norms.[14] Thus, municipal norms contested from the point of view of international human rights law are often evaluated with regard to general principles relating to necessity and proportionality.[15] Good faith and reasonableness[16] are used as a standard for the interpretation of discretionary powers of states, notably when the latter have extraterritorial effect or affect rights or interests of third states. *Third*, general principles of law influence the formation of conventional and customary rules of international law, and sometimes also of rules of internal law (legislation).[17] Thus, in international humanitarian law, the whole normative process is profoundly influenced by the fact that each rule is a compromise between the countervailing principles of humanity on the one side and military necessity on the other. These are two fundamental general principles of IHL.[18] By the same token, in the context of the law relating to the expulsion of foreigners, the rules have been elaborated so as to take account of the gravity of

[11] See I Stribis, *La manifestation des lacunes en droit international* (Athens, 2009).

[12] P Guggenheim, *Traité de droit international public*, vol I, 2nd edn (Geneva, 1967) 296–97.

[13] As to the latter, see the classical reasoning of the *Trail Smelter* arbitral tribunal (1941), *RIAA*, vol III 1963ff. The principle was repeated by the ICJ some years later in the *Corfu Channel* case, Merits, (1949) *ICJ Reports* 22, and later became a pillar of international environmental law.

[14] H Lauterpacht, *The Development of International Law by the International Court* (London, 1958) 158ff; W Friedmann, 'The Uses of General Principles in the Development of International Law', (1963) 57 *AJIL* 286.

[15] See eg W Kälin and J Künzli, *The Law of International Human Rights Protection* (Oxford, 2009) 99ff; FG Jacobs and RC White, *The European Convention on Human Rights*, 2nd edn (Oxford, 1996) 304ff.

[16] O Corten, *L'utilisation du 'raisonnable' par le juge international* (Brussels, 1997). See, on this issue, eg the *Iron Rhine Railway* case (2005) XXVII *RIAA* 100ff, in particular § 204.

[17] See P Reuter, *Droit international public*, 6th edn (Paris, 1983) 119.

[18] C. Rousseau, *Le droit des conflits armés* (Paris, 1983) 21.

the motives of expulsion and therefore of proportionality.[19] *Fourth*, general principles allow the judge to blow some flexibility into the law to be applied and sometimes even to develop international law.[20] This need is characteristic of new areas into which international law progressively extends.[21] The development of the modern law of maritime delimitation around the concept of 'equitable principles' (between 1969 and the 1990) is an interesting example.[22] For a long time, the international law of environmental protection has remained anchored in the main principle of the law of neighbourhood, namely: *sic utere tuo ut alienum non laedas*. In other words, a state may not use or allow the use of its territory in a way trespassing on the territory of neighbouring states, if the damage crosses the threshold of a certain gravity. Only progressively has that body of the law been enriched by a much larger perspective, where however the principle *sic utere tuo ut alienum non laedas* has continued to play a dynamic role.[23]

(iv) *Unifying function*. The application of the same or similar general principles across the different branches of the law—and even across the legal orders—accentuates the unity of the legal phenomenon. In addition to the axiological and systematic unity mentioned above, there comes a certain practical unity of common legal experiences and of common legal language. The general principles allow a degree of fluidity of the master ideas of the law throughout its provinces. By way of analogies, these key ideas can be transported from one legal branch to the other.[24] The principles are in this regard like a currency which allows exchanges. Thus, it has been demonstrated how general principles have contributed to a progressive interrelation of private and public law, which were anciently separated with significantly greater rigidity.[25] Necessity and proportionality, or good faith/reasonableness, are

[19] This subject matter has considerably gained in political controversy in the last years and is now under consideration at the ILC: see www.legal.un.org/ilc/.

[20] See eg the classical works by H Lauterpacht, *Private Law Analogies and Sources of International Law* (London, 1927); and B Cheng, *General Principles of Law—As Applied by International Courts and Tribunals* (London, 1953). For good faith, see in particular S Rosenne, 'The Perplexities of Modern International Law' (2001) 291 *RCADI* 466.

[21] This has for a long time been the case in the context of international contracts: see eg P Weil, 'Principes généraux du droit et contrats d'Etat', *Essays in Honor of B Goldman* (Paris, 1982) 387ff.

[22] P Weil, *Perspectives du droit de la délimitation maritime* (Paris, 1988).

[23] On the international law of environment and its development, see eg U Beyerlin, *Umweltvölkerrecht* (Munich, 2000); P Sands, *Principles of International Environmental Law*, 2nd edn (Cambridge, 2003); AC Kiss and D Shelton, *International Environmental Law*, 3rd edn (New York, 2004); PW Birnie, AE Boyle and C Redgwell, *International Law and the Environment*, 3rd edn (Oxford, 2009); see now also D Bodansky, J Brunée and E Hey (eds), *The Oxford Handbook of International Environmental Law* (Oxford, Oxford University Press, 2007).

[24] Analogy is a fundamental tool of human reasoning in general, and of legal reasoning in particular. It was used extensively by the glossarors of the Middle Ages, when trying to harmonise the various passages of the *Corpus Juris* by 'concordantia discordantium' and by 'procedere ad similia': see A Steinwenter, 'Prolegomena zu einer Geschichte der Analogie', *Essays in Honor of F Schulz*, vol II (Weimar, 1951) 345ff.

[25] W Friedmann, *The Changing Structure of International Law* (London, 1964) 281ff.

some principles common to all legal science. An impressive example of this unifying and centripetal function of principles can be seen in the law of international spaces. This law has been formatted by UN General Assembly resolutions where the mention of principles outweighed by far the precise technical elaboration in detailed norms. Thus, the law of outer space is governed by principles such as non-appropriation, freedom of use, peaceful use, due regard to the activities of other states, exploration and exploitation as a common heritage of mankind, cooperation, etc. One finds these principles in Resolutions 1721 (XVI) of 1961, 1962 (XVII) of 1963 and 2222 (XXI) of 1967, and later in the Outer Space Treaty of 1967.[26] The legal regime of the deep seabed is to some extent similar. The 'common heritage of mankind' aspect has been emphasised in Resolution 2749 (XXV) of 1970 and in articles 133ff of the Montego Bay Convention on the Law of the Sea.[27]

(v) *Correcting function*. General principles may add precision to the scope of application of a conventional or customary rule of international law, and sometimes have even derogatory force.[28] This occurs in the context of supreme principles, not of auxiliary or subsidiary ones.[29] When the legal operator must reconcile a plurality of norms applicable at the same time to the same facts, principles will often guide his way.[30] Equity has performed this function in some cases. It may temper an unjust rigour in the application of one norm by taking account of other norms. Thus, the legal operator could develop an 'equitable exception' by a careful distinguishing. In a highly interesting decision of the Swiss Federal Tribunal,[31] the question arose in the context of a limitation imposed by federal legislation (the so-called *lex Friedrich*) on the owners of land to freely dispose of their properties. This legislation applied to the purchase of Swiss land by foreigners. The federal legislator (the legislation had been adopted by popular vote, against the advice of the Government) had omitted to harmonise this new law with a series of existing treaties. One among these treaties was the Agreement of 1862 between France and Switzerland relative to the Dappes valley. This valley had been definitively ceded to France in 1862, which in

[26] R Wolfrum, *Die Internationalisierung staatsfreier Räume* (Berlin, 1984) 269ff.

[27] AC Kiss, 'La notion de patrimoine commun de l'humanité' (1982-II) 175 *RCADI* 99ff. Pt XI of the 1982 Convention has in the mean time been modified by a more market-oriented legal régime: see eg DH Anderson, 'Resolution and Agreement Relating to the Implementation of Pt XI of the UN Convention on the Law of the Sea: A General Assessment' (1995) 55 *ZaöRV* 275ff. For the effect of this revision on the Law of the Sea Tribunal, see T Treves, 'The Law of the Sea Tribunal: Its Status and Scope of Jurisdiction after November 16, 1994' (1995) 55 *ZaöRV* 421ff.

[28] A Favre, *Principes du droit des gens* (Freiburg, 1974) 295.

[29] M Akehurst, 'The Hierarchy of the Sources of International Law' (1974/1975) 47 *BYIL* 278–79.

[30] A Verdross and B Simma, *Universelles Völkerrecht*, 3rd edn (Berlin, 1984) 389.

[31] *Office fédéral de la Justice v Morel et Commission vaudoise de recours en matière foncière*, Judgment of 15 July 1982: (1983) 34 *ASDI* 199–200.

turn had retroceded certain lands to Switzerland. The lands retroceded had been acquired by the Canton of Vaud. Must the new federal legislation be applied to these lands, or can one argue that French purchasers would have a right to acquire such lands in which they had a long-standing equitable interest? The Federal Tribunal starts by emphasising that the Treaty of 1862 did not contain an express provision on such a right of purchase, since at the time it was supposed to exist under generally applicable legislation; the restrictions issued one century later could not be foreseen.[32] But the whole spirit of the Treaty was manifestly based on the existence of such a right. It had been a fundamental basis for retroceding the lands to Switzerland.[33] The federal legislation ought thus to be interpreted restrictively, so as to conciliate it with the Treaty. The Tribunal thus accepts an 'equitable exception' for a special case which the legislator had manifestly not considered. Behind the technical arguments of the Tribunal, there loom largely the principles of equity, good faith and reasonableness. They allowed the flexibilisation of a too-rigorous norm.

(vi) *Adapting function*. The more a norm is formulated in general and abstract terms, the longer it will be able to last over time; conversely, the more individualised and concrete the formulation of the norm, the less it will be equipped to survive the erosion of time. The general norm does not contain precise and situated normative elements. Such elements would need to be constantly adapted in regard of changing social conditions. The general norm rather encapsulates constant aspects of human life and elementary conditions of justice, such as the duty to hear the other party (*audiatur et altera pars*), respect for the pledged word, the protection of legitimate expectations, etc. Each epoch can then elaborate the meaning and reach of such general injunctions, eg by determining what it considers to be a 'legitimate' expectation. Contrariwise, the more the norm contains concrete elements, the more it is rooted in a particular socio-political context. This is the reason why the general principle of good faith can traverse many centuries with little alterations, while a concrete administrative provision on technical matters will require to be constantly adapted. What has been said explains that general principles, which are among the most general and abstract norms of the legal system, grant a certain degree of permanence and unity of the law across time. The particular norms which must be

[32] ibid.

[33] ibid, 200: 'On peut donc supposer que, si la législation suisse sur l'acquisition des immeubles par des personnes à l'étranger avait existé en 1862, les négociateurs du traité concernant la vallée des Dappes n'auraient pas manqué de soumettre à un régime particulier les transferts de terrains situés dans la partie de territoire cédée à la Suisse. … Dès lors, on se trouve aujourd'hui en présence d'une lacune proprement dite, qu'il y a lieu de combler selon le principe général énoncé à l'article premier [du Code civil, c'est-à dire: *modo legislatoris*]'. Summing up: the Federal Tribunal considers that if the federal legislation restricting the purchase of land had existed in 1862, the treaty would have made an exception for the French purchasers; thus, there is now a gap in the law, which has to be filled by the judge acting as a legislator. The gap is filled by the principles mentioned.

changed, adapted or flexibilised can sometimes be remoulded in the light of the general principles and their concretisations. This metabolic function is all the more important in a legal order which is defective from the standpoint of available mechanisms of change. It is true that most international norms are *derogable*, ie the general rule can be substituted inter partes by a special provision. But the *modification* of the general norm itself remains often utterly difficult. Multilateral treaties suppose unanimous consent to be modified with effect *erga omnes partes*; bilateral treaties can be changed by the consent or the subsequent practice of two states; customary norms of general reach suppose a sufficiently general practice and legal opinion (it is however not necessary that the new practice and opinion are actually displayed by a vast majority of states, it being sufficient that some states practice and consider legal a certain course, and the majority of other states do not oppose or protest that course, especially when they are particularly affected by it). In the end result, international law, centred on individualistic sovereignty, has always suffered from a distinct lack of means of peaceful change. In this arid environment, the general principles offer themselves as vectors of a minor—but not necessarily less effective—process of legal change. They may induce new interpretations of old-style norms; insert into the body of the law new equitable exceptions; create new norms by judicial development of the law; etc. The principles have thus a soothing effect on the characteristic illness of international law consisting in the tendency to constantly privilege the yesterday over the tomorrow. In short terms, the principles may contribute to keeping the law at least to some degree up to the exigencies of time. Certainly, one must not exaggerate this function. The judge is not the legislator, and he or she cannot simply reinvent the law as he or she sees fit. But the issue is elsewhere: between the all and the nothing lies the something; and sometimes it is possible to adapt and slightly reshuffle, even if it is not possible to rebuild.

Some examples will follow. It may occur that a certain domain of the law has become too rigid in view of recent social developments. It may at the same time be difficult to expect a formal modification of the law. The jurisprudence has then sometimes—as we have seen in the previous section—attempted to adapt the law. It could try to do so by instilling into its body some equitable exception justified by new circumstances. The latter could be linked back to some hypothetic will of the lawgiver: 'if the new facts had been known, the legislator would have…'. The rule on the exhaustion of local remedies in the context of diplomatic protection offers an example. In the *Panevezys-Saldutiskis Railway* case (Preliminary Objections, 1939), the PCIJ admitted that there are exceptions to that rule, eg when the municipal tribunals are not in a position to decide or when the remedy cannot lead to a change in the decision.[34]

[34] PCIJ, ser A/B, no 76, p 18.

This means that the rule of exhaustion of local remedies has been tempered when confronted with situations where it would be unreasonable or inequitable to require its application. International practice shows that many other equitable exceptions to this rule have been accepted in the growing case law, albeit in a piecemeal and sometimes haphazard way. The rule has been said to be inapplicable in the following cases: direct damages from state to state, including damage to diplomatic personnel or other persons covered by international immunities;[35] where damage is caused outside the territory of the wrongdoing state (since it would be inequitable to require an alien to exhaust remedies in a foreign territory with which he or she has had no voluntary contact);[36] where it is excluded by a treaty;[37] where the defendant renounces the benefit of the rule after the judicial organ has been seized[38] (renunciation may be implicit if there are clauses providing for the arbitration of a class of disputes); where there are no appropriate remedies for the dispute at stake,[39] in particular if the remedies are illusory or ineffective[40] by reason of objective circumstances (municipal judicial organisation,[41] state of municipal law,[42] nature of the competent organ,[43] excessive delays,[44] substantial risk to have the damage increasing,[45] etc) or by reason of subjective circumstances (the dependence of the tribunals upon the executive, the bad faith or notorious xenophobia of the judges,[46] etc);

[35] *Phosphates in Morocco* case (1938), PCIJ, ser A/B, no 74, p 28. The interpretation and application of a treaty, even in the context of individual rights and obligations, is never subjected to the rule: *Switzerland v Germany* (1958) 25 *ILR* 42ff; *Aerial Services*, France/US (1978) 54 *ILR* 322ff; *Ireland v UK*, ECtHR (1978) 58 *ILR* 263.

[36] This is a controversial matter: see CF Amerasinghe, *Local Remedies in International Law* (Cambridge, 1990) 138ff.

[37] *Amoco* case (1982) 1 *Iran/US Claims Tribunal Reports* 493. This is also the case under the ICSID system under the Washington Convention of 1965, art 26: (1965) 4 *ILM* 536. See also the *Uzielli* case (1963) 40 *ILR* 149ff; *Gallardo* case (1981) 67 *ILR* 578.

[38] *Müller v Austria* (1974), Communication no 5849/72, European Commission of Human Rights Report.

[39] *Altesor v Uruguay* (1982) 70 *ILR* 253; *Nielsen v Denmark* (1961), Communication no 343/57, European Commission of Human Rights Report; *Englert v FRG* (1987) ECtHR, Series A no 123, 51–53; *Velasquez Rodriguez*, Inter-American Court of Human Right (1988) 95 *ILR* 233ff, 270ff. See also the concluding observations of the Belgian Government in the *Barcelona Traction* case, *ICJ Pleadings*, vol I, pt III, 218–19, and vol III, 602.

[40] See CF Amerasinghe, *Local Remedies in International Law* (Cambridge, 1990) 166ff, 193ff.

[41] This may occur, for example, if the supreme tribunal depends on the executive on a particular question whose international legality is disputed: see the *Salvador Commercial Company* case (1902) XV *RIAA* 476–77; *Valentine Petroleum* case (1967) 44 *ILR* 91–92.

[42] Eg when the decision flows from a formal law for which the judge has no power of review: see the *Rhodope Forests* case (1933) III *RIAA* 1405.

[43] Eg acts of government: *Finnish Shipowners* (1934) III *RIAA* 1490ff.

[44] *El Oro* (1931) V *RIAA* 191 (nine years). See CF Amerasinghe, *Local Remedies in International Law* (Cambridge, 1990) 203ff.

[45] *De Sabla* (1933) 28 *AJIL* 607, implicitly.

[46] *Brown* (1923) VI *RIAA* 120ff, 129. See CF Amerasinghe, *Local Remedies in International Law* (Cambridge, 1990) 193ff.

where the remedy is only one for the revision of the judgment, and not an ordinary appeal or cassation;[47] possibly also where the question is limited to points of law to the exclusion of any point of fact;[48] where an estoppel impeaches the plea that the remedies have not been exhausted;[49] etc. Moreover, the rule of exhaustion is satisfied even when the municipal procedures do not have exactly the same subject matter as the international procedures, provided that the substance of the demand has been presented on the internal level and that there has been maximum possible action in the light of internal procedures and laws.[50] The conjunction of all these exceptions, developed in the case law, has blunted the sharp edge of the rule and brought it in line with equitable considerations. A German author had proposed as early as the 1930s that the rule should be set aside each time there are 'valid motives' to dispense the aggrieved party from its observation.[51] Overall, the developments mentioned placed the rule directly under the control of equity and ultimately *inter fauces justitiae*. Equity has penetrated the normative injunction to the point of dominating it altogether. This means that a general principle of law has served as the vehicle for a transformation of the law, in substitution to the formal legislator.

Another example can be found in the *Norwegian Fisheries* case (1951). The applicable rule of international law is to measure maritime zones from baselines situated on the coastline. These lines follow the low water mark. However, there exist some extremely tortuous coastlines, replete with irregularities, fjords, islets, rocks, fringes, banks and other complications. It would be difficult to draw practicable maritime lines by following the haphazard course of such coasts. This is the reason why many states have in such circumstances had recourse to straight baselines. Is this practice compatible with the rule of international law? This is far from being obvious. The practice of straight lines is at variance with the rule discussed. It moreover allows a coastal state to claim areas of the high seas by extending the reach of its maritime zones. When seized of the question, the ICJ admitted nevertheless that such straight baselines are compatible with international law under some conditions. An equitable and reasonable exception is thereby carved out of the rule. The conditions for the acceptability of straight baselines are defined by the Court in a passage resembling an act of judicial legislation.[52] These conditions are as follows: (1) the straight baselines must not depart significantly from the general direction of the coastline; (2) they may enclose certain waters so intimately

[47] *Salem* (1932) II *RIAA* 1190.

[48] *Aerial Services* case, France/US (1978) XVIII *RIAA* 469.

[49] See R Kolb, *La bonne foi en droit international public* (Paris, 2000) 565ff.

[50] *Elettronica Sicula (ELSI)*, (1989) *ICJ Reports* 46, § 59.

[51] E Kaufmann, 'Règles générales du droit de la paix' (1935-IV) 54 *RCADI* 457.

[52] As the Court had already done for the conditions of validity of reservations to multilateral treaties: *Genocide Convention* opinion, (1951) *ICJ Reports* 20ff.

> linked with the coast that it is justified to treat them as internal waters; (3) economic interests of the coastal state attested by a long usage can be taken into account.[53] The conditions outlined by the Court were finally inserted by the formal legislator into article 4 of the 1958 Geneva Convention on Territorial Waters and later in article 7 of the 1982 Montego Bay Convention on the Law of the Sea. The principles of reasonableness, of equity, of practicability, of good faith and of legal security have influenced the judicial reasoning.

Overall, it can thus be concluded that general principles appear in various different complexions and that they perform various important functions within a legal order. They tend to shape the reasoning of the lawyer, in civil law countries as pillars of the legal order, in common law countries sometimes simply as *rationes decidendi* distilled from the analysis of precedents. Whether the principle is 'already there' and can be used for deductive and other reasoning, or whether it must first be shaped by the analysis of the case law, in both cases their role should not be neglected. True, it is often less visible in a non-codified system (such as also international law) than in a codified system. But visibility is not necessarily tantamount to real impact.

[53] (1951) *ICJ Reports* 132–33.

2

The Three Meanings of Good Faith in Public International Law

The term 'good faith' has three distinct meanings in international law. In other words, a perusal of international documents shows that the term is used with three different shades: as a mere legal fact related to an erroneous subjective belief; as a vague standard for evaluating the reasonableness or the normality of behaviour; and to designate a powerful general principle of the law whose main normative content is the protection of legitimate expectations freely created in another subject by some deliberate course of conduct. In the first sense, the term has no normative content of its own. It is just the element of a norm, ie a fact which a norm supposes to attach legal consequences to that fact. In the second sense, the term has but little normativity. It could easily be replaced by other concepts, such as 'reasonableness'. In the third sense, the principle has its most intimate and typical legal cloth, and also its highest degree of normativity. The principle here requires some type of conduct, or at least attaches consequences to some type of conduct. The generality of the behavioural injunction is such (eg the protection of legitimate expectations) that the principle generates sub-principles and sub-rules in the various branches of international law, with the aim to further or secure the general normative content designated mainly by the idea of legitimate expectations. Let us now turn to each of these aspects of the term 'good faith'.

I. Good Faith as a Subjective Legal Fact

In the narrowest sense, good faith designates a state of mind consisting in an erroneous representation of legally relevant facts.[1] The gist of the matter lies in the lack of knowledge by some subject on some such fact, which is thought to exist while it does not, or which is thought to be without defects while it is not. Subjective good faith refers therefore to a doctrine of 'erroneous beliefs'. Such errors of fact can lead to a legal protection of the subject suffering from the erroneous representation,

[1] See the developments in Kolb, *Bonne* 115ff.

when the latter cannot be attributed any fault. Good faith here means a subjective or psychological legal fact. Example: I may suppose that the seller of some good is the owner and that he therefore can cede the title of property to me; I may however be ignoring the fact that the object was stolen and that the person trying to lure me into the transaction is therefore not the lawful owner. In legal terms, I can be said to have purchased the object in good faith, i.e. ignoring the preceding theft. When according to the circumstances I could and should have believed in the ownership if the seller, i.e. when there is no negligence in my judgment, the legal order sometimes protects the property title I have acquired.[2] The subjective fact of good faith is here a condition for acquiring the property. If I had not been in good faith, either because I knew of the theft, or because I should have been more prudent in view of the circumstances, the property cannot pass under the heading we are here analysing.

To some extent, there is a bridge which can be built between the subjective good faith and good faith as a principle. The main point of the norms of law containing references to subjective good faith is to protect the erring subject when there is no fault which can be attributed to it. In that sense, these norms protect 'legitimate expectations'. Under that perspective, there is a path leading from one notion to the other. But the conceptual difference remains: good faith designates a fact to which the law attaches some consequences; and the other time it designates a normative proposition which makes the injunction to protect legitimate expectations in some defined contexts. On the one hand there is a fact and on the other a norm.

In international law, the notion of good faith in the subjective sense is known and applicable in several contexts. Some of the areas in which the notion applies are interwoven between international and municipal law. However, subjective good faith remains overall a rather marginal phenomenon in that legal order.[3] It certainly features much less prominently than good faith as a legal standard or as a legal principle. The 'erroneous belief' theory is much more suitable to natural persons, having a personal psychology, and also to a legal order garnered with judges able to ascertain what a person thought and knew, than it is for the international legal order which regulates the political relations between powers and among complex legal persons. In the latter, the jurisprudence is somewhat 'rougher';[4] macro-phenomena take the place of micro-enquiries; and moreover, there is a greater need for objectivised principles and rules, based on specific results or means,

[2] This is the position under civil law. In common law, a stolen object cannot be acquired in good faith, apart from the rules on prescription. See RK Paterson, 'Canada', in T Kono (ed), *The Impact of Uniform Laws on the Protection of Cultural Heritage in the 21st Century* (Leiden, 2010) 233, with references.

[3] As to which see Zoller, *Bonne.*

[4] Remember the famous phrase of WE Hall, *A Treatise on International Law*, 8th edn (Oxford, 1924) 395, fn 2, on international law as the 'rough jurisprudence of nations'. Certainly, international law has been much refined since then, so as to become a fully fledged legal order. See on that issue G Abi-Saab, 'Cours général de droit international public' (1987-VII) 207 *RCADI* 123ff. But Hall's phrase still has some justification in various contexts, as the one we are dealing with here.

guaranteeing a simpler application and some concomitant legal certainty. Thus, it is not wholly surprising that in many branches of international law, subjective criteria have been progressively smoothed out and objective standards have finally triumphed. The law of state responsibility is a good example: the requirement of 'fault', so frequently discussed in the past, has given way to the objective regime of responsibility for breach of obligation with the work of the ILC.[5]

Here are some examples of the application of good faith as a subjective fact centred on excusable erroneous belief. Before we turn to these examples, there is one issue to be shortly clarified. Whether the acquisition of territory by acquisitive prescription (prolonged passivity of the title-holder combined with effective administration *à titre de souverain* by some other state) is a recognised norm of the international legal order is debated in legal doctrine. What is not truly debated any more, however, is that subjective good faith (ie ignorance that some other state held a title) is not a condition for prescription. Subjective good faith thus does not play a prominent role in this context. We will return to that question later in this book.[6] There are however some other areas where this type of good faith is relevant, examined below.

A. The Ancient Rule *Pirata Non Mutat Dominium* and Related Rules

Let us start with a historical example, drawn from the corpus of classical international law. A recurring matter to be decided by tribunals had been whether the bona fide buyers of certain goods and assets could acquire the title to them. In the eighteenth century, the rule developed that assets seized by pirates remained the property of their lawful owners.[7] If however bona fide purchasers acquired these assets, international law would avoid disturbing the title they acquired under the relevant municipal law. The condition for that protection was the existence of subjective good faith, ie ignorance of the piratical seizure. This rule has been codified in the mean time, for example in article 19 of the Geneva Convention on the High Seas (1958) and in article 105 of the Montego Bay Convention on the Law of the Sea (1982).[8] An equivalent rule has been applied in other contexts of transfer of property, eg the seizure of assets under neutrality laws[9] or the transfer of property contrary to rules on belligerent occupation.[10] A recent example can

[5] See the short explanations in J Crawford, *State Responsibility* (Cambridge, 2014) 60–62.

[6] Ch 6, section I.

[7] See BA Wortley, 'Pirata non Mutat Dominium' (1947) 24 *BYIL* 258ff.

[8] The latter reads as follows: 'On the high seas, or in any other place outside the jurisdiction of any State, every State may seize a pirate ship or aircraft ... The courts of the State which carried out the seizure may decide upon the penalties to be imposed, and may also determine the action to be taken with regard to the ships, aircraft or property, subject to the rights of third parties acting in good faith'.

[9] *Kronprins Gustaf Adolf* case, arbitration, (1932) II *RIAA* 1288–89.

[10] J Robinson, 'Transfer of Property in Enemy Occupied Territory' (1945) 39 *AJIL* 226–27, 230.

be found in Resolution 2240 (2015) of the UN Security Council.[11] This resolution allows member states to take measures against smuggling and people trafficking from the coast of Libya. Paragraph 8 of the Resolution authorises member states for a period of one year to seize vessels engaged in such a course of conduct, but at the same time underscores that 'further action with regard to such vessels … will be taken in accordance with applicable international law with due consideration of the interests of any third parties who have acted in good faith'. Thus, such a vessel may not be confiscated or destroyed if it belongs to a person who was unaware that it was used to commit the said offences, ie a person whose good faith can be established.

B. Rules on the Effects of Nullity of Treaties

In case of voidness of a treaty, the relevant law provides for a return of the status quo ante. That means that if acts have been performed in reliance on the validity of the treaty, each party may require any other party to establish as far as possible in their mutual relations the position that would have existed if the acts had not been performed.[12] Article 69, § 2, letter b, of the VCLT of 1969 introduces the following qualification: 'acts performed in good faith before the invalidity was invoked are not rendered unlawful by reason only of the invalidity of the treaty'. This proviso affirms that acts in performance of the treaty done in good faith (ie without the knowledge of the reasons or pleas of invalidity, but rather in the belief of validity of the treaty) remain valid.[13] The other party must compensate the bona fide subject, by means which are not specified in the VCLT, eg performance of its own mirroring obligations, replacement or reparation, or by other agreed means. This proviso stabilises treaty relations and protects the faithful treaty party.[14] There remain important questions related to the interpretation of this subparagraph,[15] but the point here was only to show that the notion of good faith on which it is based corresponds to the subjective and fact-related type.

C. Rupture of a Blockade in the Law of War

It often occurred that the subjective good faith of a captain was advanced in order to demand the release of a ship which had violated a coastal blockade.

[11] S/RES/2240 of 9 October 2015.

[12] Art 69, § 2, letter a, of the VCLT of 1969. See the short commentary of ME Villiger, *Commentary on the 1969 Vienna Convention on the Law of Treaties* (Leiden, 2009) 853ff.

[13] Ibid, 861–62. See also art 70, § 1, letter b, of the VCLT, 1969.

[14] C Rozakis, 'The Law of Invalidity of Treaties' (1974) 16 *AVR* 163.

[15] Kolb, *Bonne*, 120.

The argument was in essence that the captain had been unaware of the proclamation of the blockade and thus acted in good faith. In a series of cases, seized ships were released on this basis. For example, Italy acted upon that practice.[16] Aspects of subjective good faith were also raised with respect to the true destination of goods, enemy or neutral.[17]

D. Ignorance of Entry into Force of a Truce or Armistice

For centuries, it took a long time before military detachments fighting far away from the centre, in the mountainous regions or at sea, could be informed of the conclusion and entry into force of a truce or an armistice. If such detachments continued fighting notwithstanding the existence of such truce or armistice, the law considered the latter not to be breached, since the persons involved acted in subjective good faith, ie in ignorance of the facts.[18]

E. Quantum of the Compensation for Unlawful Acts

Within the body of the law of international responsibility, subjective good faith has not been accepted as a circumstance precluding wrongfulness. In other words, the excusable error on the lawfulness or unlawfulness of a conduct is not such a circumstance. Rather, the maxim *ignorantia juris nocet* is applied.[19] Conversely, subjective good faith has sometimes been taken into account as one element in the calculation of the amount of compensation due for the commission of an internationally wrongful act. Thus, in the *Romano* case (1898), the arbitrator rejected the claim for loss of profit on the grounds that 'it was a matter of one who caused damage, but acted in good faith, in the belief that he was exercising acts of jurisdiction in his own territory'.[20]

[16] R Ago and M Toscano, *La prassi italiana di diritto internazionale, Prima Serie*, 1861–1887, vol II (New York, 1970) p 1037, no 1155 and p 1050, no 1166. See also ibid, *Seconda Serie*, 1887–1918, vol IV (New York, 1980) p 2111, no 2901, p 2189, no 1968; etc.

[17] C Calvo, *Le droit international théorique et pratique*, 5th edn, vol IV (Paris, 1896) 304, 309.

[18] ibid, 380.

[19] See the following arbitrations: *Coquitlam* case (1921); *Jessie, Bayard and Pescawha* case (1921); *Wanderer* case (1921); *Kate* case (1921); *Favourite* case (1921): (1921) VI *RIAA* 47, 59, 74, 81, 84. Further, in the *Land and Maritime Boundary* case (*Cameroon v Nigeria*) (2002), Nigeria had pleaded for a full exoneration of responsibility by reason of the fact that it acted in 'reasonable mistake' or 'honest belief' on a piece of territory which the Court might find to belong to Cameroon: (2002) *ICJ Reports* 451, § 311. The ICJ considered that by the ordered withdrawal of the Nigerian forces, the injury suffered by Cameroon would be sufficiently addressed; it thus did not need to rule further on that point: ibid, 452, § 319.

[20] *Romano* (1898) XV *RIAA* 13.

F. Presumption of Good Faith

It is often stated that good faith is presumed. Reference is made here to a fact, ie to subjective good faith as opposed to bad faith or detrimental knowledge. In other words, a presumption of good faith makes sense not with regard to a normative principle, but with regard to a psychological fact which can be present or absent. The law has not to be proved; it is normally for the judge to establish it (*jura novit curia*). International case law has often stated that good faith is presumed.[21] This means that the onus of proof does not lie on the state wishing to establish its good faith (the ignorance of a relevant fact), but on the other state, which has to show that its counterpart knew or should have known that fact, ie has at least been negligent in this regard.[22] The presumption we are dealing with favours the stability of international transactions and is based on the socially useful consideration that regularity is the rule and fraud the exception. It avoids a too frequent divorce between the legal duty and the effective conduct. Finally, it seems equitable to assume correctness and honesty in case of doubt. This presumption of regularity and correctness consequently also reinforces the confidence of the state in judicial proceedings. The presumption can however be rebutted. It is also subjected to equitable exceptions in certain subject matters where knowledge must more easily be imputed, eg in the context of contraband of war.[23]

To a certain degree, the notion opposed to subjective good faith is 'bad faith'.[24] In the narrow sense, bad faith refers to the knowledge of the fact which breaches the operation of a legal norm requiring subjective good faith, eg of the norm allowing one to acquire property, which is breached when I know that the asset I want to buy was stolen. On this plane, both notions, good and bad faith, mirror each other and are placed on the same subjective footing. Absence of bad faith here designates good faith.[25] In the broader sense, bad faith refers also to hidden motives, fraud, injurious or arbitrary conduct,[26] non-respect for the law, intentions to harm, undisclosed motives, and the like.[27]

[21] See e.g. the *Lake Lanoux* arbitration, (1957) XII *RIAA* 305; or the *Navigational and Related Rights* case (*Costa Rica v Nicaragua*), (2009) *ICJ Reports* 267, § 150.

[22] Thus, Germany could rely on its good faith in regard to the liquidation of certain assets in Polish Upper Silesia: *Certain German Interests in German Upper Silesia* (1926), German Memorial, PCIJ, ser C, no 11-I, 375–76.

[23] See JB Moore, *A Digest of International Law*, vol VII (Washington DC, 1906) 623 and the case law quoted in Kolb, *Bonne* 127, fn 250.

[24] See mainly M Gounelle, *La motivation des actes juridiques en droit international public* (Paris, 1979) 192ff.

[25] See C Fernandez De Casadevante Romanì, *La interpretación de la normas internacionales* (Pamplona, 1996) 43ff.

[26] Arbitrary conduct is sometimes equated to conduct in bad faith: see eg Dissenting Opinion Hackworth, *Administrative Tribunal of the ILO* advisory opinion, (1956) *ICJ Reports* 121.

[27] In this larger sense, for example, art 53 (unlike art 64) of the VCLT of 1969 sanctions the conclusion of a treaty in defiance of the international public order by the nullity of the treaty in all its parts. The existence of a norm of *jus cogens* being here known to the parties, the voiding of the whole treaty

It has been claimed that it is almost impossible for a judge to find that a sovereign state has acted in bad faith, since that judgment would be almost injurious.[28] It is true that a judge will rarely issue a blunt statement that a state has acted in bad faith. Such a course could be self-defeating, inflaming hostility and provoking resistance by the condemned state. However, findings of absence of good faith in the subjective sense obviously occur[29] (and are in legal technique equivalent to a finding of bad faith), and tribunals have even reached out by affirming that they would make a relevant finding where indispensable. Thus, in the *Tacna Arica* case (1925), the arbitrator said that: 'While there should be no hesitation in finding such intent or bad faith, if established, and in holding the Party guilty thereof to the consequences of its action, it is plain that such a purpose should not lightly be imputed'.[30] This statement is tantamount to recalling the presumption of good faith. In short terms, there is nothing non-justiciable in the notion of bad faith. We may also recall that there are subject areas of international law where the notion of bad faith is largely implicit in some norm, as is the case in the context of the prohibition of denial of justice,[31] and that it has also been regularly used in the law of international investments.[32]

There remains a last question to be shortly mentioned and considered. Can there be good faith on both sides of a transaction (as there existed the question if a war could be 'just' on both sides), and if that is the case what would be the legal consequence? If such a situation occurs, it seems intuitive that no legal 'sanction' can be pronounced against any party. Thus, the arbitral tribunal in the *Maritime Delimitation* case (*Guinea v Guinea-Bissau*) (1985) affirmed that the highly divergent interpretations of a provision by the two parties reflected entirely bona fide positions and thus no negative consequences could be drawn against either party.[33] Conversely, if both parties can be shown to have acted in bad faith, neither should benefit from the operation of a legal norm claimed to their advantage, and both could be subjected to some form of legal sanction, to be apportioned in context.

and the refusal to allow separation of clauses under art 44 of the VCLT is after all a sanction for bad faith in the larger sense. See A Gomez Robledo, 'Le ius cogens international: sa genèse, sa nature, ses fonctions' (1981-III) 172 *RCADI* 122.

[28] P Cahier, 'Cours général de droit international public' (1985-VI) 195 *RCADI* 90.

[29] See eg the *Orinoco Navigation Company* arbitration, (1910) XI *RIAA* 240 (the tribunal however avoided the term 'bad faith' while asserting the relevant knowledge precluding the operation of the presumption of good faith). In the *Application of the Interim Accord* case (*FYROM v Greece*, 2011), the ICJ considered an argument that the applicant had acted in bad faith, but did not find that argument substantiated in the present case: (2010–11) *ICJ Reports* 685, § 132.

[30] *Tacna Arica* (1925) II *RIAA* 930. Because bad faith should not lightly be imputed, a series of arbitrations examined the issue and finally rejected the plea of bad faith on the facts of the case: see eg *Case Concerning Claims Arising out of Decisions of the Mixed Graeco-German Arbitral Tribunal set up under Article 304 in Part X of the Treaty of Versailles*, arbitration, (1972) XIX *RIAA* 27ff.

[31] AV Freeman, *The International Responsibility of States for the Denial of Justice* (London, 1938) 84ff. See eg the *Chattin* case, referring explicitly to bad faith: (1927) IV *RIAA* 286–87.

[32] See below, Ch 10.

[33] *Guinea v Guinea-Bissau* (1985) 77 *ILR* 661.

II. Good Faith as an Objectivising Legal Standard

The law operates in a social environment made up by living entities with their values, conceptions, behaviours and expectations. It needs in many cases to refer to social norms in order to operationalise legal norms. What is meant by 'reasonable'? What is meant by 'good morals'? What is to be considered 'abusive' or 'oppressive'? What is 'legitimate'? What is 'proportional'? What is 'due'? On such notions, there cannot exist a once-and-for-all answer valid everywhere and at all times. The legal norm must be referred back to the feelings and conceptions predominant in a given society, ie of the 'reasonable man', of *quod plerumque fit*, or the like. The legal standard, which refers back to social understandings, is thus a sort of window towards social facts. The latter are not simply taken as a statistical given, but are considered from a normative perspective, ie by what appears the reasonable and informed view of the social body as a whole.[34]

From this perspective, what is required by good faith can be considered as a legal standard making reference to such normal or expected social behaviour.[35] There are indeed some vague references to good faith as 'correct' and 'expectable conduct', or as 'legitimate' conduct, which are legally no more than references to social conduct as described above. The term 'good faith' could here be replaced by equivalent ones, such as 'reasonable', 'appropriate', 'loyal', and so on. Good faith is here not taken in a truly technical meaning. It is a vague reference to correctness. Thus, the arbitral tribunal in the *Rainbow Warrior* case (1990) emphasised that France had make no 'efforts in good faith' to obtain New Zealand's consent to the removal of its two agents detained on the island of Hao.[36] The term 'good faith' could here be replaced without any loss by the term 'reasonable efforts'. And what is reasonable depends on the standards of diligence predominant in international society. Another example can be found in the *KPMG v Davison* case (New Zealand Court of Appeal, 1996), where the Court held that in situations of concurring jurisdiction of states there is a good faith duty requiring moderation in the unilateral exercise of such jurisdiction.[37] In other words, the jurisdiction must be 'reasonably' used. Another example can be found in the *Blaskic (Subpoenae)* case (1997). There, the Appeals Chamber of the ICTY held that there was a bona fide duty of cooperation of a state with the Tribunal in the context of the delivery of documents allegedly raising security concerns.[38] This is tantamount to saying that the state shall reasonably cooperate. As often, good faith here tempers insolent unilateralism. It is understandable that this quite vague type of good faith abounds

[34] See the very thorough study by S Rials, *Le juge administrative français et la technique du standard* (Paris, 1980).

[35] See, eg L Siorat, *Le problème des lacunes en droit international* (Paris, 1958) 406.

[36] *Rainbow Warrior* (1990) XX *RIAA* 260, § 94.

[37] *KPMG v Davison* (1996) 104 *ILR* 545 (Judge Cooke).

[38] *Blaskic (Subpoenae)* (1997) 110 *ILR* 728–29, § 68.

in diplomatic and political documents.[39] It is however not particularly interesting for the purposes of this study, and can thus be left to rest.

III. Good Faith as a General Principle of Law

The general principle of good faith in international law has three distinct contents, the first being the most prominent:[40] 1) good faith protects the legitimate expectations of another subject generated through a deliberate conduct, whatever the true intentions or will of the acting subject;[41] 2) good faith also protects certain common interests against attacks by excessively individualistic claims and pretentions (prohibition of abuse of rights); and 3) good faith inhibits the capacity of a subject to draw advantages of a non-loyal and incorrect conduct infringing reciprocity and equality (*nemo ex propria turpitudine commodum capere potest*: no one can profit from his own wrong). The operation of the principle consists mainly in creating and nourishing a series of sub-principles, norms, and maxims which will realise these general aims of the principle throughout the legal order: eg by some pre-contractual obligations, by acquiescence and estoppel, by an interpretation of the text according to the spirit rather than excessively focused on the letter, by prohibiting the abuse of rights or of procedure, by doctrines of reasonable time for withdrawal from a legal compact, by the doctrine of the binding force of unilateral engagements, by the prohibition of perfidy in the law of armed conflict, and the like. The principle tends thus to create specific norms which will transport and operationalise its main legal idea in the various subject areas of the law. The main spin of the principle is thus a powerful, seminal and foundational legal conception, which will tend to irradiate into the whole legal order.

The most frequent legal idea attached to the principle of good faith is the one linked to the protection of *legitimate expectations* freely created by a subject and on which another subject could and should have relied.[42] This part of the principle is linked with the conception of 'legal security'. Security, ie certainty and

[39] See eg *Documents diplomatiques français, 1932–1939*, Deuxième Série, vol VII (Paris, 1972) 530 where the French Minister of Foreign Affairs wished to see the German Reich giving some additional guarantee of good faith in the context of the Locarno settlement.

[40] See Kolb, *Bonne* 143ff.

[41] It can thus be seen that good faith is the counterpart of the principle of intention/will in international law.

[42] Sometimes, this principle was applied in political practice, eg when the US—and in particular President Wilson—insisted on not changing a position contained in an armistice, and which the US led the enemy to believe in, simple because the US had the might to do so: see P d'Argent, *Les réparations de guerre en droit international public* (Brussels, 2005) 65. Conversely, it has been held that the argument of good and bad faith is mainly a political and moral argument states use in order to discredit other states by accusing them of bad faith: G de Lacharrière, *La politique juridique extérieure* (Paris, 1983) 108. This may manifestly occur, but such a political use of the term does not detract from its parallel operation in the legal order as a legal concept.

foreseeability, are fundamental needs of individuals and social groups. The action an individual projects and finally undertakes is based on the expectation of normal conduct of other subjects or of conduct that can be required in a certain context. The orientation of human behaviour is significantly driven by the internalisation of external signs. The understanding of their meaning allows individuals to act and to participate with efficacy of social interaction. Society in itself is but a network of regularities resulting in a certain order. Life in common is possible only under the condition of such regularities. Just as the universe could not exist if it were not governed by certain physical laws, so society would fall into chaos if there were no regularities nourished by expectations. There are various aspects manifesting the importance of security.

1. Legal *sociology* defines norms as generalised expectations of conduct accompanied by sanctions. Thus, the expectation (which is mid-way between a pure fact and a pure ought) becomes the central pivot for the definition of norms. It concerns a real psychological fact in the mind of individuals; but it differs from the mere effectiveness of real situations in that it contains a normative element. The generalisation of social expectations allows a stabilisation of society. Regularity condenses itself into rules. Moreover, expectations reduce the domain of complexity: they allow a subject to avoid anticipating each time all the possible avenues of conduct and result, and to concentrate on the expectable and legitimate behaviour in regard to the social role of the other persons. The sociological definition of norms is thus grafted upon the idea of the security of inter-individual interaction.[43] The same could be said of economic interaction, which is a special aspect of social interaction. Apart from devices geared at securing a certain flexibility for unforeseen developments (eg safeguard clauses), economic interaction is fundamentally based on the foreseeability of exchanges and transactions. Without such foreseeability, the

The principle of legitimate expectations is also applicable in the domestic legal orders, in private and public law. For Switzerland, see for example the still seminal study by B Weber-Dürler, *Vertrauensschutz im öffentlichen Recht* (Basle, 1983). For the common law countries, see eg the rich case law on the invocation of legitimate expectation of application of treaties which are ratified by a state but are not yet formally applicable for the reason that implementing legislation is lacking: *Teoh* (1995) 104 *ILR* 460ff (Australian High Court); *AG v Jospeh and Boyce* (2006) 134 *ILR* 542ff (Pollard J) (Caribbean Court of Justice (Appellate Jurisdiction)); and the more restrictive precedents in *R v DPP, ex p Kebilene* and *HL* (1999) 122 *ILR* 440–42, 456–59 (England, High Court); *Ahani v The Queen* (2002) 124 *ILR* 398, § 22 (Ontario Superior Court of Justice, Canada); *R (Bancoult) v Foreign Secretary (No 2)* (2008) 138 *ILR* 650ff (Lord Hoffmann) (House of Lords, England); *Baker v Canada* (1999) 148 ILR 607–08 (L'Heureux J) (Supreme Court of Canada). The issue of legitimate expectations under municipal law has also arisen in the context of the grant of diplomatic protection: see *R (Abbasi) v Foreign Secretary* (2002) 126 *ILR* 713–24, § 99–103 (England, Court of Appeal), the Court finding no abuse of discretion nor any legitimate expectation. See further *Kaunda v President* (2004) 136 *ILR* 503, § 168 (Ngcobo J) (South African Constitutional Court); *R (Al-Rawi) v Foreign Secretary* (2006), England, Court of Appeal, ibid, 654ff.

[43] *Encyclopedia of Social Sciences*, vol 11 (New York, 1968) 204ff, 208ff; N Luhmann, *Rechtssoziologie*, vol I (Reinbeck, 1973) 53ff.

exchange of goods is hampered, as times of important monetary upheavals or other types of crisis show.

2. Security also plays an eminent role in *anthropology and psychology*. The foreseeability of conduct and the faculty to harmonise one's own acts and aspirations with the external world are important factors of psychic stability. Security reduces anguish and the pressure of having to take all too frequently complex decisions. The weight of having to balance up constantly all the innumerable alternatives is considerably reduced.[44] This need for stability is more pronounced in human beings than in (other) animals. The latter are more importantly driven by instinct. The human being, being less determined by instinctive conduct, suffers from a deficit of inner security. The institutions of culture (including the law) must compensate the deficits wrought by nature.[45] Brutal social upheavals provide evidence for this: the growing insecurity ushers into disorder and tension; all exchanges suffer, from black markets to hyper-inflation; the individual shows traumatic signs, anxiety and fear, leading often to aggression and hate. Periods of rejection of received certainties are also periods of violence. This is true to a large extent also for animal life.[46] The study of animals living in groups has shown that they subject themselves to an often rigid social order, based on hierarchy and the prohibition of fallacious conduct. The security and credibility of the signs emitted by each member of the group is central to the ability of the whole group to survive to the many external threats. It is in such cases essential to be able to rely on the conduct of the other members of society. Security, moreover, allows for improvement in the efficacy of social life by the division of tasks. This sharing of tasks supposes that the legitimate confidence placed in the correct execution of the roles is honoured in most cases.
3. Finally, security is also a cardinal notion of *moral* life. Legitimate expectations create confidence and faith; it should not be deceived or deluded. *Fides est credulitas*, as Isidor of Seville rightly observed.[47] The duty to honour the confidence created is at the root of the contractual bond (*pacta sunt servanda*, good faith).[48] It stands to reason that such a duty is intimately linked with notions of justice and correctness. These are at bottom cardinal moral values.

Consequently such a notion of security could not be indifferent to the *law* either. As has been said: 'Trust lies at the basis of society';[49] or: 'Law of every type relies

[44] U Beer, *Optimisten leben länger* (Geneva, 1985); M Koller, *Sozialpsychologie des Vertrauens* (Bielefeld, 1990); K Salmelaaro and J Nurmi, 'Uncertainty and Confidence in Interpersonal Projects', *Journal of Social and Personal Relationships*, vol 13 (1996) 109ff.

[45] A Gehlen, *Moral und Hypermoral* (Frankfurt, 1969) 95ff.

[46] K Lorenz, *Über tierisches und menschliches Verhalten* (Munich, 1974); K Lorenz, *Vergleichende Verhaltensforschung* (Vienna, 1978; GE Pugh, *The Biological Origin of Human Values* (London, 1977); GS Stent (ed), *Morality as Biological Phenomenon* (Berlin, 1978); EO Wilson, *Sociobiology* (Cambridge, 1982).

[47] Isidor of Seville, *De Differentiis*, I, 486.

[48] Cicero, *De officiis*, lib I, cap VII.

[49] J de Louter, *Le droit international public positif*, vol I (Oxford, 1920) 470, a phrase attributed to TD Woolsey.

on the fulfilment of expectations'.[50] On the one hand, there is security attached to the legal order and its functioning, ie to its legal norms and institutions (objective legal security). Thus, questions of the number of norms, their systematisation, the degree of their clarity, their rapid or slow change and transient legal regimes, the quality of the enforcement mechanisms, the chance to see a norm enforced, etc, are part of this limb. As these matters are not specifically linked to good faith, we may abstain from further analysing them. On the other hand, there is also *security between the parties* (*fides*) (subjective legal security). Modern legal orders create rights and duties flowing from a social interaction in which one subject holds a conduct arousing legitimate expectations in some other subject. The confidence in a certain regularity of legally relevant conduct is protected under the guise of good faith. The law does not allow the true but hidden will of the subject acting in the first place to displace the socially legitimate expectation created by the effective conduct. The subject is bound by the manifestation, representation or appearance deliberately or objectively created. It is this 'subjective' legal certainty, realised through the doctrine of legitimate expectations, that will form the main thread of analysis in Part II of this study. It will there be seen that international law has developed a series of tools which aim at protecting this confidence between the subjects of the law caught up in an infinite network of varying interactions.

This legal idea of the protection of legitimate expectations is not merely a refined notion of legal civilisation, developed in recent years under the pressure of increased relationships between states or under the guise of globalisation constraints. It is a traditional legal idea which grows parallel to the strengthening of a legal order. In other words, needs for the protection of trust and confidence are eternal problems a society faces, and not only issues for a post-modern society. Some older arbitral precedents shall now illustrate the point. In the *Port of Portendick* case (1843),[51] France had given assurances that some of its ports in Senegal would remain open. However, in view of the eruption of local turmoil, the ports were eventually closed. British ships having sailed towards Portendick in reliance on the previous assurances were now forced to refrain from entering the port, and thereby suffered loss. The arbitrators did not question the legal right of France to close the port. However, in view of the previous assurances, a notification of the closure at the earliest possible time should have been made. Since it had not, France was condemned to compensate the loss. The 'trust and confidence that

[50] G Schwarzenberger, 'The Fundamental Principles of International Law' (1955-I) 87 *RCADI* 290. Conversely, it has been claimed that the doctrine of legitimate expectations cannot be applied to international law since it would fall into natural morality and thus be utopian: M Koskenniemi, *From Apology to Utopia—The Structure of the International Legal Argument* (Helsinki, 1989) 288–90. But this statement comes only from the completely odd and useless starting point of that author. Each normative proposition is to some extent 'utopian'; but this has not impeded the existence of laws since the dawn of civilisations.

[51] A De La Pradelle and N Politis, *Recueil des arbitrages internationaux*, vol I (1798–1855) (Paris, 1905) 512ff, 526.

a State may reasonably place in the word of another'[52] were here protected; this is further shown by the fact that the arbitration tribunal rejected the claims for reparation by those ships which had unofficially received knowledge of the closure of the port. There was here an absence of subjective good faith, which made them unworthy of protection. In the *Aboilard* case (1905),[53] the arbitrator was faced with a concession contract which was finally annulled because municipal legislature refused to give its consent. However, the Haitian government had given important assurances to the investor, who decided to invest in the concession on the faith of these guarantees. The arbitration tribunal decided to allow reparation of the injury sustained on account of these legitimate expectations. In the *DJ Adams* case (1921), the Canadian Government abstained for a prolonged period of time from applying a certain piece of ancient UK municipal legislation which prohibited the entry of foreign fishing ships into Canadian ports. When the US complained of the seizure of one of its ships after a change of policy was effected, the arbitrators did not condemn Canada to pay damages on account of the fact that the captain of the ship had had knowledge of the change of policy (absence of subjective good faith). However, it stated as a matter of principle:

> As a matter of international law, where for a long continued period a Government has, either contrary to its laws or without having any laws in force covering the case, permitted to aliens a certain course of action, it cannot, under the principles of international law, suddenly change that course and make it affect those aliens already engaged in forbidden transactions as the result of that course and deprive aliens of their property so acquired, without rendering themselves liable to an international reclamation.[54]

A doctrine against 'sudden change' is here foreshadowed. Finally, in the *Schufeldt* case (1930), Guatemala pleaded the voidness of a contract of concession concluded with a foreign investor. For many years, the investor had incurred important and costly expenses on the faith of the validity of the concession. The arbitrator awarded damages on other legal grounds, but *obiter* also took cognisance of the good faith related argument of the investor:

> The Guatemala Government, having recognized the validity of the contract for six years and received all the benefits to which they were entitled under the contract and allowed Schufeldt to go on spending money on the concession, is precluded from denying its validity, even if the approval of the legislature had not been given to it.[55]

Many other later statements to the same effect could be produced, one of the most generally known being that of the ICJ affirming the legally binding character of

[52] B Cheng, *General Principles of Law as Applied by International Courts and Tribunals* (London, 1953) 139.

[53] *Aboilard* (1905) 12 *RGDIP*, Annex, Documents, 15.

[54] *DJ Adams* (1919–22) 1 *Annual Digest of Public International Law Cases* (now *ILR*) 237–38. See also (1921) VI *RIAA* 85ff.

[55] *Schufeldt* (1930) II *RIAA* 1094. The arbitrator said in this regard: 'I have no doubt that this contention of the United States is sound and in keeping with the principles of international law' (ibid).

unilateral promises on the basis of the necessary trust and confidence in international legal relations.[56]

One further question deserves a short mention at this juncture. What are the limits to the operation of the principle of good faith? There are internal and external limits. The most important internal limit is the 'legitimacy' of the expectations.[57] The norms seek to protect only those who deserve protection. This deservingness is a notion centred upon a normative analysis and a value judgment. It depends on the full context. Thus, if there is absence of subjective good faith, there is a good reason for not allowing the principle of legitimate expectations to operate; the expectation is not legitimate. Equally, the degree of development of a state and its legal services may to some extent be taken account of when judging whether legitimate expectations were created towards another state (i.e. on what that other state could legitimately rely).[58] It is also possible to exclude the expectations doctrine by express clauses, eg if the Security Council of the United Nations inserts a clause reserving to itself the right to do something, eg to lift an immunity at a later stage; the true meaning of such clauses can be to exclude the crystallisation of legitimate expectations to the contrary.[59] The most important external limit is linked to the prevalence of public order norms. *Inter partes* security has to give way to the nullity of legal acts when contrary to *jus cogens*.[60] Thus, acquiescence or estoppel are legally irrelevant to cure liberties taken with fundamental principles of international law, such as the prohibition of genocide or of torture. As was already affirmed by H Lauterpacht in the context of the freedom of the high seas (which is however not a *jus cogens* norm and whose statement could be criticised on that account):

> On the other hand, it is probably true to say that the absence of protest is irrelevant if the action of the State claiming to acquire title is so wrongful in relation to any particular State or so patently at variance with general internal law as to render it wholly incapable of becoming the source of legal right … Thus, for instance, if a State were to proclaim an exclusive right of navigation, jurisdiction or exploitation of what is regarded by the generality of States as part of the high seas, the absence of protest would hardly make any difference to the legal position.[61]

[56] *Nuclear Test* cases, (1974) *ICJ Reports* 268, § 46 and 473, § 49.

[57] One of the areas of international law in which the question of what is 'legitimate' in the context of expectations has often been analysed is the international law on investments: see below, Ch 10.

[58] See eg the arguments in Dissenting Opinion Wellington Koo, *Preah Vihear* case, (1962) *ICJ Reports* 89ff; Dissenting Opinion Spender, ibid, 128–29. See also MS McDougal, HD Lasswell and JC Miller, *The Interpretation of International Agreements and World Public Order* (Dordrecht, 1994) 345–48; S Ratner, *The Thin Justice of International Law* (Oxford, 2015) 193; P Jessup, *The Price of International Justice* (New York, 1971) 15–16.

[59] See S Heselhaus, 'Resolution 1422 (2002) des Sicherheitsrates zur Begrenzung der Tätigkeit des Internationalen Strafgerichtshofs' (2002) 62 *ZaöRV* 911–12.

[60] A Orakhelashvili, *Peremptory Norms in International Law* (Oxford, 2006) 77, 367ff.

[61] H Lauterpacht, 'Sovereignty over Submarine Areas' (1950) 27 *BYIL* 397–98.

3

The Degree of Normativity of the Principle of Good Faith

Normativity designates the presence of a prescriptive substance (an 'ought') which can be rendered operational by way of concretisations through more detailed rules,[1] or which lends itself to direct application by a legal operator.[2] The more the one or the other is present in a given context, the more the legal proposition bearing that content will be considered 'normative'. From this perspective, legal facts have no normativity; and legal norms have varying degrees of normativity. Therefore, it can be said that subjective good faith, as a legal fact, is deprived of normativity of its own. It is limited to be an external element necessary for the operation of a legal proposition. The normativity lies in the latter, not in the former. Conversely, objective good faith, ie good faith as a principle of international law, is intensely normative. There are two aspects which make the principle of good faith an intensely normative notion. First, as a fundamental principle of international law, it is a sort of structural given, a necessary content of each legal system. It does not flow from practice only, like most norms of customary international law, but is presupposed by practice and could not be validly altered by it. Thus, it has been said: 'It stands to reason that good faith … cannot be observed by empirical methods. As an ever-present element of any legal system, it constitutes a rationalisation of a certain way of correct conduct required of everyone.'[3] There is here a maximal

[1] See, eg P Reuter, 'Principes de droit international public' (1961-II) 103 *RCADI* 442.

[2] This may depend on the precision of the norm. E Kaufmann has thus for example considered that the more a rule depends on considerations of formal equality (commutative justice), the easier it is to apply it directly in a single case, and the more a rule depends on considerations of redistribution of wealth or the like (distributive justice), the less it will be prone to direct application, needing instead an intermediary concretisation by the legislator. See E Kaufmann, 'Règles générales du droit de la paix' (1935-IV) 54 *RCADI* 510.

[3] C Tomuschat, 'Obligations Arising for States Without or Against Their Will' (1993-IV) 241 *RCADI* 322. On the *jus cogens* character of the principle, see Kolb, *Bonne* 158ff; the principle is logically and legally non-derogable. As was laconically stated by G Schwarzenberger, 'The Fundamental Principles of International Law' (1955-I) 87 *RCADI* 326: 'A fundamental principle which can be eradicated from international law only at the price of the destruction of international law itself forms a necessary part of the international public order'. In the same vein: 'hanc si tollas, tollis mutua inter principes commercia … et tollis ipsum ius gentium', C Van Bynkershoek, *Quaestiones iuris publici* (1737), lib II, cap X (a sentence which has often been quoted with approval or replicated: see eg L Casanova, *Del diritto internazionale*, vol II (Florence, 1870) 23; R Phillimore, *Commentaries Upon International Law*, 3rd edn, vol II (London, 1882) 877). Clearly not all concretisations of good faith are themselves peremptory. Thus, acquiescence and estoppel can be derogated by agreement and are themselves subject to peremptory norms of international law.

distance between the fact and the norm: the latter is not nourished by some factual practice; it is rather axiomatic. Second, good faith is fundamentally normative also in its intimate legal substance, which is 'protect legitimate expectations', 'do not allow the abuse of subjective legal positions', 'do not allow to take advantage from your own wrong', etc. These key legal ideas are then concretised through a series of legal norms in the various areas of international law. Behind these many concretising norms, running like planets in the system, there remains the sun of the founding principle, which irradiates its normative idea into them and exercises its gravitational pull on their movements. The norms concretising the general genetic code are never ended or static. There is a constant flow of development and attunement in accordance with new social needs. Thus, the ICJ could in 1974 affirm the binding legal nature of unilateral promises by founding itself directly on the principle of good faith.[4] At a time when soft law instruments developed, doctrines of 'taking account of resolutions in good faith', estoppel applied to such texts, and other related notions developed.[5] When investment law and WTO law developed, elaborate doctrines of legitimate expectations were seeing the light of day under the guise of 'fair and equitable treatment' or directly under a legitimate expectations heading.[6] The legal order thus flexibly strives to realise the normative content of the principle—which reflects a permanent concern of justice and legal certainty—across the various legal subject matters as they develop over time.

There remains the question as to whether the principle of good faith can also be directly applied by the legal operator in the sense of creating rights and obligations of its own. According to certain authors[7] and to a quite constant jurisprudence of the ICJ,[8] good faith is a principle of interpretation or a foundation for other legal principles and norms,[9] but it does not create in itself duties to act or abstain, i.e. subjective rights or obligations. This view however is too narrow. If good faith can found new norms and principles, which in their turn can be applied to specific cases, it is hard to exclude a normative reach of the principle itself—since it operates *longa manu* through the concretisations. In other terms, a neat separation

[4] *Nuclear Test* cases, (1974) *ICJ Reports* 268, § 46 and 473, § 49.

[5] See below, Ch 7, section II.

[6] See below, Chs 10 and 11.

[7] J Combacau and S Sur, *Droit international public*, 8th edn (Paris, 2008) 110: 'règles fondamentales qui, sans être directement opératoires elles-mêmes, engendrent des règles plus précises—ainsi la bonne foi…'.

[8] See the case concerning *Border and Transborder Armed Actions* (*Nicaragua v Honduras*), (1988) *ICJ Reports* 105, § 94: 'The principle of good faith is … not in itself a source of obligation where none would otherwise exist'. See also eg the *Maritime and Land Boundary* case (*Cameroon v Nigeria, Preliminary Objections*), (1998) *ICJ Reports* 297, § 39. To the same effect, eg J Verhoeven, 'Considérations sur ce qui est commun, Cours général de droit international public', (2008) 334 *RCADI* 146. It has also—again to the same effect—been held that the principle of good faith is not a primary norm of international law, but is limited to direct the interpretation and application of primary norms: E Sciso, *Gli accordi internazionali confliggenti* (Bari, 1986) 301.

[9] See C Rozakis, *The Concept of Jus Cogens in the Law of Treaties* (Amsterdam, 1976) 22: 'By definition a general principle is not a norm. It is a general statement induced from or giving rise to a number of rules of law; but it is not itself a norm in the sense that it has no legally binding character as such'.

between the normativity of the concretising norms and the non-normativity of the founding principles is somewhat artificial. Consider the argument of the ICJ in the *Nuclear Test* cases of 1974, already mentioned, where the obligations arising out of a unilateral promise are directly based on the binding nature of the promise, but indirectly on the principle of good faith as protective of legitimate expectations.[10] The whole formulation of the Court revolves around good faith as an agent of creation of obligations and of rules. We have also seen that the same principle has been directly applied in case law, as occurred in the previously mentioned *Port of Portendick* case.[11] It is certainly true that good faith operates mainly through a network of intermediate principles and norms and rather rarely through a direct application of its own substance to a particular case. But the principle maintains itself always in the background as a fallback option eventually justifying some legal obligation arising out of its normative substance (almost as an equitable default rule). It is therefore submitted that the arbitrators who directly applied legitimate expectations considerations to concession contracts or to the closure of ports did not thereby commit a legal mistake. In short terms, good faith is normative also under the limb of the possibility of its direct application as an obligation-creating norm. Areas like the one of international investment law or international commercial law are good examples for the principle of good faith applied directly as a principle yielding legal obligations.[12]

[10] Here is the reasoning of the Court: 'One of the basic principles governing the creation and performance of legal obligations, whatever their source, is the principle of good faith. Trust and confidence are inherent in international co-operation, in particular in an age when this co-operation in many fields is becoming increasingly essential. Just as the very rule of *pacta sunt servanda* in the law of treaties is based on good faith, so also is the binding force of an international obligation assumed by unilateral declaration. Thus interested States may take cognizance of unilateral declarations and place confidence in them, and are entitled to require that the obligation thus created be respected'. *Nuclear Test* cases, (1974) *ICJ Reports* 268, § 46 and 473, § 49.

[11] Above, Ch 2, section III.

[12] See below, Ch 7, section IV and Ch 10.

4

The Delimitation of Good Faith with Respect to Other Principles of International Law

I. Good Faith and *Pacta Sunt Servanda*

It is broadly agreed that *pacta sunt servanda* is the rule on the binding force of contractual or conventional bonds.[1] What is its exact relation to the principle of good faith? For some authors, *pacta sunt servanda* flows from the principle of good faith; the latter underlies the former and founds it.[2] This conception has historical roots. In classical Roman law there was no general rule of *pacta sunt servanda*; rather the rule was *ex nudo pacto actio non oritur*.[3] Only named contracts with varying degrees of formalism were considered legally binding. In the evolution of civil law at the end of the middle Ages, under the powerful impulsion of canon law, it was considered that the word pledged should per se bind the promisor. The development of modern commerce buttressed this evolution. Thus, the trust in the word deliberately given was seen as the root of the *pacta* rule. In other words, good faith was considered the reason why the compact should be legally and morally binding. This development of the law found a particular resonance in nascent international law. There, the contractual formalism of Roman law had no place; it was held that sovereigns should bind themselves by the simple pledge given, not by being subjected to civil law formalisms.[4]

For some other authors, good faith does not add anything to the *pacta sunt servanda* rule. Either the obligation is executed and *pacta* satisfied, whence good

[1] On the historical roots of that rule, see Kolb, *Bonne* 86ff.

[2] TO Elias, *The Modern Law of Treaties* (New York, 1974) 41; JF O'Connor, *Good Faith in International Law* (Aldershot, 1991) 107, 117, 119. Other authors are quoted in Kolb, *Bonne* 93.

[3] 'No action arises from a mere pact.' See G Diosdi, *Contract in Roman Law From the XII Tables to the Glossators* (Budapest, 1981); H Dilcher, 'Der Typenzwang im römischen Vertragsrecht', (1960) 77 *Zeitschrift der Savigny-Stiftung für Rechtsgeschichte, Romanistische Abteilung* 272ff; B Schmidlin, 'Zum Gegensatz zwischen römischer und moderner Vertragsauffassung: Typengebundenheit und Gestaltungsfreiheit', in *Essays in Commemoration of the Sixth Lustrum of the Institute for Legal History of the University of Utrecht* (Assen, 1979) 111ff.

[4] This is eg the sense of a phrase such as 'all international treaties are covenants bonae fidei'. See R Phillimore, *Commentaries Upon International Law*, 3rd edn, vol II (London, 1882) 94.

faith is superfluous; or the obligation is not executed and *pacta* violated, whence again good faith does not make any valuable contribution. In short, it is not possible to execute an obligation in bad faith—since that would be tantamount to not executing it at all.[5]

Both conceptions are too narrow. As to the first, good faith may well be the founding principle, and *pacta* an expression of it. But there does not follow an identity of the two rules. There still remains the necessity to consider the legal-operational differences between both. As to the second conception, it is manifestly based on an error. *Pacta* is nothing more than a formal injunction to execute an obligation. But it does not determine what must be substantively done in order to satisfy the obligation, a problem which it supposes to be already solved. Thus, other rules and principles—among which good faith—must still apply so as to determine what exactly is the extent of the obligation incurred, e.g. by the device of bona fide interpretation, and the like. Thus, for example, to accept that there is a contractual obligation not to construct fortifications at the port of Dunkirk (as was the case following the Treaty of Utrecht, in 1713), while starting to erect such fortifications one mile of distant at Mardyck, is not fulfilling the obligation of disarmament[6]—this is determined not by the mere text of the treaty but by considerations of its spirit and by good faith. Once this operation is achieved, *pacta* comes into play so as to ensure the binding force of the obligation as it has been determined.

What, then, are the differences, between both principles? The following ones appear to be the most important:

(i) Good faith is not limited to the law of treaties or to the execution of obligations. It has a series of other applications centered mainly on the legitimate expectation limb, such as acquiescence and estoppel, the prohibition of perfidy, etc.
(ii) As already mentioned, within the law of treaties, good faith goes beyond *pacta*. The latter is but a formal injunction to execute the due, a sort of blanket[7] to be filled by concrete content. Good faith is one of the rules for filling that blanket. Further, good faith can also limit the principle *pacta* by providing for exceptions to the duty to honour a contractual obligation, for example through the doctrine *rebus sic stantibus*[8]
(iii) Good faith applies also to the creation of obligations, and here precedes chronologically and logically the principle *pacta*. Thus, some obligations are created with regard to soft law instruments and unilateral acts (hence, the term *pactum* is here enlarged); or with regard to legitimate expectations

[5] H Kelsen, *The Law of the United Nations* (London, 1951) 89.

[6] See R Phillimore, *Commentaries Upon International Law*, 3rd edn, vol II (London, 1882) 102–03; Zoller, *Bonne* 81.

[7] G Dahm, *Völkerrecht*, vol I (Stuttgart, 1958) 13.

[8] The latter is seen by some authors as a concretisation of good faith considerations: see, eg A Verdross, *Die Quellen des universellen Völkerrechts* (Freiburg, 1973) 133–34; P De Visscher, 'Cours général de droit international public' (1972-II) 136 *RCADI* 87.

created (see the cases mentioned above, from *Portendick* to *Schufeldt*); or still, good faith may command not to attach importance to formal clerical errors in the context of the creation of an obligation.[9]

Thus, however close the two principles may be, they have distinctive features and operate in different ways within the international legal order.

II. Good Faith and Equity

This is not the place to develop at length the interesting concept of equity.[10] We may summarise its complexion and function within the legal system as follows. There are two main functions of equity: the correction of excessively rigid rules (corrective equity); and the balancing of all relevant circumstances in an area deprived of detailed legal rules (autonomous equity).

First, equity is a fact-related concept: distinct from strict or formal justice, and strict or formal application of the legal rules, it offers the sensitivity of a spontaneous feeling of fairness, especially in atypical cases where the strict application of formal justice or of relevant rules might cause hardship. Thus, a legal rule may provide for the confiscation of any car engaged in drug trafficking. It may occur in a single case that a car was thus used by the grandchild of an elderly lady, without the knowledge of the latter, and is confiscated for transportation of a very small amount of drugs for personal use. The car may here be vitally important for the elderly lady, since it allows her to drive regularly to the hospital where she receives vital treatment. If the law makes no equitable exceptions but commands in all cases the confiscation of the car, we would probably all have a spontaneous feeling of injustice and inequity. But not all situations are as harsh as this one. 'Corrective equity', as we termed it, which could soften the excessively hard contours of the formal law, can be used by the legal operator at different stages of the application of the law. It can pour into the interpretation of a rule, so as to take account of equitable factors and to choose the most equitable construction of the rule within the four corners of what the text allows (equity *intra legem*). Thus, if a delimitation line has to be drawn in the desert, and the course of the *uti possidetis* line is not entirely clear in a relevant area, so that there is a certain leeway in the interpretation of the title, the judge will probably avoid drawing the line in such a way as to leave all five oases in the possession of one state; rather a line will be chosen which distributes these points 4-1 or 3-2.[11] Similarly, equitable considerations may be

[9] *Bank of Brussels v Discount Company and Bank of Dresden* arbitration: 'It would be contrary to the principle of good faith, which should govern the relations between the Offices, to attach a judicial consequence to such a clerical error'; (1929) 5 *Annual Digest of Public International Law Cases* 428.

[10] See Kolb, *Bonne* 99ff.

[11] See the considerations of Judge G Abi-Saab (Separate Opinion), *Territorial Dispute (Burkina Faso v Mali)* (1986) *ICJ Reports* 662–63.

used to fill gaps within the law (equity *praeter legem*). Thus, if the two parties require the judge to delimit all the relevant areas between them, but in a certain sector there is no applicable title, this gap may be filled by the judge through equitable considerations.[12] Finally, the extent to which equity can be used to correct a formally applicable but excessively strict piece of legislation (as in our example with the car, above) depends on a series of considerations, such as the mandate and general position of the judge, the applicable principles of the legal order, and the like. For elementary reasons of legal security, it is rare that a judge or legal operator is allowed to discard a formally applicable rule under equitable considerations. But he or she might smuggle into the law some equitable exception, by some dynamic or elsewise courageous interpretation. One possibility which may be open is to declare that the law did not intend to cover such atypical cases, which then creates a gap to be filled by equity.

Second, equity may operate free-standing, ie not in relation to an extant (and possibly too strict) rule. There are some areas of the law which are not yet permeated by too many or by too directive legal rules. In such areas, the law commands the legal operator to balance up all the relevant circumstances and to shape a legal rule in context. To do so, the operator will have recourse to considerations which seem fair and equitable in context. It is in this way that a law of maritime delimitation was progressively shaped under the polar star of 'equitable principles'.[13] This type of equity is sometimes called 'autonomous equity', for the reason that it is not defined in opposition to or in relation to an applicable rule of (strict) law.

What are the relations between the principles of good faith and equity? In many cases, authors affirm that both principles are intimately linked.[14] Good faith and equity are often mentioned together as principles softening excessive formalisms within the legal rules.[15] It also occurs that good faith and equity are mentioned vaguely to cover the same 'equitable' ground, especially in concession contracts.[16] Comparison of the two principles is rendered difficult by the many layers which both manifest: subjective good faith, good faith as legal standard, principle of good faith, corrective and autonomous equity. However, the gist of the difference lies between the two objective principles. Equity designates the conditions for deriving the 'justice of the particular case'. Its focus is always individualising and fact-intensive. Good faith, on its part, is centred on the softening of the socially unwelcome consequences of an excessive preponderance given to the (possibly undisclosed) will of one subject, by protecting the legitimate expectations of the

[12] See eg the *Land, Island and Maritime Frontier Dispute (El Salvador v Honduras)* (1992) *ICJ Reports* 514–15, where the Court had recourse to a line set out in a non-ratified treaty to fill such a gap.

[13] See R Kolb, *Case Law on Equitable Maritime Delimitation, Digest and Commentaries/Jurisprudence sur les délimitations maritimes selon l'équité, Répertoire et commentaires* (La Haye, 2003); P Weil, *Perspectives du droit de la délimitation maritime* (Paris, 1988).

[14] L Delbez, *Les principes généraux du contentieux international* (Paris, 1962) 98; Zoller, *Bonne* 14.

[15] *Cayuga Indians arbitration* (1926) VI *RIAA* 180.

[16] E Paasivirta, *Participation of States in International Contracts* (Helsinki, 1990) 59ff.

other subjects. Good faith also tempers the exercise of rights when done in a way which gravely contravenes the collective interest. Often, good faith operates itself as strict law. Thus, for example, an acquiescence or estoppel protecting legitimate expectations may in a particular case work some inequity for third world states not enjoying the developed legal services necessary to react so as to protect their own rights.[17] In short, equity has as its core an individualisation or smoothing of abstract or strict norms, while good faith tempers individualistic voluntarism.

There are a series of further differences between both concepts. For example, equity is more totalising in perspective, since it takes account of an unlimited number of considerations drawn from the relevant context.[18] Good faith, on its part, is centered on legitimate expectations, trust created, avoidance of abuse and harm to the collectivity, immoral conduct. It however also occurs that both concepts converge. For example, it is true that in the interpretation, equity tends to seek justice and good faith the prevalence of the spirit over excessive literality; but to some extent both notions converge in what has been called 'considerations of fairness, reasonableness and policy'.[19] Thus, there is overall a complex relationship between the two principles, even if each one has and retains its own distinctive features.

[17] See eg the arguments in Dissenting Opinion Wellington Koo, *Preah Vihear* (1962) *ICJ Reports* 89ff; Dissenting Opinion Spender, ibid, 128–29. See also MS McDougal, HD Lasswell and JC Miller, *The Interpretation of International Agreements and World Public Order* (Dordrecht, 1994) 345–48; S Ratner, *The Thin Justice of International Law* (Oxford, 2015) 193; P Jessup, *The Price of International Justice* (New York, 1971) 15–16.

[18] See the impressive list of considerations on which the arbitrator relied in the *Region of Brcko* arbitration (1997). According to Annex II of the Dayton Agreements of 1995, a line of demarcation had to be established in the zones controlled by the parties, Serbia and Bosnia. To say the least, their relations were strained. The parties did not manage to find an agreement. The issue was thus brought to arbitration according to the mentioned Annex V of the Dayton Agreement. The region of Brcko, where the disagreement had manifested itself, was considered vital by both sides. The procedure of the tribunal was punctuated by incidents and ill-will. The two 'national arbitrators' refused to sign the award; it therefore emanates only from its President, Sir Robert Owens. The tribunal refused to apply merely the law. It had recourse to equity, which its constitutive instrument allowed it to apply. It therefore took into account a series of circumstantial factors of extra-legal nature, such as: the tension reigning in the area; the allegiances of the population; economic interests; the psychological value of the region for the parties; the importance of the lines of communication for those parties; and the interests of the international community to a lasting a peaceful settlement. In view of these factors, the tribunal decided that a partition of the area, as envisaged in the Dayton Agreement, was still premature. The arbitrator opted rather for a temporary solution of joint administration under international control. He added: 'not being required to proceed solely on the basis of legal rules, the Tribunal is authorized to render an award that, in its view, best reflects and protects the overall interests of the parties and that has the strongest likelihood of promoting a long-term peaceful solution'. See (1997) 36 *ILM* 428ff, quote at ibid 431, § 97.

[19] I Brownlie, *Principles of Public International Law*, 4th edn (Oxford, 1990) 26 (5th edn 1998, p 25).

Part II

Good Faith in the Various Subject Areas of Public International Law

5

Good Faith and the Sources

It is a commonplace to affirm that good faith is inherent in contractual bonds[1] and that it plays a fundamental role in the law of treaties.[2] Good faith is indeed paramount in all legal areas permeated by reciprocity and bilateralism. Compacts, in particular, create a legal relationship of trust and confidence. The parties come closer to each other than other subjects of a society, which are not bound by (common) agreements. Thus, relationships of increased loyalty and protection of legitimate trust are crystallised within the law.[3] However, as we will see, good faith plays a role also in all other sources of law or obligations. This is so because all these sources are concerned with will, consent and interaction of subjects, which is a fundamental playground of good faith. Thus, the principle is paramount also in the context of soft law obligations, unilateral promises and other unilateral acts, as it is in the formation of customary international law. Let us first turn to the conclusion of treaties, then to the interpretation and execution of treaties, and later to the other sources. We will present the most important concretisations of good faith in these areas.[4]

I. Good Faith and Pre-Conventional Obligations (Article 18 of the VCLT)

Article 18 of the VCLT of 1969 reads as follows:

> A State is obliged to refrain from acts which would defeat the object and purpose of a treaty when: (*a*) it has signed the treaty or has exchanged instruments constituting the treaty subject to ratification, acceptance or approval, until it shall have made its intention clear not to become a party to the treaty; or (*b*) it has expressed its consent to be bound

[1] P Guggenheim, *Traité de droit international public*, vol I (Geneva, 1967) 28–29.

[2] CC Hyde, *International Law—Chiefly as Interpreted and Applied by the United States*, vol II (Boston, 1922) 71: '[Good faith and high purpose is] the only intelligible theory on which enlightened States could be deemed to conclude treaties with each other'. See also Zoller, *Bonne* 47; PM Dupuy, 'L'unité de l'ordre juridique international' (2002) 297 *RCADI* 126–27.

[3] Müller, *Vertrauensschutz* 154–55, 164.

[4] For a more detailed discussion, see Kolb, *Bonne* 179ff.

by the treaty, pending the entry into force of the treaty and provided that such entry into force is not unduly delayed.[5]

In brief, the common enterprise of an agreement and the investments it inevitably triggers, creates between or among the concerned states a bond of trust meaning in the first place that no one of these states shall, in a disloyal way, attempt to

[5] On this provision, see: J Nisot, 'La force obligatoire des traités signés, non encore ratifiés' (1930) 57 *JDI* 878ff; Harvard Research, 'Law of Treaties' (1935) 29 *AJIL* 778ff (art 9); B Cheng, *General Principles of Law—As Applied by International Courts and Tribunals* (London, 1953) 106ff; R Bernhardt, 'Völkerrechtliche Bindungen in den Vorstadien des Vertragsschlusses' (1957/58) 18 *ZaöRV* 652ff; W Morway, 'The Obligation of a State not to Frustrate the Object of a Treaty Prior to its Entry into Force' (1967) 27 *ZaöRV*, 451ff; JP Cot, 'La bonne foi et la conclusion des traités' (1968) 4 *RBDI*, 140ff; JP Cot, 'La bonne foi en droit international public' (1968/69) *Cours de l'IHEI (Paris)* 39ff; J Nisot, 'L'article 18 de la Convention de Vienne sur le droit des traités' (1970) 6 *RBDI* 498ff; C Verdon, 'Les obligations précontractuelles dans le droit des traités' (PhD thesis, Geneva, 1972); P Cahier, 'L'obligation de ne pas priver un traité de son objet et de son but avant son entrée en vigueur', *Essays in Honor of F Dehousse*, vol I (Paris, 1979) 31ff; M Rogoff, 'International Legal Obligation of Signatories to an Unratified Treaty' (1980) 32 *Maine Law Review* 266ff; T Hassan, 'Good Faith in Treaty Formation' (1981) 21 *Virginia JIL*, 443ff, esp 450ff; T Vassalli di Dachenhausen, *La culpa in contrahendo nel diritto internazionale* (Naples, 1983); P McDade, 'The Interim Obligation Between Signature and Ratification of a Treaty: Issues Raised by the Recent Actions of Signatories to the Law of the Sea Convention with Respect to the Mining of the Deep Seabed' (1985) 32 *NILR*, 5ff, esp 9–28; JS Charme, 'The Interim Obligation of Article 18 of the VCLT: Making sense of an Enigma' (1991) 25 *The George Washington Journal of International Law and Economics*, 74ff; R Platzöder, 'Substantive Changes in a Multilateral Treaty Before its Entry into Force: The Case of the 1982 U.N. Convention on the Law of the Sea' (1993) 4 *EJIL*, 390ff; P Palchetti, 'Article 18 of the 1969 Vienna Convention: A Vague and Ineffective Obligation or a Useful Means of Strengthening Legal Cooperation?' in E Cannizzaro (ed), *The Law of Treaties Beyond the Vienna Convention* (Oxford, 2011) 25ff. See also: O Hoijer, *Les traités internationaux*, vol I (Paris, 1928) 136ff; G Dahm, *Völkerrecht*, vol III (Stuttgart, 1961) 70–71, 80–81; AD McNair, *The Law of Treaties* (Oxford, 1961) 199ff; AP Sereni, *Diritto internazionale*, vol III (Milan, 1962) 1413ff; K Holloway, *Modern Trends in Treaty Law* (London, 1967) 56ff; JP Müller, *Vertrauensschutz im Völkerrecht* (Köln, 1971) 154ff; TO Elias, *The Modern Law of Treaties* (New York, 1974) 26; E Zoller, *La bonne foi en droit international public* (Paris, 1977) 48ff; M Gounelle, *La motivation des actes juridiques en droit international public* (Paris, 1979) 204ff; I Sinclair, *The Vienna Convention on the Law of Treaties*, 2nd edn (Manchester, 1984) 13, 19, 43, 86, 99, 109; S Bastid, *Les traités dans la vie internationale: Conclusions et effets* (Paris, 1985) 50; P Reuter, *Introduction au droit des traités*, 2nd edn (Paris, 1985) 62–63; ME Villiger, *Customary International Law and Treaties* (Dordrecht, 1985) 321ff; *Restatement of the Law Third, The American Law Institute*, vol I (St Paul, ALI, 1987) 174ff (s 312); R Kolb, *La bonne foi en droit international public* (Paris, 2000) 182ff; A Aust, *Modern Treaty Law and Practice*, 2nd edn (Cambridge, 2007) 116ff; ME Villiger, *Commentary on the 1969 Vienna Convention on the Law of Treaties* (Leiden, 2009) 242ff; L Boisson de Chazournes, AM La Rosa and M Mbengue, 'Article 18' in O Corten and P Klein (eds), *The Vienna Conventions on the Law of Treaties—A Commentary*, vol I (Oxford, 2011) 369ff; O Dörr, 'Article 18' in O Dörr and K Schmalenbach (eds), *Vienna Convention on the Law of Treaties, A Commentary* (Berlin, 2012) 219ff; R Kolb, *The Law of Treaties—An Introduction* (Cheltenham, 2016) 43–46. On the drafting history, see S Rosenne, *The Law of Treaties—A Guide to the Legislative History of the Vienna Convention* (Leyden, 1970) 171ff. For some practice, see M Nash Leich (ed), *Digest of US Practice in International Law* (Washington DC, 1980) 398ff, 690ff, 701; M Whiteman, *Digest of International Law*, vol XIV (Washington DC, 1970) 42–43, 47–48.

The normative content of art 18 VCLT is often applied by analogy to other areas of international treaty law, eg to suspended treaties: see F Bestagno, *La clausole di salvaguardia economica nel diritto internazionale* (Milan, 1998) 196; or to treaties already in force: Dissenting Opinion Fleischhauer, *Gabcíkovo-Nagymaros* (1997) *ICJ Reports* 206 and Separate Opinion Keith, *Pulp Mills* (2010-I) *ICJ Reports* 127, § 17 (and see below, section VI).

directly or indirectly defeat the object and purpose of the treaty while it is not yet in force and thus not yet legally executory. If such a state does not want to participate any more to the treaty it has signed but not yet ratified, it ought to formally notify that it renounces ratification to the treaty-partners or possibly to withdraw its signature. Conversely, it should not take the liberty to torpedo the treaty by acts and deeds which must be considered to be disloyal. The issue is plainly one of good faith taken in the sense of protection of legitimate expectations of a minimally loyal behaviour. Further, another aspect of good faith comes to fore, namely the protection of the object and purpose of a transaction against frustration by unilateral acts of some state or states. Legitimate expectations and non-unilateralism to defeat the common enterprise are here the essence of the applicable principle of good faith.

Consider the following situations. Two states agree to reduce by 50 per cent some customs dues on a certain asset by 1 January 2017, the day on which the treaty shall enter into force. State A increases its customs dues on the said asset by 100 per cent on 30 December 2016. It is not yet bound by the treaty, and thus its action is not breaching the latter. However, this action defeats the object and purpose of the treaty and is also manifestly an act of bad faith. Indeed, state A will in our example not have conceded any true reduction on the dues, while state B will have done so. Take another example. State A cedes a part of its territory to state B for the exploitation of some resources which lie there. It receives proper consideration in view of the resources ceded. Pending the entry into force of the treaty, it accelerates the exploitation of the resources, so as to leave only a small fraction of what was expected to the other state once the treaty enters into force. Take yet another example. Two states agree to allow the free navigation of a part of a common river. Before the treaty enters into force, state A engages in a series of costly works for the amelioration of the navigability of the river, the construction of new ports, etc. State B, on its part, constructs a series of structures which render impossible the navigation of the river in the relevant section. The common aspect of all these situations it that the workability of the treaty, once it will enter into force, is heavily jeopardised or rendered nugatory. But there also remain many open questions: must there be an intention to deprive the treaty of its efficacy, or is it sufficient to objectively cause this result? What is the object and purpose of the treaty, ie which are its essential provisions? When the realisation of the treaty's purpose is rendered more difficult but not nugatory, what is the legal position? Must one take into account the reversibility of the action, ie the capacity to restitute or return to the status quo ante once the treaty enters into force? Can article 18 VCLT exceptionally command also action rather than simple abstention, when the former is necessary to save the object and purpose of the treaty commitment? Can such a duty more easily be admitted when the other party or parties have freely engaged in such positive action? Must one balance up the relative importance of the preservation of some objects of the treaty as against the potential urgency of contrary action for the concerned state? Can the probability of ratification or entry into force of the treaty be taken account of for configuring the strength of article 18

VCLT obligations? Can the doctrine *rebus sic stantibus* be applied by analogy to the article 18 VCLT obligations? These and further questions must be answered in the light of the underlying principle of good faith-legitimate expectations.[6] One has to ask what type of expectations the parties could and should have had considering context. These expectations have an objective and a subjective limb. Objectively, the parties may legitimately expect a reasonably loyal behaviour with regard to the treaty as it appears to the neutral observer. This is a general legal standard, to be appreciated by what can and must on average be expected from treaty partners. Subjectively, the parties may legitimately expect what has been represented to them in the concrete case by the deeds, utterances and other behaviour of the other party or parties.

Some general aspects of article 18 VCLT may be noted.

— *First*, article 18 does not make specific provisions of the treaty provisionally applicable. Provisional application is regulated by article 25 VCLT. If states agree to provisional application, the treaty obligations apply as such, according to the precise scope of the collateral agreement on provisional application. Article 18 VCLT is limited to imposing some extra-treaty obligations under general international law, and not to impose application of treaty provisions.[7] Its aim is to protect the object and purpose of the common compact as a whole. The rule under article 18 does therefore not normally require a state *to act* in a specific way; it requires only *abstention* from some type of action.[8] Consequently, it is also not normally possible to say that a state should take positive measures in order to further the object and purpose of the treaty, or in order to remove obstacles to the proper implementation of the treaty which have occurred in the meantime without responsibility of the state. The opposite could be true only if legitimate expectations have been created to the opposite. And the opposite is true if the state has intentionally created these obstacles.

— *Second*, many acts and deeds can or do impact in some way on the treaty and on its object and purpose. The chain of causality and foreseeability may be shorter or longer. Article 18 requires abstention only for acts which have the direct effect of frustrating the operation of the treaty once it entered into force. If acts and deeds have a speculative impact on the treaty objectives and main rules, article 18 VCLT has not been violated. A state does not subject itself to the obligation to abstain from a whole series of policy actions which could have some more or less remote impact on treaties it has signed.

[6] That this is the governing principle for the application of art 18 VCLT is generally admitted in legal doctrine. See the many authors quoted in Kolb, *Bonne* 206, fn 167.

[7] However, art 18 VCLT can be applied to the agreement providing for provisional application after its signature and before it is in force.

[8] JP Cot, 'La bonne foi et la conclusion des traités' (1968) 4 *RBDI* 155ff; T Hassan, 'Good Faith in Treaty Formation' (1981) 21 *Virginia JIL* 452; R Bernhardt, 'Völkerrechtliche Bindungen in den Vorstadien des Vertragsschlusses' (1957/58) 18 *ZaöRV* 682–83.

— *Third*, the obligation under article 18 VCLT applies to a signatory state only for the time it has not notified to the other parties its intention not to become a party to the treaty (ie not to ratify it). Once a state has openly stated that it 'exits' the common treaty enterprise, as it is entitled to do under the law of treaties, it no longer has any pre-conventional obligations.[9] The issue is manifestly one of fair dealing: the intention not to ratify should be openly stated, and not channelled through some 'perfidious acts' more or less indirectly torpedoing the object and purpose of the common enterprise. This also means that a state does not have to 'un-sign' a treaty (as the US did for the Rome Statute of the ICC)[10] in order to be freed from its obligations under article 18 VCLT. Un-signing has mainly a political motivation. Legally, it is sufficient to notify the depositary that the state renounces its ratification.
— *Fourth*, subjective bad faith of the state is neither required nor necessary.[11] The standards under article 18 VCLT are objective. This is also the case for the good faith standard geared towards the protection of legitimate expectations.
— *Fifth*, the obligation under article 18 VCLT is now part of customary international law.[12] It has been frequently invoked in judicial and diplomatic practice. However, it has not had an enormous impact on the law of treaties. It is unusual for states to play fast and loose with treaties they freely signed and which they have in any event an easy means to exit if they desire.
— *Sixth*, contrary to what has been sustained,[13] the ratification of the treaty by a state is not a condition for (retroactively) sanctioning its deeds contrary to article 18 VCLT and related customary international law. In other words, the obligation not to frustrate the object and purpose of a treaty pending its entry into force is a free-standing obligation under international law[14] and is not conditional on the later ratification of the treaty. The pre-conventional obligations are not a retroactive effect of ratification.

[9] This occurred in the *Dutch Seamen's Welfare Foundation v Minister of Transport* case before the Netherlands Council of State, (2007) 38 *NYIL* 498, § 2.4. See also the Report of the competent Minister as to the reasons of non-ratification: (2008) 39 *NYIL* 269–70.

[10] JR Worth, 'Globalization and the Myth of Absolute National Sovereignty: Re-Considering the Un-Signing of the Rome Statute and the Legacy of Senator Bricker' (2004) 79 *Indiana Law Journal* 245ff; ET Swaine, 'Unsigning' (2003) 55 *Stanford Law Review* 2061ff. The same occurred with Russia in 2016.

[11] But some authors consider it to be necessary, eg Zoller, *Bonne* 77; P McDade, 'The Interim Obligation Between Signature and Ratification of a Treaty: Issues Raised by the Recent Actions of Signatories to the Law of the Sea Convention with Respect to the Mining of the Deep Seabed' (1985) 32 *NILR* 22. The ILC did however not require such a subjective bad faith: (1966-II) *YbILC* 202. See also Müller, *Vertrauensschutz* 154ff.

[12] See eg ME Villiger, 'Article 18' in ME Villiger (ed), *Commentary on the 1969 Vienna Convention on the Law of Treaties* (Leiden, 2009) 252; O Dörr, 'Article 18' in O Dörr and K Schmalenbach (eds), *Vienna Convention on the Law of Treaties, A Commentary* (Heidelberg, 2012) 221. See also the analysis of L Boisson de Chazournes, AM La Rosa and M Mbengue, 'Article 18' in O Corten and P Klein (eds), *The Vienna Conventions on the Law of Treaties, A Commentary*, vol I (Oxford, 2011) 372ff, ultimately reaching the same result.

[13] See eg W Wengler, *Völkerrecht*, vol I (Berlin, 1964) 222–23; R Quadri, *Diritto internazionale pubblico*, 5th edn (Naples, 1968) 160.

[14] Müller, *Vertrauensschutz* 162ff.

— *Seventh*, once the treaty enters into force for a state, the interim obligation of article 18 VCLT in principle ceases to apply. When the state is bound to positively apply all the provisions of the treaty, the lesser duty not to frustrate the object and purpose of the treaty may seem to have no place any more. We shall however see in the chapter devoted to the execution of treaties[15] that the object and purpose of the treaty is a separate asset with regard to the black letter provisions. It enjoys protection also once the treaty enters into force—perhaps even a fortiori. Moreover, if the treaty is suspended on any grounds, the obligation under article 18 VCLT is applied by analogy during the phase of suspension, when there is a legitimate expectation that the treaty obligations could be resumed.[16]

There are interesting applications of these pre-conventional obligations in ancient and recent diplomatic practice. As an example of the former, in the report of the Attorney General and Queen's Advocate of the UK dated 15 May 1857, we read the following passage:

> That Altho' the Convention between Her Majesty and the Republic of Honduras has not yet been ratified, yet the ratifications, when exchanged, will relate back to, and confirm the Convention ... No Act can in the meantime be properly done by Her Majesty, whilst the ratification of the Treaty is under consideration, which may at all affect any of the stipulations of the Treaty.[17]

And in 1864, Lord Palmerston affirmed that the mere signature of a treaty bound the signatory, 'whilst the ratification is under consideration, not to do anything which might affect any of the stipulations of the treaty'.[18] Later, the principle was affirmed in many diplomatic exchanges, eg by Canada,[19] the Netherlands,[20] Switzerland,[21] Italy,[22] the US,[23] the UN,[24] etc. The older case law is also quite

[15] Below, section VI.

[16] Art 72, § 2, of the VCLT: 'During the period of the suspension the parties shall refrain from acts tending to obstruct the resumption of the operation of the treaty'. See ME Villiger, *Commentary on the 1969 Vienna Convention on the Law of Treaties* (Leiden, 2009) 890; S Wittich, 'Article 72' in O Dörr and K Schmalenbach (eds), *Vienna Convention on the Law of Treaties, A Commentary* (Heidelberg, 2012) 1233–34; P Couvreur and CE Berdud, 'Article 72' in O Corten and P Klein, *The Vienna Conventions on the Law of Treaties, A Commentary*, vol II (Oxford, 2011) 1637–39.

[17] P McDade, 'The Interim Obligation Between Signature and Ratification of a Treaty: Issues Raised by the Recent Actions of Signatories to the Law of the Sea Convention with Respect to the Mining of the Deep Seabed' (1985) 32 *NILR* 11.

[18] *Hansard*, HC Deb (Third Series), vol 174, col 787, quoted by McDade, ibid, p 11, fn 27.

[19] (1978) 16 *CYIL* 366.

[20] (1975) 6 *NYIL* 283.

[21] (1977) 33 *ASDI* 150–51.

[22] R Ago and M Toscano, *La prassi italiana di diritto internazionale, Terza Serie (1919–1925)*, vol I (Rome, 1995) 342–44.

[23] M Nash Leich (ed), *Digest of United States Practice in International Law, 1980* (Washington DC, 1986) 398–99, 701. See also Nash Leich, ibid, *1979* (Washington DC, 1983) 691.

[24] See the Report of the UNSG with relation to the revision of Pt XI of the Law of the Sea Convention of 1982, UN Doc A/48/950, 1994, Annex I, § 6.

rich but unequally relevant.[25] The leading case is *Megalidis* (1928), decided by a Greco-Turk Mixed Arbitral Tribunal.[26] It concerned the seizure of assets belonging to Mr Megalidis pending the entry into force of a treaty. The discussion concentrated on the duty of Turkey to restitute these assets once the treaty had entered into force. The tribunal decided in favour of restitution on account of the doctrine of pre-conventional obligations.[27] This jurisprudence had been preceded by (and was founded on) the *Ignacio Torres* arbitration (1871),[28] thc *German Reparations according to Article 260 of the Treaty of Versailles* arbitration (1924)[29] and the *Tacna Arica* arbitration (1925).[30] The often-quoted *Certain German Interests in Upper Polish Silesia* case (1926)[31] of the PCIJ is not a good precedent on the issue. The Court did not decide the issue, since in its view there was no treaty obligation not to alienate certain assets, and thus there could also be no pre-conventional obligation to abstain from such conduct.[32] The same is true for the *Kemeny* arbitration (1928), which concerns the provisional application of a treaty, and not the pre-conventional obligations.[33] There are finally also a series of older municipal law decisions, which do recognise the pre-conventional obligations, eg in *Polish State Treasury v Von Bismarck* (1923),[34] Polish Supreme Court, or in *Termination of Employment* case (1956),[35] Austrian Supreme Court.

There is now newer national case law. It puts into focus issues related to provisional application and the impact of a conduct on the future ability to apply the treaty. In the *FG Hemisphere Associates v Congo (Stock VP)* case (2010),[36] statements to maintain absolute immunity while having signed the UN Immunities Convention of 2004 were not held to be defeating the object and purpose of the Convention. China had simply continued its former policy on foreign immunities pending ratification. No legitimate expectation had been created that it would alter its own conduct while the treaty was not in force. It must be added that there

[25] See Kolb, *Bonne* 189ff for a detailed discussion.

[26] *Megalidis* (1928) VIII *Recueil des décisions des Tribunaux arbitraux mixtes institués par les traités de paix* 386ff.

[27] 'Qu'en outre, il est évident que la saisie n'a pas pu être faite dans le but de s'approprier les objets, étant donné qu'il est de principe que déjà avec la signature d'un Traité et avant sa mise en vigueur, il existe pour les parties contractantes une obligation de ne rien faire qui puisse nuire au Traité en diminuant la portée de ses clauses … Il est intéressant de faire observer que ce principe—lequel en somme n'est qu'une manifestation de la bonne foi qui est à la base de toute loi et de toute convention—a reçu un certain nombre d'applications dans divers traités…'. Ibid, 395.

[28] JB Moore, *History and Digest of the International Arbitrations to which the United States has been a Party*, vol IV (Washington DC, 1898) 3801.

[29] *German Reparations according to Article 260 of the Treaty of Versailles* (1924) I *RIAA* 522.

[30] *Tacna Arica* (1925) II *RIAA* 935.

[31] *Certain German Interests in Upper Polish Silesia* (1926) PCIJ ser A, no 7, pp 29–30.

[32] ibid, pp 38–39.

[33] *Kemeny* (1927/28) 4 *Annual Digest of Public International Law Cases* 549–50.

[34] *Polish State Treasury v Von Bismarck* (1923/24) 2 *Annual Digest of Public International Law Cases* 80.

[35] *Termination of Employment* (1956) 23 *ILR* 470–71.

[36] *FG Hemisphere Associates v Congo (Stock VP)* (2010) 142 *ILR* 254–56, §§ 103–06 (Hong Kong Special Administrative Region, Court of Appeal).

is no irreversible action here: the object and purpose of the Convention, once ratified and in force, remains intact for such future time: a restrictive immunity can be applied to all the cases after the entry into force of the Convention. If the Court had decided otherwise, that would have been tantamount to using article 18 VCLT as a device to force China into a provisional application of the Convention. In the *Clarification of Paragraph 5 of Operative Part of Constitutional Court Resolution No 3-P of 2 February 1999* case (2009),[37] the Russian Constitutional Court held that Russia was in breach of article 18 VCLT by the fact of applying the death penalty after having ratified Protocol no 6 to the ECHR on the abolition of the death penalty. However, it added that Russia had avoided a breach of international law by substituting all death penalties by other punishments. This interpretation is open to important doubts. It is not certain whether article 18 VCLT was applicable at all. Protocol no 6 was not to be applied provisionally pending its entry into force. It could therefore not be applied to the penalties already meted out (non-retroactivity). Conversely, the future implementation of that Protocol by Russia was not put into jeopardy by the acts at stake. Russia would be able to fully apply the obligations under the Protocol from the day of its entry into force. In other words, there was no defeating impact of the present acts on the ability to perform the treaty obligations once they entered into force. The death penalties concerned could have been found illegal under other grounds, but hardly under article 18 VCLT. It is also strange to consider that article 18 VCLT was violated but that Russia avoided a 'breach' of international law by not carrying out the death penalties. Either article 18 VCLT has been violated and there is a breach of international law, or the commutation of the death penalties respected the true objective of article 18 VCLT and then there was no violation of international law at all (neither under article 18 VCLT nor with regard to alleged rules of customary law on execution of death penalties).

The issue of article 18 VCLT was recently also examined by a WTO Panel. It however found no breach of the obligation not to frustrate the object and purpose of the applicable agreement. The filing of a complaint could not be considered to defeat that object and purpose.[38]

There have also been many arguments in legal doctrine whereby article 18 VCLT should be applied to certain international situations. Thus, it has been claimed that the conclusion of bilateral agreements with the US under article 98, § 2, of the Statute of the ICC, in order to paralyse the competence of the ICC by the mutual grant of immunity, is contrary to article 18 VCLT.[39] These agreements were concluded by some states while the ICC Statute was not yet in force. The claim was

[37] *Clarification of Paragraph 5 of Operative Part of Constitutional Court Resolution No 3-P of 2 February 1999* (2009) 142 *ILR* 384ff.

[38] *Peru-Agricultural Products* case (WTO, 2014), Panel Report, WT/DS457/R, § 7.88ff.

[39] L Burgorgue-Larsen, 'Les Etats-Unis d'Amérique et la justice internationale—Entre l'utilisation et l'instrumentalisation du droit international', in *Vie rencontre internationale de la Faculté des sciences juridiques, politiques et sociales de Tunis, Le droit international à la croisée des chemins* (Paris, 2004) 233ff, 258.

also that these agreements were perverting the aim of article 98, § 2, of the Rome Statute on the ICC (1998), which concerned only the agreements existing at the time of conclusion of the ICC Statute, and not later agreements on immunity squarely contrary to the Court's competence.[40]

It has sometimes been argued—as we have already seen—that states are free to not ratify a signed treaty. Therefore, it has been said, it is difficult to see why these states should not perform action which defeats the object and purpose of the treaty before ratification, since such conduct would be simply tantamount to an implicit refusal of ratification. Why should international law be formalistic on this matter?[41] Such an argument overlooks almost entirely the true meaning of the pre-conventional obligations under article 18 VCLT and their foundation in the principle of good faith. It resembles an argument which would state that a treaty containing a somewhat broad denunciation clause must not be executed since it could anyway be denounced at any time. However, the former means is not equivalent to the latter; the disguised means is not comparable to the legally provided one. The law does not preclude a result, but prohibits one particular means to get there (*Wegverbot*). It does so on account of the necessary trust and confidence of the treaty parties. These parties are entitled to expect that a state which no longer wishes to ratify the treaty will formally declare this stance, so that the other states engaged in the enterprise can immediately and fully make up their minds on the new situation. The point is thus to protect the legitimate expectations in a minimum of fair dealing. The point is not one of formalism; it is one of good faith. It is therefore unpalatable to interpret one freedom accorded by the law (to declare not to be willing to ratify) as implying the larger freedom to do anything as one sees fit (for example to destroy the object and purpose of the treaty by insidious acts). As has been rightly said: 'This interpretation overlooks the purpose of Article 18 which is precisely to ensure that States make their intentions clear by other means than by committing such acts.'[42]

II. Good Faith and the Ratification of Treaties by Conduct

Normally, ratification of a treaty is made by a formal letter sent to the depositary. However, it also occurs that one or more states in fact apply a treaty, often over a prolonged period of time, and are thereafter estopped from pleading that the

[40] On this issue, see also E David, 'La Cour pénale internationale' (2005) 313 *RCADI* 442ff.

[41] See, eg P Cahier, 'L'obligation de ne pas priver un traité de son objet et de son but avant son entrée en vigueur' *Essays in Honor of F Dehousse*, vol I (Paris, 1979) 31, 34, 36.

[42] ME Villiger, *Customary International Law and Treaties* (Dordrecht, 1985) 322. See also H Lauterpacht (1953-II) *YbILC* 111, § 2.

treaty is not binding on them. Legal doctrine and practice have coined the concept of 'ratification by conduct' for this hypothesis. Ratification is here implicit in the effective application of the treaty rights and obligations.[43] Alternatively, a state is considered having waived the requirement of ratification through its conduct. The issue is plainly one of good faith and of legitimate expectations. If a state applied a treaty for a prolonged time-span, and thereby created legitimate expectations that it considers the treaty applicable, and also reaped advantages from the application of the treaty, it cannot be allowed to plead at its discretion that the treaty had not been validly ratified. As can be seen, good faith as protection of legitimate expectations operates here as a sort of substitute principle of effectiveness: the situation as it operates in fact shall not be disturbed by formal legal arguments of municipal law. There is some consistent practice in this regard, even if the situation is somewhat exceptional.

Thus, the Indian Supreme Court has judged that a treaty could be impliedly ratified by the ratification of later agreements which suppose the applicability of the former.[44] In the *Textron* case (1981), the arbitrators accepted ratification by conduct: Iran had treated an arbitration clause as being in full force and effect, and executed the agreement containing it for a substantial period of time. It could not now plead the absence of formally perfected ratification.[45] Similarly, in the *Sandline International and Papua New Guinea* arbitration (1998), the tribunal held that a contract concluded in violation of procedural provisions of municipal law could not be invalidated when no argument of illegality had been raised for many years and the contract had been duly executed.[46] It must be considered to be ratified by conduct. In the *Loan Agreement* case (*Italy v Costa Rica*, 1998), the arbitrators discussed all the issues involved in the concept of ratification by conduct in the context of a loan agreement. They concluded that Costa Rica could not contest its validity on the grounds of irregular ratification in view of the fact that the agreement had been executed and advantages therefrom enjoyed by Costa Rica for a prolonged period during which the issue of invalidity had not been raised.[47] In the already quoted older and perfectly analogous *Schufeldt* case (1930), the arbitrator was confronted with the argument of the invalidity of a concession agreement on account of lack of parliamentary approval as required by municipal law. Thus, in a sense, the concession contract had not been validly concluded (in analogy to a lack of proper ratification). The arbitrator had this to say: 'the Guatemala Government having recognized the validity of the Contract for six years and received all the

[43] R Kolb, *La bonne foi en droit international public* (Paris, 2000) 224ff; Müller, *Vertrauensschutz* 164ff; W Karl, *Vertrag und spätere Praxis im Völkerrecht* (Berlin, 1983) 198ff; JP Cot, 'La conduite subséquente des parties à un traité' (1966) 70 *RGDIP* 658ff; G Schwarzenberger, 'The Fundamental Principles of International Law' (1955-I) 87 *RCADI* 296ff; and on the older case law, F Dehousse, *La ratification des traités* (Paris, 1935) 154ff.

[44] *Union of India v Sukumar Sengupta* (1990) 92 *ILR* 570.

[45] PM Eisemann and V Coussirat-Coustère, *Repertory of International Arbitral Jurisprudence*, vol III (Dordrecht, 1991) 1052–53.

[46] *Sandline International and Papua New Guinea* arbitration (1998) 117 *ILR* 562–63, § 11.1–11.2.

[47] *Loan Agreement* arbitration (1998) XXV RIAA 23ff, 36ff.

benefits to which they were entitled under the contract and allowed Schufeldt to go on spending money on the concession, is precluded from denying its validity'.[48] The PCIJ itself accepted implicit ratifications: in the *Certain German Interests in Polish Upper Silesia* case (1926), it judged that Poland could have become a party to an armistice convention and to the Spa Protocol, to which it was not formally a party, through its acts and conduct; yet, it denied that in the case at hand Poland had conducted itself in such a way as having implicitly ratified those agreements.[49] The ICJ, conversely, applied the doctrine of implicit ratification by deeds in the *Military and Paramilitary Activities in an Against Nicaragua* case (Jurisdiction and Admissibility, 1984).[50] As will be recalled, Nicaragua had sent a telegram to the League of Nations Secretariat, notifying its participation in the optional clause system of the PCIJ under article 36, § 2, of the Statute of Court. It also stated that the ratification instrument would be handed in later. In fact, this instrument was never received in Geneva. According to one hypothesis, it was sent by maritime courier during the war and had been lost on the sea. However, Nicaragua always behaved as if it was bound by the optional clause system. It was therefore also listed as one of the states parties to the system in the Yearbooks of the ICJ. The Court concluded through a prolonged and careful (though not uncontested)[51] reasoning that Nicaragua was bound by its conduct to the optional declaration it had made. It consequently affirmed its jurisdiction in the present case under article 36, § 2, of the Statute.

There are also municipal tribunals and institutional practice in the context of ratification by conduct. An ancient example of the former took place in the context of the protectorate of Anjouan Island which France enjoyed by virtue of some Treaties of 1885, 1887 and 1892. The last of these treaties had not been formally ratified, but had in fact been applied for some period of time. The Cour de cassation therefore considered it to have been tacitly ratified.[52] Examples of the latter have occurred in the context to membership to international organisations, which have not been based on a regular ratification of the constitutive instrument. Thus, Argentina had acceded to the League of Nations from its very beginnings (1920). However, the ratification pronounced by a declaration of its President was fouled by the fact that the constitutionally necessary approval of Parliament had not been sought. In 1920, it was all but clear that such a defective 'ratification' could be considered valid. Eventually, Parliament gave its approval in 1933. Had Argentina been a member of the League from 1920 to 1933? In international practice, Argentina

[48] *Schufeldt* (1930) II *RIAA* 1094.

[49] *Certain German Interests in Polish Upper Silesia* (1926) PCIJ, ser A, no 7, pp 28–29.

[50] *Military and Paramilitary Activities in an Against Nicaragua* (1984) *ICJ Reports* 399ff. See also JG Merills, 'The Optional Clause Revisited' (1993) 64 *BYIL* 199.

[51] See eg Dissenting Opinion Oda, ibid (1984) *ICJ Reports* 484ff; Dissenting Opinion Jennings, ibid, 540ff; Dissenting Opinion Schwebel, ibid, 588ff.

[52] (1894) 1 *RGDIP* 64ff, 66–67: 'Dans tous les cas, le traité doit avoir force obligatoire lorsqu'il a été régulièrement exécuté des deux parts ... [Le] consentement apparaît par l'exécution du traité au moins autant que par sa ratification.'

had been considered to have indeed been a member since 1920, having participated in the Assemblies, voting regularly on the items proposed, chairing various organs, contributing to the budget of the organisation, and so on. There are several legal constructions that justify the result thus reached. First, it is possible to claim that the Presidential declaration of 1920 was internationally valid notwithstanding the lack of parliamentary approval (a sort of retroactive application of the substance of article 46 VCLT, 1969); second, it is possible to claim that the authorisation of 1933 had a retroactive effect and cured the defect of its absence between 1920 and 1933 (albeit the declaration contained no such wording); third, it has been said that in view of its conduct Argentina would be estopped from claiming not to have been a member of the organisation; or, fourth, it has been claimed that Argentina's prolonged behaviour within the organisation was legally tantamount to a ratification by deeds.[53] Whichever the argument chosen (or the combination thereof), the legal result is that a sort of informal regularisation took place.

It stands to reason that an implicit ratification can be accepted only in rare and clear cases, lest the ratification requirement, which is an important instrument of control and even of democracy, be emptied of its proper function.[54] However, it would be contrary to good faith, which governs treaty law, to allow a state to apply a treaty for a prolonged period of time and yet to permit it thereafter to plead that the treaty did not bind it. This would allow that state to play fast and loose with the treaty commitment, honouring it as long as it has an interest, and repudiating it at will at any given moment as a function of a change of interests. The doctrine of ratification by conduct rightly impeaches such an outcome.

Finally, we may mention that there is also some old authority for the proposition that if a treaty is in fact executed, but a state later refuses to ratify it, the latter state would in any case be obliged, under the principle of good faith, to pay damages to the aggrieved state.[55] This occurrence may manifestly be avoided through the doctrine of ratification by conduct.

[53] Several arguments were indeed presented: see MO Hudson, 'The Argentine Republic and the League of Nations' (1934) 28 *AJIL* 125ff; WH Kelchner, *Latin American Relations with the League of Nations* (Boston, 1930) 47ff. A similar situation occurred with regard to Guatemala's membership of the Organization of American States. The US delegate to the UN Security Council however argued that Guatemala had acquired that membership by tacit ratification through its conduct. See LB Sohn, *Cases on United Nations Law*, 2nd edn (New York, 1967) 903: 'The Government of Guatemala has regularly exercised the privileges and enjoyed all the advantages of membership in the Organization of American States, including those of attending and voting in the meetings … We hear today that Guatemala, after years of posing as a member of that Organization, now for the first time claims that it is not technically a member thereof. To have claimed and exercised all the privileges of membership for a number of years, and then to disclaim the obligations and responsibilities is an example of duplicity which, surely, the Security Council should not condone.'

[54] Such indirect ratification is not lightly to be presumed: *North Sea Continental Shelf* cases (1969) *ICJ Reports* 25–26.

[55] L Casanova, *Del diritto internazionale*, vol II (Florence, 1870) 7–8.

III. Good Faith and the Conclusion of a Treaty in Violation of Municipal Law (Article 46 of the VCLT)

Article 46 of the VCLT of 1969 reads as follows:

> 1. A State may not invoke the fact that its consent to be bound by a treaty has been expressed in violation of a provision of its internal law regarding competence to conclude treaties as invalidating its consent unless that violation was manifest and concerned a rule of its internal law of fundamental importance. 2. A violation is manifest if it would be objectively evident to any State conducting itself in the matter in accordance with normal practice and in good faith.[56]

[56] On the issue here at stake, see: P Chailley, *La nature juridique des traités internationaux* (Paris, 1932) 167ff; F Dehousse, *La ratification des traités* (Paris, 1935) 138ff; Harvard Draft, 'Article 21' (1935) 29 *AJIL* 992ff; L Fairman, 'Competence to Bind the State to an International Engagement' (1936) 30 *AJIL* 439ff; JM Jones, 'Constitutional Limitations upon the Treaty-Making Power' (1941) 35 *AJIL* 462ff; P de Visscher, *La conclusion de traités internationaux* (Brussels, 1943) 151ff; JM Jones, *Full Powers and Ratification* (Cambridge, 1946) 134ff; G Balladore Pallieri, 'La formation des traités dans la pratique internationale contemporaine' (1949-I) 74 *RCADI* 469ff; H Rolin, 'Les principes de droit international public' (1950-II) 77 *RCADI* 421ff; G Sperduti, 'Rilevanza internazionale delle disposizioni costituzionali sulla stipulazione dei trattati e i suoi limiti' *Essays in Honor of T Perassi*, vol II (Milan, 1957) 303ff; H Blix, *Treaty-Making Power* (London, 1960) 223ff; AC Gialdino, 'Imputazione giuridica e buona fede nella conclusione dei trattati' (1960) 43 *RDI* 427ff; AD McNair, *The Law of Treaties* (Oxford, 1961) 58ff; I Seidl-Hohenveldern, 'Transformation or Adoption of International Law into Municipal Law' (1963) 12 *ICLQ* 101ff; WK Geck, *Die völkerrechtlichen Wirkungen verfassungswidriger Verträge* (Köln, 1963); L Ferrari Bravo, *Diritto internazionale e diritto interno nella stipulazione dei trattati* (Naples, 1964); WK Geck, 'The Conclusion of Treaties in Violation of the Internal Law of a Party' (1967) 27 *ZaöRV* 429ff; K Holloway, *Modern Trends in Treaty Law* (London, 1967) 105ff; L Wildhaber, 'Provisions of Internal Law Regarding Competence to Conclude Treaties' (1967/68) 8 *Virginia Journal of International Law* 94ff; J Hostert, 'Droit international et droit interne dans la Convention de Vienne sur le droit des traités du 23 mai 1969' (1969) 15 *AFDI* 92ff, esp 100ff; RD Kearney, 'Internal Limitations on External Commitments. Article 46 of the Treaties Convention' (1969/1970) 4 *The International Lawyer* 1ff; C Rousseau, *Droit international public*, vol I (Paris, 1970) 108ff; P Cahier, 'La violation du droit interne relative à la compétence pour conclure des traités comme cause de nullité des traités' (1971) 54 *RDI* 226ff; L Wildhaber, *Treaty-Making Power and Constitutions* (Basle, 1971); P de Visscher, 'Cours général de droit international public' (1972-II) 136 *RCADI* 94ff; TO Elias, *The Modern Law of Treaties* (New York, 1974) 142ff; H Mosler, 'The International Society as a Legal Community' (1974-IV) 140 *RCADI* 54ff; T Meron, 'Article 46 of the Vienna Convention on the Law of Treaties (*Ultra vires* Treaties): Some Recent Cases' (1978) 49 *BYIL* 175ff; I Sinclair, *The Vienna Convention on the Law of Treaties*, 2nd edn (Manchester, 1984) 169ff; P Cahier, 'Cours général de droit international public: Changements et continuité du droit international' (1985-VI) 195 *RCADI* 184ff; P Reuter, *Introduction au droit des traités*, 2nd edn (Paris, 1985) 24–25; L Ferrari Bravo, 'Alcune riflessioni sui rapporti fra diritto costituzionale e diritto internazionale in tema di stipulazione di trattati', in *Essays in Honor of R Ago*, vol I (Milan, 1987) 273ff; B Conforti, 'Cours général de droit international public' (1988-V) 212 *RCADI* 95ff; L Oppenheim (R Jennings and A Watts, eds), *International Law*, 9th edn (London, 1992) 1285ff; A Aust, *Modern Treaty Law and Practice*, 2nd edn (Cambridge, 2007) 312ff; ME Villiger, *Commentary on the 1969 Vienna Convention on the Law of Treaties* (Leiden, 2009) 583ff; M Bothe, 'Article 46' in O Corten and P Klein (eds), *The Vienna Conventions on the Law of Treaties—A Commentary*, vol II (Oxford, 2011) 1090ff; T Rensmann, 'Article 46' in O Dörr and K Schmalenbach (eds), *Vienna Convention on the Law of Treaties, A Commentary* (Berlin, 2012) 775ff; R Kolb, *The Law of Treaties—An Introduction* (Cheltenham, 2016) 91ff.

This provision deals with ratifications which have been made in violation of procedural rules of the municipal legal order related to the ratification of treaties ('irregular ratifications'). In other words, article 46 VCLT concerns the breach of provisions of internal law regarding competence to conclude treaties and the effect of this breach on the validity of the treaty in international law. Notice that article 46 VCLT concerns only provisions relating to the competence to conclude treaties. It does not touch on the material compatibility of the treaty provisions with municipal law, ie all the possible conflicts of the content of the treaty with internal law provisions. This latter issue is one of conflict of norms between legal orders and not one of validity of the treaty.

There are many provisions of internal law concerning the conclusion of the treaty, where breaches of the law may occur. Some examples may illustrate the point: (i) the full powers for negotiating and signing the treaty were not issued by the authorised person or office;[57] (ii) the treaty ought to have been presented to the approval of the Parliament but the executive has omitted to do so; (iii) Parliament did not approve the treaty, yet the executive ratified it; (iv) the vote in Parliament did not reach the quorum, but this fact has been discovered only later; (v) some Parliamentarians were corrupted when voting on the approval of the treaty and their votes were finally decisive; (vi) the executive submitted by mistake or on purpose an incomplete, truncated, or otherwise faked version of the treaty to be approved to Parliament; (vii) ratification was performed by a person or through a procedure which is contrary to a municipal law provision; (viii) some municipal provisions on the publicity of the treaty, before being allowed to ratify it, were breached; (ix) the procedural provisions related to approval and ratification was not followed correctly; etc.

The main issue in this context has always been the extent to which international law refers back to municipal law on these points. Consequently, two sharply opposed theories and practices were upheld, one 'constitutionalist' (invalidity of the treaty) the other 'internationalist' (validity of the treaty). For some authors, international law refers entirely back to municipal law on the whole question of conclusion of treaties. Because of their constitutional autonomy, states are left free to define the conclusion procedures as they see fit. These procedures are then incorporated into international law by *renvoi*. Thus, any violation of municipal law is automatically also a violation of international law. As a sanction, the treaty

In the old literature, see: D Anzilotti, 'Volontà e responsabilità nella stipulazione dei trattati internazionali' (1910) 5 *RDI* 3ff; L Bittner, *Die Lehre von den völkerrechtlichen Vertragsurkunden* (Berlin, 1924) 81ff; A Cavaglieri, *Lezioni di diritto internazionale* (Naples, 1925) 329ff; D Anzilotti, *Cours de droit international* (Paris, 1929) 359ff. On the role of good faith, see in particular: G Dahm, *Völkerrecht*, vol III (Stuttgart, 1961) 21ff; JP Müller, *Vertrauensschutz im Völkerrecht* (Köln, 1971) 191ff. On the drafting history at the ILC: S Rosenne, *Developments in the Law of Treaties, 1945–1986* (Cambridge, 1986) 142ff; S Rosenne, *The Law of Treaties—A Guide to the Legislative History of the Vienna Convention* (Leyden, 1970) 266ff.

[57] On this point, see art 7 VCLT, 1969, notably § 1, letter b, and § 2, where the legitimate expectations in the capacity of certain persons are protected.

will be invalid (constitutionalist theory).[58] However, if all defaults in the municipal law procedures led to an invalidation of international treaties, the latter would suffer from an important blind spot of legal uncertainty. The confidence of the treaty partners in the common enterprise could suffer serious drawbacks. For other authors, consequently, the reference to municipal law is only a limited one. International law is a separate legal order and defines for itself the reasons for invalidity of legal acts. The principle of stability of treaties, and the protection of the trust of the treaty partners, explains that in international law municipal law defaults cannot be *sic et simpliciter* relevant for voiding the treaty (internationalist theory).[59] A series of arguments buttress this solution: (i) the absence of a clear international practice for voiding treaties in all situations characterised by internal law breaches on the conclusion of the treaty; (ii) the fact that the opposite solution would push contracting states to ask for guarantees as to the respect of internal law provisions; this would lead to a tendency to unwelcomely intervene into internal affairs of other states in order to secure the treaty conclusion process; (iii) the fact that the other contracting states in principle ignore the municipal law of their partners and ought not to be obliged to know it; (iv) the fact that any different regulation would lead some states to voluntarily commit some default in the process of conclusion in order to have an argument, in the future, to void the treaty when they see it most fit (and it would be exceedingly difficult for treaty partners to prove that the breach had been made on purpose). However, on the other hand, if the defaults in the internal law procedures were entirely ignored and the treaty considered internationally valid in each case, the reference to municipal law and the constitutional autonomy of states would have been curtailed to a large extent. The democratic aim of the procedures of control of the executive in the context of ratification of treaties would suffer an important inroad. Indeed, whatever the violation of municipal law, the treaty would be valid.

[58] See eg H Triepel, *Völkerrecht und Landesrecht* (Leipzig, 1899) 236ff; J de Louter, *Le droit international public positif*, vol I (Oxford, 1920) 474; J Spiropoulos, *Traité théorique et pratique de droit international public* (Paris, 1933) 238; G Scelle, *Précis de droit des gens*, vol II (Paris, 1934) 439; K Strupp, 'Les règles générales du droit de la paix' (1934-I) 47 *RCADI* 360; FO Wilcox, *The Ratification of International Conventions* (London, 1935) 41ff; C Fairman, 'Competence to Bind the State to an International Engagement' (1936) 30 *AJIL* 443ff, 452ff; JM Jones, *Full Powers and Ratification* (Cambridge, 1946) 154ff, 157; P Freymond, 'La ratification des traités et le problème des rapports entre le droit international et le droit interne' (thesis, Lausanne, 1947) 89ff; F Berber, *Lehrbuch des Völkerrechts*, 2nd edn, vol I (Munich, 1975) 468; J Sette Camara, *The Ratification of International Treaties* (Toronto, 1949) 112ff; L Cavaré, *Le droit international public positif*, 3rd edn, vol II (Paris, 1969) 104–05; B Conforti, 'Cours général de droit international public' (1988-V) 212 *RCADI* 97.

[59] See eg D Anzilotti, *Diritto internazionale* (Rome, 1928) 327–29; GG Fitzmaurice, 'Do Treaties Need Ratification?' (1934) 15 *BYIL* 113; M Siotto-Pintor, 'Traités internationaux et droit interne' (1935) 42 *RGDIP* 521ff; M Sibert, *Traité de droit international public*, vol II (Paris, 1951) 217ff; G Schwarzenberger, *International Law—As Applied by International Courts and Tribunals*, 3rd edn, vol I (London, 1957) 429–30; H Blix, *Treaty-Making Power* (London, 1960) 392ff; WK Geck, *Die völkerrechtlichen Wirkungen verfassungswidriger Verträge* (Köln, 1963) 411ff; WW Bishop, 'General Course of Public International Law' (1965-II) *RCADI* 340ff; K Holloway, *Modern Trends in Treaty Law* (London, 1967) 105ff, 441ff; R Monaco, 'Cours général de droit international public' (1968-III) 125 *RCADI* 157.

In order to blunt the too sharp edges of both theories and to propose a reasonable compromise solution, doctrine and practice have progressively developed the intermediate theory of 'apparent authority'.[60] In short terms, only violations of internal law of a certain gravity (the principle of proportionality is thus taken account of) that are apparent to the treaty partner (who cannot be said to have had legitimate confidence in the regularity of the treaty conclusion process in such cases) should qualify for exceptionally invalidating the treaty. The main rule is thus that municipal law defaults are not relevant for voiding the treaty on the international plane, and that only municipal sanctions against the culprits can be taken. An equitable exception applies to cases of grave violations of municipal law manifest to the other treaty partners. As a result of such arguments, the solution in article 46 is largely based on the latter view (no relevance of the internal law breach for the international validity of the treaty, but with a small concession for the invalidity of the treaty under extremely strict exceptional circumstances). In other words, there is here an objective responsibility of the defaulting state for the legitimate expectation in the validity of the treaty. That state cannot plead its own municipal wrong in order to invalidate the treaty. As can be seen, three principles or maxims of international law come together to buttress this result: proportionality, good faith and related to good faith, the maxim 'nobody can profit from its own wrong'.

Analytically, the exception to the international validity of the treaty is based on the presence of two cumulative criteria:

(i) the provision of internal law breached must be of fundamental importance. As already suggested, this is an issue of proportionality: the invalidity of a treaty is such a heavy consequence that it must be reserved to the cases where the breach of municipal law was of the gravest nature;

(ii) the violation must have been manifest for the treaty partner(s). The issue is here one of good faith as protection of legitimate expectations. Even if the violation was grave, the result of it should not go to the detriment of the treaty partner(s) when the latter were without fault on account of the fact that they could not have known about the breach. In simple words, it would be unjust to project on the treaty partners a mistake committed by yourself. The extent to which a breach is 'manifest' can be measured according to two standards:

[60] See eg J Basdevant, 'La conclusion et la rédaction des traités et des instruments diplomatiques autres que les traités' (1926-V) 15 *RCADI* 581; P de Visscher, *La conclusion de traités internationaux* (Bruxelles, 1943) 272ff; CC Hyde, *International Law—Chiefly as Interpreted and Applied by the United States*, 2nd edn, vol II (Boston, 1947) 1385–86; G Balladore Pallieri, 'La formation des traités dans la pratique contemporaine' (1949-I) 74 *RCADI* 483–84; H Rolin, 'Les principes du droit international public' (1950-II) 77 *RCADI* 425; AD McNair, *The Law of Treaties* (Oxford, 1961) 58ff, 76–77; M Sorensen, 'Principes de droit international public' (1961-III) 109 *RCADI* 68; G Dahm, *Völkerrecht*, vol III (Stuttgart, 1961) 27ff; JP Müller, *Vertrauensschutz im Völkerrecht* (Köln, 1971) 191ff; A Verdross and B Simma, *Universelles Völkerrecht*, 3rd edn (Berlin, 1984) 444ff.

(a) Objective test: a violation is objectively evident when the municipal law procedures at stake have a typical character, are generally known or correspond to usual state practice. Thus, it is objectively evident that a state would not relinquish or cede parts of its territory by a simple treaty in simplified form, without any internal consultation.

(b) Subjective test: some municipal law procedures may be less typical and less known generally, but they may be well known by some treaty partner which has regular treaty relationships with that state (eg neighbouring states with regular bilateral treaty relations). The same is true if the concerned state notified the provisions of municipal law at stake to the treaty partners. In this case, the treaty partners did know or at least ought to have known about the breach.

International practice has for a long time been uncertain and contradictory on the issue of irregular ratifications. There were precedents giving full weight to domestic law[61] and precedents affirming the international validity of the treaty, notwithstanding the violation of municipal law.[62] The same split can be found in diplomatic practice.[63] Progressively, however, the intermediate theory of 'apparent authority' gained ground, and after article 46 VCLT was adopted it became the applicable conventional and customary international law. There are already some old precedents based on that criterion. Thus, the criterion of good faith and confidence was mentioned in Swiss practice.[64] It was also applied in the context of an unauthorised agent having concluded a treaty in the *Trumbull* (1892)[65] and *Hemming* (1910)[66] arbitration cases. We may now direct ourselves on the other side of the watershed, at a time when article 46 of the VCLT had been adopted. In a legal advice of the International Law Directorate of the Swiss Foreign Ministry, it was stated that Switzerland could rely on assurances given by Republic X that a treaty concluded with Switzerland fulfilled all municipal law requirements.[67] In other words, the violation of internal law could not have been manifest to Switzerland. Article 46 VCLT could not apply. In the *Kamiar* case (1968),[68] the Israeli Supreme Court held that a state may rely on the usual constitutional practice

[61] See eg the *Cleveland Award* (1888), JB Moore, *History and Digest of the International Arbitrations to which the United States has been a Party*, vol II (Washington DC, 1898) 1957–58; *G Pinson* (1928) V *RIAA* 394.

[62] See eg the *Franco-Swiss Commercial Treaty* case (1912) XI *RIAA* 411, 418; the *Rio Martin* case (1925) II *RIAA* 724; etc.

[63] See the precedents mentioned in Kolb, *Bonne* 249–50.

[64] P Guggenheim (ed), *Répertoire suisse de droit international public*, vol I (Bern, 1975) 11–12: 'Nous devons soutenir que la Suisse ne pouvait que s'en tenir à l'affirmation des délégués de la Chine déclarant avoir les pouvoirs nécessaires pour conclure, sans autorisation parlementaire'.

[65] JB Moore, *History and Digest of the International Arbitrations to which the United States has been a Party*, vol IV (Washington DC, 1898) 3569.

[66] *Hemming* (1910) IV *RIAA* 142.

[67] (1987) 43 *Annuaire suisse de droit international* 137–38.

[68] *Kamiar* (1968) *ILR*, vol 44, p 262–263.

of another state, such as presented in the UN legislative series. This interpretation goes very far in the protection of the expectations of the treaty partner. In the *Textron* arbitration (1981),[69] Iran invoked the violation of a municipal decree on the powers of its Council of Ministers. The arbitrators, referring to article 46 VCLT, refused to countenance this argument. The provision of internal law was not sufficiently fundamental in nature; and the treaty partner could not have known of such a special decree, granting particular powers. In the *Guinea-Bissau v Senegal* arbitration (1989),[70] there had been a 1960 Agreement between Portugal and France, acting as colonial powers, on the delimitation of some terrestrial and maritime spaces. Guinea Bissau argued that the agreement should have been subject to the approval of the Parliament, since it concerned national territory. According to the Tribunal, the internal law provision concerned was clearly of fundamental importance (relating to territory); but its violation had not been manifest to the other party. Indeed, France could have relied on the effective constitutional practice in Portugal in the 1960s, when the role of the Parliament had been significantly curtailed. In actual Portuguese practice of that time, the chief of the executive, President Salazar, approved the treaties concluded. Hence, the substance of article 46 VCLT could not be applied to void the treaty. We may also notice in passing that the arbitral tribunal held that the content of article 46 reflected customary law in 1960, when the agreement here at stake had been concluded—a somewhat daring interpretation. The already quoted *Loans Agreement* case (*Italy v Costa Rica*, 1998) also discusses in depth the issue of irregular ratification and applies the principles contained in article 46 of the VCLT of 1969.[71] In the *Land and Maritime Boundary, Cameroon v Nigeria* case (2002),[72] the ICJ was confronted with the Delimitation Agreement of Maroua, concluded in 1975. The capacity of the Head of the Nigerian State to sign and ratify treaties had been restricted under domestic law. The Court concluded that the rule on the authority to sign treaties was of fundamental importance, but that the limitations put on the Head of State were not manifest to the other contracting party.[73] The treaty was therefore internationally valid. Article 46 was also mentioned in passing the *Harksen v President of South Africa* case (2000),[74] but the conditions for its applicability were once more not considered to be met. Finally, it may be noted that the ECJ emphasised twice that the relevant EC rules on the conclusion of treaties are significantly complex, so that they could hardly be manifest for the other contracting parties: *France v Commission* (1994)[75] and *European Parliament v Council* (2006).[76]

[69] PM Eisemann and V Coussirat-Coustère, *Repertory of International Arbitral Jurisprudence*, vol III (Dordrecht, 1991) 1502–03.

[70] *Guinea-Bissau v Senegal* arbitration (1989) XX *RIAA* 139ff, esp 142, § 59.

[71] (1998) XXV RIAA 35ff.

[72] (2002) *ICJ Reports* 430–31, §§ 265–68.

[73] ibid, 430, § 265.

[74] *Harksen v President of South Africa* (2000) 132 ILR 565–66, §§ 26–27 (South African Constitutional Court).

[75] *France v Commission* (1994) 30 *ILR* 101ff.

[76] Cases C-317/04 and C-318/04 *European Parliament v Council* (2006).

There is thus now a consolidated pattern of case law firmly settled and neatly entrenched on the lines of article 46 VCLT. It will be noticed that no tribunal ever found the exceptional rule, allowing the invalidation of a treaty, to be applicable. More than once, it could be established that the provision at stake was of fundamental importance, so that the first condition of the exceptional rule was fulfilled. However, in these cases, the second condition could not be considered to be fulfilled, namely the one requiring that the violation be manifest to the treaty partner(s). This practice clearly shows the extent to which the rule we are here discussing is permeated by the principle of good faith as protection of legitimate expectations. This latter principle is the foundation of the rule and provides at the same time an important limitation on its practical operation. Overall, the doctrine of 'apparent authority' thus works in practice largely as would the internationalist doctrine, which considers that the violation of municipal law rules on the conclusion of treaties is immaterial to the international validity of the treaty. But there is the addition of a small safety valve, which is still awaiting successful application.

IV. Good Faith and the Loss of the Right to Claim the Invalidity of a Treaty (Article 45 of the VCLT)

There are several grounds on which a treaty can be claimed to be void or which allow a treaty party to suspend or withdraw from a treaty (articles 46–50, 60–62 VCLT). What happens if the treaty party, which is put on notice of a ground of invalidity or of suspension/termination, keeps silent for a prolonged time and continues to apply the treaty? Article 45 of the VCLT purports to give a response to this query:

> A State may no longer invoke a ground for invalidating, terminating, withdrawing from or suspending the operation of a treaty under articles 46 to 50 or articles 60 and 62 if, after becoming aware of the facts: (*a*) it shall have expressly agreed that the treaty is valid or remains in force or continues in operation, as the case may be; or (*b*) it must by reason of its conduct be considered as having acquiesced in the validity of the treaty or in its maintenance in force or in operation, as the case may be.[77]

Cases of absolute nullity (articles 51–53 of the VCLT) are excluded from this regulation: bilateral legitimate expectations cannot prevail over public order.

[77] On this provision, see Zoller, *Bonne* 319ff; Kolb, *Bonne* 258–60; M Kohen and S Heathcote, 'Article 45' in: O Corten and P Klein (eds), *The Vienna Conventions on the Law of Treaties—A Commentary*, vol II (Oxford, 2011) 1064ff; ME Villiger, *Commentary on the 1969 Vienna Convention on the Law of Treaties* (Leiden, 2009) 572ff; K Odendahl, 'Article 45' in O Dörr and K Schmalenbach (eds), *Vienna Convention on the Law of Treaties, A Commentary* (Berlin, 2012) 765ff; R Kolb, *The Law of Treaties—An Introduction* (Cheltenham, 2016) 112–14.

Analytically, article 45, letter b), is a matter of applying estoppel or acquiescence, ie of good faith protecting legitimate expectations and treaty stability.[78] There is also the maxim that a state should not benefit from its own contradictory behaviour[79] ('no one shall take advantage of its own wrong'). The decisive question in the application of this provision is to what extent the treaty partners could and should have considered the actual behaviour of the concerned state as an acquiescence. As can be seen, good faith once more protects the 'other' parties. It refers to the face value of a behaviour as it must be reasonably understood externally (other-relatedness).[80] Therefore, it is conceptually wrong to require that the behaviour of the concerned state must manifest an 'intention' to confirm the validity or the permanence of the treaty.[81] A real intention is not necessary: when you behave in a certain way, you are considered by the virtue of good faith to be bound (acceptance is thus objectively imputed, if at all). Legally, this can manifestly be called acceptance. But it is an acceptance beyond the expression of will. Moreover, conduct can be both active and passive at the same time, ie application of the treaty and silence on the grounds of invalidity or termination. It can also be merely passive attitudes, if the treaty needs no actual application during a certain time. If the aggrieved state is coerced, its silence cannot legally be considered as acquiescence (analogy to articles 51 and 52 of the VCLT). Acquiescence must be established according to the mentioned criteria; it is not simply presumed.

In order to apply article 45, letter b), the concerned party must know the facts allowing invalidation or withdrawal. Constructive knowledge is sufficient, ie negligent ignorance will not provide an excuse.[82] The exact moment in time when this knowledge is acquired may be difficult to determine. However, such knowledge will often be crystallised through some diplomatic exchanges or correspondence, where the different positions are formulated; thus the moment may often be determined with some objectivity.

Notice that there is no fixed time-span for the application of the rule. A state can react at any time the grounds of invalidity or withdrawal manifest themselves, no matter how long time ago the treaty has been concluded. There is also no exact time for the reaction of the aggrieved state after the discovery of the fact, the standard being that it must react in 'reasonable time' if it wants to avoid acquiescence. What is a reasonable time depends on the circumstances. Certainly, the reaction must be overall reasonably swift. In other words, there must be valid reasons for having delayed the reaction. Article 45 applies to all motives of relative nullity (articles 46–50 VCLT), including fraud. Even if a state has been subjected to fraud, it must make up its mind whether it wants to keep or to void the treaty. It cannot remain

[78] See eg S Rosenne, *Breach of Treaty* (Cambridge, 1985) 7, 70.

[79] K Odendahl, 'Article 45' in O Dörr and K Schmalenbach (eds), *Vienna Convention on the Law of Treaties, A Commentary* (Berlin, 2012) 765.

[80] Correctly, ibid, 772.

[81] See however and slightly contradictorily, ibid, 772.

[82] See *Norwegian Fisheries* (1951) *ICJ Reports* 138–39.

silent and adopt contradictory attitudes, albeit in a case of fraud it has been the victim of an attitude contrary to good faith in the first place.[83] In other words, there is no *tu quoque* compensation here. In the VCLT of 1986, related to treaties concluded by international organisations, the relevant rule (article 45) has been slightly modified so as to take account of the practice of the 'competent organ' of the organisation. It is this practice which will create 'legitimate' expectations.[84]

Acquiescence to maintaining a treaty has been applied under customary international law a long time before its codification in article 45 VCLT. Thus, in the old case of the Treaty of Lima (1836) between the US and Peru, a treaty had been observed for nine years by Peru after a violation of its municipal law in the context of the conclusion of the treaty had taken place and was known.[85] As we have already seen, in the *Textron* arbitration (1981) the Tribunal held that an agreement had been ratified by subsequent conduct. The violation of the municipal law during its conclusion could not be pleaded after a substantial time had elapsed and the treaty had been considered as being valid, the reason of invalidity not being invoked albeit it was known.[86] In the *Land and Maritime Boundary between Cameroon and Nigeria* case (2002), a correction inserted in a treaty (Declaration) showed that this treaty was considered by the parties to be valid.[87] It could therefore not be voided thereafter. Finally, in the *Territorial and Maritime Dispute* (*Nicaragua v Colombia*, Preliminary Objections, 2007), a treaty was contested on account of violations of municipal law in the context of conclusion and also on account of coercion. The Court recalled that Nicaragua had for over 50 years treated this 1928 Agreement as being valid. The Court however did not quote article 45 VCLT, which was not retroactively applicable to a treaty concluded in 1928 (and notice also that coercion was not generally prohibited in the law of 1928). The Court moreover did not engage in an analysis of the date at which the defaults of the treaty came to the knowledge of the aggrieved party. Seemingly, Nicaragua must have known them since the beginning: thus, coercion could not go unnoticed. In substance, this is all the same an application of the legal idea contained in article 45 VCLT. It must be added, however, that coercion could not be cured today under the umbrella of article 45 VCLT. Treaties concluded under coercion are now considered to be absolutely void and not curable (articles 51–52 VCLT).

[83] There has been some debate on this issue at the Vienna Conference leading to the adoption of the VCLT: see Kolb, *Bonne* 259.

[84] P Manin, 'La Convention de Vienne sur le droit des traités entre Etats et organisations internationales ou entre organisations internationales' (1986) 32 *AFDI* 466.

[85] JM Jones, 'Constitutional Limitations upon the Treaty-Making Power' (1941) 35 *AJIL* 465–66.

[86] PM Eisemann and V Coussirat-Coustère, *Repertory of International Arbitral Jurisprudence*, vol III (Dordrecht, 1991) 1502–03.

[87] *Land and Maritime Boundary between Cameroon and Nigeria* (2002) *ICJ Reports* 431, § 267.

V. Good Faith and the Interpretation of Treaties

As was said a long time ago by Sir Robert Phillimore, 'the interpretation is the life of the dead letter'.[88] By extension, it can be said that the interpretation is the life of the law as a whole. Legal work consists of interpretation. Norms have to be interpreted in order to be applied to single cases. The process is caught in a parallelogram of comprehension and of volition: as an interpreter, I try to understand what meaning the law-creator attached to the norm; but I eventually also give the norm the meaning as I see it myself. The point of this section is not to analyse the process of interpretation. It is rather to determine what the principle of good faith contributes to this complex process of understanding and shaping of legal prescriptions.[89]

To start with, we may notice that the role of good faith in interpretation has been judged from opposite perspectives. For some authors,[90] good faith is the only true rule of interpretation, all the more detailed rules and maxims being only specifications of the former. Conversely, for other authors good faith does not add anything to the process of interpretation, either because it is not a material legal rule[91] or because it is limited to requiring the execution of the obligations due.[92] A perusal of international legal writings and of international practice shows that good faith has two main meanings in the context of interpretation, in addition to a series of subordinate functions.[93] The two main aspects are: (i) the primacy of the spirit of the treaty over an excessive attachment to the black-letter wording; and

[88] R Phillimore, *Commentaries Upon International Law*, 3rd edn, vol II (London, 1882) 95.

[89] On the issue of good faith in interpretation, see: B Cheng, *General Principles of Law—As Applied by International Courts and Tribunals* (London, 1953) 114ff; G Schwarzenberger, 'The Fundamental Principles of International Law' (1955-I) 87 *RCADI* 300ff; S Neri, *Sull'interpretazione dei trattati nel diritto internazionale* (Milan, 1958) 285ff; R Bernhardt, *Die Auslegung völkerrechtlicher Verträge—insbesondere in der Rechtsprechung internationaler Gerichte* (Köln, 1963) 23ff; L Cavaré, 'La notion de bonne foi et quelques-unes de ses applications en droit international public' (1963/1964) *Cours IHEI Paris* 22ff; C Rosseau, *Droit international public*, vol I (Paris, 1970) 269–70; JP Müller, *Vertrauensschutz im Völkerrecht* (Köln, 1971) 127ff; TO Elias, *The Modern Law of Treaties* (New York, 1974) 40ff; E Zoller, *La bonne foi en droit international public* (Paris, 1977) 78ff, 202ff; R Kolb, *La bonne foi en droit international public* (Paris, 2000) 260ff; R Kolb, *Interprétation et création du droit international* (Brussels, 2006) 419ff, 606ff; R Gardiner, *Treaty Interpretation* (Oxford, 2008) 147ff; ME Villiger, *Commentary on the 1969 Vienna Convention on the Law of Treaties* (Leiden and Boston, 2009) 425–26; O Dörr, 'Article 31' in O Dörr and K Schmalenbach (eds), *Vienna Convention on the Law of Treaties, A Commentary* (Berlin, 2012) 548–49. See also Dissenting Opinion Torres Bernardez, *Fisheries Jurisdiction (Spain v Canada, Jurisdiction)* (1998) *ICJ Reports* 670ff, § 234ff.

[90] G Balladore Pallieri, *Diritto internazionale pubblico*, 8th edn (Milan, 1962) 310. Some authors consider that good faith is limited to being a principle of interpretation: see JES Fawcett, 'The Legal Character of International Agreements' (1953) 30 *BYIL* 396–98.

[91] H Kraus, Response, (1950-I) 43 *Annuaire de l'Institut de droit international* 445.

[92] H Kelsen, *The Law of the United Nations* (London, 1951) 89; AP Sereni, *Diritto internazionale*, vol I (Milan, 1956) 117. See the contrary and correct position of M Virally, 'Review Essay: Good Faith in Public International Law' (1983) 77 *AJIL* 132.

[93] Conversely, it has rightly been emphasised that good faith is overworked when almost all legal tools and maxims for interpretation are said to flow from it: I Tammelo, *Treaty Interpretation and Practical Reason* (Sydney, 1967) 33–34. It must also be stressed that good faith can have distinctive special

(ii) the search for a reasonable interpretation, in the sense of what a honest and reasonable party could and should have understood with regard to the text as it has been adopted. The first limb is directed mainly at negatively eliminating interpretations which are abusive and often made in bad faith. In a sense, we are here in the context of the prohibition of abuse of rights. The second limb is directed at positively ensuring the most reasonable interpretation in view of what the parties reasonably must have understood by their compact. We are here in the context of the protection of legitimate expectations. To the two main limbs of good faith as a principle of interpretation, international practice has added some other more limited functions. Let us analyse them all, one after the other.

1. *Primacy of the spirit over the letter*. The issue is not to engage in abstract and speculative 'spiritism'; it is taking account of what Celsus, the important Roman jurist, had to say: *Scire leges non est verba eorum tenere, sed vim ac potestatem*[94] ('knowing the laws is not to cling to their letter but to understand their spirit'). It may indeed occur that one party clings to the wording in an abusive and fraudulent way, so as to be able to circumvent the true obligations incurred.[95] A protection against such abusive constructions is particularly important in a legal order which is largely based on self-interpretation of commitments by each legal subject.[96] The ancient manuals of international law refer to breathtaking examples of fraudulent interpretations in the Antique world: a promise to repatriate prisoners of war was indeed fulfilled, but only after having been killed;[97] an agreement to restitute half of a fleet was honoured by cutting the ships down their middle;[98] a promise not to shed blood if a garrison surrendered had been made, and so the men were burnt alive;[99] a cease-fire for 30 days was concluded, and attacks were perpetrated by night;[100] in a peace treaty, it was written that each party would restitute the towns taken during the war, but later one party claimed to keep certain town on the grounds that they had freely surrendered;[101] etc. Other famous historical examples include that of France, which had engaged herself by the Treaty of Utrecht (1713) to destroy the port and fortifications of Dunkirk, and not to reconstruct them. France fulfilled this obligation literally, but then proceeded to construct an

functions in the context of interpretation in a municipal legal order. Thus, in the US, interpreting in good faith can mean interpreting according to the expected reciprocal meaning of terms contained in the treaty, and not according to the meaning the US legal order attaches to some terms, ie unilaterally. See DJ Bederman, *Classical Canons—Rhetoric, Classicism and Treaty Interpretation* (Aldershot, 2001) 215ff.

[94] *Digest*, 1, 3, 17. See also Corinthians, II, 3, 6: 'The letter killeth, but the spirit giveth life'.
[95] See the many references in Kolb, *Bonne* 264.
[96] Zoller, *Bonne* 580.
[97] Thucydides, *Peloponnesian War*, Book II, Ch VI, § VII.
[98] H Grotius, *De jure belli ac pacis* (1625), Book II, Ch XVI, § 5.
[99] HW Halleck, *International Law*, 4th edn, vol I (London, 1908) 324.
[100] P Belli, *De re militari et de bello tractatus* (1563), Part I, Ch III.
[101] R Redslob, *Histoire des grands principes du droit des gens* (Paris, 1923) 55.

even more powerful military port at Mardyck, a distance of only some miles from Dunkirk. After further negotiations, however, this project was eventually abandoned.[102] Another example occurred during World War I: Germany had claimed that the use of asphyxiating gases contained in 'cylinders' was not unlawful, since the law of war prohibited only the use of such gases through 'projectiles'.[103] A fraudulent interpretation is sometimes well hidden behind a technical argument. The judge will then most times reject it diplomatically, without emphasising its inappropriateness or any bad faith. Thus, Canada tried to argue that a single investment was not covered by a treaty provision that used the plural form ('investments'). The arbitral Tribunal had this to say: 'The Tribunal rejects Canada's argument that the plural form of the language of Article 1102(2) [of the applicable agreement] places a single investment outside the Article's coverage'.[104] The Tribunal recalled the use of such language as discrimination against 'women' or 'children', which did not preclude the unlawfulness of a single discrimination. Further, it would be contrary to good faith to insist on a clerical error in the text, to the detriment of the contracting party. The maxim which must prevail is *falsa demonstratio non nocet*. Thus, an arbitral tribunal had this to say: 'It would be contrary to the principle of good faith which should govern the relations between the offices, to attach a juridical consequence to such a clerical error'.[105] Once more, good faith tempers here an excessive attachment to the text to the detriment of the spirit or of the true object of consent.

2. *A reasonable interpretation*. Good faith protects the legitimate confidence of each party in a reasonable use of the terms contained in the treaty. Thus, each party must be able to rely on the *usus loquendi*, ie on what it could and should have been reasonably understood by the terms used in context.[106] This reliance on the most reasonable and expectable use of terms does not rule out a special sense of the words; but such a sense must be specifically shown to have been contemplated by the parties.[107] The principle of good faith here reinforces the main aim of the rule on the 'ordinary meaning' or 'natural meaning'

[102] Zoller, *Bonne* 81; WE Hall, *A Treatise on International Law*, 8th edn (Oxford, 1924) 393–94.

[103] See the *Krupp* trial (1948), *Trials of War Criminals before the Nuremberg Military Tribunals under Control Council Law No 10*, vol XI (Washington DC, 1950) 1376.

[104] *Pope & Talbot v Canada (Merits of Phase 2)*, (2001) 122 *ILR* 359, § 36.

[105] *Bank of Brussels v Discount Company and Bank of Dresden* (1929) 5 *Annual Digest of Public International Law Cases* 428 (Mixed Arbitral Tribunal).

[106] See the literature quoted in Kolb, *Bonne* 272. There is this characteristic phrase in GF de Martens, *Précis du droit des gens modern de l'Europe*, vol I (Paris, 1864) 165: 'la bonne foi, qui doit présider à tous les traités des nations, défend de prendre les mots dans un sens inusité, à moins d'en avertir'. This seems to have been plainly misunderstood by the Appellate Body of the WTO in the *EC Computer Equipment* case (1998) WT/DS62(and 67 and 68)/AB/R, § § 83–84, when it stated that the interpretation according to legitimate expectations is inconsistent with art 31 of the VCLT 1969, since it would rely on the subjective and unilateral expectation of one party instead of the common intention of the parties. The point is not to explore the true subjective projection of one party; it is to ask what the reasonable expectation created is, in view of the most natural meaning of the words used.

[107] Art 31, § 4, of the VCLT 1969.

of words as emphasised in article 31, § 1, of the VCLT of 1969; it may even be said to be at the origin of the 'natural' or 'ordinary' meaning doctrine.[108] The tool of 'reasonable interpretation' is particularly important where a text gives each party a certain leeway of appreciation, or even some degree of discretionary power. In such cases, it is important to ensure that the granted power is not used to defeat the convention by the instilment of too great a share of unilateralism. The case law is quite rich on this issue of 'reasonable interpretation'. A somewhat older precedent is the *North Atlantic Coast Fisheries* case (1910), decided by an arbitral tribunal. Under a treaty of 1818, Great Britain had accorded certain rights related to fisheries to US citizens, while maintaining for itself the right to regulate the whole subject matter. The arbitral tribunal emphasised that Great Britain was bound by the treaty commitments to exercise its regulatory power in a reasonable way and in good faith.[109] It checked whether the regulations adopted by Great Britain fulfilled these standards. An analogous approach was applied by the ICJ in the *Rights of US Citizens in Morocco* case (1952)[110] and by the arbitral tribunal in the *Rainbow Warrior* case (1990).[111] In some arbitrations, the 'reasonable interpretation' took more directly into account the 'reasonable consequences' which must flow from an appropriate interpretation exercise. Thus, in the *Amco Asia Corporation v Republic of Indonesia* case (1983), decided by an ICSID tribunal, it was said that: 'Any convention … should be construed in good faith, that is to say by taking into account the consequences of their commitments the parties may be considered as having reasonable and legitimately envisaged'.[112] Under the same limb of good faith, any interpretation which leads to absurd results in regard of the object and purpose of the treaty is legally wrong.[113] Overall, the principle of good faith here ushers largely into the standard of 'reasonableness'. But the protection of legitimate expectations remains a corollary and essential criterion.

3. *Other functions of good faith*. International practice has extended the reach of good faith in interpretation to some other aspects. Here are some examples. *First*, it has been claimed that an interpretation which goes clearly against the established will of one or more than one party as to the sense of the provision

[108] See S Sur, *L'interprétation en droit international public* (Paris, 1974) 74. See also the *Brazilian Loans* case (1929) PCIJ ser A, no 21, p 114.

[109] *North Atlantic Coast Fisheries* (1910) XI *RIAA* 187, 188.

[110] *Rights of US Citizens in Morocco* (1952) *ICJ Reports* 211.

[111] *Rainbow Warrior* (1990) 82 *ILR* 543, § 63 and 562, § 94.

[112] *Amco Asia Corporation v Republic of Indonesia* (1984) 23 *ILM* 359. See also *Soabi v Senegal* (1988), in R Rayfuse (ed), *ICSID Reports*, vol II (Cambridge, 1994) 205–06: 'An arbitration agreement must be given, just as with any other agreement, an interpretation consistent with the principle of good faith. In other words, the interpretation must take into account the consequences which the parties must reasonably and legitimately be considered to have envisaged as flowing from their undertakings'. Further precedents are mentioned in Kolb, *Bonne* 271–72.

[113] I Sinclair, *The Vienna Convention on the Law of Treaties*, 2nd edn (Manchester, 1984) 120.

at the time the treaty was drafted would be contrary to good faith.[114] Good faith can also form the basis for the construction of a hypothetical common intention, where such one cannot be established as a matter of fact.[115] *Second*, there is a powerful field of application for good faith as protection of legitimate expectations in the context of an interpretation which takes account of the effective behaviour of the parties and the interpretation to which they have committed themselves over time by their deeds. It would be manifestly contrary to good faith to adopt a certain interpretation of a treaty provision for a prolonged time and to change attitude in an opportunistic way at a chosen and self-serving moment.[116] An international operator will avoid to countenance such a course of conduct by referring to the general principle of good faith. Consequently, the arbitral tribunal deciding the *Italian-Swiss Commercial Treaty* case (1911) interpreted the expression 'new wine' contained in the treaty according to the long-term interpretation upheld by Switzerland and to which Italy had not objected.[117] *Third*, it has been claimed that rules such as effect utile[118] or the construction of a clause in a way which avoids the adoption of an illegal outcome,[119] are expressions of the principle of good faith. The principle of good faith has here a less distinctive role. *Fourth*, it has been said that the traditional rule of interpretation *contra proferentem* (ie that in case of doubt, the solution adopted shall be to the detriment of the party which drafted the treaty and thus had the advantage of controlling the whole process) is but an outflow from the principle of good faith.[120] Its main basis is in the context that he who has the advantages shall also bear the risk. The issue is as much one of good faith (there is a legitimate expectation that the drafting party should have been clearer if it wanted to impose the more detrimental sense of the words for the other party) as one of equity (there is a reasonable apportionment of the relative advantages and burdens). *Fifth*, an interpretation which would create disequilibrium between the treaty commitments, eg by amplifying the advantages and disadvantages between the parties (ie an interpretation which would on the one side create an advantage

[114] Pleadings of P Reuter, *Temple of Preah Vihear* (1962) II *ICJ Pleadings* 195.

[115] '[In cases of absence of common intent] the principle of good faith and consideration of the general purpose of the treaty may legitimately provide a substitute for any lack of common intention. The principle of good faith impels the assumption of a common purpose': H Lauterpacht, *Collected Papers*, vol IV (Cambridge, 1978) 437–38.

[116] FG Jacobs, 'Varieties of Approach to Treaty Interpretation' (1969) 18 *ICLQ* 333.

[117] *Italian-Swiss Commercial Treaty* (1912) XI *RIAA* 262. See also the *Russian Indemnity* case (1912), ibid, p 446; *Seaman* case (1963) 34 *ILR* 199–201.

[118] See the *Revaluation of the German Mark* case (1980) XIX *RIAA* 126. In legal writings, see eg H Lauterpacht, *The Development of International Law by the International Court* (London, 1958) 290.

[119] *In favorem validitatis* interpretation: see the Greek Memorial in the *Lighthouses* case (1934) PCIJ ser C, no 74, p 199; Separate Opinion Seferiades, ser A and B, no 62, p 47. In the *Russell* case (1931) it was said: 'Treaty stipulations will not be regarded as a nullity unless the language clearly makes them so. It will not be presumed that the framers of a treaty have done a vain thing…' ((1931) IV *RIAA* 810).

[120] See JP Cot, 'La bonne foi et la conclusion des traités' (1968) 4 *RBDI* 144; Müller, *Vertrauensschutz* 150–51.

with seems disproportionate with regard to the disadvantage caused to the other party), should be rejected as much on the basis of the hypothetical common intention of the parties as on good faith. This was decided in the *Dispute on the Repartition of Goods* (1953) by the Franco-Italian Conciliation Commission.[121] *Sixth*, good faith requires a party not to attempt to profit unduly from ambiguities and misunderstandings to the detriment of the other party.[122] As these examples show, good faith is a flexible principle which can be called into action on many fronts when a need arises. In the context of interpretation, it straddles legitimate protection-related arguments, prohibition of abuse of rights, and equitable considerations.

VI. Good Faith in the Execution of Treaties

There are certain legal norms flowing from good faith which impose obligations on the treaty parties in the execution phase. These duties extend beyond the mere interpretative aspects mentioned above. There are different types of duties. We will review the most important ones here.

A. General Duty of Cooperation

The main duty is very general in nature and flows from the treaty bond itself. The latter creates a lesser or greater amount of legitimate expectations with regard to the necessary cooperation for solving problems in the execution of the treaty. Thus, according to the increasing degree of common purposes in the treaty, there is a stronger obligation to take due regard of the positions of the other parties and to cooperate with them in a proper implementation of the common bond. Consequently, as has been emphasised: 'Good faith performance or enforcement of a contract emphasizes faithfulness to an agreed common purpose and consistency of the *justified expectations* of the other party…'.[123] Or, as has been said by an arbitral tribunal:

> [According to a provision in the agreement] the contracting parties resolve to work in good faith to resolve any difficulty that could arise in the course of implementing this Agreement … The fact that the provision presently discussed is not applicable in the instant case does not mean that the Parties do not have to work in good faith to resolve any difficulty which may arise in implementing the agreements which bind them. As it

[121] *Dispute on the Repartition of Goods* (1953) XIII *RIAA* 521.

[122] FG Jacobs, 'Varieties of Approach to Treaty Interpretation' (1969) 18 *ICLQ* 333.

[123] Dissenting Opinion Brower, *International Systems and Controls Corporation, case no. 494* (1990), *Iran/US Claims Tribunal Reports*, vol 24, p 86 (italics added).

was already stressed, such an obligation is a general principle of international law, codified in the Vienna Convention, and applicable to every treaty.[124]

This general obligation to cooperate has found certain more precise expressions in the following three contexts. *First*, there may be an obligation under good faith to inform the treaty parties of certain facts and events. This is the case in particular for facts or events jeopardising the execution of the treaty. The arbitral tribunal in the *Rainbow Warrior* case (1990) emphasised this duty in the context of the precipitate repatriation of the two French agents from the island of Hao, contrary to the treaty commitments. *Second*, if there is no specific time-span indicated for a withdrawal from the treaty to take effect, the principle of good faith imposes a 'reasonable time' so as to protect the effectiveness of the treaty bond and therefore to protect also legitimate expectations. The ICJ has judged this issue in the *1951 Agreement between the WHO and Egypt* advisory opinion (1980)[125] and later in *Military and Paramilitary Activities in and Against Nicaragua (Jurisdiction and Admissibility)* (1984),[126] in the latter context for an optional declaration of jurisdiction formulated pursuant to a treaty provision. *Third*, in certain exceptional circumstances the principle of good faith may impose a duty to renegotiate certain issues or to agree on treaty adjustments. Thus, for example, it has been said that it would be contrary to good faith to take advantage of a considerable devaluation of the money in a concession contract. The parties were thus directed to new adjustments.[127]

B. *The Duty not to Defeat the Object and Purpose of the Treaty after its Entry into Force*

An important obligation in the execution phase relates to the preservation of the object and purpose of the treaty.[128] As we have already discussed, there is a bona fide obligation of signatories not to defeat the object and purpose of a treaty pending its entry into force.[129] To some extent, this obligation continues to bind the treaty parties after the treaty has entered into force and has become executory. There is a distinction between the black-letter provisions of the treaty and its object and purpose, ie the underlying conditions for its proper execution.[130] Not all can be written down in the text, even by the most prudent drafters. Certain matters

[124] Case *A 15, Iran v USA* (1986), *Iran/US Claims Tribunal Reports*, vol 12, p 61.

[125] *1951 Agreement between the WHO and Egypt* (1980) *ICJ Reports* 92ff.

[126] *Military and Paramilitary Activities in and Against Nicaragua (Jurisdiction and Admissibility)* (1984) *ICJ Reports* 415ff, esp § 60.

[127] *Franco-Hellenic Lighthouses arbitration* (1956) XII *RIAA* 226. See also the amicable composition in the *Société européenne d'entreprises v Yugoslavia* case (1956), in PM Eisemann and V Coussirat-Coustère, *Repertory of International Arbitral Jurisprudence*, vol III (Dordrecht, 1991) 923.

[128] See the developments in Kolb, *Bonne* 283ff.

[129] See above, Chapter 5.

[130] The following judgment is manifestly erroneous: 'De deux choses l'une, en effet: ou bien les dispositions du traité sont violées, et il n'est pas besoin de son objet et de son but; ou bien elles ne le

must and do remain presupposed. It would be contrary to good faith to be free to defeat these underlying conditions for a proper execution, while taking care not to breach any black-letter injunction. The manifest problem with the whole subject matter is to determine with some degree of legal certainty where the protected sphere of these 'underlying conditions' bounds on the sphere of freedom of the states parties, ie the sphere where they have not undertaken an express or implied legal commitment. This issue must mainly be solved with regard to the underlying principle of good faith: what could and ought reasonably to be expected from the parties when engaging into this treaty? What must be considered to be an abusive attitude, which the legal order should not countenance? Some further general considerations as to how to determine the reach of the prohibition will be offered after the discussion of international practice.

The obligation at stake here was discussed generally in the ILC under the lead of H Waldock.[131] International practice shows that the doctrine of the protection of the object and purpose of a treaty after its entry into force has been applied in different contexts. But that practice also shows that there remain doubts as to the precise extent of the obligation. A first example of the application of the doctrine can be found in some anti-terrorist conventions, where the principle *aut dedere aut judicare* is established by a black-letter law provision. These conventions establish a duty to prosecute and, if guilt is found, to punish. However, the conventions do not contain any provision on the right of states parties to exercise their faculty to commute a criminal sentence or to grant a presidential grace. It stands to reason that the skilled use of such devices could easily turn into a mere sham the conventional obligation to prosecute and punish. The reasoning has here to take account of the object and purpose of the treaty and of the implied necessity to have it function properly.[132] A second example—a famous one—can be found in the *Military and Paramilitary Activities in and Against Nicaragua* (Merits, 1984).[133] Nicaragua had pleaded that the overt hostility of the US violated the object and purpose of the Friendship, Commerce and Navigation Treaty of 1956 between the two states. According to Nicaragua, there existed an international customary obligation to abstain from acts which would impede the proper execution of an applicable treaty.[134] The difficulty of its argument in the present case was the breadth

sont pas, mais comment son objet et son but pourraient-ils alors être illégalement méconnus?' J Verhoeven, 'Le droit, le juge et la violence' (1987) 91 *RGDIP* 1224.

[131] See ibid, 284–85. See also DW Greig, 'Nicaragua and the United States: Confrontation over the Jurisdiction of the International Court' (1991) 62 *BYIL* 254ff; H Thirlway, 'The Law and Procedure of the ICJ (1960–1989): Treaty Interpretation and Other Treaty Points' (1992) 63 *BYIL* 48ff; C Lang, *L'affaire Nicaragua/Etats-Unis devant la CIJ* (Paris, 1990) 265ff; S Rosenne, *Developments in the Law of Treaties, 1945–1986* (Cambridge, 1989) 139ff.

[132] See eg JA Frowein, 'The Present State of Research Carried Out by the English-Speaking Section of the Centre for Studies and Research' in Hague Academy of International Law (ed), *Legal Aspects of International Terrorism* (Dordrecht, 1989) 84.

[133] *Military and Paramilitary Activities in and Against Nicaragua (Merits)* (1986) *ICJ Reports* 135ff.

[134] ibid, 135, § 270.

of the object and purpose of that treaty, as evidenced in its preamble: 'to further peace and cooperation between both States'. Through a teleological projection, such aims could potentially prohibit any type of act that seems contrary to their (full) realisation—ie an unlimited set of acts, considered somewhat unfriendly, and thereby concomitantly limiting in an unprecedented way the freedom of the state to act according to its policy choices. Such a course would mean extending the reach of the treaty commitments beyond any foreseeable bound. Moreover, such an approach would jeopardise the security and predictability of treaty relations, and also hamper the conclusion of treaties of amity. Finally, the recourse to generally stated aims and purposes is often the result of a poor degree of agreement on any concrete clauses to be inserted in the treaty. The more the parties disagree and state general aims instead of clear and applicable obligations, paradoxically the more a robust doctrine of the protection of the object and purpose of the convention would produce a series of obligations introduced by the backdoor of powerful teleological considerations. All these aspects would clearly upset proper treaty relations and the intentions of the parties to a treaty. But must one conclude that there is no room at all for an obligation not to defeat the object and purpose of such a treaty after its entry into force? That would seem to go too far, to throw out the baby with the water. In our case, the ICJ elaborated a 'principle of specialty' in the context of the object to be protected, allowing restraint of the acts which could be said to be prohibited. It expressed the principle thus:

> There must be a distinction, even in the case of a treaty of friendship, between the broad category of unfriendly acts, and the narrower category of acts tending to defeat the object and purpose of the Treaty. That object and purpose is the effective implementation of friendship in the specific fields provided for in the Treaty, not friendship in a vague and general sense.[135]

In other words, the Court distinguishes between the general object of the treaty, which is friendship, and the special object of the treaty, which is to act or abstain to act in the concrete subject matters covered by it. The first object is too vague to give rise to implied obligations to protect the object and purpose; the second objects are precise enough to give rise to such derived obligations. Thus, the Court held that some specific acts, such as the mining of ports of Nicaragua or direct attacks on such ports, were contrary to the 'whole spirit' of the treaty and constituted a violation of its object and purpose.[136] Such conduct did not violate any black-letter law provision in the treaty; however, it rendered its whole application increasingly nugatory. The *Nicaragua* case is consequently a precedent for the obligation not to defeat the object and purpose of a treaty in the execution phase.

There are different aspects which have to be taken into account by the legal operator when he or she tries to breathe life into the doctrine here at stake. In the first place, the type of object and purpose of the treaty must be carefully considered.

[135] ibid, 137, § 273.

[136] ibid, 138, § 275.

The more the aims and purposes are general, and the less any obligation of preservation should be implied; and vice versa. Compare in this regard the finalities of a treaty of amity with the one of a treaty on extradition. In the concretisation of the mentioned standard, the legitimate expectations of the treaty parties in regard to their commitments have to be taken into account: what could and should the parties reasonably have expected? In the second place, the importance of the contrary acts for the state performing them, or purporting to perform them, has to be considered. At the same time, the legal operator should take into account the precise expected effect of these acts on the treaty and the proper causality between the acts and the defeating of the object and purpose. Only direct causation could qualify for a prohibition, while remote and speculative effects on the treaty object could not lead to an implied prohibition. In the third place, the operator has to consider each provision of the treaty and the accepted subsequent practice of the parties. If a black-letter provision expressly allows a certain conduct, it cannot be said to be prohibited as defeating the object and purpose of the compact, since the parties have accepted that conduct.[137] They are the masters of the treaty and can thus allow an imperfect realisation of the treaty's object and purpose. The legal operator cannot upset these party's intentions. It may also be possible to take into account other treaties concluded by the same parties on similar subject matters in order to see whether they contain express clauses allowing a certain course of conduct. In the fourth place, a legal operator should have recourse by analogy to the practice and law surrounding article 18 VCLT.[138] The latter provision may be relevant for example in determining whether only abstentions or also some action to salvage the object and purpose of the treaty can be required. Such issues have been discussed in the context of the pre-conventional obligations as set out in article 18 VCLT.

[137] See ibid, 136, § 272. Some problems may arise: 'If an act which the parties do *not* wish to forbid is sufficiently close to the definition in the treaty of acts which it is to forbid, provision may be made that the treaty "does not preclude" such action; and in such case it cannot be caught as "action likely to defeat the object and purpose". If however action in the same sphere is thought to fall right outside the treaty's prohibitions, it will not be mentioned; and then there may be a risk that it may be found to be calculated to "defeat the object and purpose"': H Thirlway, 'The Law and Procedure of the ICJ (1960–1989): Treaty Interpretation and Other Treaty Points' (1992) 63 *BYIL* 52. This problem must be solved through a careful interpretation. The doctrine of the object and purpose can also have a quite different configuration in the context of treaties defining an objective (eg the transfer of certain assets) and providing for a series of means to reach that objective on the one hand and of treaties declaring that a certain objective is in itself unlawful (eg any alienation of political independence, *Customs Régime between Germany and Austria*, advisory opinion, PCIJ, ser A and B, no 41, p 37ff) on the other hand. In the first case, means not mentioned must be considered allowed or prohibited by an interpretation of the treaty; in the second case, any means are prohibited by the treaty. In both cases, the issue of the 'means' is not to be solved under the object and purpose-doctrine under consideration, but under an interpretation of the treaty black-letter provisions, including the consideration of the object and purpose as a device of interpretation. Conversely, the protection of the general aim of the treaty can sometimes give rise to an application of the 'non-defeating' doctrine: eg acts which lead to the destruction of the assets to be transferred or which render inoperative the channels of transfer.

[138] DW Greig, 'Nicaragua and the United States: Confrontation over the Jurisdiction of the International Court' (1991) 62 *BYIL* 267.

C. The Obligations of Rectitude

There are finally a series of scattered obligations of rectitude during the execution phase of a treaty, which flow from the general principle of good faith. Here are three examples.

— *First*, when a provision sets up one or more conditions for the realisation of a certain result, the party benefitting from the result may be tempted to provoke the realisation of the condition(s) and the other party may conversely be tempted to impede its/their realisation. If such conduct occurs, the legal operator may well legally treat the condition as not having been realised in the first case, but realised in the second case.[139] By the same token, the ICJ has considered that for reasons of good faith a right of (unilateral) denunciation could not be implied in a treaty. The treaty provided for the competence of the Court if Iceland adopted certain unilateral measures, namely the extension of its fisheries area. The aim was to protect the rights of the other treaty parties. If the right of denunciation was implied, this would have been tantamount to saying that Iceland could have first ridded itself of the treaty obligations and thereafter adopted the conduct which according to the treaty should open the way to a scrutiny by the Court. Since the treaty would have lapsed, Iceland would avoid being subjected to that judicial scrutiny. Such an interpretation would have manifestly upset the treaty regime and allowed an action which was plainly contrary to the legitimate expectations of the parties. This is the true reason for which the Court rejected it.[140]

— *Second*, a party must execute all the provisions of the treaty and cannot pretend to selectively accept only the ones which are beneficial to it. This would be contrary to the principle of good faith and the legitimate expectations of the treaty parties. It would also be contrary to the maxim that he who has the advantages must also bear the burdens (*qui habet commoda, ferre debet onera*). Consequently, a state could not successfully plead that it succeeded (through state succession) only in some provisions of the treaty and not in other ones, according to the benefits it could now draw from the various provisions.[141] The treaty regime is a single whole. It must be taken as such and not split up selectively.

[139] See the pleadings in the *Tacna Arica* case of 1925 mentioned in H Lauterpacht, *Private Law Sources and Analogies of International Law* (London, 1927) 291.

[140] *Fisheries Jurisdiction (UK v Iceland, Jurisdiction)* (1973) *ICJ Reports* 15–16, § 28–29. See also H Thirlway, 'The Law and Procedure of the ICJ (1960–1989): Treaty Interpretation and Other Treaty Points' (1992) 63 *BYIL* 64–65.

[141] See *K v Socialist Republic of Vietnam* (1984) 40 *ASDI* 177 (Court of Appeal of the Canton of Bern). See also the *Aegean Sea Continental Shelf* case (1978) *ICJ Reports* 33, § 78, in the context of an argument which accepted a dynamic interpretation of terms in the context of one provision, but refused it in the context of another provision.

— *Third*, if a party through its deliberate conduct renders impossible the proper execution of a treaty, it should not be freed of the treaty obligations, but be obliged to apply the treaty provisions in a way that (maximally or reasonably) approximates the originally intended result, while assuming responsibility for the breach. The doctrine has been expressed in well-pondered terms by Sir Hersch Lauterpacht: 'It is a sound principle of law that whenever a legal instrument of continuing validity cannot be applied literally owing to the conduct of one of the parties, it must, without allowing that party to take advantage of its own conduct, be applied in a way approximating most closely to its primary object'.[142] This doctrine was thoroughly discussed in the ICJ *Gabcikovo-Nagymaros* case of 1997, to which we will return in the chapter devoted to the maxim that no one shall be allowed to reap advantages from their own wrong (a further outflow of the principle of good faith).[143] The main point is not to allow the party to benefit from its breach—which is plainly an issue of good faith. The maxim also has a forward-looking reach: by not rewarding such conduct, it seeks to avoid incentivising it.

VII. Good Faith in the Modification of Treaties

Treaty commitments sometimes span long periods of time. The original meanings of treaty terms must often be adapted to new circumstances. However, a formal modification of a treaty is often burdensome and riddled with problems: it may take a long time; procedures may be complicated and costly; a formal conference may open up Pandora's boxes and undo more of the treaty regime than was wished; a new agreement, if adopted, will take many years to enter into force; it may not be ratified by all parties to the old treaty, thus leading to a complex split of treaty relations.[144] It may often be much easier, more flexible, more discreet, and more successful, to leave things to be sorted out by the subsequent practice in the application of the treaty. The states parties may thereby progressively crystallise certain patterns of expectations in the context of the treaty, which constantly evolve and have a sufficient degree of common basis. Thus, problems which may be of principle in a conference can be reduced to practical issues in the context of concrete cases of application. This shrinking in dimension allows the easier solving of such issues.

The ILC Draft on the VCLT of 1966 had contained an article 38. It was formulated as follows: 'A treaty may be modified by subsequent practice in the application

[142] Separate Opinion H Lauterpacht, *Admissibility of Hearings of Petitioners by the Committee on South West Africa* advisory opinion (1956) *ICJ Reports* 46.

[143] See below, Ch 6, section 4.

[144] On this last point, see art 40, § 4, of the VCLT.

of the treaty establishing the agreement of the parties to modify its provisions'.[145] By applying the treaty, the parties implicitly express themselves on its content. Since the parties can modify the treaty without any requirement of form, concordant applicative practice can evidence some 'implied intention' to modify the compact. Alternatively, this common practice can be considered under the principle of good faith: legitimate expectations in the proper meaning of the various contents of the treaty are created; assertive practice meets with silent acquiescence and new normative patterns emerge. Article 38 in the Draft had indeed a solid basis in international state, arbitral and judicial practice.[146] Nevertheless, it was deleted at the Vienna Conference of 1969. The reasons were not all directed against the substance of the rule. They were the following:[147] (i) the modification by subsequent practice is a customary law procedure, and the VCLT does not deal with unwritten law; (ii) the stability of treaties could be undermined if 'practice' could change the black letter law; (iii) the competence to engage a state by a treaty could be short-circuited in the modification phase if various state organs could contribute, through their practice, to amend the provisions of a treaty.[148]

The process of changing a constituent text by subsequent practice had been developed in the era of the Covenant of the League of Nations.[149] Article 1, § 2, of the Covenant was reinterpreted to mean that states that did not govern themselves freely (non-democratic states) could be admitted as members. This opened the door of membership to Siam and Abyssinia. Article 16 of the Covenant was weakened by resolutions of the Assembly which provided that each state was free to qualify for itself the *casus foederis vel garantiae*. The Council gradually obtained predominance in the organisation by reducing the role of the Assembly. The right of the Organisation to conclude treaties (*jus tractatus*) was permitted in practice, for example in the context of the mandate agreements or the treaty between the League and Switzerland concerning League personnel (1926). The right of the Organisation to enter into diplomatic relations was also admitted in practice. Consequently, a diplomatic mission was sent by the League to Mosul and the Åland Islands.

145 (1966-II) *YbILC* 236.

146 W Karl, *Vertrag und spätere Praxis im Völkerrecht* (Berlin, 1983).

147 Kolb, *Bonne* 297ff for a more detailed account.

148 It is to be regretted that these reasons led to the suppression of the provision. None of the objections is truly well-founded. As to the first, the relevant practice is so closely linked with the treaty that it ought to have been considered. Moreover, some provisions of the VCLT recall the role of customary international law in the context of treaties, eg art 38 of the VCLT as it now stands. As to the second objection, the stability of treaties is undermined merely by unilateral action. It is not jeopardised by subsequent practice which evidences an 'agreement' as in the wording of the ILC Draft. As to the third objection, the competence to engage the state remains fully reserved. Subordinate state organs cannot engage the state in matters of modification of the treaty. It is however true that the higher authorities have to control the lower ones. If they do not object to a practice for a prolonged period of time, they will be considered to have acquiesced. See mutatis mutandis for estoppel: *Preah Vihear* (1962) *ICJ Reports* 25, 34; A Verdross and B Simma, *Universelles Völkerrecht*, 3rd edn (Berlin, 1984) 507.

149 See W Schücking, 'Le développement du Pacte de la Société des Nations' (1927-V) 20 *RCADI* 359ff.

In the Charter of the UN, one finds the same propensity to effect changes by a subsequent practice informally accepted to be law.[150] One can mention the voting procedure in the Security Council (article 27 § 3): the abstention of a permanent member is not counted as a veto. Similarly, peacekeeping operations, with the specific rules that applied thereto, were introduced into the Charter in an informal manner. There was also a new interpretation given to article 42 as authorising member states to use force under a sort of 'mandate' of the United Nations. The powers of the General Assembly by virtue of Resolution 377 (V), called 'Uniting for Peace' or 'Dean Acheson', rebalanced the domains of action between the Assembly and the Council. A constitutional practice thus developed: nowhere in the Charter is the mechanism 'Uniting for Peace' found. Article 12 § 1 of the Charter, subordinating the General Assembly to the Security Council when the latter organ is seized of a dispute, has also been the object of exceptions and flexible interpretation. The Assembly more than once took position on a crisis notwithstanding that the Council was still formally seized of the question or even acting upon it. The era of decolonisation affected United Nations practice in the 1950s. It modified the Charter in a profound way, notably in Chapter XI relative to non-autonomous territories. A more recent example is a re-evaluation of human rights law, including the 'responsibility to protect' individuals against grave and systematic violations against their physical integrity. Among the aims of the Charter, human rights law has gained more weight than it enjoyed in the drafting-era of the Charter.

The jurisprudence on subsequent treaty practice modifying the treaty is very rich.[151] Here are some examples.

In the *US/France Air Transport Services Agreement Arbitration* (1963),[152] the US had for years operated an air route and a frequency of flights departing from the text of the applicable bilateral agreement. The French authorities tolerated this practice for many years without any objection whatsoever. The Tribunal thus considered that the agreement had been changed by subsequent practice and acquiescence. In other words, it was not open to France to contest the modified meaning of the treaty, since that would have been contrary to good faith, considering its previous conduct.

In the *Temple of Preah Vihear* case (1962),[153] the ICJ considered a Treaty of 1904 which placed a boundary on the watershed of a chain of mountains. Siam (Thailand) thereafter through a series of acts accepted or failed to object to a

[150] See B Simma et al (eds), *The Charter of the United Nations, A Commentary*, 3rd edn (Oxford, 2012).

[151] See Kolb, *Bonne* 301ff.

[152] *US/France Air Transport Services Agreement Arbitration* (1963) 38 *ILR* 182ff, 248ff. See also the *Italy and US Air Transport Arbitration* (1965) 45 *ILR* 393.

[153] (1962) *ICJ Reports* 34. See also the *Taba* arbitration between Egypt and Israel (1988) 80 *ILR* 224ff, 297–98, § 209–11; and the *Kasikili/Sedudu Island* case, (1999-II) *ICJ Reports* 1076ff, § 50ff. See also the *Delimitation of the Eritrea and Ethiopia Border* case, arbitration by the Eritrea and Ethiopia Boundary Commission, (2002) 130 *ILR* 37ff. In municipal law, see eg *Judgment no 6/99* of the German Federal Constitutional Court, dated 22 January 2001.

different course of the boundary. This course of conduct evidenced that the treaty and the boundary had thus been modified. As the Court noted, Siam had acquiesced in that boundary and could not subsequently be allowed to contest it, since that would have been contrary to good faith.

In the *Namibia* advisory opinion of 1971,[154] the ICJ held that the abstention of permanent members of the Security Council was not to be counted as a veto—contrary to what the clear text of article 27, § 3, of the Charter affirms. This text had been modified by the subsequent practice within the Council. No objection against the new practice had been raised in the UN membership. It had thus been accepted by acquiescence.

An interesting diplomatic precedent can be found in a Legal Note of the Swiss International Law Directorate at the Ministry of Foreign Affairs concerning the Swiss-German Convention on social assistance of 1997.[155] Germany had formally delegated the execution of this Convention to subordinate state organs. It was thus clear that the acts of the lower organs were imputable to the higher authorities. The regional German office had constantly accepted without any objection a certain practice of reduction of the reimbursements paid by Switzerland. This limitation was accepted on a reciprocal basis, the German authorities having adopted the same practice. The conclusion was that the treaty had been modified by concordant subsequent practice. The Legal Note emphasised that it would be contrary to good faith to allow any contrary position on this point at this stage.

In the *UNESCO Taxes Regime* arbitration (2003),[156] the issue turned upon the taxation of certain retired staff members of UNESCO after their retirement on French territory. France refused to grant the tax exemption provided for in article 22 of the Headquarters Agreement of 1954 between itself and UNESCO, arguing mainly that the exemption applied only to staff members still in employment. The arbitral tribunal accepted France's position. The tribunal checked whether the subsequent practice of the treaty parties changed the meaning of the text it had reached through its exercise of interpretation. On the facts of the present case, the tribunal held that the practice was insufficiently clear and unambiguous to modify informally the 1954 Agreement.[157] It did not further consider the argument on the legitimate expectations not of the parties to the Agreement, but of the individual staff members.[158] It is indeed doubtful whether such non-treaty party expectations can be legally relevant.

[154] (1971) *ICJ Reports* 22.

[155] (1998) 8 *RSDIE* 630. See also the *Houston Contracting Company* case (1988) 20*Iran/US Claims Tribunal Reports* 56–57: 'The Tribunal therefore concludes that the contractual provisions of Clause 42 of the General Conditions were not observed by the Parties in practice and, given this past conduct, it would be inequitable to allow those provisions to be accepted as a bar to payment of the remaining claims for extra work'.

[156] (2003) 107 *RGDIP* 221ff or (2003) XXV *RIAA* 233ff.

[157] (2003) XXV *RIAA* 256ff.

[158] See however the Separate Opinion Valticos, ibid 266.

A careful perusal of the practice shows that the doctrine according to which the subsequent practice manifests a tacit 'common intention of the parties' is in many cases a fictional construction.[159] The main point for the legal operator is to *objectively* judge the conduct of the parties according to the legitimate expectations created. It is true that the fictional intention-construction here has also its advantages. The legal operator will in such cases be able to hide behind what he emphatically qualifies as the 'intention of the parties', telling those parties that he does nothing more than to give effect to their own will. Such a course can have a soothing effect, reassuring the states as to the full respect of their own law-making power and sovereignty.[160] The truth however lies elsewhere: the legal operator will consider whether the practice is such that allowing a state to deny its normativity would be a breach of faith, of reasonableness and of legitimate expectations. If that is the case in his or her judgment, the operator will wrap up the matter as a new 'common intention' of the parties and solve the point in the full orthodoxy of apparent legal positivism. This course may be accepted in a world of touchy sovereign states. But analytically, no one should be blind as to the real instruments of legal craftsmanship. In most cases, the subsequent practice results from a series of more or less clear or amorphous conducts, to which the other parties react or do not react. To reduce this process, spread over time and made up of very heteroclite acts and omissions, to the simple complexion of an instantaneous legal act appears more often than not highly artificial. The issue is plainly not one limited to a legal act (a tacit agreement); it is rather one about a customary process engrafted upon the treaty (the subsequent practice). The *opinio juris* in this case flows automatically from the fact that the implementation of a treaty is at stake: the treaty implementation is a legal matter by definition. In other words, we are here confronting a special type of customary law, which is limited to the treaty parties and where the legal opinion is implicit. Good faith arguments, acquiescence by prolonged silence, estoppel, and similar considerations are more important in this context than abstract conceptions on invisible implied intentions. The main point is that a prolonged practice by treaty parties creates a legitimate expectation as to its continuity. The stability of the mere text has then to give way to the still more fundamental continuity of the effective and uncontested conduct. Legal principles outweigh here the role of the parties' real (and unascertained) will.

Another point concerns the issue of the 'common' practice or agreement. Article 38 of the ILC Draft had required that the subsequent practice reveals the 'agreement' of the parties, ie their *common* agreement (agreement of all the parties).

[159] See JP Cot, 'La conduite subséquente des parties à un traité' (1966) 70 *RGDIP* 645; W Karl, *Vertrag und spätere Praxis im Völkerrecht* (Berlin, 1983) 143ff; Müller, *Vertrauensschutz* 171ff. But it may certainly occur that a modified treaty replaces an older one by some way of real tacit agreement, ie real exchanges of mind of the holders of the treaty-making competence.

[160] On the need to reassure states so as not to make them shy away from international justice, see H Waldock, 'General Course on Public International Law' (1962-II) 106 *RCADI* 104ff; H Lauterpacht, *The Development of International Law by the International Court* (London, 1958) 75ff. On the role of fiction in this context, see generally J Stone, 'Fictional Elements in Treaty Interpretation' in J Stone, *Of Law and Nations—Between Power Politics and Human Hopes* (New York, 1974) 194ff.

If that is translated into the world of the legal fact constituted by the customary process, rather than remaining in the world of the legal act of a tacit agreement, what meaning does the word 'common' obtain? How can the commonness of the practice be ascertained in a process rather than an act? The issue is largely the same as it is for the formation of new customary international law itself. The practice must not positively emanate from all treaty parties. That is to say that not every single party has to engage in that practice. It is enough that such a practice is regularly followed by a number of treaty parties and that the other parties do not protest it.[161] The practice then becomes 'common' by the aggregate of those who effectively engage in it and of the other parties which acquiesce through their silence. As is known, silence is only relevant in the legal order when there is a legal duty to speak out: *qui tacet consentire videtur, si loqui potuisset ac debuisset*. In our context, the duty to speak out and to protest flows from the common treaty bond. It is again a matter of good faith: the treaty parties engaged in a certain practice have the legitimate expectation, and thus the right, to see their attitudes contested if that is the position of some other treaty party. Through its silence, a state party to a treaty accepts new legal facts. As can be seen, this is a harsh doctrine: states have to be vigilant about their common treaty commitments and timely react to evolutions they disagree with. This supposes a certain staffing and proper functioning of the relevant legal services, which may be problematic for poorer states. However, the needs of a quickly evolving world, and the concomitant needs of flexibility within the treaty enterprises, render this duty to protest an indispensable asset of modern treaty relations.

Overall, as can be seen, the subject matter of subsequent practice—in treaty matters of elsewhere—is permeated profoundly by considerations of good faith protecting the legitimate expectations of the treaty 'community'. The treaty bond is a continuously unfolding commitment. It is not enough to conclude a treaty and to think that the bond created is other than a living organism. The equilibrium between stability and change, and the balance between the interests of the treaty partners, is largely a matter of good faith. In this context, it is only in the last drafting phase of this or that judgment that the easy and subservient 'intention of the parties' argument can offer its nominal—albeit partially welcome—services. As we have seen, the gist of the matter most often lies elsewhere.

VIII. Good Faith and the Doctrine *Rebus Sic Stantibus*

There were different constructions of the doctrine of 'fundamental change of circumstances' before the matter was eventually codified in article 62 of the VCLT

[161] See JP Cot, 'La conduite subséquente des parties à un traité' (1966) 70 *RGDIP* 634–35; W Karl, *Vertrag und spätere Praxis im Völkerrecht* (Berlin, 1983) 111ff. For customary international law, see M Akehurst, 'Custom as a Source of International Law' (1974/75) 47 *BYIL* 16–18, 38ff. See also DJ Bederman, 'Acquiescence, Objection and the Death of Customary International Law' (2010) 21 *Duke Journal of Comparative and International Law* 31ff.

of 1969.[162] The most classical doctrine was linked to the construction of a tacit clause: when a treaty is concluded, the parties intend an underlying tacit understanding according to which the treaty commitment can be terminated if certain unforeseen events occur, which fundamentally alter the extent of the mutual commitments to the detriment of one party and to the benefit of the other. This tacit clause was upheld mainly by the positivistic authors; they sought to always refer to the will of states.[163] An alternative view was based on the idea that an objective legal norm of customary international law allowed an equitable adjustment of the conventional commitments in the case of such unforeseen later events.[164] The main criticism levied by the latter school of thought against the former is to have recourse to a manifestly fictional element.[165] Finally, an intermediary theory has seen the light of day. It is based on a standard of good faith, ie the legitimate expectations of the parties.[166] This standard operates by a judgment on what the expectations of the parties ought to have reasonably been when considering the content of the treaty and the entity of the changes in the surrounding environment. Thus: 'The treaty is ended because we can infer from its terms that the parties ... would, if they had foreseen [the event which has occurred], have said that the treaty ought to lapse'.[167] The search cannot be for the real intentions of the parties, if the fiction is to be avoided. The exercise must be a normative one, considering objectively what the parties could and should have expected in view of the concrete relations as they are stipulated in the agreement. The matter can also be looked at under the perspective of the prohibition of abuse of rights, which is equally a matter of good

[162] Here is the text of art 62: '1. A fundamental change of circumstances which has occurred with regard to those existing at the time of the conclusion of a treaty, and which was not foreseen by the parties, may not be invoked as a ground for terminating or withdrawing from the treaty unless:

(*a*) the existence of those circumstances constituted an essential basis of the consent of the parties to be bound by the treaty; and

(*b*) the effect of the change is radically to transform the extent of obligations still to be performed under the treaty.

2. A fundamental change of circumstances may not be invoked as a ground for terminating or withdrawing from a treaty:

(*a*) if the treaty establishes a boundary; or

(*b*) if the fundamental change is the result of a breach by the party invoking it either of an obligation under the treaty or of any other international obligation owed to any other party to the treaty.

3. If, under the foregoing paragraphs, a party may invoke a fundamental change of circumstances as a ground for terminating or withdrawing from a treaty it may also invoke the change as a ground for suspending the operation of the treaty.'

[163] See eg D Anzilotti, *Corso di diritto internazionale* (Rome, 1928) 407.

[164] See eg G Schwarzenberger, 'The Fundamental Principles of International Law' (1955-I) 87 *RCADI* 273; G Schwarzenberger, *International Law—As Applied by International Courts and Tribunals*, 3rd edn, vol I (London, 1957) 543.

[165] But it has also been said that the objective norm of customary international law is as much fictional as the implied intention-doctrine: O Lissytzyn, 'Treaties and Changed Circumstances' (1967) 61 *AJIL* 922.

[166] Müller, *Vertrauensschutz* 212ff; Lissytzyn, ibid, 896ff; C Rabl-Blaser, *Die Clausula Rebus Sic Stantibus im Völkerrecht* (Zurich, 2012) 59–60.

[167] JL Brierly, *The Law of Nations*, 6th edn (Oxford, 1963) 336.

faith: does the refusal of one party to adapt the treaty (or to have it lapsed) appear in context as an abusive attitude.[168]

There are some traces of such an application of good faith in the case law, but overall the doctrine of *sic stantibus* has been very rarely applied, especially since 1969.[169] In the *Pensions of Officials of the Saar Territory* arbitration (1934), it was held that: 'if subsequently and unexpectedly circumstances had so changed that the performance of the contract would no longer reasonably correspond to what was originally intended, and if, accordingly, it would be contrary to good faith to uphold the claim'.[170] Further, in the *Italian Consortium* case (1987), an International Chamber of Commerce Tribunal referred in this context to the principles of good faith and the prohibition of abuse of rights, as recognised also under Libyan, Swiss and German Law.[171] Overall, good faith is once more called into action to temper excessively will-oriented constructions to the benefit of 'shared expectations' doctrines.

We may also notice that according to article 62, § 2, VCLT a fundamental change of circumstances 'may not be invoked as a ground for terminating or withdrawing from a treaty: ... (b) if the fundamental change is the result of a breach by the party invoking it'. Letter (b) applies the legal maxim according to which no one can profit from his own wrong (*nemo ex propria turpitudine commodum capere potest*).[172] Paragraph 2, letter b only envisages the situation where the fundamental change is brought about by a breach of treaty or a breach of any other international obligation owed to any other party to the treaty. The breach need not be a material breach in the sense of article 60 VCLT.[173] However, material breaches are more likely to provoke situations such as envisaged here. The conclusion of a new treaty contradicting earlier obligations suffices for the purposes of § 2, letter b.[174] The understanding at the Vienna Conference was that any changes provoked bona fide would not lead to a loss of the right to invoke the changed circumstances—but conversely that changes not brought about bona fide would automatically be tantamount to a violation of the treaty.[175] This however must not always be the case. The change can relate to conduct which is not prohibited under the treaty. It is then a matter of interpretation to what extent it could be

[168] W Sauer, *Völkerrecht und Weltfrieden* (Stuttgart, 1948) 155. The Swiss Federal Tribunal has often had recourse to this criterion in the context of municipal law: see eg ATF (*Arrêts du Tribunal fédéral, série officielle*) 97 II, 398; ATF 107 II, 348.

[169] See C Rabl-Blaser, *Die Clausula Rebus Sic Stantibus im Völkerrecht* (Zurich, 2012).

[170] *Pensions of Officials of the Saar Territory* arbitration (1934) III *RIAA* 1566.

[171] *Italian Consortium* (1987) 114 *JDI* 1014–17.

[172] On this maxim, see R Kolb, 'La maxime "nemo ex propria turpitudine commodum capere potest" (nul ne peut profiter de son propre tort) en droit international public' (2000) 33 *RBDI* 84ff. See also in our context C Rabl-Blaser, *Die Clausula Rebus Sic Stantibus im Völkerrecht* (Zurich, 2012) 376ff.

[173] *Contra*: ME Villiger, *Commentary on the 1969 Vienna Convention on the Law of Treaties* (Leiden, 2009) 776.

[174] T Giegerich, 'Article 62' in: O Dörr and K Schmalenbach (eds), *Vienna Convention on the Law of Treaties, A Commentary* (Berlin, 2012) 1094.

[175] ibid, 1095.

subsumed as a breach of positive corollary obligations under the treaty. Moreover, the question remains as to whether a party should prevent the occurrence of the change if it is able to do so. This will be the case only if the party is under an international obligation, under good faith or under some rule of international law (including the treaty), to prevent the change.[176] The existence of such an obligation will not be common.

Finally, if a fundamental change is invoked, the principle of good faith requires the readiness of that state to negotiate about the fate of the treaty.[177] Further, the change must be invoked within a reasonable time, since otherwise the state will be considered to have acquiesced in the permanence of the treaty (or alternatively that the change was not considered to be fundamental).[178] These rules are based on the operation of the principle of good faith-legitimate expectations.

IX. Good Faith and the Birth of Customary International Law

The importance of customary law in a given society is in inverse proportion to the degree of centralisation and institutionalisation of that society. In a society characterised by the lack of centralised organs and by a centrifugal split of power arenas, customary law remains a fundamental source of the legal order.[179] In such societies, legal norms arising from practice and spontaneous social interaction—and not through the enactment of a legislator—are bound to play a pre-eminent role.[180] International society is in precisely such a position. The formal dimensions of the legal norms are diluted by the pattern of various 'practices'. They are replaced by flexibly and spontaneously emerging norms, a process which carries with it a certain degree of legal uncertainty.[181] However, the process by which customary norms are established remains difficult to describe or catch up in legal

[176] ibid, 1095.

[177] See Kolb, *Bonne* 313; C Rabl-Blaser, *Die Clausula Rebus Sic Stantibus im Völkerrecht* (Zurich, 2012) 380ff.

[178] Kolb, *Bonne* 314, with relevant case law; Rabl-Blaser, ibid, 379–80.

[179] H Waldock, 'General Course on Public International Law' (1962-II) 106 *RCADI* 39.

[180] R Ago, 'Science juridique et droit international' (1956-II) 90 *RCADI* 946ff. On the specificities of the doctrine of R Ago: J Kunz, 'Roberto Ago's Theory of a Spontaneous International Law' (1958) 52 *AJIL* 85ff; AP Sereni, 'Dottrine italiane di diritto internazionale' *Essays in Honor of T Perassi*, vol II (Milan, 1957) 277ff, 284ff; F Münch, 'A propos du droit spontané' *Essays in Honor of G Sperduti* (Milan, 1984) 147ff; See also G Barile, 'Diritto internazionale et diritto interno—Diritto della coscienza e diritto della volontà' (1956) 39 *RDI* 449ff; P Ziccardi, 'La consuetudine internazionale nella teoria delle fonti giuridiche' *Comunicazioni e studi*, vol X (Milan, 1960) 187ff, 224ff. And see generally E Pecourt Garcia, *Tendencias actuales de la doctrina italiana de derecho internacional público* (Valencia, 1965) 108ff.

[181] G Barile, 'La rilevazione e l'integrazione del diritto internazionale non scritto e la libertà di apprezzamento del giudice' *Comunicazioni e studi*, vol V (Milan, 1953) 143ff.

terms. The dominant theory refers to the two well-known elements of 'practice' and '*opinio juris*', but it leaves open many hard questions.[182]

In this context, the principle of good faith as protection of legitimate expectations has provided some insight into the customary process, without necessarily purporting to displace the traditional theory of the two elements. The emergence and hardening of customary rules is in this perspective perceived as one aspect of the continuous interaction between the subjects of the law, with their deeds and omissions, as well as their claims, opinions, intentions and expectations. As has been graphically explained in a much celebrated formula, which can be transposed from the specific subject matter in which it was placed to the formation of customary international law in general:

> From the perspective of realistic description, the international law of the sea is not a mere static body of rules, but rather a whole decision-making process, a public order which includes a structure of authorized decision-makers as well as a body of highly flexible, inherited prescriptions. It is in other words, a process of continuous interaction, of continuous demand and response, in which the decision-makers of particular nation states unilaterally put forward claims of the most diverse and conflicting character to the use of the world's seas, and in which other decision-makers, external to the demanding state and including both national and international officials, weigh and appraise these competing claims in terms of the interests of the world community and of the rival claimants, and ultimately accept or reject them. As such a process, it is a living, growing law, grounded in the practices and sanctioning expectations of nation-state officials, and changing as their

[182] On the formation of customary international law, see the explanations and bibliography in T Treves, 'Customary International Law' in R Wolfrum (ed), *The Max Planck Encyclopedia of Public International Law*, vol II (Oxford, 2012) 937ff. See also MH Mendelson, 'The Formation of Customary International Law' (1998) 272 *RCADI* 155ff. There are mainly four schools of thought in this regard: (i) custom as a legal act, ie a tacit agreement evidences *rebus ipsis et factis*; (ii) custom as flowing from the conjunction of the two elements of practice and legal opinion (see P Guggenheim, 'Les deux éléments de la coutume en droit international public' *Essays in Honor of G Scelle*, vol I (Paris, 1950) 275ff), a doctrine forged in the Middle Ages by the jurists working on the Code of Justinian in order to limit the role of local usages with respect to imperial law (see E Lambert, *Etudes de droit commun législatif ou de droit civil comparé*, série I, *Le régime successoral* (Paris, 1903) 110ff; F Senn, 'La leçon de la Rome Antique sur le fondement de la force obligatoire de la coutume' *Essays in Honor of E Lambert*, vol I. (Paris, 1938) 218ff; B Schmiedel, *Consuetudo im klassischen und nachklassischen römischen Recht* (Graz, 1966); D Nörr, 'Zur Entstehung der gewohnheitsrechtlichen Theorie', in *Essays in Honor of W Felgenträger* (Göttingen, 1969) 353ff); (iii) custom as laws spontaneously emerging in the social body and reflected in the legal conscience of peoples (see G Scelle, 'Essai sur les sources formelles du droit international' *Essays in Honor of F Gény*, vol III (Paris, 1934) 400ff); (iv) custom as the outflow of legitimate expectations in social interactions. As to the latter doctrine, see IC McGibbon, 'Customary International Law and Acquiescence' (1957) 33 *BYIL* 115ff; G Sperduti, 'Prescrizione, consuetudine e acquiescenza in diritto internazionale' (1961) 44 *RDI* 3ff, 9ff; E Suy, *Les actes juridiques unilatéraux en droit international public* (Paris, 1962) 249ff, 260ff; ZS Slouka, *International Custom and the Continental Shelf* (The Hague, 1968) 15ff, 169ff; H Günther, *Zur Entstehung von Völkergewohnheitsrecht* (Berlin, 1970) 127ff, 138ff; B Simma, *Das Reziprozitätselement in der Entstehung des Völkergewohnheitsrechts* (Munich, 1970) 45ff, 73–74 [summary in English]; A D'Amato, *The Concept of Custom in International Law* (Ithaca NY, 1971) 73ff, 199ff; JP Müller, *Vertrauensschutz im Völkerrecht* (Köln, 1971) 77ff; Kolb, *Bonne* 315ff.

demands and expectations are changed by the exigencies of new interests and technology and by other continually evolving conditions in the world arena.[183]

In this continuous process of demand and response, normative patters emerge through the creation of legitimate expectations as to future conduct, and thus through legal instruments such as reliance, acquiescence or estoppel. Ultimately, all these institutions are rooted in the doctrine of good faith as the depositary of the reasonable expectations doctrine. As we have already seen, a significant amount of conduct by states implies a plea that this conduct is lawful or even obligatory. When such conduct impacts on the legally protected interests of other states, international law requires from the latter a reaction. If such reaction is omitted, the other states will be considered to have acquiesced in the conduct. As has thus rightly been said: 'Protests and acquiescence play a central role in the formation of customary international law'.[184] In a nutshell, under this view (which may be inserted into the two elements doctrine or made autonomous), a communication process composed of acts, omissions, claims, silences, acceptances, reservations, and the like, may usher into a certain regularity; this regularity will at a certain stage provoke the normative expectation in the subjects of the legal order that future conduct will conform to the standards thus established. This legitimate reliance transforms a regularity of fact into a rule of law.[185] As can be seen, in this theory on the formation of customary international law, the more inward-oriented 'opinio juris' is translated into the more outward-reaching 'legitimate reliance': the unilateral and subjective acceptance of the rule by each subject individually gives to some extent way to the collective reliance and expectation of a plurality of subjects.[186] Consequently, it can be observed once more that good faith has the function to displace the centre of legal interest from a subjective inner fact (a

[183] M McDougal, 'The Hydrogen Bomb Tests and the International Law of the Sea' (1955) 49 *AJIL* 356–57. See also: H Lauterpacht, *International Law— Collected Papers*, vol I (Cambridge, 1970) 63–64: 'A course of action, constantly pursued and believed to be dictated by duties of neighborliness, reasonableness and accommodation, may, in the interest of international stability and good faith, assume the complexion of binding international custom'; P Reuter, *Droit international public*, 6th edn (Paris, 1983) 111–12: 'La répétition d'une attitude déterminée engendrant auprès des Etats prenant la même attitude, l'attente légitime du même comportement: la règle coutumière serait la conséquence d'un besoin de sécurité sociale'; ME Villiger, *Customary International Law and Treaties* (Dordrecht, 1985) 29ff, 29–30: 'In a first stage, some States engage in a given practice ... In a second stage, States react with further conduct, claims and counter-claims, and thereby uphold the practice, for instance, in the expectation that other States will again accord reciprocity. Other States may come to rely on the conduct of a State, and the latter will then be bound by the expectations which its conduct has raised in other States'; E Decaux, *La réciprocité en droit international* (Paris, 1980) 117; U Fastenrath, *Lücken im Völkerrecht* (Berlin, 1991) 110ff.

[184] M Akehurst, 'Custom as a Source of International Law' (1974/1975) 47 *BYIL* 38. See also IC McGibbon, 'Customary International Law and Acquiescence' (1957) 33 *BYIL* 115ff.

[185] Müller, *Vertrauensschutz* 78, 85ff.

[186] U Scheuner, 'Internationale Verträge als Elemente der Bildung von völkerrechtlichem Gewohnheitsrecht', *Essays in Honor of FA Mann* (Munich, 1977) 416: 'Damit [*Vertrauensschutz*] verlagert sich das Element der normativen Annahme einer Regel durch den handelnden Staat auf die Erwartung anderer Staaten auf die Konstanz einer Übung'. See also U Fastenrath, *Lücken im Völkerrecht* (Berlin, 1991) 104–05, 110ff, 210.

will) to an external objective fact (the normatively reasonable expectations of the others). In this sense, will and faith are two opposing poles in constant interaction.

A criticism levied against the presented theory is that interactions leading to legitimate expectation can certainly be a source of particular obligations between some states, but that the theory does not explain in a satisfactory way how such particular norms pass the stage to become objective norms of general international law.[187] However, in a decentralised society such as the international one, the distinction of sources of law and sources of obligation[188] is only a relative one. The borders between both concepts remain in constant shift and flux. Moreover, the leap between the particular rule and the general one can be taken by collective acquiescence (silence) as well as by praying in aid the traditional practice/legal opinion theory, which the reasonable expectation doctrine does not intend to entirely displace.

It must at the same time be conceded that the reasonable expectations theory, valuable as it is in catching the eye to an aspect of the growth of unwritten rules, cannot purport to provide a sufficient explanation for the formation of all customary rules. This is manifest for the axiomatic customary rules at the apex of the system (eg *pacta sunt servanda*); but it is also true for a series of other rules, eg for customary rules hardening into existence in the course of a formal codification process. The formation of customary law is too multi-faceted and complex a process to be caught up in one-size-fits-all. The doctrine of legitimate expectations presented here must thus remain one element in a vaster edifice. Overall, it can mainly be said that this doctrine offers a quite realistic explanation of the progressive emergence of many (not all) customary rules in the body of international law. Under this limited perspective, it deserves some keen attention.

X. Good Faith and Unilateral Acts

There are many types of unilateral act within a legal order. The ones interesting us in this chapter in the perspective of the international legal order are characterised by the following features: (i) only unilateral *legal* acts shall be analysed, ie manifestations of will attributable to one or more than one legal subject and purporting to create legal effects according to the expressed will (this category thus excludes material unilateral acts, ie mere factual acts and omissions, not of a normative nature); (ii) only unilateral acts having an *external reach* shall be considered, ie the addressees of the legal act are third subjects; (iii) only *autonomous*

[187] Scheuner, ibid, 416–17; M Bos, 'The Identification of Custom' (1982) 25 *GYIL* 41–42. Even the proponents of the legitimate expectations theory emphasise that it is particularly well-suited for regional custom, prescriptive situations and other particular rules: Müller, *Vertrauensschutz* 81.

[188] On the distinction, see MH Mendelson, 'Are Treaties Merely a Source of Obligation?' in WE Butler (ed), *Perestroika and International Law* (Dordrecht, 1990) 81ff.

legal acts are at stake, and thus not unilateral acts taking place in the context of a treaty bond, such as signature, ratification, reservations, etc, the latter being part of the law of treaties. With regard to their effects, unilateral legal acts are generally distinguished in acts creating new rights and obligations (promise and recognition), acts extinguishing rights and obligations (renunciation) and acts confirming rights or obligations (protest and notification, if the latter is considered to be a unilateral normative act at all).[189] What is the basis of obligation of such unilateral acts? Why, for example, is a promise legally binding? And is it binding at all?

Several responses to this question have been attempted: (i) there is no legally binding force of autonomous normative unilateral acts;[190] (ii) the binding force of unilateral normative acts is limited to the treaty-context;[191] (iii) the binding force of such acts depends on the will of the declaring state;[192] (iv) the binding force of such acts flows from objective norms of customary international law or from general principles of law (*promissio est servanda*);[193] (v) the binding force of such acts, mainly promise, flows from the principle of good faith as a norm for the protection of legitimate expectations, including the principle of estoppel.[194] The legitimate expectations thus create a certain degree of confidence and legal

[189] See E Suy, *Les actes juridiques unilatéraux en droit international* (Paris, 1962) 42–43. On such unilateral acts in general, see V Rodriguez Cedeno and MI Torres Cazorla, 'Unilateral Acts of States in International Law' in R Wolfrum (ed), *The Max Planck Encyclopedia of Public International Law*, vol X (Oxford, 2012) 163ff, with a bibliography.

[190] See eg JW Garner, 'The International Binding Force of Unilateral Oral Declarations' (1922) 27 *AJIL* 493; P Ziccardi, *La costituzione dell'ordinamento internazionale* (Milan, 1943) 418–19; G Biscottini, *Contributo alla teoria degli atti unilaterali nel diritto internazionale* (Milan, 1951) 158ff; G Cansacchi, *Istituzioni di diritto internazionale pubblico*, 5th edn (Turin, 1963) 216. In the case law, see eg the *Island of Lamu* case (1889), in H La Fontaine, *Pasicrisie internationale* (Bern, 1902) 335ff.

[191] See eg AP Sereni, *Diritto internazionale*, vol III (Milan, 1962) 1350ff; R Quadri, *Diritto internazionale pubblico*, 5th edn (Naples, 1968) 569ff.

[192] See eg G Bosco, 'Il fondamento giuridico del valore obbligatorio del diritto internazionale' (1938) 30 *Rivista di diritto pubblico* 626ff, 633–34.

[193] See eg C Rousseau, *Droit international public*, vol I (Paris, 1970) 416ff.

[194] Some authors insist on estoppel, eg G Schwarzenberger, *International Law—As Applied by International Courts and Tribunals*, vol I (London, 1957) 553: 'The typical minimum effect of unilateral acts is to create an estoppel. It prevents the subject of international law, to which the unilateral act is imputable, from acting contrary to its declared intent'. See also GG Fitzmaurice, 'The Law and Procedure of the ICJ, 1951–54: Treaty Interpretation and Other Treaty Points' (1957) 33 *BYIL* 230: '[A Declaration will be binding if it is held out] as an instrument on which others may rely and under which the declarant purports to assume such obligation. Particularly will this be so where other countries have, on the faith of the Declaration, changed their position or taken action on the basis of it'; M Bothe, 'Rechtsfragen der Rüstungskontrolle im Vertragsvölkerrecht der Gegenwart' *Berichte der deutschen Gesellschaft für Völkerrecht*, vol 30 (Heidelberg, 1990) 71: 'Solche politisch verbindlichen Erklärungen können dazu über den Weg des *Vertrauensschutzes*, auf der Grundlage des estoppel-Prinzips, rechtliche Verbindlichkeit erlangen. Hierzu ist aber erforderlich, dass eine Vertrauenssituation geschaffen wurde und dass derjenige, der auf die Erklärung der anderen Seite vertraut hat, selbst im Hinblick auf dieses Vertrauen eigene Positionen verändert hat'; A Miaja de la Muela, 'Los actos unilaterales en las relaciones internacionales' (1967) 20 *REDI* 431.

Many other authors rather insist on the principle of good faith and on legitimate expectations beyond the strict conditions of estoppel. See eg EC Stowell, *International Law* (New York, 1931) 131, 134ff; GC Venturini, 'La portée et les effets juridiques des attitudes et des actes unilatéraux des Etats' (1964-II) 112 *RCADI* 402; S Carbone, *Promessa e affidamento nel diritto internazionale* (Milan, 1967)

stability around the unilateral promises or around similar acts of states. A criterion is thereby indicated for determining why—and perhaps also to what extent—unilateral legal acts are binding.

International practice acknowledges this role of reliance on good faith in the context mainly of unilateral acts creating new rights and obligations, such as promises. The focus here again is shifted to some extent away from the mere inner will of the declaring state to consider also what the receiving state(s) could and should have understood when confronted with the declarations at stake. There is a certain amount of state practice and of case law sustaining the reliance-doctrine. The Swiss Directorate of International Law made the statement that unilateral acts are binding on the legal basis of good faith and legitimate expectations.[195] The same is true of certain municipal case law, such as the *West Rand Central Gold Mining* case (1905), decided by the English King's Bench Division.[196] The leading international case is the judgment by the ICJ in the *Nuclear Test* cases (1974).[197] The Court first stated that a promise will become legally binding when

53ff, 132ff; S Carbone, 'Promise in International Law: A Confirmation of its Binding Force' (1975) 1 *ItYbIL* 169–170; TM Franck, 'Word Made Law: The Decision of the ICJ in the Nuclear Test Cases' (1975) 69 *AJIL* 616ff; J Leutert, 'Einseitige Erklärungen im Völkerrecht: Ein Beitrag zur Lehre vom Vertrauensschutz' (PhD thesis, Bern, Diessenhofen, 1979); U Fastenrath, *Lücken im Völkerrecht* (Berlin, 1991) 104ff, 210; C Tomuschat, 'International Law: Ensuring the Survival of Mankind on the Eve of a New Century' (1999) 281 *RCADI* 344, 346; Müller, *Vertrauensschutz* 112. See also the terms used in R De Nova, 'Considerazioni sulla neutralità permanente dell'Austria' *Comunicazioni e studi*, vol VIII (Milan, 1956) 11: 'L'atto di notifica fa uscire la dichiarazione … dalla sfera del promittente e la immette come autentica promessa nel circuito internazionale facendo sorgere corrispondenti aspettative e determinando quel concreto affidamento in cui si può scorgere la ragione d'essere della obbligatorietà della promessa'; E Suy, *Les actes juridiques unilatéraux en droit international public* (Paris, 1962) 151: 'C'est dans cette confiance dans la parole donnée que se trouve le fondement de validité de la promesse … L'intérêt supérieur de la sécurité des rapports internationaux exige que la promesse soit obligatoire dès qu'elle est connue par les sujets intéressés et cet intérêt se traduit dans le principe de la bonne foi qui doit régir toutes les relations internationales'; P Reuter, *Droit international public*, 6th edn (Paris, 1983) 164: 'Cette affirmation [of the binding force of promises] est basée sur le principe de la bonne foi et plus spécialement sur l'obligation de respecter les convictions que l'on fait naître par son comportement'. Further references in Kolb, *Bonne* 328–29.

[195] (1983) 39 *ASDI* 186. The same principle was applied later in the context of tax restitution: see (2000) 10 *RSDIE* 631.

[196] Per Lord Alverstone: 'We can well understand that, if by public proclamation or by convention the conquering country has promised something that is inconsistent with the repudiation of particular liabilities, good faith should prevent such repudiation'. See LC Green, *International Law Through Cases*, 4th edn (New York, 1978) 41.

[197] *Nuclear Test* (1974) *ICJ Reports* 253ff, 457ff. On these judgments, see H Falsafi, 'L'affaire des essais nucléaires devant la CIJ' (PhD thesis, Neuchâtel, 1978); S Sur, 'Les affaires des essais nucléaires' (1975) 79 *RGDIP* 972ff; B Bollecker-Stern, 'L'affaire des essais nucléaires français devant la CIJ' (1974) 20 *AFDI* 299ff; TM Franck, 'Word Made Law: The Decision of the ICJ in the Nuclear Test Cases' (1975) 69 *AJIL* 612ff; R MacDonald and B Hough, 'The Nuclear Test Case Revisited' (1977) 20 *GYIL* 337ff; P Lellouche, 'The Nuclear Test Cases: Judicial Silence v Atomic Blasts' (1975) 16 *Harvard International Law Journal* 614ff; D Khosla, 'Nuclear Test Cases: Judicial Valour v Judicial Discretion' (1978) 18 *Indian JIL* 322ff; WA Kewenig, 'Der Internationale Gerichtshof und die französischen Kernwaffenversuche', in *Essays in Honor of E Menzel* (Berlin, 1975) 323ff; P De Visscher, 'Remarques sur l'évolution de la jurisprudence de la CIJ relative au fondement obligatoire de certains actes unilatéraux', in *Essays in Honor of M Lachs* (The Hague, 1984) 459ff. See also S Carbone, 'Promise in International Law: A

the declaring state intends to confer it such legal force.[198] In the key passage, the Court added that the legal force of such promises is also based on the principle of reliance on good faith:

> One of the basic principles governing the creation and performance of legal obligations, whatever their source, is the principle of good faith. Trust and confidence are inherent in international co-operation, in particular in an age when this co-operation in many fields is becoming increasingly essential. Just as the very rule of *pacta sunt servanda* in the law of treaties is based on good faith, so also is the binding force of an international obligation assumed by unilateral declaration. Thus interested States may take cognisance of unilateral declarations and place confidence in them, and are entitled to require that the obligation thus created be respected.[199]

The question therefore arises—and has indeed been asked—of the exact relation between the will element and the element of reliance on good faith. The ICJ referred to both in the 1974 cases, and it did not clearly sort out the role of each. It is therefore not surprising that all the possible interpretations on the relationship of the two elements have been defended in legal doctrine. A careful analysis of the judgment tends to show that the paragraph devoted to the 'will' deals with the conditions of existence of a promise as a legal act. A legal act is based on an expression of will; and hence a legally binding promise supposes such a will. It is not by accident that the Court analyses this element in the context of the distinction between legal acts and mere political declarations.[200] Then the Court moves to the legal basis for the binding force of such declarations. In this context, it elaborates on good faith and reliance.[201] It could be said that the latter consideration is legally superfluous: if the legal act exists only when the declaring state intends to be bound, that will also explains the binding force of the act and good faith is no longer necessary to establish the legal bond. However, the legal construction of the Court would exceptionally allow to postulate a binding force even absent a will to be bound (ie absent a legal act) when the declaring state has aroused the legitimate confidence of other subjects that it is bound. In a sense, this was precisely the case in the *Nuclear Test* cases: it is more than doubtful whether in that case France ever considered that it was undertaking a firm legal obligation. But the Court could find such a binding force in consideration of the objective and 'other-oriented' effect of the declarations considered under the lens of good faith. As has been aptly said:

> [an] intention cannot be determined solely by reference to the speaker's state of mind but must also take into account that of the listeners … if a state speaks, through an ostensible

Confirmation of its Binding Force' (1975) 1 *ItYbIL* 166ff; AP Rubin, 'The International Legal Effects of Unilateral Declarations' (1977) 71 *AJIL* 24ff. References to pleadings and individual opinions in other cases of the PCIJ and ICJ which follow the criterion of good faith, see Kolb, *Bonne* 330.

[198] (1974) *ICJ Reports* 267, § 43, and 472, § 46, the Court referring to the 'intention' of the declaring state.

[199] ibid, 268, § 46 and 473, § 49.

[200] ibid, 267, § 43 and 472, § 46.

[201] ibid, 268, § 46 and 473, § 49.

> agent, and the statement contains an express commitment to a course of conduct by that state, it should not be necessary to inquire whether the state intends to be bound but merely whether other States with an interest at stake could reasonably assume that the statement constituted a commitment'.[202]

This is also the opinion of authors such as Khosla,[203] Mössner[204] or, forcefully, Fastenrath.[205] At a minimum, this reliance-creating utterance must be considered a form of 'constructive intention' or 'imputed intention'. The better explanation is however to consider that the binding force directly rests in the good faith-reliance principle, so as to avoid excessive legal fictions. As we have already seen, it may in many cases clearly be useful to hide between the lofty and lenitive assertion of some intention, so as to reassure the states that the judge or operator is not creatively revising their commitments. It must however be conceded that what actually occurs is better explained by the objective approach (reliance) than by the subjective one (will). It must be added that in most cases there will be no gulf between both elements. The state will have some form of intention to be bound, and because that intention is somehow implied or conveyed, the third actors may have legitimate expectations in the binding nature of the act.

The argument that such objective criteria are too vague and allow the legal operator to engage in arbitrary constructions has but little weight. The matter is rather one of keeping the right measure. Abuse can never be wholly avoided. If one clings to the mere 'intention doctrine', abuse is open to the declaring state: it can conclusively plead that it did not intend to undertake a legal obligation (and such an inner fact cannot be disproved by a third state) and rid itself of any commitment, no matter how much others were entitled to rely on its representations. The objective appraisal of a conduct *pro externo* is a less arbitrary criterion. It has also been argued that the 'good faith approach' is too narrow, since it reduces the question as to the binding force of a promise to the degree in which concrete other states in effect relied upon the representations of the declaring state. The binding force of the promise then becomes a circumstantial matter. Thus, it would be impossible to explain how such promises become generally binding on the basis of such a narrow and subjective expectations construction.[206] This criticism is based on a misunderstanding. The principle of good faith does not operate only on the basis of the effective reliance created in a concrete addressee. It also operates on the more abstract level of a synthetic judgment according to which in view of the circumstances each other relevant subject of law could and should have relied on

[202] TM Franck, 'Word Made Law: The Decision of the ICJ in the Nuclear Test Cases' (1975) 69 *AJIL* 616, 617.

[203] D Khosla, 'Nuclear Test Cases: Judicial Valour v Judicial Discretion' (1978) 18 *Indian Journal of International Law* 322–23, 342ff.

[204] J M. Mössner, *Einführung in das Völkerrecht*, (Munich, 1977) 19, the legitimate expectation created prevails on the *animus sibi vincolandi*.

[205] U Fastenrath, *Lücken im Völkerrecht*, (Berlin, 1991) 105–106, 210.

[206] See W Fiedler, 'Zur Verbindlichkeit einseitiger Versprechen im Völkerrecht' (1976) 19 *GYIL* 47–48.

the promise.[207] This is a judgment based on reasonableness rather than on effectiveness. To be sure, both criteria can be useful according to the concrete legal question posed; but the objective criterion is the one interesting us here.

The next question is which doctrine of legitimate protection applies in this context? The stricter one centred upon estoppel, or the larger one centred directly upon good faith? Both legal instruments are based on the protection of legitimate expectations, ie ultimately on the principle of good faith. But estoppel is a more special doctrine, supposing a 'detrimental reliance' by the addressees in the specific case. For the reasons exposed above, the binding force of legal acts such as promises cannot be based on the idiosyncratic reactions of single members of the international society. For this reason, the ICJ in the *Nuclear Test* cases was right to entirely forgo the notion of estoppel and to rely on the larger notion of good faith.

Overall, it can be seen that the foundation of the binding force of unilateral legal acts which have a law-creating effect relies importantly on the notion of good faith-reliance. The aim of the principle is to explain the basis of the legal obligation and also the precise extent to which such an act can be said to be legally binding. The intention to confer a binding force to such an act is the starting point of a positive law analysis. But this criterion has to be integrated in a larger whole, taking into account the extent to which third states or other addressees could rely on the assertions made. In case of incongruence between the two circles, will and reliance, the latter shall prevail and create obligations even where the real will could not be established. This 'surplus' of obligation is the most distinctive effect of good faith in the context of unilateral acts. It also shows once more that it is wrong to claim that good faith does not create obligations where there existed none before.

XI. Good Faith and Acquiescence

Legal life is dominated by innumerable facts. The legal order must establish which of these facts have what effect. In a decentralised society such as the one regulated by international law, where the law shifts and metabolises by a continuous exchange of demands and responses rather than by centralised legislative acts and regular judicial qualifications, the disorder created by facts is greater than in the more significantly tamed municipal legal order. In international law, 'facts' will not normally be opposable to subjects of the law, unless accepted by them. Their sovereignty precludes the possibility to bind states to facts which they have not contributed to produce or which they have not recognised. In this context, the

[207] See correctly JD Sicault, 'Du caractère obligatoire des engagements unilatéraux en droit international public' (1979) 83 *RGDIP*, 684: 'La confiance dont il s'agit ici n'est pas, en effet, la confiance effective des destinataires de la promesse (*reliance*) mais la confiance qu'ils doivent pouvoir avoir dans le caractère obligatoire de la promesse'.

doctrine of normative acquiescence[208] has an eminent role to play as an alternative to formal and express recognition. It creates a device for the opposability of facts to a subject and therefore oils and smoothens the wheels of the international legal order.

There are different concepts of acquiescence. At the lowest level, acquiescence may simply mean an express or tacit acceptance.[209] It is then designating a real or fictional expression of will. The concept here is synonymous to 'consent' or to 'recognition'. It is certainly better to avoid the term 'acquiescence' in this context so as to prevent any confusion; the better word here is clearly consent. There are also authors[210] considering acquiescence as part and parcel of a complex set of presumptions of acceptance. Thus, for example, silence in the face of a mandatory notification of facts is tantamount to acceptance; if the notification was merely optional, there is no more than a rebuttable presumption of acceptance; if a state

[208] On acquiescence in international law, see notably: A Cavaglieri, 'Il decorso del tempo ed i suoi effetti sui rapporti giuridici internazionali' (1926) 18 *RDI* 169ff, 184ff; IC McGibbon, 'The Scope of Acquiescence in International Law' (1954) 31 *BYIL* 143ff; DW Bowett, 'Estoppel Before International Law and its Relations to Acquiescence' (1957) 33 *BYIL* 197ff; IC McGibbon, 'Customary International Law and Acquiescence' (1957) 33 *BYIL* 115ff; G Sperduti, 'Prescrizione, consuetudine, acquiescenza' (1961) 44 *RDI* 3ff; M Waelbroeck, 'L'acquiescement en droit des gens' (1961) 44 *RDI* 38ff; KJ Partsch, 'Qualifiziertes Stillschweigen' in K Strupp and HJ Schlochauer (eds), *Wörterbuch des Völkerrechts*, vol III (Berlin, 1962) 391–92; J Bentz, 'Le silence comme manifestation de volonté en droit international public' (1963) 67 *RGDIP* 44ff; J Barale, 'L'acquiescement dans la jurisprudence internationale' (1965) 11 *AFDI* 389ff; P Cahier, 'Le comportement des Etats comme source de droits et d'obligations', *Essays in Honor of P Guggenheim* (Geneva, 1968) 237ff; FV Kramer, 'Actos convencionales y no convencionales—Ratificación, acquiescencia y estopell', *Essays in Honor of E Jiménez de Aréchaga (El derecho internacional en un mundo en transformación)*, vol II (Montevideo, 1994) 963ff; I Sinclair, 'Estoppel and Acquiescence' *Essays in Honor of RY Jennings* (Cambridge, 1996) 104ff; H Das, 'L'estoppel et l'acquiescement: assimilations pragmatiques et divergences conceptuelles' (1997) 30 *RBDI* 607ff; NS Marques Antunes, 'Acquiescence' in R Wolfrum (ed), *The Max Planck Encyclopedia of Public International Law*, vol I (Oxford, 2012) 53ff. See further: H Lauterpacht, 'Sovereignty over Submarine Areas' (1950) 27 *BYIL* 393ff; GG Fitzmaurice, 'The Law and Procedure of the ICJ, 1951–54: General Principles and Sources of Law' (1953) 30 *BYIL* 27ff; E Suy, *Les actes juridiques unilatéraux en droit international public* (Paris, 1962) 61ff; RY Jennings, *The Acquisition of Territory in International Law* (Manchester, 1963) 36ff; G Venturini, 'La portée et les effets juridiques des attitudes et des actes unilatéraux des Etats' (1964-II) 112 *RCADI* 374ff; YZ Blum, *Historic Titles in International Law* (The Hague, 1965) 38ff, 129ff; G Zimmer, *Gewaltsame territoriale Veränderungen und ihre völkerrechtliche Legitimation* (Berlin, 1971) 31ff; JP Jacqué, *Éléments pour une théorie de l'acte juridique en droit international public* (Paris, 1972) 210ff; W Karl, *Vertrag und spätere Praxis im Völkerrecht* (Berlin, 1983) 276ff; H Thirlway, 'The Law and Procedure of the ICJ (1960–1989): General Principles and Sources of Law' (1989) 60 *BYIL* 29ff; VD Degan, *Sources of International Law* (The Hague, 1997) 348ff; M Kohen, *Possession contestée et souveraineté territoriale* (Paris, 1997) 355–56; G Distefano, *L'ordre international entre légalité et effectivité* (Geneva, 2002) 201ff; C Tams, 'Waiver, Acquiescence and Extinctive Prescription' in J Crawford, A Pellet and S Olleson (eds), *The Law of International Responsibility* (Oxford, 2010) 1035ff. In the context of good faith, see in particular: Müller, *Vertrauensschutz* 35ff; Kolb, *Bonne* 339ff. See also the study of PCW Chan, 'Acquiescence and Estoppel in International Boundaries: Temple of Preah Vihear Revisited' (2004) 3 *Chinese Journal of International Law* 421ff.

[209] See eg Blum, op cit, 131–32; A Orakhelashvili, *Peremptory Norms in International Law* (Oxford, 2006) 398ff.

[210] See eg A Cavaglieri, 'Il decorso del tempo ed i suoi effetti sui rapporti giuridici internazionali' (1926) 18 *RDI* 188ff.

has accidental knowledge of a fact, its acceptance of that fact by silence depends upon the circumstances and there is at best a reasonable presumption of acceptance in case of silence. It must however be said that there are no precise norms of international law establishing such presumptions.[211] The system of presumptions thus presented hardly deserves that name. It is at best a set of elements for interpretation.

The notion of acquiescence which interests us here has been aptly defined in the following terms: '[proposition] of binding effect resulting from passivity and inaction with respect to foreign claims which, according to the general practice of States usually call for protest in order to assert, preserve or safeguard rights'.[212] In other words, acquiescence is a principle of law attributing certain effects to silence when certain conditions are met, and not the mere fact of consent. It is a doctrine of 'qualified silence', ie of silence to which legal effects are attributed. These legal effects flow from the need of a proper functioning of the legal order, and in particular from the necessity of some stability of legal relations,[213] and most importantly also from the need of protecting legitimate expectations of the actors of the international arena.[214] Whence: *qui tacet consentire videtur si loqui potuisset ac debuisset.*[215] The reader will notice that this type of acquiescence is not based on a legal act; it is not an expression of will. Therefore, a real will of a subject to accept the facts at stake is not required. Rather, this type of acquiescence is based on a legal norm which imputes to a subject the consequences which would have flown from its acceptance of a set of facts when this subject has remained silent for a prolonged time once confronted with these facts and where there was

[211] G Cansacchi, *La notificazione internazionale* (Milan, 1943) 285–86.

[212] JP Müller and T Cottier, 'Acquiescence' in *EPIL* (2nd edn), vol 7, p 5. In the words of G Sperduti, 'Prescrizione, consuetudine e acquiescenza in diritto internazionale' (1961) 44 *RDI* 8: 'l'acquiescenza è un comportamento pratico che si limita ad attestare l'assenza di volontà contraria ad un'altrui pretesa o ad una certa situazione quando, tenuto conto delle circostanze del caso, ed anzitutto della pubblicità della pretesa e della notorietà della situazione, era da attendersi la manifestazione … di una volontà contraria…'.

[213] H Lauterpacht, 'Sovereignty over Submarine Areas' (1950) 27 *BYIL* 395–96: 'The far-reaching effect of the failure to protest is not a mere artificiality of the law. It is an essential requirement of stability—a requirement even more important in the international than in other spheres; it is a precept of fair dealing in as much as it prevents States from playing fast and loose with situations affecting others; and it is in accordance with equity in as much as it protects a State from the contingency of incurring responsibilities and expense, in reliance on the apparent acquiescence of others, and being subsequently confronted with a challenge on the part of those very States'.

[214] Müller, *Vertrauensschutz* 38–39. See also the precise words of ML Alaimo, 'Natura del consenso nell'illecito internazionale' (1982) 65 *RDI* 269: 'Tutte le volte in cui viva è apparsa la preoccupazione di considerare prevalente il comportamento anteriore di uno Stato rispetto a quello successivamente tenuto … si è fatto ricorso al principio generale della buona fede, intesa nel senso oggettivo di affidamento. L'esigenza della certezza del diritto nelle relazioni internazionali ha comunque indotto la giurisprudenza a ritenere preminente la circostanza che uno Stato ha lasciato sorgere da un certo suo comportamento l'affidamento di un altro Stato piuttosto che ricercare l'eventuale coincidenza fra quel comportamento ed un'effettiva volontà'.

[215] *Corpus iuris canonici, Liber Sextus, regula iuris* 43. See *Dig* 19, 2, 13, § 11 (Ulpien). *Is, qui tacet, non fatetur sed nec utique negare videtur* (*Liber Sextus, regula* 46; *Dig*, 50, 17, 142, Paulus).

a legal duty to react in order to uphold the position of non-opposability of these facts. Acquiescence taken in this sense is consequently normative: it is a legal norm flowing from the principle of good faith-reliance and accepted as a free-standing rule of international law in relevant practice. It is therefore appropriate to call it a doctrine of 'normative acquiescence', in contradistinction to acquiescence as a real consent. Plainly, if the word 'acquiescence' was not frequently used to mean a form of consent, it would be superfluous to add the epithet 'normative' to it. Since that is not the case, the epithet is not unnecessary.

This doctrine of 'qualified silence' operates through the conjunction of three legal elements: time (prolonged silence), knowledge of the facts and duty to speak.

A. Time

The backbone of acquiescence lies in the prolonged silence or passivity opposed to the claims of another subject. Thus, the time-dimension is an essential element of the principle.[216] The loss of subjective rights induced by its application is justified only because some fault can be imputed to the passive subject: it had time to react but did not do it; there was moreover a duty to react, and it was not honoured; the reliance and stability thus created shall not now, after considerable time has elapsed, be disturbed. In this sense, acquiescence is often linked to legal processes such as prescription, the consolidation of imperfect titles and the emergence of local customary law.[217] The amount of time required for the operation of the principle depends on the circumstances. There is a certain length of time which must pass; but the exact amount of time required varies according to factors such as:

(i) the frequency and intensity of the conduct to be opposed (the greater it is, the quicker a reaction can be reasonably expected);
(ii) the nature of the legal relationship and the degree to which the need of stability, security and confidence is felt within that relationship (the greater these needs and the quicker a reaction is necessary: eg close ties of cooperation versus loose obligations of coexistence);
(iii) the importance of the interests and rights at stake (the greater their importance, the less time may be required: eg sensitive territorial rights, eg important amounts of investment made);
(iv) the intensity of the relationship between the parties (the closer it is and the more quickly a protest may be necessary: eg neighbouring relations);

[216] Thus, if the period of time may be short, it cannot be entirely absent. There is no 'instant acquiescence'. If there indeed is an instantaneous 'acquiescence' this is tantamount to finding a tacit consent. Notice however that 'instantaneous acquiescence' has sometimes been sustained: see eg JP Müller and T Cottier, 'Acquiescence' in *Encyclopedia of Public International Law* (2nd edn) vol 7 (1984) 6.

[217] See RY Jennings, *The Acquisition of Territory in International Law* (Manchester, 1963) 36ff; DHN Johnson, 'Acquisitive Prescription in International Law' (1950) 27 *BYIL* 347–48.

(v) the effective knowledge of the facts rather than the constructive knowledge of the fact (calling for a quicker reaction, eg when a state has been put on notice by a diplomatic note).[218]

In a curious ontogenesis, time itself becomes a relevant factor: the more it has already elapsed, and the stronger the acquiescence argument.[219] Overall, the acid test is whether at a given time a legitimate expectation in the consolidation of the attitude has emerged, or alternatively whether it would appear abusive to allow a party which for that time had been silent to now change its attitude to the detriment of the other party/ies. It has also to be noted that in practice most often a set of actions and deeds is added to a set of abstentions and passivity. The deeds may reinforce the legal meaning of passivity: eg, if a boundary is not only not protested against, but certain official visits take place, compliments are exchanged, etc., acquiescence appears to be all the more established.[220]

Some examples of the case law may now be given. First, in the *Norwegian Fisheries* case (1951), the peculiar system of maritime boundaries practised by Norway had been the object of a general tolerance for more than 60 years.[221] This state of affairs was sufficient to find an acquiescence. Second, in the *Arbitral Award Made by the King of Spain* case (1960), it was held that the validity of an arbitral award could not be impugned after six years of silence accompanied by many acts signalling its positive acceptance.[222] Third, in the *Temple of Preah Vihear* case (1962), the silence in the face of a boundary drawn contrary to the relevant provision in the delimitation treaty was considered to have been accepted, through a tolerance of more than 50 years.[223] Fourth, in the *Territorial and Maritime Dispute* case (*Nicaragua v Colombia*, Preliminary Objections, 2007), Nicaragua had been silent for more than 50 years on the validity of a treaty. It had at the same time conducted itself in a way which was incompatible with a belief that the treaty was void. Hence its claim that the treaty was invalid could not be heard.[224] In the first case (*Norwegian Fisheries*), the passivity had been upheld for a very long time; thus, a legitimate expectation in the acceptance could build up. In the second case (*King of Spain*),

[218] On such factors, see P Reuter, 'Pleadings for Cambodia, *Temple of Preah Vihear* case' (1962) I *ICJ Pleadings* 203; Müller, *Vertrauensschutz* 39; G Sperduti, 'Prescrizione, consuetudine e acquiescenza in diritto internazionale' (1961) 44 *RDI* 9.

[219] G Schwarzenberger, 'The Fundamental Principles of International Law' (1955-I) 87 *RCADI* 257: 'With the passing of time, the probability that passivity means acquiescence increases'.

[220] See *Temple of Preah Vihear* (1962) *ICJ Reports* 6ff. On this case in our context: Müller, *Vertrauensschutz* 22ff; JP Cot, 'L'affaire du *Temple de Préah Vihéar* (fond)' (1962) 8 *AFDI* 217ff; E Pecourt Garcia, 'El principio del 'estoppel' y la sentencia del Tribunal Internacional de Justicia en el caso del *Templo de Preah Vihear*' (1963) 16 *REDI* 153ff; JHW Verzijl, 'Case Concerning the Temple of Préah Vihéar' (1962) 9 *NTIR* 238.

[221] *Norwegian Fisheries* case (1951) *ICJ Reports* 138–39. In particular, the UK has not protested against these limits from 1869 to 1933.

[222] *Arbitral Award Made by the King of Spain* (1960) *ICJ Reports* 203, 210ff, the period spanning from 1906 to 1912.

[223] *Temple of Preah Vihear* (1962) *ICJ Reports* 23, 27ff, the period spanning from 1908 to 1958.

[224] *Territorial and Maritime Dispute (Nicaragua v Colombia, Preliminary Objections)* (2007-II) *ICJ Reports* 859, § 79–80.

the validity of an arbitral award was at stake; the needs of stability are at their apogee with regard to such legal acts;[225] and therefore, a relatively short period of passivity, but also accompanying deeds, appeared to be entirely sufficient to allow the argument of acquiescence. In the third case (*Preah Vihear*), the passivity was accompanied by a series of active deeds, which pointed in the same direction, namely acceptance; thus, fifty years seemed a time long enough to build up a legitimate expectation, even if in this case national territory (ie a sensitive matter) was at stake. The same is true for the fourth case (*Territorial and Maritime Dispute*).

B. Knowledge of the Facts

It is reasonable and fair to expect a reaction to facts (and also to sanction passivity) only when a subject has knowledge of those facts. If it had not, it could not be expected to react. This is the main meaning of the formula *si loqui potuisset*: one can speak only if one knows the underlying facts. However, a subject may not protect its rights by simply failing to take notice of the facts surrounding it. Thus, according to a significant doctrinal opinion, the silence remains imputable to a subject if it should have known the facts by using the usual standards of due diligence (presence of non-excusable negligence).[226] To the real knowledge of facts is thus added the 'constructive knowledge' of facts. Both lead to an imputation of silence and to the operation of normative acquiescence. Notice that the addition of constructive knowledge is itself a matter of good faith: it would be preposterous to allow a subject to plead its ignorance of the facts if that ignorance is due to its proper fault (no one can take advantage of its own fault). Such a course would moreover incentive the subjects not to take cognisance of international facts—a truly inappropriate doctrine for international affairs. A precedent for constructive knowledge can be found in the famous *Norwegian Fisheries* case (1951). To the argument of acquiescence presented by Norway, the UK had responded with the argument that it had ignored the particular system of baselines practised by Norway. The Court had this to respond:

> The Court is unable to accept this view. As a coastal State on the North Sea, greatly interested in the fisheries in this area, as a maritime Power traditionally concerned with the law of the sea and concerned particularly to defend the freedom of the seas, the United Kingdom could not have been ignorant of the Decree of 1869 which had at once provoked a request for explanations by the French Government.[227]

[225] *Expedit rei publicae, ut finis sit litium: Codex Justinianum*, 7, 52, 2, Caracalla.

[226] See eg Müller, *Vertrauensschutz* 41; J Bentz, 'Le silence comme manifestation de volonté en droit international public' (1963) 67 *RGDIP* 86ff; J Barale, 'L'acquiescement dans la jurisprudence internationale' (1965) 11 *AFDI* 402ff; *contra*, with hardly convincing arguments, P Cahier, 'Le comportement des Etats comme source de droits et d'obligations', *Essays in Honor of P Guggenheim* (Geneva, 1968) 237ff. For many further references, see Kolb, *Bonne* 346.

[227] *Norwegian Fisheries* case (1951) *ICJ Reports* 139. See also, in support of that position, Separate Opinion Alvarez, ibid, 152 and Dissenting Opinion McNair, ibid, 171ff.

The due diligence standard is evidently open to contextual interpretation. Could the standard of negligence be softened when a state is generally underdeveloped and when it is moreover in the midst of a bloody civil war? This had been pleaded in the *Territorial Dispute (Eritrea v Yemen)* case (1998).[228] This precedent tends to show that tribunals will be slow to lower the applicable standard, so much as there is a need for a certain international stability. The fault of ignorance will be extinguished only when there is some force majeure or material impossibility which can be shown to the satisfaction of the judge or arbitrator (*ad impossibile nemo tenetur*). An improper organisation of the state is thus not an argument for dispensing that state from the internationally applicable legal duties. A civil war or other events of the same type may certainly be more easily be accepted as excuses under the mentioned standards, but as such they are not recognised as factors inhibiting the operation of the doctrine of normative acquiescence. Ultimately, the arbitral tribunal in the *Territorial Dispute* case accepted constructive knowledge with regard to a published Petroleum Agreement between Yemen and Shell, since 'with a sufficient diligence it could have been known to Ethiopia', which however failed to issue a protest.[229] The argument that Ethiopia was a poor country ridden by civil war did not alter this finding. This precedent thus perfectly fits the *Norwegian Fisheries* jurisprudence.

C. Silence in Face of a Duty to React

There is no general rule in international law according to which each silence leads to acquiescence.[230] In other words, acquiescence attaches legal consequences not to silence in general, but to a 'qualified silence', ie to a silence held although there was a legal duty to react in order to protect one's own rights.[231] The silence is relevant *si loqui potuisset ac debuisset*; note the conjunctive in the past, 'if it could and should have spoken' at the relevant time in the past (and not: *si loqui debuit ac potuit*,

[228] *Territorial Dispute (Eritrea v Yemen)* (1998) 114 *ILR* 102.

[229] ibid.

[230] Such a rule has however been—rarely—upheld: see eg J Kunz, 'Protest' in: K Strupp (ed), *Wörterbuch des Völkerrechts*, vol II (Berlin, 1924) 329. *Contra*, rightly, D Anzilotti, *Corso di diritto internazionale* (Rome, 1928) 309.

[231] See the many references in Kolb, *Bonne* 347. See the *Pulau Ligitan and Pulau Sipadan* case (2002) *ICJ Reports* 650, § 48, the Court holding that the UK had no duty to react when a document had not been officially communicated to it. By the same token, a state has no duty to protest against maps deprived of probative value: see *Territorial and Maritime Dispute between Nicaragua and Honduras in the Caribbean Sea* (2007-II) *ICJ Reports* 692, § 97, argument of Nicaragua. Contrariwise, silence kept during the negotiations of a peace treaty on the issue of reparations can be interpreted as a waiver: see P d'Argent, *Les réparations de guerre en droit international public* (Brussels, 2005) 224, fn 757, for the '2+4 Treaty' on Germany (1990). If a state fails to object to a certain course of conduct, but indicates that in its view the question is not yet settled, no acquiescence can be derived: *Polish Postal Service at Danzig* advisory opinion (1925) PCIJ ser B, no 11, pp 31–32.

'if it could and should speak' now). The silence is relevant only if there is a legal duty to oppose a claim or to react to an adverse fact by way of protest.[232] Customary international law provides for such a duty to react in three cases. The first two cases are based on specific norms while the last is based on a general clause.

— *First*, the duty to react can be based on a norm contained in a treaty, eg in opting out-systems,[233] or article 20, § 5, of the VCLT of 1969 requiring a reaction to a reservation within 12 months if some other treaty party does not want to accept it.[234] Similarly, under article 89, § 2, of the Rules of Court (1978), the ICJ shall in some circumstances fix a time-limit within which the respondent may state whether it opposes a discontinuance of the proceedings; if there is no objection before the expiration of that time-limit, acquiescence will be imputed.[235] Still, article 5, § 1, of the Vienna Convention on Diplomatic Relations of 1961, stipulates that absence of objection to the multiple accreditation of a diplomat within a reasonable time is tantamount to acquiescence.[236]
— *Second*, such a duty may flow from some generally accepted practice within an institutional setting. Thus, the interpretations of the Secretariat of the ILO on international conventions on labour, communicated to the member states, are considered to have been accepted by the latter if there is no objection.[237]
— *Third*, the duty to react can flow directly from general international law under the aegis of the principle of good faith.[238] There is such a duty to react each time, according to the circumstances, it appears to be contrary to good faith to keep silent and thereafter to claim that certain facts cannot be opposed to

[232] H Lauterpacht, 'Sovereignty over Submarine Areas' (1950) 27 *BYIL* 393ff. See the *Palmas* case (1928) II *RIAA* 866; *Honduras Boundaries* (1933) II *RIAA* 1327ff; *Pensions of Officials of the Saar Territory* (1934) III *RIAA* 1563; *Venezuelan Preferential Rights* (1904) IX *RIAA* 109; *Fabiani* (1905) X *RIAA* 120; the *Cravairola Alp* case, in H La Fontaine, *Pasicrisie internationale* (Bern, 1902) 208.

[233] See J Klabbers, *An Introduction to International Institutional Law*, 2nd edn (Cambridge, 2009) 199–200.

[234] '[A] reservation is considered to have been accepted by a State if it shall have raised no objection to the reservation by the end of a period of twelve months after it was notified of the reservation or by the date on which it expressed its consent to be bound by the treaty, whichever is the later'. See the short commentary in ME Villiger, *Commentary on the 1969 Vienna Convention on the Law of Treaties* (Leiden, 2009) 293.

[235] See, under the old art 69 of the Rules of Court of 1948, the *Barcelona Traction* case (New Application, Preliminary Objections), (1964) *ICJ Reports* 20.

[236] See the Legal Note of the Swiss Directorate of Public International Law to the Department of Foreign Affairs, 2 December 1980, (1981) 37 *ASDI* 263.

[237] See CW Jenks, 'The Interpretation of International Labour Conventions by the International Labour Office' (1939) 20 *BYIL* 133; CW Jenks, 'The Corpus Iuris of Social Justice' in: CW Jenks, *Law, Freedom and Welfare* (London and New York, 1963) 121–22; N Valticos, *Droit international du travail*, 2nd edn (Paris, 1983) 134–35.

[238] J Bentz, 'Le silence comme manifestation de volonté en droit international public' (1963) 67 *RGDIP* 59.

oneself. There are different contextual factors to be considered in establishing this duty:

(i) the past pattern of conduct of the concerned state, which can lead to a legitimate expectation that in similar circumstances a similar attitude will be followed, eg that a protest will be voiced where it had been analogously voiced in the past;

(ii) the nature of the legal relationship, when the need of legal stability and certainty is particularly important as for example for the validity of arbitral awards;

(iii) the closeness of the relations of the parties between or among themselves, which can sharpen the expectations (eg neighbourhood, alliances, vassalage, etc);

(iv) the importance and gravity of the interests at stake for the third state, eg when the latter engages in onerous and intense activities in the belief of the existence of its rights;

(v) if the claim of a third entity affects the legally protected interests of another subject of law there is a duty to react.[239]

— As can be seen, these factors correspond in part to the ones which are to be taken into account for the computation of the relevant time-span for admitting an acquiescence. Notice that there is no duty to react if and when the attitude of the other subject of law remains ambiguous, unclear and uncertain. A protest may here be entered *ex abundante cautela*, but there is no legal disadvantage if none is made. A protest could not be expected in good faith in the face of such an unclear attitude.[240]

In the formula *si loqui potuisset ac debuisset* (which the ICJ used in the *Temple* case of 1962),[241] there are two limbs: can and shall. The 'can' refers to the knowledge of the relevant facts (see above) but also to the absence of coercion. If there is coercion or impossibility,[242] a subject cannot speak (freely); and thus the silence will not be imputed to that subject for the purposes of an acquiescence. It would also be possible to say that in such cases there is simply no duty to speak out. The second term is 'shall'. This is the truly controlling concept. It explains that we are dealing here with a normative doctrine, not simply with a tacit but real intent. Thus, for example, a state must not react to a writ from a municipal tribunal to appear, since it can rely on the general understanding that it is the matter of the territorial state to respect its jurisdictional immunities. Silence in face of the summation to appear cannot therefore be interpreted as acquiescence. There cannot

[239] See eg M Akehurst, 'Custom as a Source of International Law' (1974/75) 47 *BYIL* 40; L Oppenheim (R Jennings and A Watts, eds), *International Law*, 9th edn (London, 1992) 1195.

[240] See the *Mount Fitzroy Boundary (Argentina/Chile)* (1994) 113 *ILR* 78–79.

[241] *Temple* (1962) *ICJ Reports* 23.

[242] Thus, for example, the doctrine of acquiescence cannot be applied to the UN Security Council. The fact that the Council does not react to an armed aggression does not mean that it acquiesces into it; the Council may just be impeded to speak out by a veto, possibly that of the state being itself the aggressor. See Y Dinstein, *War, Aggression, Self-Defense*, 3rd edn (Cambridge, 2001) 272.

be any legitimate expectation to that end, and international practice buttresses this position.[243]

International case law illustrates the preceding positions. In the *Grisbadarna* case (1909), Sweden's passivity had a particular relevance in regard of the neighbourhood of the two concerned states and of the considerable investments on the spot made by Norway.[244] In the *Norwegian Fisheries* case (1951), the long-standing maritime power tradition of the UK and its particular interest in the fisheries of the concerned region founded—and also increased—the expectation of a reaction on its part.[245] In the already quoted *King of Spain Award* case of 1960, as well as in the *Temple* case of 1962, the duty flowed from a particular exigency of legal stability with regard to the arbitral awards on the one side, and the stability of boundaries on the other.[246]

A further interesting precedent is the *Territorial Dispute* arbitration between Eritrea and Yemen (1998). The duty to react was here qualified by a series of contextual factors:[247] (i) the remoteness of the island whose sovereignty was contested, its uninhabited character and the lack of lines of communication near the island; (ii) the fact that patrols took place at night during darkness; (iii) the fact that many patrols were conducted at high speed; (iv) the fact that civil hostilities were in progress. It may be asked whether all these factors really impacted on the duty to protest (or the significance of lack of protest), or whether they should not rather have been analysed under the heading of knowledge of the relevant facts.

There are two arguments cautioning for a limitation or for exceptions to this overall approach on the duty to react. First, it has been argued that states sometimes abstain from protesting because they know that their protest will be ineffective.[248] This statement manifestly begs the question. In reality, the protest may well be wholly ineffective in the sense that it is unable to reverse the facts created by some other entity. But it is not ineffective from the legal point of view, in that it protects the protesting state from being considered to have acquiesced in the facts. Second, it has been said that a protest is often omitted in order not to strain the relations with some other state, eg a powerful ally or enemy, or some other subjectively important state.[249] But the price to pay for such policy-considerations is the possible loss of a right through acquiescence.[250] Good faith-reliance is stronger than equity-considerations related to power, which remain legally elusive. The need

[243] See eg H Damian, *Staatenimmunität und Gerichtszwang* (Berlin, 1985) 40.

[244] *Grisbadarna* (1909) XI *RIAA* 147ff.

[245] *Norwegian Fisheries* (1951) *ICJ Reports* 139.

[246] On the stability of boundaries, see G Abi-Saab, 'La pérennité des frontières en droit international' (1990) 64 *Relations internationales* 341ff. For a critical analysis, see G Giraudeau, *Les différends territoriaux devant le juge international, Entre droit et transaction* (Leiden, 2013) 281ff.

[247] *Territorial Dispute* (1998) 114 *ILR* 84, § 306.

[248] A D'Amato, *The Concept of Custom in International Law* (Ithaca NY, 1971) 195–96.

[249] See eg the argument of France (through A Gros) in the *Minquiers and Ercrehos* case, (1953) II *ICJ Pleadings* 261ff (he however also quotes some protests).

[250] As has been rightly noted: 'La concezione dell'acquiescenza … comporta che, se acquiescenza si è avuta, non valga poi a privarla di efficacia la dimostrazione che essa fu dovuta a questa o quella particolare ragione': G Sperduti, 'Prescrizione, consuetudine, acquiescenza' (1961) 44 *RDI* 8.

for clarification and reliance is pre-eminent with respect to the various possible calculi of foreign policy which a state can make. This is borne out by international practice, the *Temple* case of 1962 being authority for that.

International case law is extremely rich with regard to judgments or awards making some place to acquiescence arguments. For example, the following cases can be mentioned: *Montijo* (1875),[251] *Grisbadarna* (1909),[252] *Palmas* (1928),[253] *Sovereignty over Certain Frontier Land* (1959),[254] *Arbitral Award Made by the King of Spain* (1960),[255] *Temple of Preah Vihear* (1962),[256] *Rann of Kutch* (1968),[257] *Continental Shelf (Tunisia/Libya)* (1982),[258] *Delimitation of the Maritime Boundary in the Gulf of Maine Area* (1984),[259] *Fileting in the Gulf of Saint-Laurent* (1985),[260] *Land, Island and Maritime Frontier Dispute (El Salvador/Honduras)* (1992);[261] etc.

The norms on acquiescence are not *jus cogens*. Acquiescence can be altered by a contrary treaty provision; and it can also be altered by practice of the concerned states. Thus, article 4, § 2, of the Antarctic Treaty of 1959 excludes acts or omissions (silences) for territorial claims over that continent. The land shall remain subjected to the regime provided for in the treaty itself.[262] By the same token, practice has accepted that provisional de facto or *modus vivendi* lines in maritime spaces, pending the final delimitation of the boundary, shall not give rise to binding obligations under the doctrine of acquiescence. If it were otherwise, no state would any more agree to such provisional lines for fear of being thereafter trapped. Consequently, the provisional administration and exploitation of such areas would thus be jeopardised. An acquiescence can however operate as to the *provisional* nature of such lines; but it cannot be transformed, if there are no special circumstances, into an acquiescence as to the *final* boundary.[263]

[251] PM Eisemann and V Coussirat-Coustère, *Repertory of International Arbitral Jurisprudence*, vol I (Dordrecht, 1991) 45–46.

[252] *Grisbadarna* (1909) XI *RIAA* 155ff.

[253] *Palmas* (1928) II *RIAA* 866. Müller, *Vertrauensschutz* 51ff.

[254] *Sovereignty over Certain Frontier Land* (1959) *ICJ Reports* 209.

[255] *Arbitral Award Made by the King of Spain* (1960) *ICJ Reports* 209, 213–14. See also Separate Opinion Spender, ibid, 219–20; Separate Opinion Urrutia Holguín, ibid, 222.

[256] *Temple of Preah Vihear* (1962) *ICJ Reports* 23–24, 32 and Separate Opinion Fitzmaurice, ibid, 62–63. Müller, *Vertrauensschutz* 43ff.

[257] *Rann of Kutch* (1968) 50 *ILR* 8ff. Müller, *Vertrauensschutz* 48ff.

[258] *Continental Shelf (Tunisia/Libya)* (1982) *ICJ Reports* 83–84, 87; Separate Opinion Ago, ibid, 95ff.

[259] *Delimitation of the Maritime Boundary in the Gulf of Maine Area* (1984) *ICJ Reports* 304–05.

[260] *Fileting in the Gulf of Saint-Laurent* (1985) 82 *ILR* 619, § 37. See also Dissenting Opinion Pharand, ibid, 652, § 47: 'France's acceptance and compliance with the Canadian regulatory system constitutes an acquiescence in that system'.

[261] *Land, Island and Maritime Frontier Dispute (El Salvador/Honduras)* (1992) *ICJ Reports* 408–09, and also 577–79, with regard to the island of Meanguera. See E Decaux, 'Le différend frontalier terrestre, insulaire et maritime (El Salvador/Honduras)' (1992) 38 *AFDI* 409ff, 418ff.

[262] See the text of the Treaty, (1960) 54 *AJIL* 476ff.

[263] See *Continental Shelf* case (Tunisia and Libya) (1982) *ICJ Reports* 83–84, 87; and *Maritime Delimitation in the Area between Greenland and Jan Mayen* case (1993) *ICJ Reports* 53–56. See also the *Newfoundland and Nova Scotia* arbitration (Second Phase, 2002) 128 *ILR* 544, § 3.6. For a series of different maritime activities and estoppel and acquiescence, see the *Barbados and Trinidad and Tobago* arbitration (2006) 139 *ILR* 553–54, § 361–66.

As a last aspect, it must be noticed that acquiescence can also be used for other purposes than the one to bind a state to a certain legal position. Thus, the absence of protest can be a hint that a state does not regard itself as having sovereignty over a certain land or island, since otherwise it would in all probability have protested adverse action.[264] Similarly, the failure to protest to some petroleum agreements of the adverse party may be read by a tribunal as a further element in support for a median line in the delimitation exercise.[265]

Overall, acquiescence is a powerful legal tool for the stabilisation of international legal relations. It flows directly from the genetic code of the principle of reliance on good faith.

XII. Good Faith and Estoppel

Analogously to acquiescence, estoppel aims at stabilising bilateral legal relationships. Legitimate expectations deliberately created by some conduct should not lead to a detriment for the relying party.[266] Contrary to acquiescence, which can be collective (the Court in the *Norwegian Fisheries* case of 1951 spoke of the 'general

[264] *Territorial Dispute* arbitration between Eritrea and Yemen (1998) 114 *ILR* 84, § 307.

[265] ibid, 114, § 438.

[266] On the notion of estoppel in international law, see: W Friede, 'Das Estoppel-Prinzip im Völkerrecht' (1935) 5 *ZaöRV* 517ff; DW Bowett, 'Estoppel Before International Tribunals and its Relations to Acquiescence' (1957) 33 *BYIL* 176ff; IC McGibbon, 'Estoppel in International Law' (1958) 7 *ICLQ* 468ff; E Menzel, 'Estoppel', in K Strupp and HJ Schlochauer (eds), *Wörterbuch des Völkerrechts*, 2nd edn, vol I (Berlin, 1960) 441–42; F Mosconi, 'La dottrina dell'estoppel in diritto internazionale' (1962) 16 (4) *Diritto internazionale* 388ff; E Pecourt Garcia, 'El principio del 'estoppel' en el derecho internacional público' (1962) 15 *REDI* 98ff; E Pecourt Garcia, 'El principio del 'estoppel' y la sentencia del Tribunal internacional de Justicia en el caso del Templo de Preah Vihear' (1963) 16 *REDI* 153ff; JV Louis, 'L'estoppel devant la Cour internationale de Justice' (1965) 42 *Revue de droit international et de droit comparé* 212ff; M Akehurst, 'Le principe de l'estoppel en droit administratif international' (1966) 92 *JDI* 285ff; C Dominicé, 'A propos du principe de l'estoppel en droit des gens', in *Essays in Honor of P Guggenheim* (Geneva, 1968) 327ff; C Vallée, 'Quelques observations sur l'estoppel en droit des gens' (1973) 77 *RGDIP* 949ff; A Martin, *L'estoppel en droit international public* (Paris, 1979); YI Youakim, 'Estoppel in International Law' (PhD thesis, Cornell University, Michigan, 1985; published 1994); T Nöcker and G French, 'Estoppel: What's the Government's Word Worth? An Analysis of German Law, Common Law Jurisdiction and of the Practice of International Arbitral Tribunals' (1990) 24 *International Lawyer* 409ff; FV Kramer, 'Actos convencionales y no convencionales—Ratificación, acquiescencia y estopell' *Essays in Honor of E Jiménez de Aréchaga (El derecho internacional en un mundo en transformación)*, vol II (Montevideo, 1994) 963ff; C Brown, 'A Comparative and Critical Assessment of Estoppel in International Law' (1996) 50 *University of Miami Law Review* 369ff; I Sinclair, 'Estoppel and Acquiescence' in *Essays in Honor of RY Jennings* (Cambridge, 1996) 104ff; KS O'Brien, 'Representation in the Doctrine of Estoppel in International Law' (2011) 3 *Irish Yearbook of International Law* 69ff; JP Müller and T Cottier, 'Estoppel' in R Wolfrum (ed), *The Max Planck Encyclopedia of Public International Law*, vol III (Oxford, 2012) 671ff; A Kulick, 'Estoppel im Völkerrecht: Antworten auf drei dogmatische Fragen' (2014) 52 *AVR* 522ff; See also Separate Opinion Alfaro, *Temple of Preah Vihear* case (1962) *ICJ Reports* 39ff; and Concurring Opinion Cançado Trindade, *Right to Information on Consular Assistance* advisory opinion (1999) 154, *ILR* 339–41 (IACtHR). See further: H Lauterpacht, *Private Law Sources and Analogies of International Law* (London, 1927) 203ff; B Cheng, *General Principles of Law—As Applied by International Courts and Tribunals* (London, 1953) 141ff; H Lauterpacht,

tolerance' of states to the baseline system at stake),[267] estoppel rules almost always bilateral or local (as opposed to multilateral or general) relationships. It has up to the present never been applied to truly collective legal positions. Its requirements, namely a certain conduct, reliance by some other party on that conduct, and harm which would ensue if the former party was allowed to change its attitude without legal consequences, are so embedded in particular social interactions that an application outside bilateral or local relations between states or other subjects is hardly conceivable. Fundamentally, estoppel disallows a subject from reaping advantages or imposing burdens deriving from contradictory behaviour. It is a doctrine of qualified non-contradiction, ie the disallowance of contradiction when there has been detrimental reliance. Consequently, estoppel in international law has been defined thus: 'Estoppel operates on the assumption that one party has been induced to act in reliance on the assurances or other conduct of another party, in such a way that it would be prejudiced were the other party later

The Development of International Law by the International Court (London, 1958) 168ff; AD McNair, *The Law of Treaties* (Oxford, 1961) 485ff; RY Jennings, *The Acquisition of Territory in International Law* (Manchester, 1963) 41ff; G Venturini, 'La portée et les effets juridiques des attitudes et des actes unilatéraux des Etats' (1964-II) 112 *RCADI* 370ff; YZ Blum, *Historic Titles in International Law* (The Hague, 1965) 90ff; M Mabrouk, *Les exceptions de procédure devant les juridictions internationales* (Paris, 1966) 107ff; JP Cot, 'L'affaire de la frontière des Andes' (1968) 14 *AFDI* 238ff; C Rousseau, *Droit international public*, vol I (Paris, 1970) 387–89; WM Reisman, *Nullity and Revision* (New Haven CT, 1971) 383ff; JP Jacqué, *Éléments pour une théorie de l'acte juridique en droit international public* (Paris, 1972) 210ff; A Oraison, *L'erreur dans les traités* (Paris, 1972) 160ff; AP Rubin, 'The International Legal Effect of Unilateral Declarations' (1977) 71 *AJIL* 16ff; O Schachter, 'The Twilight Existence of Nonbinding Agreements' (1977) 71 *AJIL* 296ff; JP Jacqué, 'A propos de la promesse unilatérale', in *Essays in Honor of P Reuter* (Paris, 1981) 335ff; W Karl, *Vertrag und spätere Praxis im Völkerrecht* (Berlin, 1983) 324ff; H Thirlway, 'The Law and Procedure of the ICJ (1960–1989): General Principles and Sources of Law' (1989) 60 *BYIL* 29ff. In the specific context of the principle of good faith, see: Müller, *Vertrauensschutz* 5ff; Zoller, *Bonne* 274ff; Kolb, *Bonne* 357ff; J Leutert, *Einseitige Erklärungen im Völkerrecht* (Diessenhofen, 1979) 41ff; JP Cot, 'La bonne foi en droit international public' (1968/69) *Cours IHEI (Paris)* 47ff; L Cavaré, 'La notion de bonne foi et quelques-unes de ses applications en droit international public' (1968/69) *Cours IHEI (Paris)* 58ff.

In the municipal civil law context, see: B Stählin, 'Estoppel und Vertrauensprinzip', in *Essays in Honor of A Simonius (Aequitas und Bona Fides)* (Basle, 1955) 381ff; and E Riezler, *Venire contra factum proprium* (Leipzig, 1912); HJ Wieling, 'Venire contra factum proprium und Verschulden gegen sich selbst' (1976) 176 *Archiv für die civilistische Praxis* 334ff; HW Dette, *Venire contra factum proprium nulli conceditur: zur Konkretisierung eines Rechtssprichwortes* (Berlin, 1985); R Singer, *Das Verbot widersprüchlichen Verhaltens* (Munich, 1993). On English estoppel: G Spencer Bower and AK Turner, *The Law Relating to Estoppel by Representation*, 2nd edn (London, 1966); S Wilken and K Ghaly, *The Law of Waiver, Variation and Estoppel*, 3rd edn (Oxford, 2012). From the standpoint of comparative law, see B Fauvarque-Cosson (ed), *La confiance légitime et l'estoppel* (Paris, 2007). There are some differences between estoppel and the doctrine of *venire*, but these differences exist only at the municipal law level. In international law, the principle is applied as an outflow from good faith and without all the technicalities proper to common law estoppel.

Estoppel can be applied to all imaginable facts and deeds in international law, even remote. For example, it has been mentioned in the context of the effect of declarations of successions to treaties with regard to third States: see A Zimmermann, *Staatennachfolge in völkerrechtliche Verträge* (Berlin, 2000) 790–91.

[267] *Norwegian Fisheries* (1951) *ICJ Reports* 139.

to change its position'.[268] This party may in most cases change its position even after it has aroused reliance; but it then incurs a legal responsibility to compensate the injury which ensues from that 'sudden change'. The position is therefore not necessarily to prohibit a state to change its policies. It is only to make provision for some compensation to the injured party which legitimately relied on the continuity of the former conduct, eg because some assurances had been given. However, it also occurs that the principle of estoppel has more sweeping outcomes. It can lead to the loss of a subjective right (if that was the object of the representation and reliance) or to the fact that an international tribunal will not allow a claim which is contrary to previously aroused legitimate expectations. There are thus several possible effects of estoppel, substantive (extinction of subjective rights) or procedural (inadmissibility of a claim or of a piece of evidence).

To operate, estoppel supposes that certain conditions be fulfilled. Some of these conditions are inherent in its very notion, while other conditions are rather additions and specifications. There are three fundamental and four additional conditions. These now fall to be analysed.

A. An Initial Clear and Unequivocal Conduct or Declaration

This element of estoppel is linked to the concept of legitimate expectations: a subject can rely on the conduct of another only if the latter's attitude is 'reliable', ie is of a nature to reasonably arouse expectations of continuity or non-contradiction.[269] The clarity of a conduct depends from the nature of the acts or omissions, the

[268] H Mosler, 'General Course on Public International Law' (1974-IV) 140 *RCADI* 147. See also Kolb, *Bonne* 359: 'Le contenu du principe consiste en ce qu'une partie s'est fondée sur les assurances ou les comportements suffisamment clairs d'une autre partie, établissant que la confiance qu'elle a accordée à la conduite de l'autre l'a amenée à modifier sa position, à prendre des dispositions, d'une manière telle qu'elle subirait un préjudice si l'autre partie était autorisée à revenir sur ses comportements'. See also the lucid and learned analysis of Judge Alfaro in the *Temple of Preah Vihear* case, (1962) *ICJ Reports* 40: 'Whatever term or terms be employed to designate this principle [estoppel] such as it has been applied in the international sphere, its substance is always the same: inconsistency between claims or allegations put forward by a State, and its previous conduct in connection therewith, is not admissible (*allegans contraria non audiendus est*). Its purpose is always the same: a State must not be permitted to benefit from its own inconsistency to the prejudice of another State (*nemo potest mutare consilium suum in alterius injuriam*). A fortiori, the State must not be allowed to benefit by its inconsistency when it is through its own wrong or illegal act that the other party has been deprived of its right or prevented from exercising it. (*Nullus commodum capere de sua injuria propria*). Finally, the legal effect of the principle is always the same: the party which by its recognition, its representation, its declaration, its conduct or its silence has maintained an attitude manifestly contrary to the right it is claiming before an international tribunal is precluded from claiming that right (*venire contra factum proprium non valet*)'.

[269] For examples from the case law: Kolb, *Bonne* 363. Thus, for example, the PCIJ had to say this in the *Serbian Loans* case (1929) PCIJ ser A, no 20, p 39: 'There has been no clear and unequivocal representation by the bondholders…'. In the *Elettronica Sicula* case (1989) *ICJ Reports* 44, § 54, the Chamber of the ICJ similarly emphasised: '[T]here are obvious difficulties in constructing an estoppel from a mere failure to mention a matter at a particular point in somewhat desultory diplomatic exchanges'. See also the *Barcelona Traction* case (Preliminary Objections), (1964) *ICJ Reports* 24; and the *Argentine and Chile Frontier* case (1966) XVI *RIAA* 166. In the arbitral practice, see eg the *Feldman v Mexico* NAFTA arbitration case (2002) 126 *ILR* 45, § 63, 45, § 64, 81, § 149, the tribunal finding that there was

degree of their precision and their continuity in time.[270] When the conduct stretches in time, it is more likely to found legitimate expectations in its permanence. The situation may then correspond to a consistent practice modifying a treaty, creating a bilateral custom or establishing a prescriptive title.[271] The relevant conduct can consist of acts or omissions, declarations and legal acts, as well as of material deeds. If the conduct can be considered clear and non-equivocal depends manifestly on the circumstances, including the type of subject matter and the type of relations between the parties. Clarity of a message is not only a matter of its intrinsic quality; it is also a matter of context and cultural attunement.

Can the relevant conduct also consist in the upholding of a legal position? This has been denied with the argument that the law is a matter solely for the judge (*jura novit curia*) and that the parties can therefore not dispose of the law;[272] or that estoppel applied to a legal position would excessively hamper the free evolution of customary international law and thus the general interest in the mobility of the law.[273] Moreover, why should another party legitimately rely on what is only the expression of an opinion on the law—it could do so only at its own risk and peril.[274] These arguments are only partially convincing. The first one ignores the fact that in international law the intervention of a judge is a rare occurrence. Why should estoppel not shape to some extent (under its restrictive conditions) the bilateral position of some parties? In addition, the judge will apply the law between the parties even if estoppel is applicable here, since in that case the principle will have created new particular obligations which the judge will have to apply

no uniform, consistent and effective conduct or representation; *Newfoundland and Nova Scotia* arbitration (Second Phase, 2002) 128 *ILR* 546, § 3.10 and 549, § 3.17, the tribunal holding that there was no sufficiently clear, sustained and consistent conduct; *SGS v Pakistan* ICSID arbitration case (Objections to Jurisdiction, 2003) 129 *ILR* 416, § 122 and 438, § 177, SGS did not represent that it would not advance an alternative remedy; *SGS v Philippines* ICSID arbitration case (Objections to Jurisdiction, 2004) 129 *ILR* 484, § 109, no clear representation on the localisation of certain investments.

270 H Thirlway, 'The Law and Procedure of the ICJ (1960–1989): General Principles and Sources of Law' (1989) 60 *BYIL* 38.

271 GG Fitzmaurice, 'The Law and Procedure of the ICJ, 1951–54: General Principles and Sources of Law' (1953) 30 *BYIL* 27ff.

272 DW Bowett, 'Estoppel Before International Tribunals and its Relations to Acquiescence' (1957) 33 *BYIL* 189–90: 'The interpretation of the rights and duties of parties to a treaty, however, should lie ultimately with an impartial international tribunal, and it would be wrong to allow the conduct of the parties in interpreting these rights and duties to become a binding interpretation of them'. See also Dissenting Opinion Bedjaoui, *Delimitation of Maritime Boundary between Guinea Bissau and Senegal* arbitration (1989) XX *RIAA* 172. By the same token, an argument abandoned in the written pieces can still be raised again in the pleadings, since it concerns a question of law and in the case at stake a clear intention to abandon the argument was not shown, as little as a reliance on such an abandonment: *Territorial Jurisdiction of the International Commission of the River Oder* (1929) ser A, no 23, pp 18–19.

273 H Thirlway, 'The Law and Procedure of the ICJ (1960–1989): General Principles and Sources of Law' (1989) 60 *BYIL* 41: 'Suppose that a State has protested against an extension of maritime jurisdiction claimed by another State at a time when that extension is gaining ground but has not yet become recognized by general customary law; once that recognition has been achieved, is the State which protested to remain, so far as regards its own maritime jurisdiction, locked into the previous customary-law regime?'.

274 ibid, 43.

for example under article 38, § 1, letter a, of the ICJ Statute. As to the second argument, it is plainly defective: in most cases where a simple legal position has been taken, estoppel will not apply at all, since no detrimental reliance can be proven. Thus, customary international law is manifestly not hampered in its development, it not being a matter of bilateral adjustments. The last argument is valid to the extent it cautions for a restrictive interpretation of estoppel. However, it must be conceded that in any case the distinction between the 'law' and the 'fact' is not always crystal clear in a society where the law-making is entirely decentralised and where the sources of particular law, and of rights and obligations, are often treated as facts by international tribunals.[275] Finally, in such a fragmented society, it is all the more important that in some circumstances a 'statement of the law' made by one party should be able to create some order and command reliance by other parties. It is thus preferable not to limit estoppel a priori to matters of fact.[276] The case law buttresses this position. The ICJ, for example, considered the issue of estoppel in the context of conduct and declarations of Germany relating to a question of law, ie the applicability of the equidistance rule.[277] It did so again in the *Nicaragua* case of 1984, in the context of jurisdictional issues (jurisdiction by estoppel or acquiescence).[278]

B. A Legitimate Reliance of Another Subject on the Representation, which Induces it to Act

This requirement solidly establishes the link between the doctrine of estoppel and good faith as the protection of legitimate expectations.[279] The mere fact of a reliance is not enough; the reliance must moreover appear to be 'legitimate' with regard to the law, ie to be founded on what could reasonably be expected from a subject in the circumstances.[280] The law does not protect those who rely on all and believe every word: *vigilanti est jus scriptum*; *Trau Schau Wem*! Conversely, an incitement to rely on a certain representation is not necessary. It is sufficient that

[275] R Kolb, 'General Principles of Procedural Law' in: A Zimmermann and C Tomuschat and K Oellers-Frahm (eds), *The Statute of the International Court of Justice, A Commentary* (Oxford, 2006) 821.

[276] W Karl, *Vertrag und spätere Praxis im Völkerrecht* (Berlin, 1983) 329; Müller, *Vertrauensschutz* 10, fn 22; E Lauterpacht, 'The Development of the Law of International Organisations by the Decisions of International Tribunals' (1976-IV) 152 *RCADI* 462: 'In the international legal system the concept of "estoppel" or "preclusion" is as much applied to the content of the law as it is to matters of fact'.

[277] *North Sea Continental Shelf* cases (1969) *ICJ Reports* 26.

[278] *Military and Paramilitary Activities in and Against Nicaragua* (Jurisdiction and Admissibility) (1984) *ICJ Reports* 413–15.

[279] As was pleaded by C de Visscher in the *Jurisdiction of the European Commission of the Danube* opinion–it is necessary that the state pleading estoppel 'puisse dire à son adversaire: "votre conduite antérieure m'a induit en erreur, j'ai été trompé: c'est à cause d'elle que je me suis comporté de telle façon…"'. (1927) IV-1 PCIJ, ser C, no 13, p 182.

[280] Müller, *Vertrauensschutz* 29.

a conduct had objectively the potential to arouse legitimate reliance.[281] Whether a representation could and should have led to reliance is a matter depending on the circumstances of the case: the nature of the rights and interests at stake, the concrete relationship between the parties, the record of their past habits, etc. It also stands to reason that a conduct based on a manifest error cannot create a legitimate expectation. Any reliance would here be founded on a grave negligence or on bad faith, and thus not be 'legitimate'. Whether the representation is compatible with the law or not, or on what grounds the representation is performed, is irrelevant for the effect of estoppel.[282] However, a plainly illegal representation sharpens the duties of diligence of the relying state. But there is no reason to hold that a state cannot arouse expectations directed against the strict application of some conventional right contained in a bilateral agreement. A variation of particular law sources can perfectly lead to a legitimate expectation of a waiver or change of the relevant legal position. Conversely, it is clear that a reliance on some inroad into *jus cogens* norms or other non-derogable norms cannot be countenanced at all, since public order prevails.[283]

The case law regularly refers to this element of reliance. It is generally linked to the element of damage, to which we shall turn in due course. Thus, in the *Tinoco Claims* arbitration (1923), the arbitrator rejected an argument whereby Great Britain had not recognised the Government of Tinoco and was consequently estopped to now present a claim based on the acts of that government:

> The failure to recognize the *de facto* government did not lead the succeeding government to change its position in any way upon the faith of it ... An equitable estoppel to prove the truth must rest on previous conduct of the person to be estopped, which has led the person claiming the estoppel into a position in which the truth would injure him.[284]

The US Commissioner Perry said, in the *Santa Isabel* arbitral case of 1926: estoppel operates in favour of 'who has in good faith relied upon such conduct, and has led thereby to change his position ...'.[285] In the *Norddeutscher Rundfunk* case (1980), decided by the German Federal Administrative Court, which applied international

[281] A Martin, *L'estoppel en droit international public* (Paris, 1979) 290ff.

[282] ibid, 293.

[283] *R v HM Treasury and the Bank of England, ex p Centro-Com SRL* (1994) 117 ILR 481, where the English Court of Appeal held that the public order of sanctions meted out in implementation of the UN Security Council Resolutions under Chapter VII of the UN Charter overrode any argument on the confidence on the continuity of a governmental policy (Kennedy LJ). See I Brownlie, *International Law and the Use of Force by States* (Oxford, 1963) 244; A Orakhelashvili, *Peremptory Norms in International Law* (Oxford, 2006) 77, 367ff. This was also the gist of the position of Judge Sidwha in *Tadic*, a jurisdiction case, ICTY, Appeals Chamber (1995) 105 *ILR* 578, § 93, when he said that there can be no estoppel against the law. The point was that the absence of challenge of the jurisdiction of a criminal tribunal cannot be raised against the rules granting a compulsory jurisdiction to the tribunal.

[284] *Tinoco Claims arbitration* (1923) I *RIAA* 383–84.

[285] *Santa Isabel arbitral case* (1926) IV *RIAA* 803. See also the Separate Opinion Fitzmaurice, *Temple of Preah Vihear* (1962) *ICJ Reports* 63; Dissenting Opinion Wellington Koo, ibid, 97; Dissenting Opinion Spender, ibid, 144.

law by analogy to a treaty concluded between three German *Länder*, the judgment emphasises that a late withdrawal from that treaty would have been allowed if the other parties had brought by their deeds the withdrawing party to believe in good faith in the admissibility of such late action. The element of reliance has been mentioned in many other international judgments, such as the *Serbian Loans* case (1929),[286] the *North Sea Continental Shelf* cases (1969),[287] in the *Nicaragua* case (1984)[288] or in the *Sovereignty over Pedra Branca/Pulau Batu Putheh, Middle Rocks and South Ledge* case (2008).[289] In short terms, without such reliance there is no estoppel.

C. A Damage Resulting from the Reliance (Detrimental Reliance)[290]

For a long time, this requirement has been controversial. But eventually the international doctrine of estoppel shifted from a general and vague rule of non-contradiction to a rule on the protection of specific legitimate expectations; it took the leap from an intra-subjective rule of consistency of one's own deeds to an inter-subjective rule considering the effects of deeds on other subjects. The restriction thereby accomplished is welcome: foreign policy must change and remain flexible; it should not be bound by too rigid rules on non-contradiction, which would in any case not be realistic, or, as is elegantly said, honoured in breach.[291] A general doctrine of non-contradiction would vastly overestimate the potential and the role of law in general, and of international law in particular. Conversely, a subject should not be entirely free in its conduct. It has to take account of legitimate reliance of others and of detrimental effects on others. The dividing line between the spheres of freedom and responsibility is drawn by the modern doctrine of estoppel.

Older case law and doctrine did not always require a damage flowing from the reliance.[292] The change of position was considered per se detrimental. In the

[286] *Serbian Loans* (1929) PCIJ ser A, no 20, p 39.

[287] *North Sea Continental Shelf* (1969) *ICJ Reports* 26.

[288] *Nicaragua (Jurisdiction and Admissibility)* (1984) *ICJ Reports* 415.

[289] *Sovereignty over Pedra Branca/Pulau Batu Putheh, Middle Rocks and South Ledge* (2008) *ICJ Reports* 81, § 228.

[290] Again in the words of C de Visscher: 'L'exception n'est recevable que si celui qui l'invoque, si celui qui s'en prévaut, se trouve exposé à subir un dommage injuste, au cas où son adversaire serait admis à démontrer le bien-fondé de sa thèse'. (1927) IV-1 PCIJ, ser C, no 13, p 182.

[291] The Swiss Federal Tribunal rightly said: 'Il n'existe aucun principe général du droit international public ou du droit interne suisse suivant lequel un sujet de droit serait lié par ses propres agissements. L'idée qui veut qu'un sujet de droit ne doit pas se mettre en contradiction avec ses propres actes s'il en résulte un préjudice pour un tiers n'est admise que lorsque certaines conditions sont réunies'. See the *Nufenen* case (*Canton du Valais v Canton du Tessin*, 1980), original French version (translated from the official German judgment): (1981) 37 *ASDI* 234; English version in: (1981) 75 *ILR* 119.

[292] See A Martin, *L'estoppel en droit international public* (Paris, 1979) 71ff, 173ff, 293ff.

modern conception of estoppel, a damage flowing from some action or omission done on the faith of the representation must be shown. This shift in the construction of the concept is of paramount importance. Simple interests are turned into legally protected interests—but only when there is legitimate reliance and ensuing damage. The showing of a damage is however necessary only when estoppel is intended to have a substantial effect, ie to create rights and obligations on the one hand, and to extinguish other rights and obligation on the other hand. Contrariwise, when estoppel is limited to procedural issues, it may require that a party is not allowed to be heard with an argument which contradicts earlier statements: *allegans contraria non est audiendus*.[293] In the close knit of a judicial procedure, where the prestige of the court of justice having been seized is also at stake, estoppel moves back towards a rule of non-contradiction. In short terms, substantive estoppel always requires detrimental reliance, whereas procedural estoppel does not require such a distinct damage (the damage is inherent in the violation of procedural fairness). Consequently, a tribunal may declare inadmissible a contradictory claim or piece of evidence without further ado. It can found itself on specific procedural rules or principles, or invoke the general principle of good faith or estoppel.

An exemplary application of the detrimental reliance requirement can be found in the *R v HM Treasury and the Bank of England, ex p Centro-Com SRL* case (1994). Kennedy LJ held that there had been no reliance on some earlier policy of the government: the relevant goods were supplied without knowing from what funds they would be paid; estoppel could thus not be invoked with success, since there was no reliance on a special funding.[294] There was all the more no basis for a legitimate expectations given that there had been no published policy statement at all.[295] In the *Pope & Talbot v Canada (Interim Award)* arbitration (2000), it was held that estoppel could not be applied in view of the absence of a proper representation, of the lack of reliance and of the consequential lack of change of position.[296] The same line of argument was used in the *SGS v Philippines* case (2004): there was no clear representation and no detrimental reliance.[297] The ICJ itself abounded in the same direction in the *Land and Maritime Boundary* case *(Cameroon v Nigeria, Preliminary Objections)* (1998).[298] It came back on this issue in the *Sovereignty over Pedra Branca/Pulau Batu Putheh, Middle Rocks and South Ledge* case (2008).[299] This is an impressive set of precedents for the modern conception of estoppel.

[293] See eg *Awas Tingni v Nicaragua (Merits and Reparations)* (IACtHR) (2001) 136 *ILR* 174: 'The principle of estoppel does not allow the State to argue that the Community has no legitimate claim based on traditional or historic land tenure, since that allegation is contrary to positions maintained by the State before the Commission and before the Community on several occasions…'.

[294] *R v HM Treasury and the Bank of England, ex p Centro-Com SRL* (1994) 117 *ILR* 499.

[295] ibid, 481.

[296] *Pope & Talbot v Canada (Interim Award)* arbitration (2000) 122 *ILR* 338–39, § 112.

[297] *SGS v Philippines* ICSID arbitration, Objections to Jurisdiction Phase (2004) 129 *ILR* 484, § 109.

[298] *Land and Maritime Boundary (Cameroon v Nigeria, Preliminary Objections)* (1998) *ICJ Reports* 303–04, § 57 and 308–09, § 71–72.

[299] *Sovereignty over Pedra Branca/Pulau Batu Putheh, Middle Rocks and South Ledge* (2008) *ICJ Reports* 81, § 228.

What is the type of required damage? Only material damage? In English law, apparently only material damages were recognised as being able to found an estoppel.[300] International law differs in this regard from its municipal law counterpart. International practice shows that 'immaterial damages' are also factored in: eg the stability of arbitral awards in the *Arbitral Award of the King of Spain* case (1960);[301] the stability of boundaries in the *Temple of Preah Vihear* case (1962);[302] the disadvantage to see the Court declare itself deprived of jurisdiction in the *Nicaragua* case (1984);[303] the impossibility to oppose an argument of inadmissibility to a claim in the context of exhaustion of local remedies in the *Elettronica Sicula* case (1989);[304] etc. It is manifestly possible to construe some pecuniary damage in all such cases: thus, the lack of competence of the Court entails the loss of sums of money which were dedicated to the preparation of the case. However, such material damages are at best mediate and can hardly be said to be the controlling issue. Further, the mere interest in the respect of international law is not a protected interest in the case of estoppel. Thus, there is no detriment in the required sense if the general expectation of respect for international law has been disappointed. A state is not expected to rely on generic representations or expectations in this context. Conversely, the damage must not have materialised; it can be potential or eventual.[305] Estoppel has the aim of *avoiding* a damage. The relevant issue is the question whether the damage would have materialised but for the application of the doctrine of estoppel, which allows to eliminate it. This also shows that the damage must exist independently from the consequences of the preclusion itself. In other words, the damage cannot consist in the non-application of the preclusion flowing from estoppel. If that were allowed, no separate requirement of a damage would be upheld and we would return to a sweeping doctrine of non-contradiction.

Estoppel rules bilateral relationships. It is thus an inherently relational concept. This has its impact on the definition of relevant 'damage'. The latter is itself shaped as a relational concept. The gist of the matter is that the *relative position* of the parties has been changed by the detrimental reliance, either to the prejudice of the one which claims estoppel or to the benefit of the other, or both.[306] Thus, a collateral

300 A Martin, *L'estoppel en droit international public* (Paris, 1979) 293.

301 *Arbitral Award of the King of Spain* (1960) *ICJ Reports* 209.

302 *Temple of Preah Vihear* (1962) *ICJ Reports* 32.

303 *Nicaragua (Jurisdiction and Admissibility)* (1984) *ICJ Reports* 413–15.

304 *Elettronica Sicula* (1989) *ICJ Reports* 43–44.

305 A Martin, *L'estoppel en droit international public* (Paris, 1979) 294, 300.

306 See the very precise expression in Separate Opinion Fitzmaurice, *Temple of Preah Vihear* (1962) *ICJ Reports* 63: 'The essential condition of the operation of the rule of preclusion or estoppel … is that the party invoking the rule must have "relied upon" the statements or conduct of the other party, either to its own detriment or to the other's advantage. The often-invoked necessity for a consequent "change of position" on the part of the party invoking preclusion or estoppel is implied in this. A frequent source of misapprehension in this connection is the assumption that the change of position means that the party invoking preclusion or estoppel must have been led to change its own position, by action it has itself taken consequent on the statements or conduct of the other party. It certainly includes that: but what it really means is that these statements, or this conduct, must have brought about a

advantage obtained by one state (and the concomitant disadvantage for the other) could be sufficient to apply an estoppel.[307]

Modern case law extensively mentions the requirement of a damage:[308] for example the *Tinoco* case (1923),[309] the *Schufeldt* case (1930),[310] the *Barcelona Traction* case (*Preliminary Objections*, 1964),[311] the *North Sea Continental Shelf* cases (1969),[312] the *Military and Paramilitary Activities in and Against Nicaragua* case (Competence and Admissibility, 1984),[313] the *Gulf of Maine* case (1984),[314] or the *Land and Maritime Boundary* case (*Cameroon v Nigeria, Preliminary Objections*) (1998).[315]

There are four additional, but more secondary conditions for the successful invocation of an estoppel. These are linked to the concrete application of the concept and are not expressive of its constitutive elements.

D. A Causality Link

There must exist a certain nexus between the initial representation, the action or omission flowing therefrom, and the damage created.[316] The change of attitude must not have occurred merely on occasion but rather because of the initial representation; and the damage must be the direct consequence of the changed attitude.

change in the relative positions of the parties, worsening that of the one, or improving that of the other, or both'. See also Martin, op cit, 297ff; RY Jennings, *The Acquisition of Territory in International Law* (Manchester, 1963) 41ff.

307 See eg the pleadings by the US and UK in the *Monetary Gold Removed From Rome* case (1954) *ICJ Pleadings* 151 and 91: 'To hold otherwise would permit the applicant State to improve its own position, at the expense of others, by first invoking a tribunal's jurisdiction and then denying it'. In the *Temple of Preah Vihear* case, the ICJ mentions the advantage of benefitting from a stable boundary: (1962) *ICJ Reports* 32. It is however unclear how this advantage changed the respective position of the parties, since it was a shared advantage: cf H Thirlway, 'The Law and Procedure of the ICJ (1960–1989): General Principles and Sources of Law' (1992) 63 *BYIL* 45. Probably the better position is that the Court relied here on acquiescence, which does not suppose a change of positions.

308 See the many cases mentioned in A Martin, *L'estoppel en droit international public* (Paris, 1979) 293ff.

309 *Tinoco* (1923) I *RIAA* 383–84. And see Martin, op cit 142ff.

310 'The Guatemala Government having recognized the validity of the contract for six years and received all the benefits to which they were entitled under the contract and allowed Schufeldt to go on spending money on the concession is precluded from denying its validity…': *Schufeldt* (1930) II *RIAA* 1094.

311 *Barcelona Traction (Preliminary Objections)* (1964) *ICJ Reports* 24–25.

312 *North Sea Continental Shelf* cases (1969) *ICJ Reports* 26. See also Separate Opinion Padilla Nervo, ibid, 96: Dissenting Opinion Tanaka, ibid, 173–74. See also J Lang, *Le plateau continental de la mer du Nord* (Paris, 1970) 51ff.

313 *Military and Paramilitary Activities in and Against Nicaragua* (Competence and Admissibility) (1984) *ICJ Reports* 415.

314 *Gulf of Maine* (1984) *ICJ Reports* 305.

315 *Land and Maritime Boundary (Cameroon v Nigeria, Preliminary Objections)* (1998) *ICJ Reports* 303, § 57.

316 A Martin, *L'estoppel en droit international public* (Paris, 1979) 300–01.

The relevant causality is not merely a natural phenomenon. It is based on legal considerations, notably as to proximity of cause and effect. Thus, it is not sufficient that there is a natural link between the relevant positions, ie that the one could not exist without the other (*conditio sine qua non*). The attitude and damage must moreover appear as reasonable consequences of the initial representation in the light of the experience of life and the ordinary course of events.[317] In other words, and as already suggested, the causes leading to the result must appear to be sufficiently proximate to the latter. Thus, for example, the damage must not appear to be too remote (length of the chain of causality) or too exorbitant (idiosyncrasy of the chain of causality in the light of what can reasonably be expected) when compared with the causing attitude. For example, a state may have taken action on the faith of some representation which now hinders it, or renders more onerous, to become a party to a multilateral convention. However, the conduct chosen as a result of this difficulty may in its turn have myriad further effects. Not all these further effects can be linked to the initial representation and lead to an estoppel—all the more since the interpretation of that notion is rather strict so as not to fall into a general rule of non-contradiction, or, worse, of responsibility for risk. The damage itself may also seem too tenuous in our case concerning difficulties in becoming a party to a multilateral convention. This is especially true when the ratification of the treaty is merely rendered more onerous (and not impossible) because some possibly minor obstacles must first be removed. Conversely, the initial representation must not be the sole cause for the conduct taken and the damage finally suffered; it is sufficient that the representation appears as the preponderant cause. The issue of causality has rarely received keen attention in the context of the doctrine of estoppel. Some consideration have however been devoted to that question during the pleadings in the *Eastern Greenland* case of 1933.[318]

E. A Free Will

The initial representation must flow from a free will and from freedom of action.[319] If there is coercion, fraud or error, the invalidation rules of the law of treaties apply by analogy.[320] Thus, in the *Salvador Commercial Company* case (1902), it was said that:

> It is of course obvious that the Salvador Government should be estopped from going behind those reports of its own officers on the subject and from attacking their

[317] G Schwarzenberger, *International Law—As Applied by International Courts and Tribunals*, vol I (London, 1957) 668ff; JHW Verzijl, *International Law in Historical Perspective*, vol VI (Leiden, 1973) 752ff; A Gattini, *Zufall und force majeure im System der Staatenverantwortlichkeit anhand der ILC—Kodifikationsarbeit, Schriften zum Völkerrecht*, vol 96 (Berlin, 1991) 48ff. See also J Crawford, *State Responsibility* (Cambridge, 2013) 492ff.

[318] See the discussion in A Martin, *L'estoppel en droit international public* (Paris, 1979) 99–101.

[319] See eg DW Bowett, 'Estoppel Before International Law and its Relations to Acquiescence' (1957) 33 *BYIL* 190.

[320] Arts 46ff of the VCLT of 1969.

> correctness without supplementary evidence tending to show that such reports were induced by mistake or were procured by fraud or undue influence. No evidence of this kind is introduced here.[321]

The door is left open for such evidence to be produced. However, even in such a case the principle of good faith could preclude a successful raising of the excuse, if the error has been committed through some negligence or if it has not been raised in a reasonable time after it was discovered (principles that 'no one can profit from his own wrong' and of acquiescence).

F. The Non-Conditioned Character of the Representation

The initial representation must be made without conditions or reservations. Otherwise, it cannot found a legitimate reliance and motivate a subject to adopt a change of conduct. For this reason, the PCIJ found only a *modus vivendi* and not a legal commitment, and even less an estoppel, in the *European Commission of the Danube* opinion (1927).[322] Again, the principle of good faith can alter the legal position, eg if a legitimate confidence was created that the initial condition is dropped. This can flow from a separate representation, giving rise to a second estoppel, or through some acquiescence to a claim presented by the other party. There may thus be estoppels in the estoppel.

G. The Attribution of the Representation

The initial representation should emanate from a state organ entitled to bind the state internationally. The applicable rules are seated in the law of treaties, notably article 7 of the VCLT of 1969. Thus, private persons cannot engage the state by some estoppel;[323] but state organs could make relevant representations in the context of dealings with such private persons. Moreover, the case law on estoppel has enlarged the entitlement to bind the state on two interlinked accounts. First, state agents with purely internal competencies can bind the state externally. Second, subordinate state agents can issue a representation giving rise to preclusion.[324] Thus, in the *France/US Air Services Agreements* case (1963), the conduct of a technician acting on behalf of the state has been taken account of in the context

[321] *Salvador Commercial Company* (1902) XV *RIAA* 473. See also the *Serbian Loans* case (1929) PCIJ, ser A, no 20, p 39 and on that case BB Cheng, *General Principles of Law—As Applied by International Courts and Tribunals* (London, 1953) 148–49. The Court here notes that the bondholder could not, materially, have exercised their rights earlier.

[322] *European Commission of the Danube* (1927) PCIJ, ser B, no 14, p 35, and DW Bowett, 'Estoppel Before International Law and its Relations to Acquiescence' (1957) 33 *BYIL* 191.

[323] *Barcelona Traction (Preliminary Objections)* (1964) *ICJ Reports* 24.

[324] A Martin, *L'estoppel en droit international public* (Paris, 1979) 278ff; JP Jacqué, *Éléments pour une théorie de l'acte juridique en droit international public* (Paris, 1972) 211ff.

of acquiescence;[325] and in the *Temple of Preah Vihear* case (1962), the ICJ affirmed that if a state does not control the conduct of its subaltern organs, it does so at its own legal risk.[326] The *Gulf of Maine* case (1984), where the Court did not consider the US bound by the written utterances of Mr Hoffmann, a subordinate staff member, can be distinguished from the main line of the case law previously mentioned. In effect, Mr Hoffmann expressly reserved the position of his higher authorities in the letter which was sent to Canada.[327] Thus, there was no clear and final representation on which the other party could rely. Consequently the incompetence of Mr Hoffmann to bind the US need not have been discussed by the Chamber of the Court. Summing up, it can be said that the higher organs of the state are 'estopped' to argue that a conduct emanated from a subordinate organ when they failed to adequately control its deeds. In such a case the representation of that subordinate agent can give rise to an estoppel vis-à-vis some other state. Again, there may an estoppel in the estoppel.

Finally, it falls to be recalled that if some element of estoppel in the technical sense of the word is lacking—eg there is no damage resulting from a reliance—a legally relevant argument can still be made on the relevant conduct. Thus, the aggrieved state may produce the evidence that the other party constantly contradicted itself in its conduct. If successful, this showing goes a long way towards weakening the position of the latter in a dispute or adjudication procedure. The invocation of inconsistencies and contradictions always produce some result in the minds of lawyers. This is then a sort of estoppel *minus quam perfectum*.[328] Notice that such an imperfect estoppel (which technically is not one) has certainly imponderable effects, but that it can have a heavy impact on the reasoning of the legal operator. Persons reasoning legally do not like contradictions; they have the bitter flavour of arbitrary action, opposed to the law.

Some authors have configured estoppel as a legal act, ie as a form of consent or tacit agreement.[329] It is sometimes added that the initial representation and the

[325] *France/US Air Services Agreements* (1963) 38 *ILR* 182ff.

[326] *Temple of Preah Vihear* (1962) *ICJ Reports 25*.

[327] *Gulf of Maine* (1984) *ICJ Reports* 306–08.

[328] DW Bowett, 'Estoppel Before International Law and its Relations to Acquiescence' (1957) 33 *BYIL* 195: 'where one or other of the foregoing essentials of a binding estoppel is absent the representation, whether by words or conduct, does not lose all value, for, although lacking conclusive effect, it may still be adduced in evidence as an admission to show a lack of consistency or weakness in a party's position'. See also the *Tinoco Claims* case (1923) 2 *Annual Digest of Public International Law Cases* (now *ILR*) 38; and the *LaGrand* and *Avena* cases, (2001) *ICJ Reports* 488–89, § 61–63 and (2004) *ICJ Reports* 38, § 45–47. Switzerland acknowledged that, on the basis of the principle of good faith, it should not oppose a certain consular practice on its territory in view of the fact that it followed the same practice itself abroad: (2002) 12 *RSDIE* 627. With regard to the acceptance of the jurisdiction of the ICJ, denied in one case and claimed in the other, see Separate Opinion Ago, *Nicaragua (Jurisdiction and Admissibility)* (1984) *ICJ Reports* 531. On such estoppels *minus quam perfecta*, see also *Beagle Channel* case (1977) XXI *RIAA* 169; (1977) 1 *NYIL* 122.

[329] See eg A Martin, *L'estoppel en droit international public* (Paris, 1979) 305–06, 307ff; J Lang, *Le plateau continental de la mer du Nord* (Paris, 1970) 55ff; A Orakhelashvili, *Peremptory Norms in International Law* (Oxford, 2006) 369ff.

reliance upon that representation create a non-rebuttable presumption that a tacit agreement has been concluded. This is a complicated construction, which hardly veils its highly fictional character.[330] If there was indeed a tacit agreement, estoppel would be legally superfluous or merely a descriptive notion of a particular way to conclude an agreement. As has been lucidly said by an eminent Common Lawyer:

> [I]n those cases where it can be shown that a party has, by conduct or otherwise, undertaken, or become bound by, an obligation, it is strictly not necessary or appropriate to invoke any rule of preclusion or estoppel ... Thus it may be said that A, having accepted a certain obligation, or having become bound by a certain instrument, cannot now be heard to deny the fact, to 'blow hot and cold'. True enough, A cannot be heard to deny it; but what this really means is simply that A is bound, and being bound, cannot escape from the obligation ....[331]

Contrary to what other sciences may be, the law is never redundant: if the binding force rests on a legal act, no further explanation for its binding character is necessary. It is legally wrong to say that a treaty binds a state because it is estopped from challenging its binding force; it is correct to say that the treaty binds the state because of *pacta sunt servanda*. The case law has thus rightly never tried to establish the existence of an agreement to apply the concept of estoppel. The reality is that in the context of estoppel it is not some will or intent which creates the legal bond, but a norm of the international legal order which attaches some consequences to a certain conduct. And this norm of international law is but a concretisation of the principle of good faith seeking the protection of legitimate expectations.[332]

In the international jurisprudence there are some famous cases dealing with estoppel. In the *Arbitral Award Made by the King of Spain* case (1960), the ICJ was confronted with an arbitral award rendered in 1906 on an issue of territorial delimitation. It had given rise to a series of declarations by Nicaragua, the succumbing party. This state expressed its satisfaction that the dispute had been solved and complimented the other party, Honduras. The King of Spain, the arbitrator, was explicitly felicitated by Nicaragua. A series of other acts manifesting an acceptance of the award followed. But in 1912, following a change of Government in Nicaragua, the award was contested and its nullity claimed. The ICJ did not accept these arguments.[333] Honduras had rightly relied on the representations of finality of the award. Manifestly, there would also have been a damage if the change of position had been accepted: the jeopardising of all the dispositions made on the reliance of the finality of the boundary. In the *Temple of Preah Vihear* case (1962), French

[330] See Martin, op cit.

[331] Separate Opinion Fitzmaurice, *Temple of Preah Vihear* (1962) *ICJ Reports* 63.

[332] See the extensive literature and case law buttressing this position in Kolb, *Bonne* 378–79. For the case law, see eg the *Gulf of Maine* (1984) *ICJ Reports* 305.

[333] *Arbitral Award Made by the King of Spain* (1960) *ICJ Reports* 209, 213. On estoppel, see also the Separate Opinion Spender, ibid, 219–20.

geographers established some maps of the common boundary, as determined by a Treaty of 1904. Apparently by accident, the lines on the maps departed in some areas from those which the treaty stipulated. Yet, Siam (Thailand) did not protest these maps or the establishment of French sovereignty over the areas at stake. For years, a series of actions, such as official visits, took place, and no contestation of the boundary occurred, up to 1958. The Court considered that Thailand was by then precluded from being heard with its claim regarding the invalidity of the maps.[334] The element of the damage was subliminal in this case: the interest of a stable boundary is a shared one. There is no change in positions here, to the detriment of one party and to the benefit of the other. It is manifest that the decision on the *Temple* case was heavily coloured by the principle of acquiescence, which does not require a detrimental reliance. The latter principle did seem relevant in view of the prolonged silence. This may explain why the Court did not search in detail for a tangible damage. The better course would have been to found the decision either on acquiescence or on estoppel, and if the latter were to be chosen, the damage would have to be defined as the annulment of all the dispositions done on the faith of the finality of that boundary. In the *Nufenen* case (1980),[335] decided by the Swiss Federal Tribunal, which concerned a boundary between two Swiss cantons and closely resembled the *Temple* case, the judges refused to apply the concept of estoppel precisely for absence of a clear damage flowing from the reliance. Instead, the Federal Tribunal relied directly on the principle of acquiescence.

The foregoing developments show that some delimitation between estoppel and acquiescence is useful. What are the exact differences between both notions? In a sense, the two concepts are intimately linked. Acquiescence produces a sort of preclusion, ie a change in the legal position to the detriment of the passive state or subject.[336] However, there are some differences in the operation of both principles.

— *First*, acquiescence concerns passivity and silence, whereas estoppel supposes deeds and acts,[337] which may be accompanied also by silences. Thus, for acquiescence the question of the 'duty to react' is paramount, but not for estoppel; in the latter, the 'detrimental reliance' is the core element. Since acquiescence is less demanding in terms of conditions to be fulfilled, it could be laudable to consider in the first place whether it can be applied, turning to estoppel only in the second place.[338] However, in many cases the record of acts and omissions is so intimately intermingled that a neat separation is

[334] *Temple of Preah Vihear* (1962) *ICJ Reports* 32. On estoppel, see also Separate Opinion Alfaro, ibid, 39ff; Separate Opinion Fitzmaurice, ibid, 62ff; Dissenting Opinion Wellington Koo, ibid, 96ff; Dissenting Opinion Spender, ibid, 142ff.

[335] *Nufenen* case (1980) 75 *ILR* 118–20, (1981) 37 *ASDI* 233–234.

[336] G Schwarzenberger, 'The Fundamental Principles of International Law' (1955-I) 87 *RCADI* 256: 'acquiescence produces an estoppel in circumstances when good faith would require that the State concerned should take active steps of some kind in order to preserve its rights…'.

[337] C Vallée, 'Quelques observations sur l'estoppel en droit des gens' (1973) 77 *RGDIP* 983ff.

[338] A Verdross and B Simma, *Universelles Völkerrecht*, 3rd edn (Berlin, 1984) 393–94.

artificial. The legal operator could apply an estoppel, which encompasses the positive deeds, when the element of detrimental reliance may reasonably be softened in regard of an existing duty to react and the finding of a number of silences opposed to adverse assertions. In other words, the operator could sometimes apply some 'acquistoppel'. The case law analysed above bears out this proposition in both the *King* and the *Temple* cases.

— *Second*, as we have seen, estoppel supposes the existence of a damage resulting from the reliance ('detrimental reliance'); acquiescence does not.[339] The protection of legitimate expectations lies in the case of acquiescence in the duty to speak out; if that is not done, the other party may *ipso facto* consider that a certain legal solution is now prevailing. No further dispositions on its part are necessary to bind the silent state to the consequences of its wrongful passivity.

— *Third*, since acquiescence is linked to a more or less prolonged silence, the element of time becomes more material than in the situation of estoppel. As has been rightly observed: 'The time element is likely to be more material in cases of acquiescence than in cases of estoppel. If there has been reliance on a statement leading to a change of the relative position of the parties, the time it has taken for this to occur is not relevant.'[340] Estoppel resembles on this account more to a legal act (such as tacit consent) and acquiescence more to a modality of customary law, ie a process where a certain practice repeated over time leads to a change in the legal positions, here in the subjective legal positions (rights and obligations).[341]

The Chamber of the ICJ in the *Gulf of Maine* case of 1984 tried to shed some light on the question of the distinction between acquiescence and estoppel. Its reasoning contains useful elements but cannot be said to be fully felicitous. Here is the utterance of the Chamber:

> The Chamber observes that in any case the concepts of acquiescence and estoppel … both follow from the fundamental principles of good faith and equity. They are, however, based on different legal reasoning, since acquiescence is equivalent to tacit recognition manifested by unilateral conduct which the other party may interpret as consent, while

[339] See eg H Thirlway, 'The Law and Procedure of the ICJ (1960–1989): General Principles and Sources of Law' (1989) 60 *BYIL* 46. See also *Gulf of Maine* (1984) *ICJ Reports* 305, § 130.

[340] Thirlway, op cit, p 46.

[341] It has thus been asked whether acquiescence is not a modality of a local or bilateral customary law: G Sperduti, 'Prescrizione, consuetudine e acquiescenza in diritto internazionale' (1961) 44 *RDI* 9ff; F Francioni, 'La consuetudine locale nel diritto internazionale' (1971) 54 *RDI* 411ff; G Cohen-Jonathan, 'La coutume locale' (1961) 7 *AFDI* 137–39. However, acquiescence (and also estoppel) are not just elements in the formation of such rules of particular customary law. The latter normally create objective rules of law, which will rule some questions also for the future; conversely, acquiescence is a source of obligations, producing the loss of a legal right in the context of subjective legal positions. But it is true that acquiescence and estoppel can be elements in the chain of formation of a customary rule, especially in the context of prescriptive titles (see Müller, *Vertrauensschutz* 77ff). The distinction between acquiescence and local customary rules is thus only relative.

> estoppel is linked to the idea of preclusion. According to one view, preclusion is in fact the procedural aspect and estoppel the substantive aspect of the same principle.[342]

The first thing to be noted is that the Chamber does not suggest that acquiescence *is* a tacit consent, ie a legal act. It merely says that it is *equivalent* to a tacit consent. This means that its legal effects are the same as if there had been a tacit consent. There is a manifest nuance between both propositions. The element of reliance on good faith appears clearly in the second part of the sentence, where the Chamber goes on to emphasise that the litmus test is whether the other party may have interpreted that silence as a tacit consent. To some extent, however, this reference to tacit consent is unhappy. It will lead a certain number of superficial commentators to consider that the Chamber has construed acquiescence as a tacit consent. At least, the Chamber could have spoken of an equivalence to recognition, avoiding the bell-sounding term 'tacit'. It may also not be entirely satisfactory to emphasise that both principles, acquiescence and estoppel, flow indistinctly from the principles of good faith and equity, without further refinement. This is too vague a statement. The truth is that an overwhelming number of legal rules flows from equity and justice, while another important number of legal rules flows ultimately from considerations of legal security or practicability. What is more important for our more concrete purposes is to consider that both acquiescence and estoppel are outflows or concretisations of the principle of good faith, taken as the fundamental norm of international law protecting legitimate expectations. The phrase that estoppel is linked to the idea of preclusion is also somewhat vague. Why should it just be linked (and how?) to an idea (or ideal?)? It would have been more precise to say that estoppel leads to a preclusion, or alternatively perhaps also consists in a preclusion (*forclusion*, in French). To some extent, this is also true for acquiescence. In this regard, it can be said that the legal effects of both principles are the same: a legal subject is bound by its previous behaviour, ie cannot change it without consequences of responsibility. Finally, the 'view' according to which acquiescence is procedural and estoppel substantive is quite odd. In the view of most legal commentators, it would be rather the other way round, acquiescence being substantive and estoppel procedural. However, as we have seen, in international law both principles often operate on the substantive level and sometimes touch on procedural questions. The particular sentence, which the Chamber just throws there, hardly adds any clarification to the matter. On the other hand, the Chamber goes on to clarify—in the sentence after the passages quoted above—that acquiescence does not suppose a separate damage, which is entirely true. Overall, it may perhaps be allowed to say with much respect that the Chamber did not offer a great contribution to the distinction between the two principles.

[342] (1984) *ICJ Reports* 305, § 130. On the configuration of these two principles, see also the Separate Opinion Wolfrum in *M/V Saiga (no 2) (Admissibility and Merits)* (1999) 120 *ILR* 230ff (ITLOS).

The statements of the WTO Panel in the *Guatemala—Cement II* case (2000) are shorter and more precise:

> We note that acquiescence amounts to qualified silence, whereby silence in the face of events that call for a reaction of some sort may be interpreted as a presumed consent. The concept of estoppel … is akin to that of acquiescence. Estoppel is premised on the view that where one party has been induced to act in reliance on the assurances of another party, in such a way that it would be prejudiced were the other party later to change its position, such a change in position is estopped, that is precluded.[343]

This statement can be faulted only on the choice of the too narrow word 'assurances'. Such assurances can manifestly give rise to an estoppel; but other forms of conduct may equally lead to a preclusion.

In the context of application of estoppel, there is also rich case law in other tribunals or decisional organs. An interesting case arose in the *Well Blowout Control Claim* (UN Claims Commission for Iraq, 1996).[344] It was held that Kuwait and its corporation KPC were estopped from presenting a claim of another corporation which had to be deemed to be included in the demands made for Kuwait's oil sector as a whole. There was no formal *res judicata* in this case, since there was no identity of the claimants and respondents. The principle of estoppel therefore substantively took the place of the *res judicata* principle. It can be noted that the Commission did not meticulously analyse the conditions of representation and detrimental reliance. The principle of estoppel was founded on equitable considerations nourished by the principle *ne bis in idem*.

There is also a distinction to be made between the operation of estoppel and of the maxim *nemo auditur propriam turpitudinem allegans* ('no one can profit from his own fault'). Both notions are often conflated, as the treatment of a very famous passage of the PCIJ in the *Chorzow Factory* case (1927) shows.[345] However, in the case of *nemo auditur propriam turpitudinem allegans*, the initial representation is characterised by an unlawful act or by a legally relevant immoral act. Thus, the element of 'detrimental reliance' disappears. The issue is not to protect a legitimate expectation in the first place, but rather to sanction an illegality or a fault. It stands to reason that in the past, when the damage element of estoppel was not yet developed as a requirement of that notion, both notions were closer together than they are today.

Finally, it may be noted that some treaty clause may allow to preclude certain conduct without examining all the technical conditions of estoppel. Thus, clauses

343 Panel Report, WT/DS156/R, § 8.23.

344 (1996) 109 ILR 505, § 61.

345 See eg B Cheng, *General Principles of Law—As Applied by International Courts and Tribunals* (London, 1953) 151ff; IC McGibbon, 'Estoppel in International Law' (1958) 7 *ICLQ* 480; M Scerni, *I principî generali di diritto riconosciuti dalle nazioni civili nella giurisprudenza della Corte permanente di Giustizia internazionale* (Padova, 1932) 127.

of 'fair and equitable treatment' contained in investment agreements may make recourse to estoppel residual.[346] A contradictory or otherwise odd conduct can be subsumed under other headings of such clauses, eg the prohibition of abuse of rights or procedure, or of arbitrary action, non-discrimination, and the like. The treaty clause is here *lex specialis* and it may allow a preclusion on eased conditions, eg without analysing to what extent there has been detrimental reliance (an exercise which can be wearying).

[346] *Occidental Cy v Ecuador* (2004) 138 *ILR* 85, § 196.

6

Good Faith and the Jurisdiction of States

Jurisdiction or competence is a legally recognised power or duty to do something. In international law, the jurisdiction of states connotes a bundle of rights of action and of protection. Contrary to a subjective right, the notion of competence also includes an element of duty. A competence is therefore a functional notion: it is conferred in order to realise certain aims rooted in the public interest. This was stressed in the celebrated dictum of M Huber in the *Island of Palmas* case (1928), where the rights conferred by sovereignty are matched by the duty to protect the rights of other states in the territory where that state enjoys its sovereignty.[1] There are several issues with regard to the creation and loss of competences, or with regard to the exercise of competences, which are based on, or at least trigger, considerations of good faith. Some of them flow from the notion of reliance on good faith (legitimate expectations), as is the case of 'acquisitive prescription'. Others flow from the necessary link between the exercise of a competence and the aims for which it was granted, as in the notion on abuse of rights. In other words, good faith displays two main functions in the context of competences: the protection of legitimate expectations and the protection of aims and purposes.

I. Good Faith in the Doctrine of Acquisitive Prescription

The question of the existence of a doctrine of prescription in international law has been and remains controversial.[2] In truth, the issue turns heavily on aspects of terminology. For some authors, prescription is essentially linked to a legally

[1] *Island of Palmas* (1928) II *RIAA* 839.

[2] On acquisitive prescription in international law, see mainly: E Audinet, 'De la prescription acquisitive en droit international public' (1896) 3 *RGDIP* 313ff; H Ralston, 'Prescription' (1910) 4 *AJIL* 133ff; P Fauchille, *Traité de droit international public*, tome I, partie 2 (Paris, 1925) 754ff; H Lauterpacht, *Private Law Sources and Analogies of International Law* (London, 1927) 116–17; M Sørensen, 'La prescription en droit international' (1932) 3 *Acta Scandinavica Juris Gentium* 145ff; PA Verykios, *La prescription en droit international public* (Paris, 1934); A Schnitzer, *Staat und Gebietshoheit* (Zurich, 1935) 87ff; DHN Johnson, 'Acquisitive Prescription in International Law' (1950) 27 *BYIL* 332ff; DHN Johnson, 'Consolidation as a Root of Title in International Law' (1955) *Cambridge Law Journal* 215ff; R Pinto, 'La prescription en droit international' (1955-I) 87 *RCADI* 391ff; L Oppenheim and

prescribed time-span, at the end of which a given legal consequence ensues. For example, the former owner of an object may lose its right over it while another subject, in continuous control of the object, will acquire rights over that object. It stands to reason that such a time-span-oriented concept of prescription does not exist in general international law. No time-span is therein generally defined for acquiring or losing rights on a certain object, such as mainly territory. But prescription can also signify the creation and concomitant loss of a legal title because of a prolonged passivity in the face of adverse claims or in the face of the assertion of adverse rights on the spot. Such a doctrine of prescription is rooted in the concepts of acquiescence and estoppel. For example, acquiescence may here lead to the loss of a territorial right and the creation of a new territorial title in the other state. But acquiescence is not the sole condition for the acquisition of territorial rights. There are other conditions to be met (eg a continuous and pacific exercise of public power over a territory), which justify the present analysis under

H Lauterpacht, *International Law, Peace*, vol I, 8th edn (London, 1955) 575ff; J Charpentier, *La reconnaissance internationale et l'évolution du droit des gens* (Paris, 1956); AG Roche, 'The Minquiers and Ecrehos Case' (PhD thesis, Geneva, 1959) 19ff, 35ff; G Sperduti, 'Prescrizione, consuetudine e acquiescenza in diritto internazionale' (1961) 44 *Rivista di diritto internazionale* 3ff; S Bastid, 'Les problèmes territoriaux dans la jurisprudence de la Cour internationale de Justice' (1962-III) 107 *RCADI* 435ff; RY Jennings, *The Acquisition of Territory in International Law* (Manchester, 1963) 20ff; M Satow, 'Die Ersitzung in der völkerrechtlichen Theorie und Praxis' (1964) *Internationales Recht und Diplomatie* 72ff; YZ Blum, *Historic Titles in International Law* (The Hague, 1965) 6ff; JA Barberis, 'La prescripción adquisitiva y la costumbre en el derecho internacional' (1967) 57 *Revue de droit international, de sciences diplomatiques et politiques* 233ff; J Symonides, 'Acquisitive Prescription in International Law' (1970) 3 *Polish Yearbook of International Law* 111ff; JP Müller, *Vertrauensschutz im Völkerrecht* (Köln, 1971) 54ff; G Zimmer, *Gewaltsame territoriale Veränderungen und ihre völkerrechtliche Legitimation* (Berlin, 1971) 46ff; G Dahm, J Delbrück and R Wolfrum, *Völkerrecht*, 2nd edn (Berlin, 1989) 365ff; L Oppenheim (RY Jennings and A Watts, eds), *International Law, Peace*, vol I, 9th edn (London, 1992) 705ff; PK Menon, 'Title to Territory, Traditional Modes of Acquisition by States' (1994) 72 *Revue de droit international de sciences diplomatiques et politiques* 13ff; M Kohen, *Possession contestée et souveraineté territoriale* (Paris, 1997) 17ff; SP Sharma, *Territorial Acquisition, Disputes and International Law* (La Haye, 1997) 107ff; LI Sanchez Rodriguez, 'L'uti possidetis et les effectivités dans les contentieux territoriaux et frontaliers' (1997) 263 *RCADI* 253ff; AR Ibrahim, 'The Doctrine of Laches in International Law' (1997) 83 *Virginia Law Review* 647ff; M Kohen, '*Uti possidetis*, prescription et pratique subséquente à un traité dans l'affaire Kasikili/Sedudu devant la Cour internationale de Justice' (2000) 43 *GYIL* 253ff; NSM Marques Antunes, *Estoppel, Acquiescence and Recognition in Territorial and Boundary Dispute Settlement* (Durham, 2000); G Distefano, *L'ordre international entre légalité et effectivité* (Geneva, 2002) 277ff; J Wouters and S Verhoeven, 'Prescription' in R Wolfrum (ed), *The Max Planck Encyclopedia of Public International Law*, vol VIII (Oxford, 2012) 420ff. See also YL Emerich, 'Comparative Overview on the Transformative Effect of Acquisitive Prescription and Adverse Possession: Morality, Legitimacy, Justice' (2015) 67 *Revue internationale de droit comparé* 459ff. In the context of good faith, see eg Kolb, *Bonne* 399ff and R Kolb, 'La prescription acquisitive en droit international public' in Université de Neuchâtel (ed), *Le temps et le droit* (Basle, 2008) 149ff. See also the many other mentions in various studies, eg K Strupp, 'Der Streitfall zwischen Schweden und Norwegen (Grisbadarna)' in W Schücking (ed), *Das Werk vom Haag, Die gerichtlichen Entscheidungen*, II Serie, vol I, Pt 2 (Munich, 1917) 132. See finally also Diss Op Dugard, *Sovereignty over Pedra Branca/Pulau Batu Putheh, Middle Rocks and South Ledge* case (2008) *ICJ Reports* 145ff, § 30ff.

On the classical authors in international law and the Roman law roots of the modern doctrine of prescription, see Kolb, *Bonne* 399–402.

a separate heading than acquiescence,[3] namely precisely under some concept of 'prescription' or of 'consolidation of titles through conduct'. Consequently, prescription is the result of a sum of passive and of active conducts, and not merely of passivity. Prescription mainly means the acquisition of sovereignty by the pacific and continuous exercise of state power over a territory, which is not contested by the holder of the formal title for a prolonged period of time. The title then shifts, or more precisely there is the loss of one title to territory and the creation of a new one. Notice however that prescription can also be used with respect to other legal positions than sovereignty over a territory, eg for fishing rights, historical bays, rights of passage, servitudes, etc.[4]

The institution of prescription is rooted in the necessity of legal stability and certainty.[5] A prolonged state of affairs creates its own equities. It would be unjust and often impracticable to disturb them after a long time has elapsed. *Quieta non movere; ne dominia rerum diutius in incerto essent.* Prescription in municipal law allows adaptation of the legal title to the effective state of affairs. But rather than allowing mere effectiveness to triumph, the law sets conditions under which the fact will be allowed to create new law. In international law, the gist of the legal institution of prescription slightly shifts. It remains a legal tool for securing security and congruence between the fact and the law. However, since there is no time-limit which triggers the legal consequences, the institution of prescription remains more closely rooted to the equities and specificities of the single case. It is here in the first place a 'bilateralist' tool for the adjustment of claims to territory in the light of conduct and silence, ie of principles such as acquiescence, estoppel or recognition. In other words, international law prescription has two hats: it is intended to improve legal security *and* to protect specific legitimate expectations in complex patterns of assertive and passive behaviours.

[3] There are however authors doubting of any autonomy of the notion of prescription in international law with respect to acquiescence/estoppel: see eg Müller, *Vertrauensschutz* 54ff; A Verdross and B Simma, *Universelles Völkerrecht*, 3rd edn (Berlin, 1984) 758; G Sperduti, 'Prescrizione, consuetudine e acquiescenza in diritto internazionale' (1961) 44 *RDI* 3ff, 8; RY Jennings, *The Acquisition of Territory in International Law* (Manchester, 1963) 36ff; IC McGibbon, 'The Scope of Acquiescence in International Law' (1954) 31 *BYIL* 152ff; IC McGibbon, 'Some Observations on the Part of Protest in International Law' (1953) 30 *BYIL* 306ff. The better view seems that prescription is founded on acquiescence and estoppel, but distinguishes itself from those notions by the other concomitant conditions, such as an effective possession of territory and the exercise of state functions therein. See to that effect *R v Seven named Accused* (2004) 127 *ILR* 272–73 (Pitcairn Island Supreme Court), where the two aspects 'exercise of sovereignty' and 'acquiescence' are analysed. And see *Sovereignty over Pedra Branca/Pulau Batu Putheh, Middle Rocks and South Ledge* (2008) *ICJ Reports* 96, § 276.

[4] Johnson, Acquisitive, op cit, 332.

[5] H Grotius, *De iure belli ac pacis* (1625), lib II, cap IV, §§ 1, 9; E de Vattel, *Le droit des gens* (1758), liv II, cap XI, §§ 147, 149; R Phillimore, *Commentaries Upon International Law*, 3rd edn vol I (London, 1879) 361–62; PA Verykios, *La prescription en droit international public* (Paris, 1934) 23ff; DHN Johnson, 'Acquisitive Prescription in International Law' (1950) 27 *BYIL* 333; AP Sereni, *Diritto internazionale*, vol II (Milan, 1958) 605; H Lauterpacht, *International Law—Collected Papers*, vol I (Cambridge, 1970) 378; L Oppenheim (RY Jennings and A Watts, eds), *International Law, Peace*, vol I, 9th edn (London, 1992) 707.

Before engaging into an analysis of the elements of prescription in international law (or, if one dislikes that term, of creation of a title to territory by exercise of public power on the one hand and by passivity on the other hand), there is one point to be made clear. Prescription concerns the creation of a new title or the consolidation of a defective title. The subject in effect administering a territory *à titre de souverain* is not possessing a title at all, or at least not a perfect title, over that territory. If that state does possess a perfect title, there is no issue of prescription: the holder of the title and the state in fact administering the territory are the same. Prescription rather concerns situations where a piece of land is in fact administered as a sovereign by a state which has no perfect title on it, while the state holding that perfect title remains passive in face of the adverse assertions. This is the situation which gives rise to the operation of the principle and which manifestly interests the principle of reliance on good faith. There are four elements which must be discussed in the context of prescription. They form the body of that norm.

A. A Continuous, Pacific and Public Exercise of Sovereign Power Over a Territory

The exercise of public authority over a piece of land must be made as a sovereign over that land (unless prescription concerns other rights than sovereignty). In other words, the display of public power must be accompanied by an *opinio juris* based on the conviction to act as a sovereign.[6] As was said by M Huber in the celebrated *Island of Palmas* arbitration (1928): 'practice as well as doctrine, recognizes … that the continuous and peaceful display of *territorial sovereignty* … is as good as a title'.[7] Sovereign acts are for instance the adoption of legislation, the granting of concessions, local administration, the perception of taxes, the exercise of criminal and civil jurisdiction, the keeping of public and civil registers, the establishment of customs authorities, and the like. This exercise of sovereign power must occur on a territory on which there exist already some adverse legal titles, perfect or inchoate.[8] In the case of a territory without a ruler (*terra nullius*),[9] the simple act of the first effective occupation will confer the title.[10] However, even

[6] Thus, a state administering a territory as a mandate, a trusteeship, or today under UN transitional administrations, will not acquire a title to sovereignty. See eg the *International Status of South-West Africa* opinion (1950) *ICJ Reports* 131–33, 142–43.

[7] *Island of Palmas* (1928) II *RIAA* 839, emphasis added. See also the careful analysis in the *Kasikili/Sedudu Island* case: (1999-II) *ICJ Reports* 1101ff, § 90ff.

[8] On inchoate titles, see AS Keller, O Lissitzyn and FJ Mann, *Creation of Rights of Sovereignty through Symbolic Acts (1400–1800)* (New York, 1938).

[9] On the status of colonial territory in Africa and the titles acquired by the coloniser, see the huge study by M Hébié, *Souveraineté territoriale par traité* (Paris, 2015).

[10] See the classical study by R Ago, *Il requisito dell'effettività dell'occupazione in diritto internazionale* (Rome, 1934). On the distinction between prescription and occupation, see DHN Johnson, 'Acquisitive Prescription in International Law' (1950) 27 *BYIL* 348ff; E Beckett, 'Les questions d'intérêt général au point de vue juridique dans la jurisprudence de la CPJI (Juillet 1932—Juillet 1934)' (1934–IV) 50 *RCADI* 218ff.

in that case a prescriptive title can be preferred after a long time has elapsed, and the legality of the original occupation has become difficult to prove. Further, as was said by M Huber in the *Palmas* award:

> if the contestation is based on the fact that the other Party has actually displayed sovereignty, it cannot be sufficient to establish the title by which territorial sovereignty was validly acquired at a certain moment; it must also be shown that the territorial sovereignty has continued to exist and did exist at the moment which for the decision of the dispute must be considered as critical.[11]

The critical date for the title is thus not just immobilised at the date of occupation; it continues to unfold thereafter. Thus, the subsequent conduct can perfect a defective occupation as it can also lead to a loss of the title flowing from the initial occupation. Moreover, the display of sovereign power must be public (not clandestine),[12] and reasonably continuous, taking into account the characteristics of the territory. Once again, a classical statement can be found in the *Palmas* arbitration:

> Although continuous in principle, sovereignty cannot be exercised in fact at every moment on every point of a territory. The intermittence and discontinuity compatible with the maintenance of the right necessarily differ according as inhabited or uninhabited regions are involved, or regions enclosed within territories in which sovereignty is incontestably displayed.[13]

Space and time are relative notions: continuity in time is a function of the nature of the space at stake. Not the same type of effective presence can be asked for a metropolitan territory and a barren uninhabited island. The main point is that the territory has globally remained under the control of the acting state. Only action attributable to the state—ie performed through state organs or agents—qualifies for prescription.[14] Conversely, actions and omissions by private persons cannot lead to a title.[15] However, private action (eg traditional fishing in historic waters) can be an element to be taken account of in the context of the growth of a prescriptive title when it is interlinked with state action (eg measures of the state to protect these traditional fishing rights).[16] The question whether tribesmen are

[11] (1928) II *RIAA* 839.

[12] This requirement has but little weight in the modern world, where it is difficult to imagine clandestine exercises of sovereign power. See DHN Johnson, 'Acquisitive Prescription in International Law' (1950) 27 *BYIL* 347 or PA Verykios, *La prescription en droit international public* (Paris, 1934) 75, considering this criterion to be useless in international law (which may be going too far).

[13] (1928) II *RIAA* 840. See also the *Clipperton* case (1931 II, *RIAA* 1110; the *Eastern Greenland* case (1933) PCIJ, ser A/B, no 53, p 46; the *Rann of Kutch* arbitration (1968) 50 *ILR* 329ff, 386.

[14] DHN Johnson, 'Acquisitive Prescription in International Law' (1950) 27 *BYIL* 344–45. On the rules of attribution, see notably L Condorelli, 'L'imputation à l'Etat d'un fait internationalement illicite' (1984-VI) 189 *RCADI* 9ff; and the contributions in J Crawford, A Pellet and S Olleson (eds), *The Law of State Responsibility* (Oxford, 2010) 221ff.

[15] Thus, in the *Kasikili/Sedudu Island* case, the ICJ rejected an argument that sovereignty had been exercised on the spot through the allegiance of a local tribe, the relevant link with the state claiming this allegiance not being sufficiently proved: (1999-II) *ICJ Reports* 1105–06, § 98.

[16] *Norwegian Fisheries* (1951) *ICJ Reports* 142.

merely private persons or exercise some state powers can be difficult to solve in a particular instance.[17]

B. The Absence of Protest

This is a fundamental element of prescription;[18] it establishes the link with the legal principles of good faith and legitimate expectations[19] and avoids clothing with the authority of the law a simple usurpation of power by the stronger state on the spot.[20] It flows from this requirement that a possession upheld in the face of constant protests by the holder of the original title cannot lead to any acquisitive prescription.[21]

The first question which must be treated is: who has a title to protest? In the ordinary situation of adverse possession, it is the holder of the title, whose silence leads to a relevant acquiescence and to the building-up of a prescriptive title.[22] On the other hand, it is admitted that when prescription touches common spaces, such as the high seas, any other state is entitled to protest (*erga omnes* effect).[23] The issue is more complicated in intermediate situations. Thus, if a territory is taken by the use of force, can the recognition or acquiescence of the title-holder allow the possessing state to build up a title? Or is the illegality of the use of force of such a nature that only the general toleration of the international community could possibly regularise the state of affairs? Considering the often-asserted *jus cogens* nature of the non-use of force rule, there is a good argument for a general standing on that issue.[24] This *erga omnes* approach has been adopted by some authors

[17] See the *Kasikili/Sedudu Island* case, quoted above, (1999-II) *ICJ Reports* 1105–06 and the Dissenting Opinion Weeramantry, ibid, 1164–65, § 33ff; Dissenting Opinion Parra-Aranguren, ibid, 1229ff, § 79ff; Dissenting Opinion Rezek, ibid, 1236–37, § 13–15.

[18] DHN Johnson, 'Acquisitive Prescription in International Law' (1950) 27 *BYIL* 345ff.

[19] It has been stated that the doctrine of prescription is based on good faith and legitimate expectations, but that this would not be so in international law where the number of states is much more limited than the number of subjects in municipal law: T Christakis, 'The State as a "Primary Fact": Some Thoughts on the Principle of Effectiveness' in: M Kohen (ed), *Secession, International Law Perspectives* (Cambridge, 2006) 162. One fails to see however the number of subjects could be relevant when the legitimate expectations argument is seen as an objective standard of conduct. The question of the protection of legitimate expectations arises already in the contact of two subjects of law, eg when they conclude a treaty.

[20] It has to be noted, however, that some arbitral precedents have sometimes down-played the element of acquiescence in favour of the element of effectiveness (with the exception of the status of maps): *Delimitation of the Boundary between Eritrea and Ethiopia* (2002) XXV *RIAA* 111, 114–15, 116, 162. This course is not warranted. A precedent more in line with the classical position can be found in the *Taba* arbitration (1988) 80 *ILR* 226.

[21] See the *Chamizal* arbitration (1911) 5 *AJIL* 806–07.

[22] DHN Johnson, 'Acquisitive Prescription in International Law' (1950) 27 *BYIL* 351.

[23] ibid. See also the *Norwegian Fisheries* case, (1951) *ICJ Reports* 139, where the Court mentions the 'general toleration of the international community'.

[24] See G Gaja, 'States having an Interest in Compliance with the Obligation Breached', in J Crawford, A Pellet and S Olleson (eds), *The Law of International Responsibility* (Oxford, 2010) 957ff; C Tams, 'Waiver, Acquiescence and Extinctive Prescription' ibid, 1042.

even more generally, considering that issues of territorial distribution are today of common interest. Thus, it has been said that

> the acquisition of sovereignty over a territory through continuous and undisturbed exercise of sovereignty over it during such a period as is necessary to create under the influence of historical development the general conviction that the present condition of things is in conformity with international order.[25]

This position may be going too far. The answer seems to lie along the following lines:

(i) when the adverse possession is the result of the violation of a fundamental rule of international law with *erga omnes* reach (notably the unlawful use of force), each state is entitled to protest; it is not even clear whether a prescription by silence could apply at all, in view of the peremptory nature of the violated norm; there are good arguments against such an application;

(ii) when the adverse possession is not the result of the violation of such a fundamental norm of international law but just of an evolution of realities on the spot, the quality to protest (and thus to acquiesce) lies with the holder of the title; acquisitive prescription can apply.

A second question is what acts amount to a 'protest'? What conduct impeaches the operation of acquiescence and prescription in the context of the territorial claims we are dealing with? It stands to reason that a formal protest fulfils all the requirements.[26] The most difficult issue is whether mere paper protests without concrete action can indefinitely interrupt the process of prescription. The majority of authors denies this and requires a minimum degree of concrete action.[27] Such action could be the introduction of some judicial claim or the conclusion of some agreement expressing on the titles to that territory.[28] But such requirements are not convincing: when a state upholds paper protests, the possessing state cannot be said to build up a legitimate expectation of undisturbed possession or sovereignty. The root of prescription, which lies in the principle of good faith, itself

[25] L Oppenheim and H Lauterpacht, *International Law, Peace*, 8th edn, vol I (London, 1955) 576. See also L Oppenheim (R Jennings and A Watts, eds), *International Law*, 9th edn (London, 1992) 706; R Monaco, *Manuale di diritto internazionale pubblico*, 2nd edn (Turin, 1971) 410; AG Roche, 'The Minquiers and Ecrehos Case' (PhD thesis, Geneva, 1959) 39, 45–46; K Von Schuschnigg, *International Law—An Introduction to the Law of Peace* (Milwaukee, 1959) 152–53.

[26] See eg IC McGibbon, 'The Scope of Acquiescence in International Law' (1954) 31 *BYIL* 143ff, 152ff; IC McGibbon, 'Some Observations on the Part of Protest in International Law' (1953) 30 *BYIL* 293ff, 306ff; E Suy, *Les actes juridiques unilatéraux en droit international public* (Paris, 1962) 71ff; PA Verykios, *La prescription en droit international public* (Paris, 1934) 99ff; L Oppenheim (R Jennings and A Watts, eds), *International Law*, 9th edn (London, 1992) 706–07.

[27] See eg DHN Johnson, 'Acquisitive Prescription in International Law' (1950) 27 *BYIL* 346; GG Fitzmaurice, 'The Law and Procedure of the ICJ, 1951–54: General Principles and Sources of Law' (1953) 30 *BYIL* 28ff; Verykios, op cit, 101; McGibbon, Protest, op cit, 310ff.

[28] As to the latter, see the *Chamizal* case (1911) 5 *AJIL* 806–07.

excludes such a course. The required frequency and force of the protests must be evaluated in the light of the intensity of the exercises of adverse public power and the strength of the claims uttered by the possessing state.[29] If the attitude of the adverse state is fluctuating or inconsistent, if it is contradicted by numerous other official acts and statements, including maps, the holder of the title is not legally obliged to protest[30]—there is here already no continuous exercise of public power over the territory in the first place. It is however clear that a protest might always have a certain usefulness, if only to make the position entirely clear and to preserve with certainty one's own legal position.

C. The Element of Time

The time element is one of the vexed questions in the context of the doctrine of acquisitive prescription.[31] No precise time-span is required. All depends on the circumstances,[32] ie the type of territory, the strength of adverse assertions, the intensity of adverse display of public functions, the existence of onerous investments made on the possessed territory in good faith,[33] the existence or absence of subjective good faith; etc.[34] This state of affairs shows that prescription in international law is not a matter of time, but a matter of acquiescence and legitimate expectations in the stability of things consolidated over time. Time is inherent in this consolidation; but it does not appear as a separate and tangible legal requirement. It is rather the dimension in which the relevant events—assertion of a claim by effective administration and silence by the holder of the title—will unfold. In short terms, the issue of time remains entirely circumstantial.

[29] Müller, *Vertrauensschutz* 58.

[30] *Mount Fitzroy Boundary, Argentina v Chile* (1994) 113 *ILR* 78–79.

[31] On time, see eg DHN Johnson, 'Acquisitive Prescription in International Law' (1950) 27 *BYIL* 347–48; PA Verykios, *La prescription en droit international public* (Paris, 1934) 85ff; L Oppenheim (R Jennings and A Watts, eds), *International Law*, 9th edn (London, 1992) 706.

[32] Oppenheim, op cit, 706: 'No general rule could be laid down as regards the length of time … Everything depended upon the individual case'. See also the *Island of Palmas* case (1928) II *RIAA* 867: 'It may suffice that such display existed … and had already existed as continuous and peaceful before that date long enough to enable any power who might have considered herself as possessing sovereignty over the island, or having a claim to sovereignty, to have, according to local conditions, a reasonable possibility for ascertaining the existence of a state of things contrary to her real or alleged rights'. Under particular international law, the parties may fix a time-span for prescription, as between the UK and Venezuela in the *British Guyana* case (1897), agreement to hold 50 years as the critical time: see H Lauterpacht, *Private Law Analogies and Sources of International Law* (London, 1927) 229ff. The agreement between the two states is published in C Parry, *The Consolidated Treaty Series*, vol 184 (New York, 1974) 189ff. In the old literature, it was already considered that the time-element was flexible and depended itself on good faith: see eg L Casanova, *Del diritto internazionale*, vol I (Florence, 1870) 178, 191.

[33] On this point, see the *Grisbadarna* case (1909) XI *RIAA* 161 and Müller, *Vertrauensschutz*p 42–43.

[34] See Kolb, *Bonne* 415–16.

D. The Element of Subjective Good Faith

Legal writings and case law emphasise that the presence of subjective good faith is not a condition for prescription.[35] Subjective good faith designates the absence of knowledge of the adverse title. Thus, even if the state holding effective possession knows that another state has or claims titles on that piece of land, it can still prevail itself of prescription in the case the formal title-holder does not contest its presence. In the stakes of the subject matter, the absence of protest weighs heavier than the absence of subjective good faith: a state can try to vindicate its own claim on the spot even if other states claim their own rights. The issue is then settled by acquiescence or recognition. But protest (even paper protest) rules out the possibility to prescribe. If there is such protest, we are confronted with a plurality of claims, and as the Chamber of the ICJ affirmed, the holder of the formal title must then be preferred.[36]

The case law is eloquent on the issue of subjective good faith. It is not mentioned in the various cases sailing under the vague flag of 'prescription', such as *Grisbadarna* (1909),[37] *Island of Palmas* (1928),[38] *Eastern Greenland* (1933),[39] *Minquiers and Ecrehos* (1953),[40] *Temple of Preah Vihear* (1962),[41] *Frontier Dispute* (Argentina/Chile, 1966),[42] *Rann of Kutch* (1968),[43] *Western Sahara* opinion (1975),[44] *Dubai/Sharjah Frontier and Territorial Dispute* arbitration (1981),[45] *Land, Island and Maritime Frontier Dispute (El Salvador/Honduras)* (1992),[46]

[35] See Zoller, *Bonne* 98ff; DHN Johnson, 'Acquisitive Prescription in International Law' (1950) 27 *BYIL* 337–38; PA Verykios, *La prescription en droit international public* (Paris, 1934) 74–75; L Oppenheim (R Jennings and A Watts, eds), *International Law*, 9th edn (London, 1992) 706, fn 6. For further literature, see Kolb, *Bonne* 416, fn 146. In the stern words of Hall: 'Instead of being directed to guard the interests of persons believing themselves to be lawful owners, though unable to prove their title, or of persons purchasing in good faith from others not in fact in legal possession, the object of prescription as between states is mainly to assist in creating a stability of international order which is of more practical advantage than the bare possibility of an ultimate victory of right' (WE Hall, *A Treatise on International Law*, 8th edn (Oxford, 1924) 143). But the point is not so much a victory of effectiveness on right; it is rather that 'right' itself shifts because of a prolonged and faulty passivity. There are some few authors requiring subjective good faith for prescription, see eg VD Degan, *L'équité et le droit international* (The Hague, 1970) 138; L Olivi, *Diritto internazionale pubblico e privato*, 2nd edn (Milan, 1911) 286.

[36] *Frontier Dispute (Burkina Faso v Mali)* (1986) *ICJ Reports* 587, § 63.

[37] *Grisbadarna* (1909) XI *RIAA* 155ff.

[38] *Island of Palmas* (1928) II *RIAA* 829ff.

[39] *Eastern Greenland* (1933) PCIJ ser A/B, no 53, p 22ff.

[40] *Minquiers and Ecrehos* (1953) *ICJ Reports* 47ff.

[41] *Temple of Preah Vihear* (1962) *ICJ Reports* 6ff.

[42] *Frontier Dispute (Argentina/Chile)* (1966) 38 *ILR* 16ff.

[43] *Rann of Kutch* (1968) 50 *ILR* 14ff.

[44] *Western Sahara* opinion (1975) *ICJ Reports* 12ff, 42ff.

[45] *Dubai/Sharjah Frontier and Territorial Dispute* arbitration (1981) 91 *ILR* 550ff.

[46] *Land, Island and Maritime Frontier Dispute (El Salvador/Honduras)* (1992) *ICJ Reports* 351ff, esp 401, 408–09, 437, 469, 525. See E Decaux, 'Le différend frontalier terrestre, insulaire et maritime (El Salvador/Honduras)' (1992) 38 *AFDI* 409ff, 418ff.

Kasikili/Sedudu Island (1999),[47] etc. There are a few cases where subjective good faith has at least been mentioned—but without giving it any effect in the decision.[48] However, it has been rightly said[49] that the presence of subjective good faith is not legally irrelevant and that it may have some collateral legal effects, such as: the required time-span in which a reaction of the other state is required could be shortened (at least when the subjective good faith is known or should have been known to the other state); subjective good faith can be taken account of in the interpretation of the title or be an equitable consideration in the context of such interpretation; the presence of bad faith can trigger certain obligations of restitution of goods and assets on the territory at stake;[50] etc. Moreover, if a tribunal is granted the power to decide *ex aequo et bono*, it can take into account the subjective good faith of one party.[51] The issue is here not one of the application of strict law but of equity.

A good example of a decision based on prescription in the sense described above is the *Frontier and Territorial Dispute Dubai/Sharjah* (1981).[52] The point was to consider the legal effect of a series of activities of Dubai in the face of prolonged silence by Sharjah. This passivity had consequences: a title is lost and a new title is created. Thus:

> What appears decisive to the Court is not that Sharjah did not assert its authority over an un-populated region by some positive action, but that it offered no opposition to the Government of Dubai treating the Al Mamzer peninsula as its own territory [...] The Court observes that there is a substantial body of case law which indicates that, when one State engages in activity, by means of which it seeks to acquire a right or to change an existing situation, a lack of reaction by another State at whose expense such activity is carried out, will result in the latter forfeiting the rights which it could have claimed. [...] The State whose rights are threatened by the actions of another State does not necessarily have to make its protest as soon as it learns about the action giving rise to the complaint, but it must be made as soon as the State realizes that these actions may be prejudicial to its rights.[53]

[47] *Kasikili/Sedudu Island* (1999-II) *ICJ Reports* 1101ff.

[48] *Frontier Dispute (Colombia/Venezuela)* (1891) I *RIAA* 292ff.

[49] M Kohen, *Possession contestée et souveraineté territoriale* (Paris, 1997) 383ff.

[50] See Separate Opinion De Castro, *Namibia* opinion, (1971) *ICJ Reports* 218.

[51] *Honduras/Guatemala Boundary* (1933) II *RIAA* 1307ff, 1311: 'In view of the nature of the territory, long uninhabited and unknown, and of the lack of authoritative delimitation, it was natural that there should have been conflicting conceptions of the extent of jurisdiction and that each Party should believe that it was entitled to advance into the unoccupied zone as its interest seemed to require. Such advances in good faith, followed by occupation and development, unquestionably created equities which enterprises subsequently undertaken would be bound to consider. When it appears that the two Parties, seeking to extend their area of possession, have come into conflict, the question of priority of occupation necessarily arises. Priority in settlement in good faith would appropriately establish priority of right'. The main mission of the tribunal had been to apply the *uti possidetis* line. It considered that in view of its equitable function, it could take account for a modification of that line only possession acquired in good faith.

[52] *Frontier and Territorial Dispute Dubai/Sharjah* (1981) 91 *ILR* 550ff, 621–25. On this case, see DW Bowett, 'The Dubai/Sharjah Boundary Arbitration of 1981' (1994) 65 *BYIL* 103ff.

[53] (1981) 91 *ILR* 622, 624.

The doctrine of prescription based on acquiescence and estoppel has been applied also to boundary disputes. The classical case in this regard is the *Temple of Preah Vihear* case (1962),[54] which has been more recently quoted with approval in the *Delimitation of the Ethiopia/Eritrea Border* case (2002).[55]

As can be seen, the doctrine of prescription under international law responds only to one type of prolonged adverse possession: the one where the assertion of rights on the spot is accompanied by passivity on the part of the holder of the formal title. If the latter recognises by some express legal act the rights of the possessor, prescription is superfluous, since recognition will itself extinguish a title and allow the creation of a new one. By the same token, if the formal holder of title protests and upholds its protest, a prescription is impossible. The dispute on the legal claims will here remain open and could (or indeed should) be solved by one of the instruments for the peaceful settlement of international disputes.[56] It is therefore only in a narrow context that the present doctrine can make its contribution to the solution of a situation characterised by contrasting claims. And by its *modus operandi*, this prescription is nothing more than an application of the principle of good faith/legitimate reliance, as is shown by the pivotal place of acquiescence and estoppel in the process.

II. Good Faith and Extinctive Prescription (Time-Bar, Laches)

The issue of time-bar or limitation in international law is again a story of good faith and not of some pre-determined lapse of a time-span.[57] There are cases where extinctive prescription corresponds to an acquisitive prescription: one state

[54] (1962) *ICJ Reports* 22ff.

[55] Arbitral Award by the Eritrea/Ethiopia Boundary Commission, *Delimitation of the Ethiopia/Eritrea Border* (2002) 130 *ILR* 35–36, § 3.9.

[56] See art 33 of the UN Charter (1945).

[57] See N Politis and C de Visscher, 'La prescription libératoire en droit international public' (1925) 32 *Rapport présenté à l'IDI, Ann IDI* 1ff, 466ff; N Politis, 'La prescription libératoire en droit international' (1925) 3 *Revue de droit international des sciences diplomatiques et politiques* 1ff; A Cavaglieri, 'Il decorso del tempo ed i suoi effetti sui rapporti giuridici internazionali' (1926) 18 *RDI* 169ff; (1931) 36-I *Travaux préparatoires pour la Session de Cambridge, Ann IDI* 435ff; A Rolin, 'Prescription extinctive', in A De La Pradelle and N Politis (eds), *Recueil des arbitrages internationaux*, vol II (Paris, 1932) 205ff; M Sørensen, 'La prescription en droit international' (1932) 3 *Acta Scandinavica Juris Gentium* 161ff; BE King, 'Prescription of Claims in International Law' (1934) 15 *BYIL* 82ff; PA Verykios, *La prescription en droit international public* (Paris, 1934) 129ff; W Roch, 'La prescription libératoire s'applique-t-elle en droit international public?' (1949) 27 *Revue de droit international, de sciences diplomatiques et politiques* 254ff; B Cheng, *General Principles of Law—As Applied by International Courts and Tribunals* (London, 1953) 373ff; R Pinto, 'La prescription en droit international' (1955-I) 87 *RCADI* 438ff, C De Visscher, 'La prescription extinctive des réclamations internationales d'origine privée (Claims)' *Essays in Honor of J Basdevant* (Paris, 1960) 525ff; AR Ibrahim, 'The Doctrine of Laches in International Law' (1997) 83 *Virginia Law Review* 647ff; K Hobér, *Extinctive Prescription and Applicable Law in Interstate Arbitration* (Uppsala, 2001). See also JC Witenberg, *L'organisation judiciaire, la procédure et la sentence*

loses one right and another acquires that right, as in the case of prescription of territory. But there are also cases where extinctive prescription is an autonomous legal figure, ie where there is only the loss of one right and no creation of a concomitant one in some other party. Thus, if a state loses the right to bring a claim under diplomatic protection by reason of its long passivity, there is no creation of rights on the other part; an entitlement is lost, and not more than that.

There are many legal reasons for some time-limitation in the legal order: (i) the stability and certainty of legal relations; (ii) equitable considerations, since it may become difficult to defend a case after a long time, the relevant pieces, evidence and proofs not being available anymore; (iii) issues of a proper administration of justice; (iv) and the protection of legitimate expectations on the part of the subject having been confronted with prolonged silence and thus being entitled to rely on the implicit representation that a claim will not be pursued.[58] In such a case, the long-time passive subject will face a procedural obstacle to bring its claim,[59] or alternatively the substantive right will be considered to have extinguished.[60] The principle of good faith is crucial especially for fixing the relevant time-limit. Since there is no generally defined limitation, expressed in some figure, the relevant time has to be shaped from case to case in view of the relevant circumstances. The key aspect is that the time elapsed must appear to amount to an 'unjustified delay' so as to have induced the other party to reasonably believe that the claim will not anymore be pursued, or alternatively that the substantive right has been waived.[61] As was said in the leading case on the subject matter: 'The claimant has so long neglected his supposed rights as to justify a belief in their non-existence'.[62] In this sense, it can be said that in international law the doctrine of extinctive prescription rests more on the sanction of a fault (culpable passivity) than on the mechanical

internationales (Paris, 1937) 138ff; A Tommasi di Vignano, *La rinuncia in diritto internazionale* (Padova, 1960) 106ff; JP Müller, *Vertrauensschutz im Völkerrecht* (Köln, 1971) 67ff; WM Reisman, *Nullity and Revision* (New Haven CT, 1971) 387ff; A Oraison, *L'erreur dans les traités* (Paris, 1972) 165ff. In art 26 of the *Harvard Draft on the Responsibility of States for Injuries to the Economic Interests of Aliens* (1961) 55 *AJIL* 580, there is the following rule: 'If the presentation of a claim is delayed, after the exhaustion of local remedies to the extent provided for in Article 19, for a period of time which is unreasonable under the circumstances, the claim shall be barred by the lapse of time'. See also, for private international law, F Hage-Chahine, 'La prescription extinctive en droit international privé' (1995) 255 *RCADI* 229ff.

58 Müller, *Vertrauensschutz* 67ff.

59 R Pinto, 'La prescription en droit international' (1955-I) 87 *RCADI* 442ff.

60 G Dahm, *Völkerrecht*, vol III (Stuttgart, 1958) 171–72.

61 Müller, *Vertrauensschutz* 70. See also DP O'Connell, *International Law*, 2nd edn, vol II (London, 1970) 1066.

62 *Gentini* (1903) IX *RIAA* 561. See also an older case of the Swiss Federal Tribunal, where it was said in the context of a fundamental change of circumstances as a cause of extinction of obligations: 'En revanche, en permettant au rapport en cause de subsister durant des décennies, la partie grevée donne à entendre qu'elle n'attribue pas elle-même aux changements intervenus la signification d'une condition conventionnelle tacite … Dès lors, les principes de la bonne foi, qui doivent également gouverner les relations entre Etats, ne lui permettent pas d'y revenir postérieurement' (P Guggenheim (ed), *Répertoire suisse de droit international public*, vol I (Bern, 1975) 183).

passing of time (limitation).[63] There is here an evident proximity to the maxim 'no one can profit from its own wrong', which flows itself from the principle of good faith. As has been said in the *Williams* case (1890):

> If such situation be fairly imputable to a claimant's laches in withholding his demand, or, in Vattel's phrase 'when by his own fault he has suffered matters to proceed to such a state that there would be danger of mistaking the truth', prescription operates and resolves such facts against him.[64]

Also: 'But where there is valid reason for the withholding the case is different ... Incapacity, disability, want of legal agencies, prevention by war, well-grounded fear, and the like' are valid reasons for delay.[65] Thus, when the delay is due to conduct of the government which now attempts to rely on it, the arbitrator will not accept any prescription.[66] Any delay incurred to give a chance to negotiation or other means of pacific settlement of the dispute cannot be considered to amount to undue delay.[67] If that was not true, international law would ultimately disincentive the use of means of pacific settlement and conversely incentive the immediate and rough pressing through of claims.[68] This would be self-defeating and inappropriate.

Extinctive prescription has been applied in the context of the presentation of claims for diplomatic protection.[69] Contrary to what has been affirmed,[70] international law does not require the legal operator to refer to the time-bar rules of the applicable municipal law. The international case law shows that the tribunals have considered the matter as a question of international law, asking themselves whether there had been reasonable reasons for the concrete delay found, so that

[63] WM Reisman, *Nullity and Revision* (New Haven CT, 1971) 392ff; B Cheng, *General Principles of Law—As Applied by International Courts and Tribunals* (London, 1953) 379, 381ff.

[64] JB Moore, *History and Digest of the International Arbitrations to which the United States has been a Party*, vol IV (Washington DC, 1898) 4196.

[65] ibid, 4195.

[66] *Cook* (1928) 22 *AJIL* 189; *Roberts* (1903) IX *RIAA* 207: 'The contention that this claim is barred by the lapse of time would, if admitted, allow the Venezuelan Government to reap advantage from its own wrong in failing to make just reparation to Mr Quirk at the time the claim arose'.

[67] WM Reisman, *Nullity and Revision* (New Haven CT, 1971) 392: 'A delay in good faith that aims at either direct resolution of the dispute or an attempt to another process of decision cannot be considered as barring a subsequent demand for arbitration'.

[68] See to the same effect and mutatis mutandis the *Nottebohm* case, (1955) *ICJ Reports* 19–20: the offer to negotiate cannot be interpreted as the implicit waiver of a defence.

[69] See the *Ambatielos* case (1956) XII RIAA 103; a relatively recent instance can be found in the *LaGrand* case, (2001) *ICJ Reports* 486–87, § 53ff, six years and a half of 'delay'. See also Dissenting Opinion Buergenthal, ibid, 556–57, § 23. Further: *Avena* (2004-I) *ICJ Reports* 37–38, § 44. See also the legal note of the Legal Bureau of the Federal Political Department of 29 December 1970: (1976) 32 *ASDI* 152–53, affirming the existence of extinctive prescription.

[70] A Tommasi di Vignano, *La rinuncia in diritto internazionale* (Padova, 1960) 114ff; R Pinto, 'La prescription en droit international' (1955-I) 87 *RCADI* 445ff. In the agreement giving rise to the Jay arbitrations between the US and the UK, in arts 6 and 7 of the Jay Treaty (1794), the rule had been accepted that no claim having lapsed under municipal law could be presented to international arbitration. The rule was applied, for example in the *Fame* case (1797): A De La Pradelle and N Politis, *Recueil des arbitrages internationaux*, vol I (Paris, 1905) 120–21.

prescription would have to be denied, or whether the passivity is undue and created a legitimate expectation, so that prescription had to be admitted.[71]

Conversely, the doctrine of extinctive prescription has rarely been applied in direct inter-state claims. States are considered to have a greater leeway in the timing of the presentation of their claims. But there is no reason to think that the doctrine could not be applied at all—even if it will be applied with circumspection. The *Arbitral Award made by the King of Spain* case (1960) can be read as an instance of 'extinctive prescription' by acquiescence and estoppel.[72] An arbitral award that is not contested for six years cannot any more be challenged thereafter. Judge Oda was prepared to apply the doctrine to a silence of 15 years in the context of its claims to restoration and reparation of exploited lands.[73] Further, in 1992, Albanian claims for war reparations formulated against Germany were countered by the latter state through the invocation of extinctive prescription.[74] An interesting claim for which issues of prescription could arise, if it were presented, are the war reparations for aggression in favour of Angola to be paid by South Africa, as recognised by a resolution of the UN Security Council.[75] Such a claim has not been presented so far. Notice that the claim of extinctive prescription has also been

[71] See the various cases mentioned in PA Verykios, *La prescription en droit international public* (Paris, 1934) 154ff, eg the *Brand* (1863), *Horatio* (1869), *Canada* (1870), *Selkirk* (1872), *Mossman* (1875), *Yeaton* (1885), *Mechanic* (1885), *Roberts* (1903) or *Tagliaferro* (1903) cases.

[72] (1960) *ICJ Reports* 213.

[73] Dissenting Opinion Oda, *Certain Phosphate Lands in Nauru (Nauru v Australia, Preliminary Objections)* (1992) *ICJ Reports* 324. The Court did not treat this aspect on the preliminary stage: ibid, 255, § 38.

[74] P d'Argent, *Les réparations de guerre en droit international public* (Brussels, 2005) 228, 817ff.

[75] At the end of the 1970s, and more especially in the 1980s, Angola was subjected to armed aggression by South Africa, even having part of its territory temporarily occupied by the enemy army. This military aggression resulted in a train of destruction, material, economic and human. The United Nations Security Council, charged by art 24, § 1, of the Charter with 'primary responsibility for the maintenance of international peace and security' reacted to this situation by adopting a series of resolutions. These declared that there had been armed aggression, the occupation of territory, loss of life and the destruction of property. The Security Council described these acts of aggression as flagrant violations of the United Nations Charter and of public international law. The resolutions in question were numbers 387 of 31 March 1976, 428 of 6 May 1978, 447 of 28 March 1979, 454 of 2 November 1979, 475 of 27 June 1980, 545 of 20 December 1983, 546 of 6 January 1984, 567 of 20 June 1985, 571 of 20 September 1985, 577 of 6 December 1985 and 606 of 22 December 1987. In Resolution 571 of 1985, the Security Council decided to set up a Commission of Enquiry to evaluate the loss and damage resulting from South Africa's invasion of Angola's territory. The objective was to ensure that 'full and adequate' reparations were paid for the human and material damage resulting from these acts of aggression (§§ 6 and 7 of the Resolution). The Commission of Enquiry delivered its report on 22 November 1985 (Doc S/17684). The Report stated that, under the letter seizing it of its task, its principal remit was to evaluate the loss and damage resulting from the South African invasion in September 1985. However, since, Resolution 571 went further than that, the Commission did not feel obliged to confine itself to that invasion alone. It indicated the resulting loss and damage, but also, where it was in a position to do so, indicated other loss and damage, resulting from previous acts. The Commission evaluated the material loss and damage in the Cazombo region (for the invasion of September 1985, at US$604,000, and in total US$1–1.5 million), in the Ondjiva region (no loss and damage resulting from the military operation of September 1985 but a total of US$5–6 million when other operations were taken into account) and in Mavinga region (US$36,084,508 for the total loss and damage) (see §§ 79 et seq of the Commission's Report). The Commission subsequently said that it was not in a position

rejected sometimes on the facts of the case, notably since the delay did not appear excessive or unjustified.[76]

Overall, the doctrine of extinctive prescription has not found an intense application international law. There are many old cases of diplomatic protection, but there is not much recent case law. It is not frequent that passivity will be interpreted as the loss of a claim of reparation or the like in international law. The haphazard and political nature of international relations has as a consequence that the notion of time is diluted. It is here more frequent that claims are processed in the long rather than the short run. The application of acquiescence or estoppel is much more frequent in the context of the assertion of a right to which no protest is opposed; the mere loss of a claim for inaction is more exceptionally admitted. However, when the strict conditions of the law are met—under good faith and legitimate expectations, or undue delay—there is no doubt that the legal operator will at least be influenced by the doctrine of extinctive prescription. Whether it will be applied depends as much on the circumstances of the case as on the sources of particular international law applicable between the parties.

III. Good Faith and the Prohibition of Abuse of Rights

The concept of abuse of rights has many facets. It connotes sometimes the exercise of a right in the mere intention to injure another subject, or the exercise of a competence for a finality for which it was not granted, or else the exercise of a right notwithstanding a considerable and disproportionate harm for another subject, or finally the arbitrary or fraudulent exercise of rights.[77] The core point is that a subjective right or a competence is *exercised* in some way that the legal

to evaluate the loss and damage resulting from the deaths and wounding of civilians (§ 92). Nor was it in a position to form a correct evaluation of the loss and damage caused to the Angolan economy, the more so since the South African aggression was continuing. The Commission did however reproduce the figure of US$10,000 million put forward in that regard by Angola (§§ 93–96). Finally, the Commission warned that it was capable of estimating only a fraction of the loss and damage caused by South Africa's acts of aggression, and that the real loss and damage was substantially higher than the estimates it was putting forward (§ 100). The Security Council, in the unanimous Resolution 577 of 6 December 1985, § 1, endorsed the Commission of Enquiry's report and expressed its approval of the Commission's work. At § 7 of the same Resolution, the Council again demanded that South Africa pay 'full and adequate' compensation for the acts of aggression perpetrated.

[76] *Armed Activities (Democratic Republic of Congo v Uganda)* (2005) *ICJ Reports* 267, § 295.

[77] On the concept of abuse of rights in international law the literature is vast. See notably: N Politis, 'Le problème des limitations de la souveraineté et la théorie de l'abus des droits dans les rapports internationaux' (1925-I) 6 *RCADI* 1 ff; G Leibholz, 'Das Verbot der Willkür und des Ermessensmissbrauches im völkerrechtlichen Verkehr der Staaten' (1929) 1 *ZaöRV* 77ff; M Scerni, *L'abuso di diritto nei rapporti internazionali* (Rome, 1930); HC Gutteridge, 'Abuse of Rights' (1933) 5 *Cambridge Law Journal* 22ff; HJ Schlochauer, 'Die Theorie des abus de droit im Völkerrecht' (1933) 17 *Zeitschrift für Völkerrecht* 373ff; S Trifu, 'L'abus de droit dans le droit international' (PhD thesis, Paris, 1940); A Voss, 'Rechtsmissbrauch im Völkerrecht. Die Theorie der Gegenstandsbedingtheit der Rechtsnorm und das Verhältnis des Rechtsmissbrauches zur Clausula rebus sic stantibus' (PhD thesis, Münster, 1940); A Schindler, 'Das

order disapproves. The existence of the right is not contested; but the exercise has effects on others or on society which cannot be countenanced. The notion has thus inherently to do with the protection of other subjects and of society at large against excessive and toxic exercises of legal positions. As with good faith-legitimate expectations, the issue is the protection of the 'other'. The gist of the

Verbot des Rechtsmissbrauchs als allgemeiner Rechtsgrundsatz des Völkerrechts' (PhD thesis, Freiburg, 1942); ERC Van Bogaert, *Het rechtmisbruik in het volkenrecht* (Anvers, 1948); J Spiropoulos, 'L'abus du droit de vote par un membre du Conseil de Sécurité' (1949) 1 *Revue hellénique de droit international* 1ff; G Van Der Molen, *Misbruik van recht in het volkenrecht* (Amsterdam, 1949); AC Kiss, *L'abus de droit en droit international* (Paris, 1953); R Laun, 'Bemerkungen zum freien Ermessen und zum détournement de pouvoir im staatlichen Recht und im Völkerrecht', *Essays in Honor of H Kraus* (Göttingen, 1953) 128ff; G Schwarzenberger, 'Uses and Abuses of the "Abuse of Rights" in International Law' (1956) 42 *Transactions of the Grotius Society* 147ff; JES Fawcett, 'Détournement de pouvoir by International Organisations' (1957) 33 *BYIL* 311ff; JD Roulet, *Le caractère artificiel de la théorie de l'abus de droit en droit international public* (Neuchâtel, 1958); B Jankovic, 'L'interdiction de l'abus de droit en droit international public' (1959) 29 *Annuaire de l'Association des anciens auditeurs de l'Académie de La Haye* 5ff; R Laun, 'Le détournement de pouvoir im Völkerrecht', *Essays in Honor of G Gidel* (Paris, 1961) 437ff; A Schüle, 'Rechtsmissbrauch' in K Strupp and HJ Schlochauer (eds), *Wörterbuch des Völkerrechts*, vol III (Berlin, 1962) 69ff; FR Bondil, 'Le détournement de pouvoir en droit international public' (PhD thesis, Aix-en-Provence, 1966); D Casanovas y La Rosa, 'Abuso de derecho, desviación de poder y responsabilidad internacional. Notas sobre la acusación de abuso de derecho y desviación de poder en el asunto de la Barcelona Traction, Light and Power Company, Ltd' (1970) 23 *REDI* 465ff; GS Taylor, 'The Content of the Rule Against Abuse of Rights in International Law' (1972/1973) 46 *BYIL* 232ff; BO Iluyomade, 'The Scope and Content of a Complaint of Abuse of Right in International Law' (1975) 16 *Harvard International Law Journal* 47ff; V Paul, 'The Abuse of Rights and Bona Fides in International Law' (1977) 28 *ÖZöRV* 107ff; H Schiedermair, 'Das Verbot des Rechtsmissbrauches und die Regelung des Transitverkehrs nach Berlin' (1978) 38 *ZaöRV* 160ff; RK Neuhaus, *Das Rechtsmissbrauchsverbot im heutigen Völkerrecht* (Berlin, 1984); M Gestri, 'Considerazioni sulla teoria dell'abuso del diritto alla luce della prassi internazionale' (1994) 77 *RDI* 5ff; M Byers, 'Abuse of Rights: An Old Principle, a New Age' (2002) 47 *McGill Law Journal* 389ff; AC Kiss, 'Abuse of Rights' in R Wolfrum (ed), *The Max Planck Encyclopedia of Public International Law*, vol I (Oxford, 2012) 20ff. See also M Scerni, *I principî generali di diritto riconosciuti dalle nazioni civili* (Padoue, 1932) 128ff; E Härle, *Die allgemeinen Entscheidungsgrundlagen des Ständigen Internationalen Gerichtshofes* (Berlin, 1933) 182ff; H Lauterpacht, *The Function of Law in the International Community* (Oxford, 1933) 286ff; G Salvioli, 'Les règles générales de la paix' (1933-IV) 46 *RCADI* 66ff; G Scelle, *Précis de droit des gens*, vol II (Paris, 1934) 37ff; H Lauterpacht, 'Règles générales du droit de la paix' (1937-IV) 62 *RCADI* 340–43, 389–91; P Guggenheim, 'La validité et la nullité des actes juridiques internationaux' (1949-I) 74 *RCADI* 250ff; RA Rolin, 'Les principes de droit international public' (1950-II) 77 *RCADI* 402ff; B Cheng, *General Principles of Law—As Applied by International Courts and Tribunals* (London, 1953) 121ff; G Schwarzenberger, 'The Fundamental Principles of International Law' (1955-I) 87 *RCADI* 304ff; H Lauterpacht, *The Development of International Law by the International Court* (London, 1957) 162ff; G Schwarzenberger, *International Law—As Applied by International Courts and Tribunals*, vol I (London, 1957) 47ff; vol III (London, 1976) 449ff; G Dahm, *Völkerrecht*, vol I, Stuttgart, 1958) 194ff; FV Garcia-Amador, 'State Responsibility: Some New Problems' (1958-II) 94 *RCADI* 376ff; L Siorat, *Le problème des lacunes en droit international* (Paris, 1958) 395ff; W Wengler, *Völkerrecht*, vol I (Berlin, 1964) 392ff; R Quardi, *Diritto internazionale pubblico*, 5th edn (Naples, 1968) 222ff; JHW Verzijl, *International Law in Historical Perspective*, vol I (Leiden, 1968) 316ff; D Carreau, *Souveraineté et coopération monétaire internationale* (Paris, 1970) 119ff; C De Visscher, *De l'équité dans le règlement arbitral ou judiciaire des litiges de droit international public* (Paris, 1972) 35ff; J Ballenegger *La pollution en droit international* (Geneva, 1975) 67ff; J Verhoeven, *La reconnaissance internationale dans la pratique contemporaine* (Paris, 1975) 617ff; E Klein, *Umweltschutz im völkerrechtlichen Nachbarrecht* (Berlin, 1976) 110ff; E Zoller, *La bonne foi en droit international public* (Paris, 1977) 109ff; M Gounelle, *La motivation des actes juridiques en droit international public* (Paris, 1979) 215ff; P Reuter, 'Quelques réflexions sur l'équité en droit international' (1980) 15 *RBDI* 179ff; JG Lammers, *Pollution of*

matter is here that the *finality* for which the rights are granted cannot be ignored. Good faith takes in this context a finalistic bent: rights and competences shall not be exercised in a way that contravenes the aim of that rights and that has inappropriate effects. The concept of abuse of rights is moreover of a negative nature. The law does not tell a subject how to exercise its rights. It rather draws an external and minimum limit which that exercise should not overstep. According to the different subject areas of the law, the negative criterion is stricter or looser: stricter eg in the scrutiny of administrative acts by an international administrative tribunal; and looser for example in the context of the drawing of maritime baselines following the general direction of the coast. The doctrine of abuse of rights ultimately rests on the conception of relativity of rights: a right is always exercised in the social space; a legal operator cannot therefore completely ignore its effects on the other subjects. There are some outer limits the legal order draws in order to temper the excessively egocentric or harmful exercise of legal positions.

According to the predominant view, the principle on prohibition of abuse of rights flows from the principle of good faith.[78] Indeed, it is often quoted in the case law together with the principle of good faith.[79] Good faith cannot countenance the exercise of a right which is gravely harmful to others and which goes beyond the sphere of what the right intended to allow. In some cases, the matter is even reduced to the principle of legitimate expectations, since a subject can reasonably rely on the fact that the other state will not abuse its legal positions.[80] However, the better explanation is that abuse of rights constitutes a separate (and negative) heading: good faith here commands the protection of the finality of rights and competences.

International Watercourses (The Hague, 1984) 572ff; S Jovanovic, *Restriction des compétences discrétionnaires des Etats en droit international* (Paris, 1988) 167ff; BD Smith, *State Responsibility and the Marine Environment* (Oxford, 1988) 83ff; W Benedek, *Die Rechtsordnung des GATT aus völkerrechtlicher Sicht* (Berlin, 1990) 383ff; P Hector, *Das völkerrechtliche Abwägungsgebot* (Berlin, 1992) 141ff; L Oppenheim (RY Jennings and A Watts, eds), *International Law*, vol I, 9th edn (London, 1992) 407ff; W Meng, *Extraterritoriale Jurisdiktion im öffentlichen Wirtschaftsrecht* (Berlin, 1994) 589ff. For the case law of the PCIJ/ICJ: GG Fitzmaurice, *The Law and Procedure of the International Court of Justice, Collected Edition*, vol I (Cambridge, 1986) 12ff, 183–84; vol II (Cambridge, 1986) 609ff, 668ff; H Thirlway, 'The Law and Procedure of the International Court of Justice (1960°89): General Principles and Sources of Law' (1989) 60 *BYIL* 25ff. And see also Kolb, *Bonne* 429ff.

Whether the concept of abuse of rights can apply to all types of internationally relevant conduct is controversial. Thus, it has been held that the highly discretionary powers of the UN Security Council could not be scrutinised under the doctrine of abuse of rights: M Zambelli, *La constatation des situations de l'article 39 de la Charte des Nationjs Unies par le Conseil de sécurité* (Basle, 2002) 101. There is however no accepted conception on such issues. For a contrary view, see eg A Orakhelashvili, 'The Power of the United Nations Security Council to Detremine a Threat to the Peace' (2006) 1 *Irish Yearbook of International Law* 73–74.

[78] See the literature quoted in Kolb, *Bonne* 440, fn 311, for example A Verdross and B Simma, *Universelles Völkerrecht*, 3rd edn (Berlin, 1984) 48.

[79] *Certain German Interests in Polish Upper Silesia* (1926) PCIJ ser A, no 7, p 30; *Fileting in the Gulf of St Laurent* case (1985) 82 *ILR* 614.

[80] See the Swiss Memorial in *Losinger* (1936) PCIJ ser C, no 78, pp 36–37.

A great number of authors recognise the existence of the principle of prohibition of abuse of rights in international law and many pleadings or individual opinions at the PCIJ/ICJ refer to that notion.[81] The decisive point—as we will see later in this chapter and in the chapters on international administrative law, WTO, international investment law or on perfidy in the law of war—is that the notion is applied in international practice. However, there are also some authors who rest on a restrictive or denying approach: (i) for some, abuse of rights is not yet a rule of positive international law but is in the process to become one (and since the time they have written may have become one);[82] (ii) some others are doubtful on the role of that principle in international law but accept that it could apply in some cases;[83] (iii) for still others the principle remains a policy abstraction having a legislative or an equitable role, but not being part and parcel of positive international law;[84] (iv) finally, some authors entirely deny the principle any foundation in international law.[85] Several arguments have been advanced against a doctrine on the prohibition of abuse of rights in international law. They must be briefly considered and rebutted.

A. The Logomachy Argument

According to this view, the doctrine of abuse of rights rests on an abuse of language and on a logical impossibility. How can there be a 'right' at all if its abuse is not tolerated? The point is then rather that the right itself does not exist: the right ceases to exist where the abuse commences. Thus, the subject 'abusing its right'

[81] See the long lists in Kolb, *Bonne* 442ff. A newer individual opinion can be found in the Dissenting Opinion Parra-Aranguren, *Gabcikovo-Nagymaros* (1997) *ICJ Reports* 231, § 22, where the judge was prepared to apply the prohibition if its elements were shown to exist.

[82] A Schüle, 'Rechtsmissbrauch' in K Strupp and HJ Schlochauer (eds), *Wörterbuch des Völkerrechts*, vol III (Berlin, 1962) 71; P Fedozzi, 'Introduzione al diritto internazionale e parte generale', in P Fedozzi and S Romano (eds), *Trattato di diritto internazionale*, vol I, 3rd edn (Padova, 1940) 529–33, esp 533.

[83] JHW Verzijl, *International Law in Historical Perspective*, vol I (Leyden, 1968) 316ff. At p 320, there is however this sentence: 'There are, however, perhaps—relatively rare—cases in which a State could correctly be accused of exercising a right abusively. A standard example of this is the casting of a negative vote in the Security Council or the General Assembly of the United Nations by a Member State, on the occasion of the request of a State for admission to the Organization on the ground … that other applicants for membership should be admitted simultaneously.' See also W Rudolf, 'Territoriale Grenzen der staatlichen Rechtssetzung' *Berichte der deutschen Gesellschaft für Völkerrecht*, vol 11 (Karlsruhe, 1973) 19–21.

[84] I Brownlie, *System of the Law of Nations: State Responsibility*, Pt I (Oxford, 1983) 51–52; BD Smith, *State Responsibility and the Marine Environment* (Oxford, 1988) 85.

[85] See notably AP Sereni, *Diritto internazionale*, vol I (Milan, 1956) 118 and vol III (Milan, 1962) 1514; R Quadri, *Diritto internazionale pubblico*, 5th edn (Naples, 1968) 222–224); A Cavaglieri, 'Règles générales du droit de la paix' (1929-I) 26 *RCADI* 543–45; C Dupuis, 'Règles générales du droit de la paix', (1930-II) 32 *RCADI* 92–95; W Wengler, *Völkerrecht*, vol I (Berlin, 1964) 392–94; JD Roulet, *Le caractère artificiel de la théorie de l'abus de droit en droit international public* (Neuchâtel, 1958) 143ff; A Lester, 'Pollution' in AH.Garretson, D Hayton and CJ Olmstaed, *The Law of International Drainage Basins* (New York, 1967) 97; RK Neuhaus, *Das Rechtsmissbrauchsverbot im heutigen Völkerrecht* (Berlin, 1984) 183–84, 185ff.

simply acts outside the bounds of its right as correctly interpreted: 'The theory of the abuse of rights seems absurd to us, because as soon as there is an abuse, the right no longer exists'.[86] The whole issue then turns into one of interpretation of the right and of its limits. But a separate doctrine of abuse of rights is unnecessary.

This argument is not convincing.[87] Whether the problem is solved through the separate intervention of the doctrine of abuse of rights or whether arguments as to the reasonable and non-abusive limits of the right are transformed into issues of interpretation, the legal operator will in both cases have recourse to a similar reasoning. In one case he or she will consider that the exercise of the right has to be limited and in the other he or she will affirm that the right does not cover a certain exercise—on the basis of considerations which are in both cases rooted in reasonableness and non-abuse. On the whole, it may even be more prudent to select the first, more restrictive, course by relying on the abuse of rights doctrine, since in that case the right of the state is not affected and only a particular exercise of the right is condemned; whereas if the operator affirms that the right does not extend at all to a certain course of conduct, this statement may often have a larger scope by denying the availability of the right in its entirety in the given context (the point rests manifestly on the concrete formulation chosen). Moreover, if the right does not extend to a certain behaviour, this does not automatically mean that the subject is acting illegally. There are also gaps in the law, where the position is in the first place 'neither permitted nor prohibited'. To fill the gap and to conclude that a certain conduct is or is not unlawful, the operator may thus in such cases need the recourse to the doctrine of abuse of rights or to some equivalent principle. Consequently, the doctrine of abuse of rights may have been chased by the door; it will come back through the window. The logomachy argument is thus at best circular.

B. The Argument of the Individualistic Nature of International Society

This argument holds that international society is based on an individualistic and egocentric pattern, where the states are sovereign, possess power and are bound by international obligations only when they clearly assumed them. The consequence of this setting of the stage is that state rights and liberties cannot be scrutinised by an operator as to proper finality or use. States have not accepted such a limitation in favour of the 'other', ie such a community-oriented international law.[88]

[86] M Seara Vazquez, *Cosmic International Law* (Detroit, 1965) 121, fn 38. See also Dupuis, op cit, 92–93; Roulet, op cit, 37, 39–40, 104, 114; K Wolff, 'Les principes généraux du droit applicables dans les rapports internationaux' (1931-II) 36 *RCADI* 518–19; C Parry, 'Plural Nationality and Citizenship with Special Reference to the Commonwealth' (1953) 30 *BYIL* 254–55.

[87] See RK Neuhaus, *Das Rechtsmissbrauchsverbot im heutigen Völkerrecht* (Berlin, 1984) 107ff; G Salvioli, 'Les règles générales de la paix' (1933-IV) 46 *RCADI* 66–68.

[88] See M Scerni, *L'abuso di diritto nei rapporti internazionali* (Rome, 1930) 69ff, 73ff and esp 79ff; A Cavaglieri, *Corso di diritto internazionale*, 3rd edn (Naples, 1934) 508.

This argument is only limitedly useful. It indicates that a certain prudence must prevail in the application of doctrines of the abuse of rights. But that is true as much in international as in internal law. A society based on freedom of the subjects cannot countenance an aggressive use of abuse of rights arguments, where some judge arrogates to himself the exacting role of saying which are the good, and which are the less good, uses of the right.[89] The intervention of the judge must be limited to cases of manifest abuse. Beyond the pale of this consideration, the argument has but little merit. First, the arguments based on the structural characteristic of international society are not normative in themselves. They cannot indicate whether a doctrine of abuse of rights exists or not in positive international law (all the more since there exists no purely individualistic society—if it did, there could be no law at all in it). It is a matter of practice and legislation to fix the place and limits of a principle of international law, not a priori speculations about the nature of international society. Second, a subjective right is always correlative to some obligation (while the opposite is not necessarily true). Thus, the issue turns always on a *relation* between two or more subjects. What could be the meaning of 'individualistic' here? There is a bond, not individualism or solipsism. Consequently, why should individualism work only to the favour of the party claiming a right and not in favour of the one burdened by the correlative obligation?[90] Both are sovereign and equal: why should a liberty operate only for the one and not the other? The only tenable view is to apply the 'individualism' to both, but by that very course the concept of individualism dissolves almost entirely. The truth then appears more clearly: the other subject must be protected against egregiously abusive exercises of a right. International practice vindicates this view, as we shall see in due course. Third, it has been claimed that the doctrine of abuse of rights is even more important in international law because of the weakness of institutional procedures and the concomitant difficulties to achieve the adjustment of conflicts in interest and rights.[91] It has also been claimed that the doctrine of abuse of rights can incite to a certain moderation in the exercise of rights[92]—precisely if it is

[89] H Lauterpacht, *The Development of International Law by the International Court* (London, 1958) 164: '[The doctrine of abuse of rights] is full of potentialities and … places a considerable power, not devoid of a legislative character, in the hands of a judicial tribunal … The doctrine of abuse of rights is therefore an instrument which, apart from other reasons calling for caution in the administration of international justice, must be wielded with studied restraint'.

[90] G Salvioli, 'Les règles générales de la paix' (1933-IV) 46 *RCADI* 69: 'On parle de caractère individualiste, mais le rapport international est un rapport entre deux sujets: auquel de ces deux sujets faut-il alors assigner la prépondérance quant à ce caractère individualiste? Pourquoi devrait-on affirmer le principe individualiste seulement en faveur d'une de ces Parties, le titulaire du droit?'.

[91] H Lauterpacht, *The Development of International Law by the International Court* (London, 1958) 162: 'particularly important in the international society in which the legislative process by regular organs is practically non-existent'. GG Fitzmaurice, 'The General Principles of International Law Considered from the Standpoint of the Rule of Law' (1957-II) 92 *RCADI* 54; G Dahm, *Völkerrecht*, vol I (Stuttgart, 1958) 195: 'bildet es gerade in der gegenwärtigen Übergangslage ein schwer entbehrliches Gegengewicht gegen die Überspannung der staatlichen Hoheitsgewalt'.

[92] E Härle, *Die allgemeinen Entscheidungsgrundlagen des Ständigen Internationalen Gerichtshofs* (Berlin, 1933) 183–84.

recognised and applied. This would have a welcome prophylactic effect in a society whose so-called 'individualistic' character tends to produce anarchy.

C. The Argument of the Ideological Divide within International Society

According to this argument, the application of a doctrine of abuse of rights supposes a value judgment in view of equitable adjustments. But international society is so split in terms of ideological and cultural values that common criteria for that value judgment are non-existent. The doctrine of abuse of rights supposes a certain homogeneity of values. It can thus exist only in municipal societies.[93]

On its face, this is a truly weak argument. Is international society not one where equity has been applied to many legal issues, from maritime delimitation to the sharing of resources and to the issues of state succession? Is municipal society not one where the split of values is often extreme, spanning from communists to liberals and then to nationalists? Are there not, in international society, elites which have often studied in the same universities and share even a common language? Be that as it may, if there really was a complete absence of common values and criteria, there could be no true law in international society. But there is such law. Overall, it can thus be said that this argument is a massive exaggeration and that the possibility of a doctrine of abuse of rights on the level of positive law is not forestalled by such dogmatic considerations.

D. The Argument of the Non-Finalistic Nature of International Legal Norms

According to this view, the international law-giver, contrary to the municipal one, does not prescribe a certain finality to be pursued by the international norms it edicts. This state of affairs renders the application of a doctrine of abuse of rights, which is a finalistic concept, out of order. It is however true that these authors admit that finalistic norms may exist in the context of particular international law, for example in the closer knit of an international organisation or within conventional relationships. But this would in any event not be true of general international law.[94]

This argument is the natural prolongation of the ones on the individualistic nature of international society and on its ideological rifts. We may thus refer to

[93] RK Neuhaus, *Das Rechtsmissbrauchsverbot im heutigen Völkerrecht* (Berlin, 1984) 187ff; W Wengler, *Völkerrecht*, vol I (Berlin, 1964) 392.

[94] See M Gestri, 'Considerazioni sulla teoria dell'abuso del diritto alla luce della prassi internazionale' (1994) 77 *RDI* 11 and 51ff; RK Neuhaus, *Das Rechtsmissbrauchsverbot im heutigen Völkerrecht* (Berlin, 1984) 83ff; W Wengler, *Völkerrecht*, vol I (Berlin, 1964) 393; M Scerni, *L'abuso di diritto nei rapporti internazionali* (Rome, 1930) 73–74, 84ff.

the arguments in rebuttal made there. More specifically, it can be recalled that the doctrine of abuse of rights was first developed in the context of private law, where the rights are mainly based on the personal freedom and not on some social finality engrafted upon them. Yet, this has never been considered to amount to a decisive obstacle to a doctrine on abuse of rights. Further, it must be emphasised that a purely 'non-finalistic' right or legal position is a contradiction in terms. Legal positions are always created with some finalities in mind. This is apparent when one thinks about the fact that 'teleological' interpretation is a general device of legal construction, applicable to all norms.[95] Finally, the distinction between general and particular international law is one of degree. If the doctrine can exist in one, it can also exist in the other. The strength of common 'finalities' may be diluted in going from the particular to the general, but it does not disappear altogether. Finally, international practice shows that considerations of abuse of rights are often applied to general norms of international law, such as the rules on expulsion, the grant or the loss of nationality, the expropriation of foreign assets, etc.

E. The Absence of a Regular Judicial Function in International Law and Legal Uncertainty

According to the first limb of this view, the doctrine of abuse of rights is fundamentally a judicial doctrine. It supposes a judge who will appreciate and apportion. In international law, the judicial function remains too marginal to accept a doctrine of abuse of rights,[96] which would lead to excessive legal uncertainty.[97]

Once more, these are arguments going to the degree rather than to the existence of the doctrine of abuse of rights. The doctrine does not depend on the judge but is simply particularly strong in its hands. This is true of all the principles of

[95] See art 31, § 1, of the VCLT, 1969.

[96] C Dupuis, 'Règles générales du droit de la paix', (1930-II) 32 *RCADI* 94: 'Entre les Etats, il n'y a pas—en principe—de juge qui s'impose, et c'est raison de plus, sans doute, de bannir la théorie de l'abus de droit du droit international, sous peine d'y multiplier les controverses irritantes et les contestations sans fin'; RK Neuhaus, *Das Rechtsmissbrauchsverbot im heutigen Völkerrecht* (Berlin, 1984) 191–94; W Wengler, *Völkerrecht*, vol I, Berlin, 1964) 394.

[97] JHW Verzijl, *International Law in Historical Perspective*, vol I (Leyden, 1968) 317: 'It has such a wide scope and is so completely impossible to define that it bristles with dangers to the certainty of the law in the international community'; W Rudolf, 'Territoriale Grenzen der staatlichen Rechtssetzung' *Berichte der deutschen Gesellschaft für Völkerrecht*, vol 11 (Karlsruhe, 1973) 21; H Lessing, 'Das Recht der Staatsangehörigkeit und die Aberkennung der Staatsangehörigkeit zu Straf- und Sicherungszwecken' *Bibliotheca Visseriana*, vol 12 (Leiden, 1937) 86: 'Es fehlt den Sätzen die Determinierbarkeit auch nur in Umrissen'; C Dupuis, 'Règles générales du droit de la paix' (1930-II) 32 *RCADI* 94: 'La théorie de l'abus de droit a le défaut d'ouvrir largement et trop largement la porte à l'arbitraire du juge, car s'il suffit au juge de dire qu'il y a abus de droit pour écarter le droit, il lui est trop aisé de substituer dans ses jugements l'équité, c'est-à-dire son équité, celle qui, pour bien intentionnée qu'elle soit, justifie l'ancien proverbe français: Dieu nous garde de l'équité des Parlements'; JD Roulet, *Le caractère artificiel de la théorie de l'abus de droit en droit international public* (Neuchâtel, 1958) 144; M Scerni, *L'abuso di diritto nei rapporti internazionali* (Rome, 1930) 83; R Quadri, *Diritto internazionale pubblico*, 5th edn (Naples, 1968) 223.

international law, such as good faith, equity, proportionality and others. The doctrine of abuse of rights is no exception in this regard. And it must be emphasised that the international judicial function has developed considerably over the last hundred years. The same is true for the danger of legal uncertainty. It cautions for a restrictive use of the doctrine—but not more than that.

F. The Argument of the Flexibility of International Norms

An additional argument is about the lack of usefulness of a doctrine of abuse of rights in an international legal order which is composed mainly of vague, flexible and indeterminate norms, which can be interpreted in a way to avoid hardship.[98]

Apart from the fact that only some norms of international law have such a character and that now many international norms are precise and rigid, it must be emphasised that the doctrine of abuse of rights has often been considered particularly important in the context of discretionary rights, ie in the area of large and vague state powers.[99] The doctrine against abuse has then the function to limit the discretionary behaviour of states so as to ensure that it does not exceed the bounds of arbitrary and malevolent action. As a matter of principle, there is a continuum of precision and flexibility in international norms. When the discretionary element prevails the doctrine of abuse of rights has the function to define outer limits; when the precision predominates, the doctrine has the function to sanction the finalities inherent in the norm against misuse of circumvention.

G. The Argument of Incompatibility with a Will-Oriented Legal Order

It has been said that good faith and the prohibition of abuse of rights in particular are non-existent in international law for the reason that they cannot be squared with the fact that this legal order is based on the autonomy of consent, whereby no obligation can be imposed on a state without its will.[100]

[98] JD Roulet, *Le caractère artificiel de la théorie de l'abus de droit en droit international public* (Neuchâtel, 1958) 114; M Scerni, *L'abuso di diritto nei rapporti internazionali* (Rome, 1930) 57–58.

[99] According to the FAO: 'The doctrine [of abuse of rights] is more likely to find grounds for application where a right is broadly defined, and no express limitations are established to its exercise' (*Doc no FI/HSF/TC/92/8:* 'Legal Issue Concerning High Sea Fishing' June 1992, in: The Netherlands Institute for the Law of the Sea (ed), *International Organizations and the Law of the Sea, Documentary Yearbook*, vol 8 (1992), p 530). Or, in the slightly too absolute words of GS Taylor, 'The Content of the Rule Against Abuse of Rights in International Law' (1972/1973) 46 *BYIL* 350. The doctrine of abuse of rights can manifestly be applied also to limited competences of states, where the particular finalities allow a powerful application of the doctrine: see J Verhoeven, *La reconnaissance internationale dans la pratique contemporaine* (Paris, 1975) 626.

[100] M Koskenniemi, *From Apology to Utopia—The Structure of the International Legal Argument* (Helsinki, 1989) 233, 281.

This argument cannot be countenanced. International practice itself shows that both these principles are applicable in international law. Indeed, the international legal order needs their operation to fulfil some necessary functions. In this sense, these principles flow from the will of the subjects of law having created this legal order. Moreover, the 'will-oriented' international legal order is but an abstraction. It cannot serve to determine which legal rules are part or not part of the positive law. To answer to that latter question, the correct way is to examine the positive law sources and not to raise dogmatic structural arguments. Consequently, it might even occur that, following a careful inventory, some norms show that the international legal order is not purely consensual. A refined theoretical explanation of its structure then becomes indispensable. In short terms, structural arguments are not normative but only descriptive.

As can be seen, there is no decisive argument against a doctrine of abuse of rights in international law. The point is rather whether positive international law has developed that principle and to what extent it has done so. This falls now to be analysed. A perusal of international practice shows that the doctrine has been applied in four different contexts:[101]

1. *The prohibition to cause intentional harm*: there are a series of conventions which expressly prohibit acts performed with the intention of harming another subject (the Roman law *aemulatio*).[102] There is also older case law on the matter. Thus, in the *Behring Sea Fur Seal* arbitration (1892), the English agent, Sir Charles Russell, admitted that a malevolent act would found an international claim against the acting state.[103] There is also case law in the context of international administrative law, which will be mentioned below.[104] The prohibition of action whose intent is to harm another subject is the core of a doctrine of abuse of rights. But the latter extends much further. A question which arises in the contexts of malevolent acts is to what extent the intention to harm must be the sole motive for action. In analogy to civil law cases, the correct answer seems to be that it must at least be the preponderant reason for action. Whether this is the case must be ascertained in the circumstances, in view of all the available evidence and by drawing reasonable inferences from the general experience of life.
2. *The détournement de pouvoir (misuse of authority)*: this type of abuse of rights comes from the French administrative jurisprudence. It refers to public law competences rather than to private law rights. The gist of the matter is the sanction of the finality of a norm: there is a *détournement* or misuse when a

[101] A long list of specific questions in which the doctrine of abuse of rights has been considered in the literature and in practice can be consulted in Kolb, *Bonne* 476–86.

[102] See eg arts 4 and 20 of the Geneva Statute on International Exchanges by Railway of 1923: L Le Fur and G Chklaver, *Recueil de textes de droit international public*, 2nd edn (Paris, 1934) 653, 658.

[103] See B Cheng, *General Principles of Law—As Applied by International Courts and Tribunals* (London, 1953) 122.

[104] Ch 7, section III.

public authority uses its powers to pursue other aims than the ones for which the power was granted.[105] Such a course of conduct leads to an illegality under abuse of rights. The question of misuse of powers has often been posed in the context of expropriation, expulsion of persons, registration of ships under a flag, and the like. Thus, in the *Lalanne Ledour* case (1902), the chief of the local customs did not allow the exportation of cattle which was to be sent by Mr Ledour to French Guyana because of an intervention by the President of Guyana. The latter had concurrent commercial interests. The arbitral tribunal concluded that there had been an abuse of authority.[106] In the *Tacna Arica* case (1925), the arbitrator recognised that the conscription of certain Peruvian personnel by Chile had the sole aim to impede these persons to vote in the imminent plebiscite on the fate of the territory.[107] In the *Fletcher Smith* case (1929), an expropriation has been condemned by the arbitrator because it was not performed in regard of a public interest but to satisfy some concurrent private investors.[108] These older cases show that the doctrine is established since a long time in international law. It is not merely the outflow of a modern refinement of public international law.[109] We may here also mention article 18 of the ECHR (1950), which under the title 'abuse of power' reads as follows: 'The restrictions permitted [to human rights] under this Convention to the said rights and freedoms shall not be applied for any purpose other than those for which they have been prescribed'.[110] Some rights listed in the Convention can, under relevant § 2 of the various provisions, be restricted for reasons of public interest or for the protection of rights and freedoms of others. The issue here is precisely to guarantee that the limitations will be made only for these public policy reasons and not for other, alien, purposes. The issue is plainly one of *détournement de pouvoir* or misuse of authority.

3. *The manifest disproportion of interests*: there are often competing claims and conduct in the context of use of territory, pollution, use of common rivers or lakes, use of common spaces such as the high seas or extra-atmospheric space, or even in the context of use of military force on the one hand and protection

[105] G Cornu, *Vocabulaire juridique*, 9th edn (Paris, 2011) 339.

[106] *Lalanne Ledour* (1902) X *RIAA* 18.

[107] *Tacna Arica* (1925) II *RIAA* 941.

[108] *Fletcher Smith* (1929) II *RIAA* 917–18. See similarly *Ballistini* (1902) X *RIAA* 18–21.

[109] For further case law and references to the many pleadings at the PCIJ and ICJ, see Kolb, *Bonne* 465.

[110] See Y Arai, 'Article 18' in: P van Dijk, F van Hoof, A van Rijn and L Zwaak (eds), *Theory and Practice of the European Convention on Human Rights*, 4th edn (Antwerp, 2006) 1093ff; FG Jacobs, RC White and C Ovey, *The European Convention on Human Rights*, 5nd edn (Oxford, 2010) 127–28; D Harris, M O'Boyle and C Warbrick, *Law of the European Convention on Human Rights*, 3rd edn (Oxford, 2014) 857ff; WA Schabas, *The European Convention on Human Rights—A Commentary* (Oxford, 2015) 623ff, with a bibliography. JF Renucci, *Droit européen des droits de l'homme*, 2nd edn (Paris, 2012) 885ff. Thus, a deprivation of nationality solely for the purpose of expulsion could constitute an evasion of the obligations under art 3 of Protocol IV to the ECHR and thus an abuse of rights: *Boudellaa v Bosnia-Herzegovina*, Human Rights Chamber, 136 *ILR* 372–74, 373, § 192.

of the civilian population on the other. The law here tries to find some equilibrium between the competing principles of *neminem laedit qui suo jure utitur* and *sic utere tuo ut alienum non laedas.*[111] In a robust vision of this function of the law, it has been said: 'There is such an abuse of right each time the general interest of the community is injuriously affected as the result of the sacrifice of an important social or individual interest to a less important, though hitherto legally recognised individual right'.[112] It is on the basis of this conception of abuse of rights that whole branches of international law have been developed, especially the principle that the use of a territory should not lead to the infringement of the rights of other states or to the creation of excessive harm on the territory of the latter.[113] The *Lake Lanoux* arbitration (1957) is a typical example of this balancing-up approach concerning the use of water and the effects of unilateral conduct on neighbouring territory.[114] The same approach has been followed in many other cases, as for example in the *Pulp Mills (Argentina v Uruguay)* case (2010)[115] or the *Indus Waters Kishenganga* arbitration (*Pakistan v India)* (2013).[116] State authorities have used the same principles in order to judge the legality of extraterritorial US legislation in the context of trust law.[117] Similarly, article 51, § 5, letter b, of Additional Protocol I of 1977 to the four Geneva Conventions of 1949, which condemns attacks causing excessive civilian collateral damage in regard of the military advantage anticipated,[118] responds to the same logic of a prohibition of abuse of rights. The issue is manifestly one of balancing up. The only collateral damage declared to be unlawful is the one which appears to be 'excessive' with regard to the military advantage anticipated.

4. *Arbitrary action, unreasonable conduct and fraud*: there is a last and more general sphere of abuse of rights. It encompasses arbitrary, unreasonable and fraudulent acts. Arbitrary conduct rests on acts which are manifestly unjustified with regard to the facts, objectively shocking exercises of a right, acts injuring the elementary legal conscience or certain discriminatory exercises

[111] See the many references in L Oppenheim (R Jennings and A Watts, eds), *International Law*, 9th edn (London, 1992) 408ff. See also among many others J Barboza, 'International Liability for the Injurious Consequences of Acts not Prohibited by International Law and Protection of the Environment' (1994-III) 247 *RCADI* 319ff.

[112] H Lauterpacht, *The Function of Law in the International Community* (Oxford, 1933) 286.

[113] See *Corfu Channel* (1949) 223 *ICJ Reports* 223 and *Trail Smelter* (1941) III *RIAA* 1963, from where the main principles of modern environmental protection law have developed.

[114] *Lake Lanoux* (1957) XII *RIAA* 281ff.

[115] *Pulp Mills (Argentina v Uruguay)* (2010-I) *ICJ Reports* 55–56, § 101, harm to the environment by construction of industrial installations.

[116] *Indus Waters Kishenganga* arbitration (*Pakistan v India)* (2013) 154 *ILR* 171ff.

[117] See W Meng, *Extraterritoriale Jurisdiktion im öffentlichen Wirtschaftsrecht* (Berlin, 1994) 416.

[118] Considered to be indiscriminate is: '(b) an attack which may be expected to cause incidental loss of civilian life, injury to civilians, damage to civilian objects, or a combination thereof, which would be excessive in relation to the concrete and direct military advantage anticipated'. On this provision, see eg Y Sandoz, C Swinarski and B Zimmermann (eds), *Commentary on the Additional Protocols of 8 June 1977 to the Geneva Conventions of 12 August 1949* (Geneva, 1987) 613ff.

of rights.[119] Unreasonable acts are those which are beyond the pale of a sharable justification. Finally, fraudulent acts are those which seek to circumvent a legal prohibition by recourse to subtle formal constructions. In a sense, the pragmatic common lawyer will refrain from seeking an excessively precise distinction between these concepts. As was graphically stated by FA Mann: 'I am not going to weary the Court with the somewhat unprofitable problem of drawing the line between abuse, arbitrariness and discrimination. These terms are often used interchangeably and all of them indicate the same idea, the same principle…'.[120] There are whole branches of international law which are based on the prohibition of 'arbitrary' action, notably in the context of human rights.[121] Thus, famously, article 6, § 1, of the Covenant on Civil and Political Rights (CCPR) of 1966 holds that 'no one shall be arbitrarily deprived of his life'.[122] It is true that to a large extent these notions have become autonomous from the concept of abuse of rights. In effect, the latter notion is not mentioned when 'arbitrary' acts are stigmatised. However, we should not ignore the fact that all these special rules have flown from a polymorph galaxy centred on good faith and the prohibition of abusive action. We may also recall the jurisprudence of the ICTY, holding that the UN Security Council could not indulge into arbitrary action.[123] Another example verging on fraud and circumvention is the modification of municipal law with a view to extract certain valuable assets from the mass of items to be transferred by state succession.[124] Similar issues have arisen in the context of fraudulent nationality in the UN Claims Commission for Iraq in the 1990s.[125] Finally, we may also emphasise that article 17 of the ECHR of 1950, under the title 'abuse of rights', is a saving clause against activities or acts aimed at the destruction of rights and freedoms provided for in the Convention.[126] This is a special type

[119] On the link between abuse of rights and arbitrary action, see eg BO Iluyomade, 'The Scope and Content of a Complaint of Abuse of Right in International Law' (1975) 16 *Harvard International Law Journal* 84ff; S Jovanovic, Restriction des compétences discrétionnaires des Etats en droit international (Paris, 1988) 193ff. Further literature in Kolb, *Bonne* 468.

[120] Pleadings by FA Mann (Belgium), *Barcelona Traction* case, VIII *ICJ Pleadings* 58.

[121] On arbitrary deprivation of nationality, see already the old statement in W Schiffer, *Repertoire of Questions of General International Law before the League of Nations, 1920–1940* (Geneva, 1942) 85, no 214.

[122] See M Nowak, *UN Covenant on Civil and Political Rights*, Commentary, 2nd edn (Kehl, 2005) 127ff; W Kälin and J Künzli, *The Law of International Human Rights Protection* (Oxford, 2009) 102–03. There are also other areas where the standard is 'arbitrariness' eg the issue of the prohibition of arbitrary interference with privacy: see the *Toonen v Australia* case, UN Human Rights Committee under CCPR, Communication no 488/1992, (1994) 113 *ILR* 340–41, § 8.3.

[123] *Tadic* (Jurisdiction) case, Appeals Chamber (1995) 105 *ILR* 465, § 28.

[124] See B Stern, 'La succession d'Etats' (1996) 262 *RCADI* 344–46.

[125] P d'Argent, *Les réparations de guerre en droit international public* (Brussels, 2005) 355. It has also been held by a Greek tribunal that the pleading of jurisdictional immunity in the face of a massacre committed by one's own military forces amounted to an abuse of rights: d'Argent, ibid, 799, but the ICJ has judged differently on that issue: *Jurisdictional Immunities of the State* (2012-I) *ICJ Reports* 100ff.

[126] See eg Y Arai, 'Article 17' in P van Dijk, F van Hoof, A van Rijn and L Zwaak (eds), *Theory and Practice of the European Convention on Human Rights*, 4th edn (Antwerp, 2006) 1083ff; FG Jacobs,

of abuse of rights: it aims at protecting the rights listed in the Convention and to safeguard the democratic institution against totalitarian and similar movements 'abusing' the rights granted with the aim of destroying human rights. In short words: no acceptance of use of human rights to destroy human rights; herein precisely lies the abuse. By the same token, there are special rules on abuse of rights within EU law.[127]

A question that has been asked is whether the notion of abuse of rights supposes a damage for a subject of the law, as does the concept of estoppel. There are different distinctions to be made here. First, there are certain types of abuse of rights which by definition suppose a damage, such as above-mentioned category 3), the disproportion of interests issue. The point is there to prohibit a certain behaviour, or to ensure reparation, when an excessive *harm* has been inflicted on another subject. A harm obviously encompasses or is in itself a damage. Conversely, there are other notions based on the abuse of rights doctrine which do not in themselves include a damage, eg the prohibition of fraudulent acts or of *détournement*. Second, much depends on the function the abuse of rights is called to display: when the issue is to claim pecuniary reparation for an unlawful act, a damage must be shown; conversely, when the abuse is claimed to obtain the nullity of a certain act, no damage must be shown.[128] Similarly, as long as the abusive act has not been executed, the claim can be geared only towards its prevention and no damage is required; once the abusive act is executed, issues of responsibility will normally be prominent and the damage may become a material consideration.[129] Overall, it cannot be said that the element of damage is an inherent requirement of the doctrine of abuse of rights.

We may conclude this chapter with some general examples of the prohibition of abuse of rights in the case law. At the PCIJ, one of the leading cases is the *Certain German Interests in Upper Polish Silesia* (1926). There the Court limited the right of Germany to dispose of certain assets in a territory where a plebiscite would be held on its remaining within Germany or shifting to Poland, by affirming that in case of an abuse of rights, the transfer or alienation of assets would amount to a violation of international law.[130] Another interesting case is the *Free Zones* case of 1930 and 1932. The Court held that France kept its full sovereignty over the free zones around Geneva and that it could therefore install any type of

RC White and C Ovey, *The European Convention on Human Rights*, 5nd edn (Oxford, 2010) 122ff; D Harris, M O'Boyle and C Warbrick, *Law of the European Convention on Human Rights*, 3rd edn (Oxford, 2014) 852ff; WA Schabas, *The European Convention on Human Rights—A Commentary* (Oxford, 2015) 611ff, with a bibliography. See also JF Renucci, *Droit européen des droits de l'homme*, 2nd edn (Paris, 2012) 885ff.

[127] See *Hungary v Slovak Republic* (2012) 153 *ILR* 118–19 (CJEU).

[128] See the Rejoinder by Guatemala in the *Nottebohm* case, (1955) I *ICJ Pleadings* 511.

[129] P Guggenheim, 'La validité et la nullité des actes juridiques internationaux' (1949-I) 74 *RCADI* 253–54.

[130] *Certain German Interests in Upper Polish Silesia* (1926) PCIJ ser A, no 7, pp 30, 37–38.

surveillance. But it cautioned that this could not amount to introduce by the backdoor customs regulations, which would be contrary to the treaty rights of Switzerland. The Court thus mentioned the doctrine of abuse of rights as a limit to the exercise of French sovereignty.[131] It may also be recalled that the Montego Bay Convention of 1982 on the law of the sea mentions the prohibition of abuse of rights in article 300,[132] while further ruling on issues of abuse of procedure (article 294) and arbitrary acts (article 297), as well as on misuse of power (article 187). This conventional regime is a complex effort to equilibrate the rights and interests of coastal and other states, in particular in the context of discretionary rights.[133]

There is also interesting case law of municipal tribunals. In the *Italy v X* case (1985), it had been held that Italy had demanded the transfer of certain historical tablets in order to manoeuver itself in the position of a defendant covered by jurisdictional immunities once the restitution would be demanded. The Court of Appeals of the Canton of Basle City accepted this plea and refused the immunity on the basis of abuse of rights. The Federal Tribunal then reversed the decision, since it considered the relevant facts not to be sufficiently proved.[134] The *Handelskwekerij GJ Bier BV v Mines de Potasse d'Alsace SA* (1979), the District Court of Rotterdam made an exemplary application of the 'disproportion of interests' abuse of rights, by applying the principle *sic utere tuo…* and by quoting the *Trail Smelter* case. The context was the pollution of the Rhine.[135]

Finally, some cases of diplomatic practice can be mentioned. In the *Polish Tourists in Beirut* case (1934), the issue was one of an arbitrary expulsion giving rise to

[131] *Free Zones* (1930, 1932) PCIJ ser A/B, no 46, p 167 and the Order of 1930, ser A, no 24, p 12.

[132] 'States Parties shall fulfill in good faith the obligations assumed under this Convention and shall exercise the rights, jurisdiction and freedoms recognized in this Convention in a manner which would not constitute an abuse of right'. On the drafting history of that provision, see Kolb, *Bonne* 475.

[133] When the Convention was negotiated, there was a delicate equilibrium to find between the many discretionary powers of the states in their coastal zones and the interests of the great maritime powers for free navigation. The latter feared that the former could abuse their discretionary powers and limit excessively their own rights. The recognition of a justiciable doctrine of abuse of rights appeared to them as a necessary counterbalancing weight to the recognition of these discretionary powers. Conversely, the coastal states feared that the maritime powers could abuse the procedural remedies offered to them so as to repeatedly contest the measures taken by the coastal states in what they considered their domain of sovereignty. The compromise has on this point been found through art 294 of the Convention. It confers to the tribunal seized the power to examine on its own behalf or on demand of one party, in a preliminary and summary ruling, the absence of abuse of procedure in the claims advanced. We are thus confronted with two cross-related compromises: discretionary powers of the coastal states against limitation of substantive abuse of rights; and preliminary check of abuse of procedural rights by the tribunal so as not to impair excessively the discretionary rights claimed. Thus, the double principle of abuse of rights has allowed to agree on a complex regime in a context of important political divergence of interests. The solutions of the conflicts were referred to future concrete situations, with a power of decision of the tribunal seized. These solutions will be easier to find in concrete cases than it would have been to create general rules in the Convention. The general principle has here a role of pacification; it functions as a midwife for the adoption of a legal regime.

[134] *Italy v X* (1985) 82 *ILR* 28 and (1986) 42 *ASDI* 60ff.

[135] *Handelskwekerij GJ Bier BV v Mines de Potasse d'Alsace SA* (1980) 11 *NYIL* 332–33. See AC Kiss, 'La pollution du Rhin: Suite (et fin?)' (1983) 29 *AFDI* 779ff.

a claim.[136] In the *French Owners of the Mont Cenis* case (1938), France complained of persecutory expropriations, which were allegedly only intended to chase the French subjects from that area. The note of the French authorities refers to the doctrine of abuse of rights.[137]

This picture shows that states and tribunals do not hesitate to rely on abuse of rights arguments, even if their frequency in general international law is not high. But this should come as no surprise, since the doctrine of abuse of rights is merely a fire-brigade provided for extreme interventions when more specialised legal arguments are not available.[138] It stands to reason that such a doctrine remains of limited application, lest the abuse of rights principle should itself become an avenue for abuse. We shall however see that in some areas of particular international law the recourse to the doctrine of abuse of rights is much more frequent and sometimes even standardised, eg in international administrative law, in WTO law or in international investment law.[139]

IV. Good Faith and the Maxim *nemo ex propria turpitudine commodum capere potest*

There is a manifest link between the principle of good faith and the legal maxim according to which nobody is authorised to take advantage of its own wrongful or faulty conduct.[140] As has been rightly emphasised: '[G]ood faith which exists in almost all legal systems ... prevents a party from profiting by its own misrepresentation' (in the original French text: 'son propre tort').[141] The maxim is a sanction

[136] See the *Note du Service juridique du Ministère des affaires étrangères*, 15 May 1934, AC Kiss, *Répertoire français de droit international public*, vol IV (Paris, 1962) no 499, p 307: 'Contrairement à ce qui a été indiqué dans la note du 13 avril, en l'absence des précisions fournies par le Consul de France à Varsovie, il apparaît donc que la mesure prise par le Haut-Commissaire de France à l'égard des ressortissants polonais dont il s'agit a nettement le caractère d'une mesure arbitraire qui engage la responsabilité internationale des Etats du Levant sous mandat français'.

[137] AC Kiss, *Répertoire français de droit international public*, vol II (Paris, 1966) no 204, p 114ff, esp 117.

[138] An example for a tribunal avoiding to enter into the argument of the parties on abuse, preferring to speak of 'different perceptions that have occasioned ancillary contentions of absence of good faith and abuse of rights' and engaging into an exercise of interpretation of the relevant provisions, see the *Iron Rhine Railway* arbitration (2005) XXVII *RIAA* 75, § 86.

[139] See below, Ch 7, sections III and IV, and Ch 10.

[140] On this maxim, see: M Scerni, *I principî generali di diritto riconosciuti dalle nazioni civili* (Padova, 1932) 125ff; B Cheng, *General Principles of Law—As Applied by International Courts and Tribunals* (London, 1953) 149ff; GG Fitzmaurice, 'The General Principles of International Law Considered from the Standpoint of the Rule of Law, General Course' (1957-II) 92 *RCADI* 117ff; IC McGibbon, 'Estoppel in International Law' (1958) 7 *ICLQ* 479ff; GG Fitzmaurice, *The Law and Procedure of the International Court of Justice*, vol II (Cambridge, 1986) 679ff; R Kolb, 'La maxime « nemo ex propria turpitudine commodum capere potest » (nul ne peut profiter de son propre tort) en droit international public' (2000) 33 *RBDI* 84ff.

[141] Diss Op Urrutia Holguín, *Arbitral Award Made by the King of Spain* case, (1960) *ICJ Reports* 222.

for wrongful or faulty acts. Thus, good faith is not based in this context on the issue of reliance and legitimate expectations. It is rather coloured by a moral bent and requires, in this context, that a subject behaves correctly. In order not to incentivise incorrect behaviour, there is a sanction meted out: 'you shall not earn rights or favourable legal positions flowing from an incorrect behaviour'. There are many Latin formulations for this basic idea: *nemo ex propria…*, *nullus commodum capere potest de sua propria injuria*, *nemo auditur propriam turpitudinem allegans*, *alterius circumventio alii non praebet actionem*, *commodum ex injuria non oritur*, *dolus suus neminem relevat*, *ex dolo malo non oritur actio*, *ex injuria jus non oritur*, *ex malitia nemo commodum habere debet*, *ex turpi causa non oritur actio*, *fraus et dolus nemini debent patrocinari*, *nemo ex suo delicto meliorem suam conditionem facere potest*, etc, as can be seen with some nuances for each expression.[142]

As has been said above, this is a maxim rather than a legal rule. In other words, the proposition has not a neatly defined scope of application within the four corners of which it would more or less invariably apply. It is rather a tool in the hands of the legal operator (or allows a claim by a subject) through which he or she can set aside a certain argument or plea in a flexible manner according to context. That is the reason why the maxim has been applied in a series of international legal situations. These must be considered under the lens of a loose galaxy of single cases stapled together by the common legal rationale of a sanction for unlawful or faulty behaviour. The sanction is typically, in analogy to procedural estoppel, that a subject will not be heard with a certain argument. The result is consequently a preclusion. This brings the maxim close to the principle of estoppel. But there are significant differences in the legal foundation and in the legal elements of both institutions. Estoppel is founded on good faith-reliance, while the maxim is based on a standard of expected correction. Moreover, estoppel is more strongly outward-looking, since it requires in most cases a detrimental reliance; contrariwise, the application of the maxim is more inward-looking and does not require such third-state reliance. Procedural estoppel, which sometimes skips the element of reliance and concentrates on the aspect of non-contradiction (*allegans contraria non est audiendus*), is a hybrid between both institutions, rooted in estoppel but clothed in the maxim *nemo…*. The point of that procedural estoppel is not mainly to protect the legitimate expectations of some other subject (hence the doing away with the element of detrimental reliance) but to protect the integrity of judicial proceedings. That integrity would be hampered if a tribunal was confronted with a lack of choice but to admit contradictory statements, which play fast and loose with facts, law and tribunal's authority.

Here are some examples of the application of our maxim in international law. We will mention different traces of the maxim in legal doctrine and practice, without taking position on whether all these applications reflect the positive law as it

[142] For these Latin maxims, see D Liebs, *Lateinische Rechtsregeln und Rechtssprichwörter*, 7th edn (Munich, 2007). See also R Kolb, 'La maxime « nemo ex propria turpitudine commodum capere potest » (nul ne peut profiter de son propre tort) en droit international public' (2000) 33 *RBDI* 91.

stands. It however remains true that all these examples can lead to an application of the maxim in appropriate circumstances. As can be seen, the spectrum of application is extremely large.

1. *Examples in the law of treaties and other agreements*: (i) the author of a fraud in the process of the conclusion of a treaty cannot demand restitution or elimination of the effects of the vitiated act (*fraus omnia corrumpit*);[143] (ii) the refusal to ratify may lead to an unlawful act if it is based on the fault of the refusing state;[144] (iii) if a state has knowledge of a ground of nullity for a treaty it has concluded, it has to invoke that ground in a reasonable time—if it does not, the delay would be due to its fault and the nullity could not be invoked anymore;[145] (iv) a state cannot invoke its negligence in failing to introduce properly a treaty obligation into its municipal law in order not to apply it;[146] (v) a state cannot invoke the lack of formal withdrawal from a contract by the other party when it itself constantly violates that contract;[147] (vi) the material breach of a treaty cannot be invoked as a motive to suspend or terminate the treaty if the state attempting to avail itself of these faculties has substantially contributed to or been the accomplice of the breach;[148] (vii) by the same token, a state cannot invoke other motives to terminate the treaty to its benefit when it has by its own fault or unlawful act substantially contributed to or caused the motive of termination;[149] (viii) if a legal consequence depends on

[143] See arts 49, 69, § 2, and 69, § 3, of the VCLT (1969); P Reuter, *Droit international public*, 6th edn (Paris, 1983) 102: 'L'auteur du dol ne peut bénéficier de la bonne foi ni demander l'élimination des effets de l'acte nul'; I Sinclair, *The Vienna Convention on the Law of Treaties*, 2nd edn (Manchester, 1984) 174.

[144] P Fauchille, *Traité de droit international public*, vol I, partie 3 (Paris, 1926) 330: 'Un refus de ratification serait certainement inadmissible s'il était dû à un fait ou à une faute de l'Etat même qui l'a émis'.

[145] See art 45 VCLT (1969) and A Maresca, *Il diritto dei trattati* (Milan, 1971) 56: 'Se tale Stato sapeva che il consenso ufficialmente espresso era viziato dalla violazione di una fondamentale norma della sua costituzione, lo Stato stesso non può successivamente invocare tale vizio al fine di non considerarsi impegnato dal consenso medesimo'; H Lauterpacht, *International Law—Collected Papers*, vol IV (Cambridge, 1978) 260–61 (*qui habet commoda debet habere onera*). This issue is plainly also one of legitimate expectations in reasonably swift action.

[146] Arts 26 and 27 VCLT (1969) and L Oppenheim (R Jennings and A Watts, eds), *International Law*, 9th edn (London, 1992) 82ff.

[147] *Sapphire International Petroleum* (1963) 35 *ILR* 185.

[148] GG Fitzmaurice, 'The General Principles of International Law Considered from the Standpoint of the Rule of Law' (1957-II) 92 *RCADI* 118. And now see the *Gabcikovo-Nagymaros* case (1997) *ICJ Reports* 67, § 110.

[149] See eg art 61, § 2, VCLT (1969), on impossibility of performance. See also *Gabcikovo-Nagymaros* (1997) *ICJ Reports* 64, § 103. See also art 62, § 2 letter b), VCLT (1969) for the fundamental change of circumstances. See M Gounelle, *La motivation des actes juridiques en droit international public* (Paris, 1979) 207–08. § 2, letter b, only envisages the situation where the fundamental change is brought about by a breach of treaty or a breach of any other international obligation owed to any other party to the treaty. The breach need not be a material breach in the sense of art 60. However, material breaches are more likely to provoke situations such as envisaged here. The conclusion of a new treaty contradicting earlier obligations suffices for the purposes of § 2, letter b The understanding at the Vienna Conference was that any changes provoked bona fide would not lead to a loss of the right to invoke the changed circumstances—but conversely that changes not brought about bona fide would automatically be tantamount to a violation of the treaty. This must however not always be the case. The change can relate

the realisation or non-realisation of a condition, the conduct of one party so as to deliberately provoke the realisation or the non-realisation of the condition will not be taken into account;[150] (ix) if a party to a treaty by its conduct renders impossible the full execution of the treaty, it could be indicated to apply the treaty in a way approaching as much as possible the original regime, so as not to allow the defaulting party to profit from its own wrong.[151]

2. *Examples in the law on jurisdiction and obligations in general*: (i) 'It is difficult to admit that a foreign ship may be seized for not having a certain document when the document has been refused to it by the very authorities who required that it should be obtained';[152] (ii) a maritime hot pursuit is not allowed when the state invoking it to its benefit is itself responsible of breach of law which leads to it;[153] (iii) a state may not fail to challenge the status of another state as a flag state of a ship at all material times and later claim the opposite on the alleged discovery of a new fact which it could have ignored only by its own negligence;[154] (iv) a right of passage cannot be suspended or terminated if the motive of termination has been caused by the state invoking it to its benefit;[155] (v) if a state ignores a fact because of its own negligence, it cannot invoke that ignorance as an excuse;[156] (vi) no extinctive prescription is allowed where the subject invoking it has impeded by its own acts that the

to conduct which is not prohibited under the treaty; it is then a matter of interpretation to what extent it could be subsumed as a breach of positive corollary obligations under the treaty. Moreover, the question remains as to whether a party should prevent the occurrence of the change if it is able to do so. This will be the case only if the party is under an international obligation, under good faith or under some rule of international law (including the treaty), to prevent the change. The existence of such an obligation will not be frequent.

Further, under the League of Nations, a state could not invoke the fact that a treaty had not been registered according to article 18 of the Covenant when it had itself failed to register that treaty: M Brandon, 'The Validity of Non-Registered Treaties' (1952) 29 *BYIL* 189.

[150] G Dahm, *Völkerrecht*, vol II (Stuttgart, 1961) 108. See also the Peruvian Pleadings in *Tacna Arica* (1925) II *RIAA* 929–30 and H Lauterpacht, *Private Law Sources and Analogies of International Law* (London, 1927) 290ff. See also, as to the application of our maxim to prevent a hypothetical profiting from the own wrong, H Thirlway, 'The Law and Procedure of the International Court of Justice (1960–1989): Treaty Interpretation and Other Treaty Points' (1992) 63 *BYIL* 64–65.

[151] See Sep Op H Lauterpacht, *Admissibility of Hearings of Petitioners*, advisory opinion (1956) *ICJ Reports* 46: 'It is a sound principle of law that whenever a legal instrument of continuing validity cannot be applied literally owing to the conduct of one of the parties, it must, without allowing that party to take advantage of its own conduct, be applied in a way approximating most closely its primary object'. See now the *Gabcikovo-Nagymaros* case, (1997) *ICJ Reports* 51ff. *Contra*: Sep Op Bedjaoui, ibid, 127–28; Op diss Herczegh, ibid, 193. And see R Kolb, 'La maxime « nemo ex propria turpitudine commodum capere potest » (nul ne peut profiter de son propre tort) en droit international public' (2000) 33 *RBDI* 98–101.

[152] *Tattler* (1920) VI *RIAA* 50.

[153] NM Poulantzas, *The Right of Hot Pursuit in International Law* (Leiden, 1969) 324–25.

[154] Sep Op Chandrasekhara Rao, *M/V Saiga (Admissibility and Merits)*, ITLOS (1999) 120 *ILR* 249; see also Sep Op Anderson, ibid, 255.

[155] Diss Op Fernandes, *Right of Passage over Indian Territory* (1960) *ICJ Reports* 143.

[156] *Norwegian Fisheries* (1951) *ICJ Reports* 139 and Sep Op Alvarez, ibid, 152 and Diss Op McNair, ibid, 171ff.

claim could be brought earlier[157] or when the delays are due to that subject;[158] (vii) an important application of our maxim is in the context of territorial changes operated by the use of unlawful force or in violation of the principle of self-determination, where there is an international legal duty of non-recognition. This is in application of the legal idea *ex injuria jus non oritur*, which finds application in the context of such qualified violations of fundamental norms of international law.[159]

3. *Examples in the context of state responsibility*: (i) circumstances precluding wrongfulness cannot be invoked to the benefit of a state which has caused these circumstances to exist;[160] (ii) a state cannot invoke with success the lack of exhaustion of local remedies when this lack is due to its own conduct;[161] (iii) a claim related to damage suffered by an alien can be inadmissible if a state has made incomplete or wrong communications relating to its nationality;[162] (iv) according to certain cases, a state cannot present a claim on behalf of one of its nationals when the latter has caused or amplified the tort for which reparation is now sought;[163] (v) the reparation to be paid may be adjusted

[157] *Chorzow Factory (Jurisdiction)* (1927) PCIJ ser A, no 9, p 31.

[158] *Roberts* (1903) IX *RIAA* 207.

[159] See J Dugard, *Recognition and the United Nations* (Cambridge, 1986) 81ff; J Crawford, *The Creation of States in International Law*, 2nd edn (Oxford) 96ff. And see the various contributions in J Crawford, A Pellet and S Olleson (eds), *The Law of International Responsibility* (Oxford, 2010) 667ff. On the principle of *ex injuria jus non oritur* in general, see A Lagerwall, *Le principe ex injuria jus non oritur en droit international* (Brussels, 2016).

[160] See arts 23, § 2, 24, § 2, and 25, § 2, letter b of the Articles on State Responsibility (2001), A/RES/56/83. See eg A Gattini, *Zufall und Force Majeure im System der Staatenverantwortlichkeit anhand der ILC—Kodifikationsarbeit, Schriften zum Völkerrecht*, vol 96 (Berlin, 1991) 98–99, 135ff. In the *Betsy* case (1797), Commissioner Pinkney stated: 'the most exceptionable of all principles, that he who does wrong shall be at liberty to plead his own illegal conduct on other occasions as a partial excuse' (JB Moore, *International Adjudications, Ancient and Modern, Modern Series*, vol IV (New York, 1931) 227). See now the *Gabcikovo-Nagymaros* case, (1997) *ICJ Reports* 35ff and 46. For the older practice of the mixed arbitral tribunals after World War I, see P d'Argent, *Les réparations de guerre en droit international public* (Brussels, 2005) 78 and fn 249.

[161] CF Amerasinghe, *Local Remedies in International Law* (Cambridge, 1990) 272ff; E Kaufmann, 'Règles générales du droit de la paix' (1935-IV) 54 *RCADI* 457–58; L Oppenheim (R Jennings and A Watts, eds), *International Law*, 9th edn (London, 1992) 525–26. See also the Swiss Memorial in the *Losinger* case, PCIJ ser C, no 78, p 41. As has been aptly formulated: 'If a State lacks effective local remedies, this accounts to a breach of the minimum standard. This omission itself constitutes an international tort and, in good faith, precludes the tortfeasor from invoking the local remedies rule' (G Schwarzenberger, *A Manual of International Law*, 5th edn (London, 1967) 177).

[162] *Flegenheimer (US v Italy)* (1958) XIV *RIAA* 378: 'It allows a Respondent State to object to the admissibility of a legal action directed against it by the national State of the allegedly injured party, when the latter has neglected to indicate his true nationality, or has concealed it, or has invoked another nationality at the time the fact giving rise to the dispute occurred, or when the national State has made erroneous communications to another State thus fixing the conduct to be followed by the latter'.

[163] So-called doctrine of clean hands: EM Borchard, *The Diplomatic Protection of Citizens Abroad* (New York, 1927) 713ff; CC Hyde, *International Law—Chiefly as Interpreted and Applied by the United States*, 2nd edn, vol II (Boston, 1947) 891ff. See also J Salmon, 'Des mains propres comme condition de recevabilité des réclamations internationales' (1964) 10 *AFDI* 225ff. See also below: Ch 8, section III.

according to the respective fault;[164] (vi) a corporation cannot complain that the government did not ensure the profitability of a factory when it contributed thereto by its own fault.[165]

4. *Examples in the context of judicial procedure*: (i) a state cannot plead that another state has not used a remedy when it itself impeded this course;[166] (ii) a state cannot rely on an objection which would be tantamount to plead the non-execution of an international obligation;[167] (iii) an international organisation can been precluded from invoking a time-bar for a claim on indemnities where it had itself caused the staff member to believe that the indemnity was not due;[168] (iv) if an individual uses and abuses all remedies offered to him in municipal law, it cannot complain at the European Court of Human Rights (and analogously elsewhere) about the length of the procedure, to the extent it is due to its own conduct;[169] (v) an individual cannot complain at a human rights court that the criminal charges were not notified to him when he himself impeded that communication;[170] (vi) a state cannot invoke at a

[164] 'If payments for work on the TIA project have been wrongfully withheld by an Agency of the Government of the Islamic Republic of Iran and if for the lack of such payment the Tribunal did not include such moneys in the dissolution value of TAMS-AFFA, then the Respondent Agency would profit by its own wrong. Conversely, if TAMS-AFFA wrongfully failed to pay tax and social security obligation and if the Tribunal did not deduct such obligations, them TAMS-AFFA would profit by its own wrong. It is a well recognized principle in many municipal systems and in international law that no one should be allowed to reap advantages from their own wrong, Nullus Commodum Capere De Sua Injuria Propria'. *Tippetts, Abbett, McCarthy, Stratton c Iran* (1984) 6 *Iran/US Claims Tribunal Reports* 227–28.

[165] *Klöckner Industrie-Anlagen GmbH v Cameroon*, ICSID arbitration, (1983) 114 *ILR* 153ff, 179: 'Klöckner cannot now complain that the Government did not ensure the profitability of the factory in the face of the precise economic problems that Klöckner had recognized but had diligently avoided calling to the attention of the Government…'.

[166] *Chorzow Factory (Competence)* (1927) PCIJ ser A, no 9, p 31: 'It is, moreover, a principle generally accepted in the jurisprudence of international arbitration, as well as by municipal courts, that one Party cannot avail himself of the fact that the other has not fulfilled some obligation or has not had recourse to some means of redress, if the former party has, by some illegal act, prevented the latter from fulfilling the obligation in question, or from having recourse to the tribunal which would have been open, to him'. See also *Philips Eindhoven v FRG* (1958) 25 *ILR* 505: 'it would by contrary to the principles of good faith for the defendant now to rely on the lack of qualification of Philips Eindhoven, since it was due to the arbitrary refusal of the custodians appointed by the German authorities and acting under their influence that Philips Eindhoven had been prevented from acquiring such qualification'. The same is true if a state insists on the necessity to negotiate before a tribunal is seized, when it rendered itself such negotiations impossible: Diss Op Weeramantry, *Lockerbie* case, (1992) *ICJ Reports* 51–52.

[167] *Jurisdiction of the Courts of Danzig* (1928) PCIJ, ser B, no 15, pp 26–27: 'Poland could not avail herself of an objection which … would amount to relying upon the non-fulfilment of an obligation imposed upon her by an international engagement'. See also the Diss Op Read, *Peace Treaties* (1950) *ICJ Reports* 244 and Diss Op Azevedo, ibid, 252–54. This position is quoted with approval by G Schwarzenberger, *International Law—As Applied by International Courts and Tribunals*, 3rd edn, vol I (London, 1957) 524.

[168] *Conrad* (1977), ILOAT, Judgment no 328.

[169] See the cases quoted in JA Frowein and W Peukert, *Europäische Menschenrechtskonvention, Kommentar*, 2nd edn (Kehl, 1996) 132.

[170] ECtHR, *Campbell and Fell* (1984) Series A no 80, § 96. By the same token, a complaint that only the Prosecutor has been heard at an audience cannot be countenanced when the accused has not availed himself of the right to be present: ECtHR, *Kampanis* (1995) Series A no 318, § 51.

human rights tribunal the lack of evidence when that evidence is in its possession but is not laid open.[171]

As can be seen, the maxim has a multifaceted character in international law. It is sometimes linked to the principle of estoppel or of prohibition of abuse of rights, or even legitimate expectations, and at other times presents itself simply as an argument in a chain of reasoning. It also occurs that the maxim condenses itself in a series of new rules of international law, for example the duty of non-recognition of certain territorial situations brought about by force or the denial of self-determination; or the rule on approximation in the execution of a treaty whose literal application has been rendered impossible by the conduct of one party.[172] Notice that the maxim has sometimes a negative and sometimes a positive reach. On its negative side, it renders inadmissible a claim or argument; on the positive side, it would require the judge to take some measures to overcome the situation in which the faulty state has placed the aggrieved state, as the doctrine of 'approximation' in the treaty execution shows. The former course is not riddled with difficulties for the judge; but the second can be delicate in an environment of sovereign states and of a relative weakness of judicial institutions. How much a judge can positively do in order to 'undo' a faulty conduct is open to contextual enquiry. Notice also that the operation of the maxim supposes a free will and a knowledge of the fault or illegality. Coercion, fraud or error in the sense of articles 48–52 VCLT, preclude the 'turpitude' and thus the operation of the maxim. Similarly, the fault may be erased when the subject had no means of recognising it. But the rule is that ignorance of the law is no excuse and that the standard of care for fault is high (*ignorantia juris nocet*). The excuse will therefore be admitted only in extreme cases. Notice further that the operation of the maxim does not suppose an unlawful act; other types of fault or immoral acts are also relevant. Thus, the US admitted that a claim in favour of one of its citizens engaged in slave trading must be dropped, even if the illegality of that trade at the time it occurred was open to discussion.[173] The fault or illegality must not flow from a single act but can also flow from an aggregate of action or of action and omission (as the *Petitioners* case with the argument of H Lauterpacht shows).[174] In any case, the fault must be the

[171] Inter-American Court of Human Rights: *Velasquez Rodríguez* (1988) Series C no 4, § 135; *Godínez Cruz* (1989) Series C no 5, § 141; *Gangaram Panday* (1994) Series C no 16, § 49: 'In proceedings to determine human rights violations the State cannot rely on the defense that the complainant has failed to present evidence when it cannot be obtained without the State's cooperation'; etc. See similarly but in another context the Sep Op H Lauterpacht, *Admissibility of Hearings of Petitioners* (1955) *ICJ Reports* 47–48.

[172] See above, number 1, ix.

[173] *Pelletier* case (1885): 'Even were we to concede that these outrages in Haytian waters were not within Haytian jurisdiction, I do now affirm that the claim of Pelletier against Haiti … must be dropped, and dropped peremptorily and immediately by the … United States … *Ex turpi causa non oritur actio…*' (*Papers relating to the Foreign Relations of the United States*, vol 26 (Washington DC, 1887) 607).

[174] (1955) *ICJ Reports* 47–48.

proximate cause of the profit to be earned and which the maxim seeks to deny. In case of lack of causal nexus, the maxim will not be applied. Thus, in the *Massey* case (1927), Commissioner Nielsen affirmed that the bad conduct of the deceased was of no relevance to the denial of justice committed with regard to his heirs after he had been assassinated.[175]

The maxim is limited in its application by certain principles and rules of international law. *First*, when its application is linked to *inter partes* adjustment of torts, the maxim is subordinated to norms of public order or other fundamental norms.[176] But it also occurs that the maxim itself gives rise to public order considerations. This is the case, for example, in the context of the duties of non-recognition, which have however become to a large extent autonomous public order norms in international law. This may be the case also in other situations: the community is interested not to allow turpitude and malevolence to prevail. In legal terms, it may occur that we end up with public order considerations on both sides, and in such a case a careful balancing-up—typical of public law—must occur.[177] *Second*, it may happen that the turpitude is not limited to one state but that there is fault or illegality on both sides. It may even occur that the fault of the defending state is greater than the one of the claiming state. If the claim was declared inadmissible on account of our maxim, a still more immoral situation could be produced in such a case. Consequently, an adjustment—on the merits—of both torts should take place to the full extent that the applicable legal rules allow it.[178] *Third*, the subject having committed the fault must try to rely on it to *its* benefit. When some third state is the beneficiary of the claim, the maxim could be inapplicable: the faulty subject does not attempt to rely on its own tort to its benefit. However, if the third state and the claiming state make common cause, this exception would not apply. There may also be circumstances where the mere relying on a tortious behaviour impedes any rights or advantages to follow, whichever the beneficiary. Conversely, it may occur that the application of the maxim will affect the rights of third states. In such a case, limitations upon its operation may be imposed so as to protect the third state. An example could be the application of the 'approximation'-doctrine in the execution of treaties when the compact is multilateral and the substitutive way of implementing the treaty has an impact on the rights of other treaty parties, or on the object and purpose of the treaty (under an analogy to article 41 VCLT, 1969). *Fourth*, the maxim is plainly not applicable when the turpitude is not attributable to the subject concerned. Thus, when Israel argued that the ICJ should not deliver the advisory opinion on the Wall in 2004,

[175] *Massey* (1927) IV *RIAA* 156.

[176] See the *Avena* case, (2004-I) *ICJ Reports* 38, § 47; see also Diss Op Weeramantry, *Gabcikovo-Nagymaros* case, (1997) *ICJ Reports* 117–18.

[177] On conflicts between *jus cogens* norms, see now JE Christofolo, *Solving Antinomies Between Peremptory Norms in Public International Law* (Geneva, 2016).

[178] See in Swiss law H Merz, 'Artikel 2 des *Zivilgesetzbuches*' in *Berner Kommentar zum schweizerischen Privatrecht, Schweizerisches Zivilgesetzbuch, Einleitung, Artikel 1-10* (Bern, 1966) 376–77.

because Palestine had 'dirty hands', the Court responded to the effect that it was not Palestine but the UN General Assembly which had requested the opinion.[179]

V. Good Faith and the Critical Date

The 'critical date' is a concept used in territorial and maritime disputes.[180] The doctrine limits the time-span during which relevant conduct for establishing a prescriptive title or for nourishing an *effectivité* can be taken into account.[181] Exercises of sovereignty occurring before that date will be considered, while exercises of public power situated after that date will be discounted. One of the aims of this legal technique is the protection of good faith and by extension of the object and purpose of the judicial proceedings (if such are initiated). If a state was allowed to produce as evidence in court conduct *à titre de souverain* after the critical date—which is normally the date of crystallisation of the dispute[182] and at latest the seizing of the judge[183]—there would be an incentive for all the parties to produce as many self-serving acts and facts as possible on the territory in dispute in order to plead a dense and increasing exercise of public power. Such a course would jeopardise the maintenance of peace and the securing of acceptable relations between the parties. It would also put under heavy strain the judicial or arbitral procedure and endanger the implementation of the final award or judgment. The link of that doctrine with good faith[184] is therefore mainly to be seen in the protection of

[179] *Wall* opinion, (2004-I) *ICJ Reports* 163–64, § 63–64.

[180] On the critical date, see eg D Bardonnet, 'Les faits postérieurs à la date critique dans les différends territoriaux et frontaliers' *Essays in Honor of M Virally* (Paris, 1991) 53ff; LI Sanchez Rodriguez, 'L'uti possidetis et les effectivités dans les contentieux territoriaux et frontaliers' (1997) 263 *RCADI* 275ff; M Kohen, *Possession contestée et souveraineté territoriale* (Paris, 1997) 169ff; GG Fitzmaurice, 'The Law and Procedure of the International Court of Justice, 1951–4: Points of Substantive Law, Part II' (1955) 32 *BYIL* 20ff; L Oppenheim (R Jennings and A Watts, eds), *International Law*, 9th edn (London, 1992) 710–12.

[181] GG Fitzmaurice, 'The Law and Procedure of the International Court of Justice, 1951–4: Points of Substantive Law, Part II' (1955) 32 *BYIL* 20: 'The "critical date" in relation to any dispute has been defined as the date after which the actions of the parties can no longer affect the issue'. Critical dates can serve different functions. For example, the issue may turn on the 'nemo dat quod non habet' principle: if there is a territorial cession, it must be determined whether on the date of the cession the ceding state had the relevant title over the territory (see the *Island of Palmas* case (1928) II *RIAA* 843, 866); further, the issue may turn on the existence of a previous title on a specific date, because if there is such a title the argument of occupation of a *terra nullius* fails (see the *Eastern Greenland* case, (1933) PCIJ ser A/B, no 53, p 45); still, the parties to a procedure may agree to a critical date or period, during which the facts and acts must be appreciated, so as to facilitate the proceedings in very complex cases; finally, the main function of the critical date, as will be elaborated in the text is to bar self-serving and unilateral acts contrary to the principle of good faith.

[182] *Sovereignty over Pulau Ligitan and Pulau Sipadan* (2002) *ICJ Reports* 682, § 135.

[183] See GG Fitzmaurice, 'The Law and Procedure of the International Court of Justice, 1951–4: Points of Substantive Law, Part II' (1955) 32 *BYIL* 20ff 29.

[184] See LI Sanchez Rodriguez, 'L'uti possidetis et les effectivités dans les contentieux territoriaux et frontaliers' (1997) 263 *RCADI* 283–84. See also *Minquiers and Ecrehos* case, (1953) I *ICJ Pleadings*

the object and purpose of legal proceedings and concomitantly in the limitation of unilateral and self-serving creation of legal facts. The protection of a common finality and the repelling of unilateralism is manifestly a core function of good faith. The aim of the critical date is not, however, to entirely freeze the dispute at some date as against all later events. Acts occurring later can be relevant either to confirm earlier acts or titles; or to manifest a recognition; or to show an acquiescence or waiver by the other party. The point of the doctrine is merely to avoid a unilateral and calculated improvement of one's own situation; it is not to impede one party to accept, acquiesce in or waive some legal pretences of the other party.[185]

In view of this aim of the doctrine, the following exceptions were admitted in the case law: (i) the critical date can be modified if the parties agree; (ii) later acts can be used if they merely confirm earlier ones (ie they 'reveal or illustrate the understanding of the situation as it was during the critical period');[186] (iii) acts and facts which do not improve the position of the party, but worsen its previous position, can still be brought to fore.[187] Notice than in complex proceedings there may be more than one critical date in accordance with different facts of the dispute: one date for the sovereignty over some islands, another date for the maritime boundary, etc.[188] As can be seen, critical dates and periods are not of an easy handling. However that may be, the main aim of most of these dates is a matter of good faith. The need to uphold good faith and to somehow restrict unilateralism provides an important criterion by which to shape the doctrine to the changing circumstances of individual cases.

551–52, 292, 294. The necessary protection of the object and purpose appears also clearly in the *Eastern Greenland* case (1933) PCIJ ser A/B, no 53, p 42.

[185] Therefore the *Minquiers and Ecrehos* Court was correct in holding: '[S]ubsequent acts should also be considered by the Court, unless the measure in question was taken with a view of improving the legal position of the Party concerned' ((1953)*ICJ Reports* 59); see also *Sovereignty over Pulau Ligitan and Pulau Sipadan* (2002) *ICJ Reports* 682, § 135.

[186] *Case Concerning the Location of Boundary Markers in Taba between Egypt and Israel* (1988) XX *RIAA* 45, § 175.

[187] *Sovereignty over Pulau Ligitan and Pulau Sipadan* (2002) *ICJ Reports* 682, § 135, *a contrario*.

[188] *Territorial and Maritime Dispute between Nicaragua and Honduras in the Caribbean Sea* (2007-II) *ICJ Reports* 699ff, § 123ff.

7

Good Faith in the Law of International Organisations

I. Article 2, § 2 of the UN Charter

Modern international law is characterised by a leap from an inorganic society to a progressively more strongly institutionalised international governance. Thus, classical international law of coexistence has enriched itself by a layer of international law of cooperation.[1] International cooperation has developed in view of certain common aspirations; it is based on some common effort; and it is thus anchored in the necessary mutual confidence concerning the effort towards some common aim. This evolution has sharpened and strengthened the finalistic or aim-oriented valence of the rules governing the area of international law concerned with international institutions. And this in turn has had profound effects on the rest of the body of international law. As was stated some years ago by JP Müller:

> The decisions of international courts show that good faith develops particular legal effects wherever states have a qualified relationship of confidence with one another, such as in the context of an arbitral or border adjustment procedure, or a vassalage relationship, *inter alia*. These effects consist of increased obligations to show mutual consideration and an increased responsibility for the confidence that has developed with regard to achieving the common objective. The relations between the members of an international organisation would likewise appear to constitute such a qualified relationship of confidence.[2]

Considering the foregoing, it stands to reason that good faith has a particular role to play in this context:[3] it will be called upon to protect the 'commonness' of the

[1] W Friedmann, *The Changing Structure of International Law* (London, 1964) 60ff; M Virally, 'Panorama du droit international contemporain' (1983-V) 183 *RCADI* 247ff.

[2] JP Müller, 'Article 2 (2)' in B Simma (ed), *The Charter of the United Nations—A Commentary* (Oxford, 1994) 93.

[3] On good faith in the law of international Organisations, see mainly LM Goodrich, E Hambro and AP Simons, *Charter of the United Nations*, 3rd edn (New York, 1969) 40–41; JP Müller, *Vertrauensschutz im Völkerrecht* (Köln, 1971) 227ff; G Schwarzenberger, *International Law—As Applied by International Courts and Tribunals*, vol III (London, 1976) 214–16; E Zoller, *La bonne foi en droit international public* (Paris, 1977) 157ff; S Rosenne, *Developments in the Law of Treaties, 1945–1986* (Cambridge, 1989) 155ff; E Zoller, 'L'article 2(2) de la Charte des Nations Unies', in JP Cot and A Pellet, *La Charte des*

effort and thus the aims of the legal relationships within the organisation against strains of excessive unilateralism by the various member states. The weight and importance of good faith will consequently vary in accordance to the depth of the proposed cooperation, the amplitude of the common finalities and the degree of integration of the organisation at stake.[4]

The best known provision on good faith in the law of international organisations is article 2, § 2, of the UN Charter. It reads as follows: 'The Organization and its Members … shall act in accordance with the following Principles: … 2. All Members, in order to ensure to all of them the rights and benefits resulting from membership, shall fulfil in good faith the obligations assumed by them in accordance with the present Charter'. This provision falls now to be analysed.

Article 2, § 2 of the UN Charter was sponsored at the Dumbarton Oaks Conference for the UN by seven Latin American states and the Netherlands.[5] The Colombian delegate emphasised: 'The United Nations … must proclaim that international life requires a minimum of morality as a normative principle of conduct for peoples. This minimum cannot be anything else than full good faith and respect for the pledged word'.[6] The point was to rebut the policy of the Axis Powers, characterised by contempt for the law ('scrap of paper' doctrine), the exaltation of force ('might before law') and excessive nationalism ('what is good for the German people is just').[7] It appears that some Anglo-Saxon delegations, notably the US, failed to understand the meaning of the term 'good faith', which clearly stems from the Roman Law tradition. For them, to say that the obligation of the Charter must be executed was enough: good faith added nothing. But the Belgian delegate, Professor H Rolin, explained the proper scope of the principle of good faith[8] and how it qualifies the obligation to execute. Thereupon, Ms Gildersleeve, from the US, replied:

> I should like to say that we have been convinced by the arguments of our friends and are now eager to support this amendment. We had not realized exactly what the words meant to those who have lived and worked in the great tradition of the Roman law. We

Nations Unies—Commentaire article par article, 3rd edn (Paris, 2005) 417ff; R Kolb, 'Article 2(2) of the UN Charter' in B Simma, D E Khan, G Nolte and A Paulus (eds), *The Charter of the United Nations, A Commentary*, 3rd edn, vol I (Oxford, 2012) 166ff. See also Kolb, *Bonne* 501ff.

4 Müller, *Vertrauensschutz* 227. Each association of states relies on this principle. See the associations in ancient Greece: G Ténékidès, 'La notion juridique d'indépendance et la tradition hellénique', in G Ténékidès, *Les relations internationales dans la Grèce antique* (Athens, 1993) 180: 'Tout statut d'association d'Etats, eût-il une base rigoureusement égalitaire, visât-il à des fins d'intérêts commun, resterait lettre morte s'il n'était pas vivifié par la *bonne foi* qui doit animer les Etats membres'; and see to the same effect the Dissenting Opinion Zoricic, *Conditions of Admission* advisory opinion (1947/1948) *ICJ Reports* 103.

5 *UNCIO*, vol 3, pp 224 (Venezuela), 269 (Panama), 328 (Netherlands), 199, 421 (Ecuador), 504 (Cuba), 562, 571 (Dominican Republic), 587 (Colombia), 596 (Peru).

6 *UNCIO*, vol 6, p 72. This delegate had already written on that subject matter during the war: JM Yepes, *Philosophie du panaméricanisme et organisation de la paix* (Neuchâtel, 1945) 266ff.

7 Yepes, *Philosophie*, op cit, 266–70.

8 See above, Ch 4, section I and Ch 5 sections V and VI.

> had thought they were quite unnecessary ... But now we realize that this is a customary phrase, which ... conveys the meaning that we are all to observe those obligations, not merely the letter of them, but the spirit of them.[9]

Finally, the provision was adopted unanimously.[10]

Article 2, § 2, deals with an obligation[11] of member states. More precisely, these states are obliged to behave in a certain way with regard to the obligations assumed in the Charter. The issue is thus an obligation about other obligations. According to the letter of article 2, § 2, the Members undertake to 'fulfil in good faith the obligations assumed by them in accordance with the present Charter', and this with a certain aim: 'in order to ensure to all of them the rights and benefits resulting from membership'. The first question is therefore one relating to the scope of the obligation to respect good faith. The 'in order' sentence is a descriptive matter, not a normative qualifier. It appears from the drafting history that this part of the sentence was added in order to show definitively why it is important to respect good faith. Since this part of the sentence is not a normative element, it would not be open to a state to argue that it is not bound to respect the principle of good faith because in its view, in that case, this would not lead to any impairment of rights and benefits of membership.[12] The obligations under the Charter have to be interpreted and implemented in good faith; it is by doing this that the rights and benefits of membership will be secured, and not the other way round. A related point is about the scope of the obligations at stake: according to the text, the obligations 'assumed in accordance with the present Charter' are covered. Since the obligations assumed under the Charter are of a sweeping nature and many of them relate to general international law (especially in article 2 of the Charter), there is no neat difference between Charter law and international law at large. The respect of international law as a whole is part of international cooperation (and this is an aim under article 1 of the Charter). Further, the drafting history shows that article 2, § 2, was indeed meant to secure respect for international law as such (no 'scrap of paper' doctrine). In this light, a broad interpretation of the words 'assumed in accordance with the present Charter' are apposite. The text is itself large enough to allow such a construction: it does not refer to 'obligations under the present Charter', but to obligations 'assumed in accordance' with it.

The next point relates to the personal scope of application. It stands to reason that article 2 directly addresses only the members of the UN, since it is a treaty concluded among them. However, article 2 can stipulate obligations for its

[9] *UNCIO*, vol 6, p 74.

[10] ibid, p 80.

[11] An obligation is a duty of one or more than one subject to act or abstain from acting in a certain way with regard to one or more than one other subjects. In the words of the *Black's Law Dictionary*: 'An obligation is a legal duty, by which a person is bound to do or not to do a certain thing'.

[12] See the similar argument under art 2, § 4, of the UN Charter, whereby a use of force that does not impair the territorial integrity, political independence or the aims of the UN is not unlawful: see A Randelzhofer and O Dörr, 'Article 2(4)', in B Simma, DE Khan, G Nolte and A Paulus (eds), *The Charter of the United Nations, A Commentary*, 3rd edn, vol I (Oxford, 2012) 215–17.

members also with regard to third states (as eg in article 2, § 4, which prohibits the use of force generally and not only with regard to members). The same is true for § 2: it is not limited to the dealings among members but requires generally from all the members a certain conduct. This is all the more understandable if one considers that the obligation of good faith reflects customary international law. Moreover, other subjects than states are also bound by this principle. Thus, good faith is a principle from which duties flow for all the organs of the UN.[13] With regard to an agreement between the World Health Organisation and Egypt, for instance, the ICJ therefore held that certain duties of cooperation in good faith applied to Egypt as the host state, as well as to the World Health Organisation.[14] Good faith also regulates the relationships between the organs of the Organisation. It gives rise to a duty of fairness, respect and mutual co-operation, and a duty to take account of the juridical acts of the various organs among themselves.[15] Good faith finally also applies to the relationships between international organisations and their staff members. As was noted by the administrative tribunal of the Organisation of American States in the *Uehling* case (1974), good faith lies at the root of the contractual bonds between such an organisation and its employee.[16] Several obligations have been derived from that general principle in the context of international administrative law: the prohibition of abuse of power or of procedure (*détournement de pouvoir*);[17] the duty to protect legitimate expectations;[18] the duty to respect promises;[19] the applicability of estoppel[20] or of the doctrine of qualified silence (acquiescence).[21] We will come back to this branch of the law in section III of the present chapter.

The gist of good faith in the law of international organisations is less to protect the legitimate confidence in bilateral settings than to require from the members a certain observance of the common pledges, and thus a readiness to compromise and cooperate in view of the accomplishment of the common aims.[22] This is a

[13] A Verdross and B Simma, *Universelles Völkerrecht*, 3rd edn (Berlin, 1984) 47; *International Law—As Applied by International Courts and Tribunals*, vol III (London, 1976) 215.

[14] *Interpretation of the Agreement of 25 March 1951 between the WHO and Egypt (advisory opinion)* (1980) *ICJ Reports* 93–96.

[15] E Klein, 'Paralleles Tätigwerden von Sicherheitsrat und IGH bei friedensbedrohenden Streitigkeiten' *Essays in Honour of H Mosler* (Berlin, 1983) 481ff.

[16] *Uehling* (1974) Judgment no 8, p 10.

[17] *Richard* (1993) Judgment no 1231 of ILOAT, p 16.

[18] *Levcik* (1974), Judgment no 192 of UNAT, pp 245ff.

[19] *Gieser* (1986), Judgment no 782 of ILOAT, p 4ff.

[20] *Banerjee* (1985), Judgment no344 of UNAT, p 13ff, also in (1985) 31 *AFDI* 463.

[21] *Waghorn* (1957), Judgment no28 of ILOAT, p 7, also in (1957) 24 *ILR* 752.

[22] A Verdross and B Simma, *Universelles Völkerrecht*, 3rd edn (Berlin, 1984) 280–81; Müller, *Vertrauensschutz* 229–30. See also the Dissenting Opinion of Judge Azevedo, *Competence for the Admission* (1950) *ICJ Reports* 23: 'by a unanimous vote, the signatories … stressed that the obligation assumed by the Members must be carried out in good faith. That is why the interpretation of the San Francisco instruments will always have to present a teleological character if they are to meet the requirements of world peace, co-operation between men, individual freedom and social progress. The Charter is a means and not an end. To comply with its aims one must seek the methods of interpretation most likely to serve the natural evolution of the needs of mankind.'

more demanding obligation of constitutional nature than the legitimate expectations doctrine of general international law. In the closer knit of an international organisation, institutionalising a given field of cooperation, the members assume more clearly defined obligations towards one another. To some extent, the good faith clause is there to blunt the too sharp edges of the principle of sovereignty enshrined in § 1 of article 2. There is a double blunt here: first, article 2, § 1, of the Charter speaks of 'sovereign equality' and not of sovereignty, recalling that the exercise of that notion must be such as to guarantee the equality of states (no absolute sovereignty); and, second, it is immediately followed by § 2, which recalls the necessary faithfulness to the common enterprise, if the organisation is to flourish at all. Without that propensity to cooperate there may be a façade of an international organisation; but there will be no organisation in flesh and blood.[23]

Good faith can concretely be called in action in an attempt to solve or smoothen certain problems the organisation faces in its day-to-day practice, eg with respect to the abusive exercise of some voting rights (*Conditions of Admission* advisory opinion, 1948),[24] with regard to the consequences of a transfer of an international organisation to another seat-state (*WHO* advisory opinion, 1980)[25] or with regard to the duty to renegotiate certain agreements (dissenting judges in the *International Status of South West Africa* advisory opinion, 1950).[26] Thus, equally, states must act carefully when they claim the ultra vires character of acts of the Organisation in order to further their own position, or generally when they indulge in more or less robust self-interpretation of their obligations. The aim is always to ensure a

[23] 'In this sense, the good-faith clause is a realistic expression of the conditions for the existence of the communal body. The fact that the principle of good faith is emphasized among the fundamental principles of the organizational law of the UN creates an awareness of the limits of technical rules and terminology, and at the same time attempts to mitigate them by appealing to the members' loyalty towards the community objectives agreed upon. One might say that the legal principle of good faith constitutes the enzyme in the organism of the institution, without which it would not be viable. The appeal for action in good faith is intended as a constant reminder that a set of treaties with such comprehensive objectives as those of the UN does not survive merely on the strength of the terms used and on its individual provisions, but only achieves its reality via the communal will of its members, for which there is ultimately no guarantee. Where, in a concrete case, there is no fundamental consensus among the community of nations on what is to be a legal obligation, or where the will to co-operate gives way to the overpowering weight of individual national interests, the substantial basis of the organization breaks down, even if the outward legality is preserved. The weakness of the good-faith clause, which is emphasized by some authors, is not so much a weakness of the legal concept, but rather an expression of the permanent risk to the community spirit to which it refers': R Kolb, 'Article 2(2) of the UN Charter', in B Simma, D E Khan, G Nolte and A Paulus (eds), *The Charter of the United Nations, A Commentary*, 3rd edn, vol I (Oxford, 2012) 172.

[24] *Conditions of Admission (advisory opinion)* (1948) *ICJ Reports* 62–63. See also G Sperduti, 'La buona fede e l'ammissione di nuovi membri nelle Nazioni Unite' (1952) 7 *Comunità internazionale* 47ff. On the abuse of voting rights and the veto, see Kolb, *Bonne* 516–17. For the scrutiny of a vote in a technical organization under the heading of *détournement de pouvoir*, see, *Constitution of the Maritime Safety Committee of the IMCO (advisory opinion)* (1960) *ICJ Pleadings* 77ff, 193ff, 249, 392, 406–08, 418, 439. See also generally Müller, *Vertrauensschutz* 234ff; E Zoller, *Bonne* 160ff.

[25] *WHO (advisory opinion)* (1980) *ICJ Reports*, 89ff.

[26] *International Status of South West Africa (advisory opinion)* (1950) *ICJ Reports* 183–85 (Judge Alvarez), 186–90 (Judge C De Visscher) and 191–92 (Judge Krylov).

certain degree of primacy to the common finalities on the manifestations of state individualism incompatible with them.[27] The principle of good faith thus allows the organs of the organisation the shaping of flexible duties and expectations with regard to member states in an attempt to find solutions to major or minor issues of contention, and sometimes even to major constitutional crises. The strength and success of the argument thus shaped will depend on many circumstantial and political factors. However that may be, the legal basis for such arguments may be found, among others, in the principle of good faith. No miracles can be expected; but there is a constitutional vehicle allowing the *legal* pursuit of such demands.

II. Good Faith and Non-Binding Resolutions

There are many potential effects of non-binding resolutions (recommendations) of an international organisation. Only the ones linked to the principle of good faith will interest us in the following lines.[28] We may immediately emphasise that these good faith effects give rise to legally weak obligations. It is not theoretically impossible for a state to give greater strength to such obligations by formulating claims, requiring justifications or possibly even adopting counter-measures for breach. But such a course is utterly improbable, considering the outer fringes of legal obligation in which we are situated. Practice shows that in general states do not attach great weight to deviance from recommendations. At the same time, however, in the context of some organisations, harder good faith obligations with regard to recommendatory resolutions have been developed. There are two main good faith effects to be analysed: (i) an estoppel flowing from an affirmative vote to the resolution; and (ii) a duty to take into account the resolution and to possibly give reasons in case of non-compliance.

A. Estoppel and Affirmative Vote

A first potential effect is an estoppel flowing from a favourable vote to a recommendation. A state having voted in favour of the recommendation might be said

[27] Kolb, *Bonne* 507.

[28] See G Dahm, *Völkerrecht*, vol II (Stuttgart, 1961) 26–27; GG Fitzmaurice, *The Law and Procedure of the International Court of Justice*, vol II (Cambridge, 1986) 710–13; FB Sloan, 'General Assembly Resolutions Revisited (Forty Years Later)' (1987) 58 *BYIL* 121–23. See also Müller, *Vertrauensschutz* 250ff; Zoller, *Bonne* 172ff and Kolb, *Bonne* 518ff. And see generally FB Sloan, *United Nations General Assembly Resolutions in Our Changing World* (New York, 1991); G Abi-Saab, 'Diplomatie multilatérale et développement du droit international—Le rôle des Résolutions de l'Assemblée générale' *Essays in Honor of J Siotis* (Brussels, 1995) 83ff; B Conforti and C Focarelli, *The Law and Practice of the United Nations*, 4th edn (Leiden, 2010) 403ff.

to be estopped from challenging its validity or content.[29] However, this conception has been vigorously contested:[30] states normally vote in favour of a resolution for a wide array of policy reasons, while being careful not to bind themselves legally.[31] Therefore, an estoppel could not be founded on such conduct, all the more since no legitimate reliance in legal consequences from the favourable vote could arise in other subjects. In simple words, all states know that the vote is a policy matter and that the fellow states will not attach legal consequences of coherence and responsibility to such conduct. To this it has been added that some treaty-making power problems might arise: a political delegate of a state in the UN General Assembly has no power to bind the state by his vote.[32] Finally, it has been added that the admission of estoppels in this context would paralyse or at least considerably hamper the work of international organisations. States would hesitate to vote a whole series of resolutions, fearing to be caught in a trap.[33] Undoubtedly, it is erroneous to affirm that a favourable vote per se creates an estoppel. There can be no automatic legitimate expectation here, nor is a detrimental reliance flowing from the mere vote. But in special circumstances an estoppel could ensue, when a state has given particular assurances to other states, eg in some declarations

[29] G Schwarzenberger, *International Law—As Applied by International Courts and Tribunals*, 3rd edn, vol I (London, 1957) 51–52, and vol II (London, 1968) 47–48: 'In form, the Resolution adopted by the General Assembly is a mere affirmation, and not an automatically binding decision. Yet, the fact that the Resolution embodies statements of a declaratory character, may be thought to estop in future members of the United Nations from challenging the binding character of the rules … In the case of members who actually voted in favour of the Resolution, such an interpretation of their vote could draw additional support from the good faith clause in paragraph 2 of Article 2 of the United Nations Charter'. See also D Thürer, 'Soft Law—eine neue Form von Völkerrecht?' (1985) 104 *Zeitschrift für schweizerisches Recht* 445–46. Some authors go further and attribute a legislative function to the UNGA (a view which has in the meantime been abandoned): TO Elias, 'Modern Sources of International Law', *Essays in Honor of P Jessup* (New York, 1972) 46, 51; TO Elias, 'The Rulemaking Process and the Future of International Law' (1981) *ASIL Proceedings* 29–30; M Bedjaoui, *Towards a New International Economic Order* (Paris, 1979) 179; Diss O Alvarez, *Effects of Awards of Compensation made by the UNAT* advisory opinion (1954) *ICJ Reports* 71–72 (on this conception: W Samore, 'The New International Law of Alejandro Alvarez' (1958) 52 *AJIL* 41ff, 44–46). For an application of good faith and estoppel to soft law in general, see eg C Tomuschat, 'International Law: Ensuring the Survival of Mankind on the Eve of a New Century' (1999) 281 *RCADI* 350.

[30] Zoller, *Bonne* 181.

[31] B Simma, 'Methodik und Bedeutung der Arbeit der Vereinten Nationen für die Fortentwicklung des Völkerrechts', in *Institut für Internationales Recht der Universität Kiel, Die Vereinten Nationen im Wandel* (Berlin, 1976) 101–02; M Mendelson, 'The Formation of Customary International Law' (1998) 272 *RCADI* 366–68.

[32] HA Smith, 'The Binding Force of a League Resolution' (1935) 16 *BYIL* 158; statements by L Condorelli and G Gaja, in A Cassese and JH Weiler (eds), *Change and Stability in International Law-Making* (Berlin, 1988) 41–42, 52, 62, 171–72. On this question, see O Asamoah, *The Legal Significance of the Declarations of the General Assembly of the United Nations* (The Hague, 1966) 64ff; J Castaneda, *Legal Effects of United Nations Resolutions* (New York, 1969) 150ff; FB Sloan, *United Nations General Assembly Resolutions in Our Changing World* (New York, 1991) 65 and 509–10, fn 307; S Bastid, 'Observations sur une "étape" dans le développement progressif et la codification des principes du droit international', *Essays in Honor of P Guggenheim* (Geneva, 1968) 136.

[33] P Dailler, M Forteau and A Pellet, *Droit international public*, 8th edn (Paris, 2009) 417.

accompanying the vote. Thus, as has been written by an eminent specialist of the subject matter:

> If an affirmative vote gives rise to reasonable expectations on the part of other states concerning a course of conduct, or if actions following the adoption of a resolution give rise to such expectations, and if the other states have acted upon these expectations, a state may be estopped or precluded from denying an obligation.[34]

In other words, estoppel does not flow *from* a vote but can arise *on occasion* of a vote. Its elements, notably a legitimate expectation created and a detrimental reliance produced, must then be shown. It stands to reason that this will be difficult to establish; but it is not impossible. An estoppel may flow from the most different state behaviours. Conduct in respect of resolutions is not excluded from the range of the principle. Notice that some other corollary effects may follow from an affirmative vote: the impossibility to contest the formal validity of the resolution; or the impossibility to contest the illegality of the attitude of states acting upon the recommendation.[35] Clear examples of an estoppel in the context of affirmative votes to recommendations have not come to the fore. But the possibility that an estoppel might operate remains. The lack of practice is mainly a reflection of the strict conditions an estoppel requires, which are particularly difficult to realise in the volatile context of votes with respect to non-binding resolutions.

B. Examine the Recommendation in Good Faith and Possibly Give Reasons for Non-Compliance

The second duty is to examine the adopted text in good faith and possibly to state the reasons for a refusal to follow the recommendation.[36] This type of duty can be

[34] FB Sloan, 'General Assembly Resolutions Revisited (Forty Years Later)' (1987) 58 *BYIL* 65 and 43, 94, 103–04, 123, 140; FB Sloan, *United Nations General Assembly Resolutions in Our Changing World* (New York, 1991) 65, 102–03; Müller, *Vertrauensschutz* 251–52; R Bindschedler, 'La délimitation des compétences des Nations Unies' (1963-I) 108 *RCADI* 345–46, 349; O Schachter, 'The Relation of Law, Politics and Action in the United Nations' (1963-II) 109 *RCADI* 16; DW Bowett, *United Nations Forces, A Legal Study of United Nations Practice* (London, 1964) 422, fn 39; E Schwelb, 'Neue Etappen der Fortentwicklung des Völkerrechts durch die Vereinten Nationen' (1966) 13 *AVR* 21; K Bailey, 'Making International Law in the United Nations' (1967) *ASIL Proceedings* 237; S Bleicher, 'The Legal Significance of Re-Citation of General Assembly Resolutions' (1969) 63 *AJIL* 447, fn 19; A D'Amato, 'On Consensus' (1970) 8 *CYIL* 115, 121; B Conforti, 'Le rôle de l'accord dans le système des Nations Unies' (1974-II) 142 *RCADI* 271ff; U Scheuner, 'Internationale Verträge als Elemente der Bildung von völkerrechtlichem Gewohnheitsrecht', *Essays in Honor of FA Mann* (Munich, 1977) 434; M Mendelson, 'The Legal Character of General Assembly Resolutions: Some Considerations of Principle', in K Hossain (ed), *Legal Aspects of the New International Economic Order* (London, 1980) 96–97.

[35] Sloan, 'General Assembly', op cit, p 114ff. For the issue of the formal validity of the resolution, see *Certain Expenses (advisory opinion)* (1962) *ICJ Reports* 176ff and Separate Opinion Fitzmaurice, ibid, 210.

[36] P Dailler, M Forteau and A Pellet, *Droit international public*, 8th edn (Paris, 2009) 418: 'Tout Etat membre est tenu, pour le moins, d'examiner la recommandation de bonne foi. Celle-ci représente en effet l'opinion de la majorité des membres de l'organisation dans laquelle l'Etat a librement choisi d'entrer et dont il a accepté les finalités' (italics omitted).

found in some constitutions of international organisations, and was developed in general terms by H Lauterpacht in the context of the South West Africa mandate. In the 1950s, in order to implement the advisory opinion of the ICJ of 1950, the UN General Assembly had adopted a series of non-binding resolutions furthering its own monitoring of the mandated territory. South Africa, the mandatory Power, sternly refused to cooperate. According to H Lauterpacht, South Africa was not entitled to entirely ignore these resolutions, as if the legal situation had been the same whether these resolutions were adopted or not. He then went on to state some good faith duties:

> The State in question, while not bound to accept the recommendation, is bound to give it due consideration in good faith. If, having regard to its own ultimate responsibility for the good government of the territory, it decides to disregard it, it is bound to explain the reasons for its decision.[37]

We may notice that South Africa held a mandate conferred on it by the League of Nations. The UN had succeeded to this mandate. South Africa could not ignore the position of its treaty partner with regard to the mandate.

These double-branch obligations (consideration/information) have in the meantime gained strong support and have been considered to reflect general duties of members of international organisations.[38] Some authors however admit only an obligation of consideration, not one of information.[39] There are also some authors rejecting entirely both sets of good faith obligations.[40] Do such obligations exist within international law? The truth of this matter is circumstantial.

[37] Separate Opinion H Lauterpacht, *Voting Procedure on Questions Relating to Reports and Petitions Concerning the Territory of South-West Africa* (1955) *ICJ Reports* 119. See also Separate Opinion Klaestad, ibid, 88, rather under the lens of moral and political duties. This type of duty has been applied elsewhere, eg to proposals of humanitarian assistance made to states by the ICRC: see F Bugnion, *Le Comité international de la Croix-Rouge et la protection des victims de la guerre* (Geneva, 1986) 410.

[38] FB Sloan, 'General Assembly Resolutions Revisited (Forty Years Later)' (1987) 58 *BYIL* 121–22; O Asamoah, *The Legal Significance of the Declarations of the General Assembly of the United Nations* (The Hague, 1966) 59–60; GG Fitzmaurice, *The Law and Procedure of the International Court of Justice*, vol II (Cambridge, 1986) 710–13; A Malintoppi, *Le raccomandazioni internazionali*, Milan, 1958) 323ff; LB Sohn, 'The Development of the Charter of the United Nations: the Present State', in M Bos (ed), *The Present State of International Law and Other Essays* (Deventer, 1973) 51; C Schreuer, 'Recommandations and the Traditional Sources of International Law' (1977) 20 *GYIL* 118; M Virally, 'Panorama du droit international contemporain' (1983-V) 183 *RCADI* 261; and M Virally, 'La valeur juridique des recommandations des organisations internationales' (1956) 2 *AFDI* 81ff, 88; BS Murty, *The International Law of Diplomacy, The Diplomatic Instrument and World Public Order* (Dordrecht, 1989) 618; S Schwager, *Empfehlungen internationaler Organisationen besonders auf dem Gebiet der europäischen Raumordnung* (Basle, 1990) 101–02; G Abi-Saab, 'Diplomatie multilatérale et développement du droit international—Le rôle des résolutions de l'Assemblée générale', *Essays in Honor of J Siotis* (Brussels, 1995) 88; etc. See also Dissenting Opinion Gros, *Namibia (advisory opinion)* (1971) *ICJ Reports* 341.

[39] RL Bindschedler, 'La délimitation des compétences des Nations Unies' (1963-I) 108 *RCADI* 346–48; G Dahm, *Völkerrecht*, t II (Stuttgart, 1961) 26–27 and fn 11.

[40] Zoller, Bonne 177ff, 180; JHW Verzijl, *International Law in Historical Perspective*, vol I (Leiden, 1968) 77: 'To my mind it is in any case impossible to acknowledge the validity under the Charter of the proposition that Recommandations of the General Assembly ... are, as such, clothed with binding force, *however limited*, as long as they remain the plaything of politics, being either acted upon or neglected according to from what quarter the political wind blows'.

The degree to which such obligations exist or can be developed depends on the applicable treaties and rules on the one hand, and on the strength of the solidarities on a certain subject matter or of a certain institution on the other hand. First, it must be considered whether the rules of the organisation state a duty to take into account and to inform on some point. If they do, the question turns into one of black-letter law obligations. This is the case, for example, in the context of article 19, § 6, of the Constitution of the ILO.[41] Second, it must be considered to what extent a subject matter is 'internationalised', as eg the situation of mandates/trusteeships, which were based on a contractual grant by the organisation to a member state. This was the context in which H Lauterpacht developed his seminal doctrine. The same may be said of the 'decisions' of the UN human rights committees under the several human rights treaties. These utterances are technically speaking recommendations, but there is a duty of good faith to take them into due account and to inform about the follow-up.[42] Third, it has to be considered to what extent a certain institution is based on a close and exacting knit of solidarities, and thus of duties of cooperation. The jurisprudence of the Court of Justice of the European Communities (now Court of Justice of the European Union) has drawn strict consequences from article 10 (formerly article 5) of the Treaty of the European Communities. This provision obliges states to abstain from taking measures jeopardising the realisation of the aims of the Treaty.[43] Such aims are sometimes concretised through recommendations of the political organs of the Union. These must then be taken into account and information upon their implementation be given.

Apart from these situations, the obligations to take into due account and to give information remain weak. The first one can be more easily admitted, but it remains somewhat impalpable. A sanction for its non-respect is hardly imaginable in practice. Some examples affirming the existence of such good faith duties in general international law must however be noticed. As will be seen, the one or the other of these examples is rather ancient, which shows that the duties of due consideration and information are not an invention of the UN age, and neither one of the eminent Judge H Lauterpacht. Thus, the Federal Department of Justice of Switzerland stated in a Report of 1923 that some non-binding resolutions by

[41] See FB Sloan, 'The Binding Force of a Recommendation of the General Assembly of the United Nations' (1948) 25 *BYIL* 10.

[42] See eg Committee of Human Rights of the CCPR, 1966, *General Comment No 33*, UN Doc CCPR/C/GC/33, 5 November 2008, §§ 14ff. See further the *Loayza Tamayo v Peru (Merits)* case, (1997) 116 *ILR* 383, § 80 (IACtHR), where the Court stated that there is for the state a duty of good faith to make every effort to comply with the recommendation of a human rights protection organ, such as the Inter-American Commission of Human Rights, and that this duty flows from the ratification of the Convention. Compare the more moderate statement in *Briggs v Baptiste* (1999) 123 *ILR* 546 (Trinidad and Tobago, Judicial Committee of the Privy Council), whereby recommendations of human rights bodies are not binding but the recommended action should be duly considered in good faith; to the same effect, *Thomas v Baptiste* (1999) 123 *ILR* 520–21, 528–30 (Trinidad and Tobago, Judicial Committee of the Privy Council).

[43] See eg Case no 804/79 (1981) *Reports* 1045.

the Central Rhine Commission should not be arbitrarily rejected by the member states.[44] Still in 1923, in the context of a draft resolution for the interpretation of article 10 of the League of Nations Covenant, the First Commission of the Assembly stated that the recommendation of the Council to be made on that issue would have to be duly taken into account by the member states with a view to securing a proper execution of their duties towards the League.[45] In the context of the elaboration of the Universal Declaration of Human Rights in 1948, which was eventually embodied in a recommendation of the UN General Assembly, the Belgian delegate to the third Committee of the UN General Assembly emphasised that no state would be bound to implement that text, but that each state would have a duty to take into due account the resolution and to consider what consequences could be given to it.[46] It must also be noted that it occurs—notably in important matters—that states justify their position with regard to recommendations of international organisations.[47] Whether this is done with *opinio juris* is open to question. But when the stakes are legally important, such a legal opinion cannot be bluntly denied.

Overall, the extent to which these two obligations of due consideration and of information are heeded in practice is not an easy question. There seems to be some difference between particular and general international law. When the constitutive instruments and rules of an organisation provide for a system of control, the degree of cooperation of member states is frequently not negligible. The duties of consideration and information take shape and place. Contrariwise, when the issue is approached under the lens of general international law, the fate of the recommendation depends on many imponderables and particularly on the strength of the political will of the majority and concomitantly on the relative isolation of the minority. These are not legal but political questions. The doctrine of due consideration and information is then but a tool which can be used, abused, or eventually neglected, by the states concerned.

III. Good Faith in International Administrative Law

The protection of staff members of international organisations has produced an important branch of international law, called administrative international law. This law is applied by a series of international administrative tribunals, being subsidiary organs of various international organisations. International administrative

[44] P Guggenheim (ed), *Répertoire suisse de droit international public*, vol I (Bern, 1975) 272.

[45] *Journal officiel, Suppl spécial no 14, Actes de la Quatrième Assemblée, Séances des Commissions, Procès-verbaux de la Première Commission* (Geneva, 1923) 27, original French version.

[46] FB Sloan, 'The Binding Force of a Recommendation of the General Assembly of the United Nations' (1948) 25 *BYIL* 30.

[47] ibid, 20.

law has been heavily influenced by the principles and rules of municipal administrative law science, especially the ones of the civil law systems. As was stated by the Court of Justice of the European Communities in the *Lachmüller* case of 1960, the principle of good faith dominates the contractual relationships between the organisation and the staff member.[48] We therefore find all typical aspects of public law good faith in this area of international jurisprudence: namely the protection of legitimate expectations, the consequences flowing from acquiescence and estoppel, the prohibition of abuse and arbitrary action, the prohibition of misuse of authority, and so on. Some examples of the very rich case law will now be given. A complete perusal of the whole body of case law is beyond the scope of this book and would require a weighty monograph of its own.

A. Détournement de Pouvoir (Abuse/Misuse of Authority) and Abuse of Rights

The condemnation of *détournement* or misuse has given rise to ongoing jurisprudence. Indeed, the number of cases where this concept has been raised is overwhelming.[49] The prohibition of *détournement* means that the judge will not accept the exercise of a competence or of a discretion when this exercise seeks to accomplish an aim which is alien to the function for which that competence or discretion was granted. As was said by the World Bank Administrative Tribunal in the celebrated *Merode* case of 1981:

> The Bank would abuse its discretion if it were to adopt such changes *for reasons alien to the proper functioning of the organization* and to its duty to ensure that it has a staff possessing 'the highest standards of efficiency and of technical competence'. Changes must

[48] (1960) VI *Reports* 989. And see CF Amerasinghe, *The Law of the International Civil Service*, vol II (Oxford, 1988) 682. On the principle of good faith and related principles in this context, see eg JES Fawcett, 'Détournement de pouvoir by International Organisations' (1957) 33 *BYIL* 311ff; MB Akehurst, 'Le principe de l'estoppel en droit administratif international' (1966) 93 *JDI* 285ff; G Schwarzenberger, *International Law—As Applied by International Courts and Tribunals*, vol III (London, 1976) 449ff; M Gounelle, *La motivation des actes juridiques en droit international public* (Paris, 1979) 210–14; CF Amerasinghe, *The Law of the International Civil Service*, vols I/II (Oxford, 1988) vol I, pp 271ff, 353ff; vol II, pp 682, 747ff; 2nd edn (Oxford, 1994) vol I, pp 277ff, 363–64; vol II, p 120ff; P Pescatore, 'Les principes généraux du droit régissant la fonction publique internationale' *Essays in Honor of M Diez de Velasco* (Madrid, 1993) 565ff. The case law of the international administrative tribunals can now be consulted online. For the UNAT, see www.untreaty.un.org/UNAT/Judgments. For the ILOAT, see www.ilo.org/dyn/triblex/triblexmain.advancedSearch.

[49] CF Amerasinghe, 'Détournement de pouvoir in International Administrative Law' (1984) 44 *ZaöRV* 439ff; Amerasinghe, *Law*, op cit, vol I, pp 260, 271ff, 353–54, vol II, pp 735–36, 757–58, 763–64, 777, 794–95, 826–27, 838–39, 888ff, 904–05, 907, 917ff, 937, 968, 991–92; Schwarzenberger, *International*, op cit, vol III (London, 1976) 449ff; Gounelle, op cit, 210ff; CW Jenks, *The Proper Law of International Organisations* (London, 1962) 94ff; MB Akehurst, *The Law Governing Employment in International Organisations* (Cambridge, 1967) 148ff. See also M Bedjaoui, 'Jurisprudence comparée des tribunaux administratifs internationaux en matière d'excès de pouvoir' (1956) 2 *AFDI* 484ff. For the recent case law, a search on the internet sites yields impressive results.

be based on a proper consideration of relevant facts. They must be reasonably related to the objective which they are intended to achieve. They must be *made in good faith and must not be prompted by improper motives.*[50]

Thus, this doctrine of misuse of power has been applied in several contexts. *First*, the tribunals have sanctioned abuses of procedure. This occurs for example when the administration takes certain decisions under an improper procedure so as to curtail some rights of the staff member, or elsewise to worsen his position. For example, the disciplinary procedure for alleged faults is not used, but the official's contract is not renewed.[51] The same is true when the staff member is affected to a useless post instead of engaging the proper steps to terminate his contract according to usual procedures.[52] The tribunals have also sanctioned the abuse of procedure by the staff member, eg in the context of dilatory and frivolous appeals.[53] *Second*, the doctrine of misuse has been applied to the merits of the staff member's rights, eg the appointment,[54] the evaluation of work,[55] questions of grade[56] and promotion,[57] questions of transfer to other posts,[58] abolition of posts,[59] questions of salary,[60] questions of non-renewal of contract,[61] questions of termination of contract,[62] etc. Many decisions were based on the existence of ill-feelings, prejudice, animosities, improper motives and personal hostility to the staff member, influencing discretionary decisions affecting that staff member.[63] In other cases, tribunals found decisions to be arbitrary, ie not justified by the facts, incoherent and insufficiently articulated.[64] This is another form of abuse of rights. As can be

[50] *Merode, Jugement no 1* (1981) *WBAT Reports* 22, emphasis added.

[51] See eg *Gausi (no 1)* (1973) ILOAT, Judgment no 223, decision without paragraphs; *Nemeth* (1974) ILOAT, Judgment no 247, § 3ff.

[52] *Richards* (1993) ILOAT, Judgment no 1231, § 24ff.

[53] *Cunio* (1983) UNAT, Judgment no 317, p 135; *Saunders (no 11)* (1995) ILOAT, Judgment no 1423, § 5.

[54] See eg *Créchet* (1988) ILOAT, Judgment no 890, § 5.

[55] See eg *Glynn* (1971) ILOAT, Judgment no 182, § 3, without the words 'abuse of authority' but in substance applying that doctrine.

[56] *Lindemann* (1989) ILOAT, Judgment no 968, § 8ff.

[57] *Carbo* (1982) ILOAT, Judgment no 519.

[58] *Quinones* (1981) ILOAT, Judgment no 447, § 4ff.

[59] *PM (no 2)* (2016) ILOAT, Judgment no 3688, § 14.

[60] *Connolly-Battisti (no 5)* (1977) ILOAT, Judgment no 323, § 29ff, arbitrariness. On the issue of salary deductions for participation in strikes, see *BJ (no 2) and others* (2016) ILOAT, Judgment no 3691, § 1ff.

[61] See eg *Rosescu* (1980) ILOAT, Judgment no 431, § 5ff, non-renewal of contract following political pressure from the state of nationality of the official, the ILOAT quashing the decision of non-renewal. See generally CF Amerasinghe, *The Law of the International Civil Service*, vol II (Oxford, 1988) 747–48. In the newer case law, see eg *A (no 2)* (2016) ILOAT, Judgment no 3703, § 1ff; *P* (2016) ILOAT, Judgment no 3679, § 1ff.

[62] *Fayemivo* (1979) UNAT, Judgment no 246, p 168ff.

[63] *Fasla* (1974) UNAT, Judgment no 158, p 367ff; *Dicancro* (1980) ILOAT, Judgment no 427, § 2ff; *Olivares Silva* (1982) ILOAT, Judgment no 495, § 1ff.

[64] *Ozorio (no 4)* (1994) ILOAT, Judgment no 1367, § 16; *Fernandez-Caballero* (1988) ILOAT, Judgment no 946, § 7ff, arbitrary action in breach of good faith. See also *N(A) (no 3)* (2016) ILOAT, Judgment no 3647, § 14, in the context of the lawfulness of appointments resulting from a competition process.

seen, the doctrine of abuse of rights, or *détournement de pouvoir*, is prominent in the case law of international administrative tribunals. It might be said that this is a strong indication of the principle of good faith in this subject area … even if this statement leads to something of a paradox!

B. Protection of Legitimate Expectations

The doctrine of reliance on good faith has in our context been applied notably as a legitimate expectation to the renewal of a contract. This doctrine of expectation is a jurisprudential creation of the administrative tribunals. Its link with the principle of good faith was acknowledged in the earliest case law,[65] the tribunals distinguishing legitimate expectation from the simple hope to be renewed.[66] Thus, it is necessary that concrete conduct by the administration has strengthened a mere factual hope so as to give an objective sense of normative expectation. An external element—as opposed to the mere inner hope—is necessary. Moreover, the conduct of the administration must be concrete and clear enough, and not vague and uncertain, or non-committal. There are different factors which may lead to a legitimate expectation: eg the excellence of the services;[67] concrete recommendations to renew the contract;[68] few specialised candidates for a significant number of posts in a given subject area;[69] the habitual practice of the organisation;[70] the importance of the organ or person having given assurances;[71] or the prolonged silence of the organisation with regard to the fate of the contract.[72] Conversely, some facts hamper the establishment of a legitimate expectation: if an assurance is given by a manifestly incompetent organ or person;[73] if the renewal of the contract has ostensibly been made dependent on the fulfilment of certain conditions;[74] or the manifest unsuitability of a candidate for a certain post.[75] The doctrine of legitimate expectation has also been applied in other contexts than the renewal of contracts. Thus, it has been held that a given interpretation of a provision—even if ill-conceived—had to be heeded with respect of a staff member who had relied in good faith on it.[76] Conversely, a clear practice can also exclude a legitimate

65 *Agarwala* (1968) ILOAT, Judgment no 121, no paragraphs, last sentence before the Decision.

66 Thus, the simple fact of being on a list for a new post does not create a legitimate expectation that the employment will follow: *Seraphides* (1971) UNAT, Judgment no 140, pp 243–44. The same is true of vague assurances to be considered: *Alexis* (1981) ILOAT, Judgment no 444, § 1.

67 *Levcik* (1974) UNAT, Judgment no 192, p 217, no XVII.

68 ibid.

69 *Robinson* (1952) UNAT, Judgment no 15, pp 49, 53, §§ 19, 29.

70 *Dale* (1969) UNAT, Judgment no 132, p 179, § 5.

71 *Perucho* (1982) UNAT, Judgment no 285, p 533, § 2.

72 *Cipolla* (1982) UNAT, Judgment no 290, p 578, § XIX.

73 *Al-Abed* (1969) UNAT, Judgment no 128, p 141ff, § IIff.

74 *Rau* (1984) UNAT, Judgment no 339, p 304, § II.

75 *Flad* (1983) UNAT, Judgment no 318, p 143, § VII.

76 *Nielsen* (1982) ILOAT, Judgment no 522, § 12 (3).

expectation as to some treatment.[77] By virtue of the same principle of legitimate expectations and good faith, a staff member is entitled to rely on a promise. Such promises are binding when they emanate from a competent or apparently competent organ, and when the applicable law has not changed in the meantime.[78] The doctrine of legitimate expectations has further been applied for example to the length of the prospective employment[79] or the status as 'non-local' agent.[80] The principle of good faith finally also requires reasonable time to be given, for example before a transfer to another post becomes effective.[81] There is a legitimate expectation that such measures will not be taken from one day to the other.

C. Nobody Should Profit from his Own Wrong

This maxim has been applied by the international administrative tribunals. In the *Conrad and others* case (1977),[82] the organisation had led the staff member to believe that he had no right to reimbursement for a certain item. When the staff member finally demanded that reimbursement, it refused to pay by invoking the lateness of the demand. The ILOAT affirmed that the organisation could not rely on its own fault, but considered this tort to be insufficiently established in the present case. Further, in the *Pinto de Magelhaes (no 3)* case (1992),[83] the organisation had pleaded that the staff member could not go back on what he had previously stated on his period of residence in Geneva in 1964, even if that now turned out to be false: *nemo auditur…* (the issue was one of local or non-local status of the staff member). The ILOAT accepted this argument but framed the issue under the principle of estoppel, holding that the staff member was now estopped from contending that he was wrongly given resident status in 1964. In the *CP* case (2004),[84] the tribunal considered that the complainant staff member could not lay the blame on the organisation for choices she had made herself, going on to state the maxim *nemo auditur suam propriam turpitudinem allegans*. It also occurs that our maxim is applied under the guise of the principle of good faith and without a separate mention. Thus, in the *D* case (2016), the ILOAT held that the organisation could not prevail itself of a time-bar for an appeal when the defendant organisation had mislead the complainant, thereby depriving him or her of the possibility to timely exercise his or her rights, in breach of the principle of good faith.[85]

[77] *Metten and others* (1985) ILOAT, Judgment no 657, § 6.

[78] *Gieser* (1986) ILOAT, Judgment no 782, § 1 See also *Farinetti, Porta and Tuzii* (1986) ILOAT, Judgment no 741, § 11.

[79] *Rogatko* (1993) ILOAT, Judgment no 1278, § 12ff.

[80] *Brocard* (1985) ILOAT, Judgment no 676, § 7.

[81] *Najman (no 5)* (1987) ILOAT, Judgment no 810, § 7, no 'due' time.

[82] *Conrad and others* (1977) ILOAT, Judgment no 328, § 2ff.

[83] *Pinto de Magelhaes (no 3)* (1992) ILOAT, Judgment no 1189, letter C and § 5 of the Considerations.

[84] *CP* (2004) ILOAT, Judgment no 2318, § 6, letter c

[85] *D* (2016) ILOAT, Judgment no 3704, § 3, with a quote of the previous jurisprudence on this point.

D. Estoppel

In the *Rothbarth* case (1947),[86] the ILOAT judged that various demands for collaboration established that a certain person was considered as part of the personnel. This could not later be contested. By the same token, an organisation has been considered to be precluded from contesting the competence of the administrative tribunal after it had formally declared its willingness to oppose the claim of a staff member.[87] Similarly, a time-bar cannot after the fact be invoked when the director had not heeded it and had examined the case on the merits.[88] Further, a staff member could not invoke a new date of birth after he had himself previously communicated a different date to the organisation.[89] The same is true for the communication of local or non-local residence.[90] In the *DD and others* case (2009),[91] the ILOAT was confronted with a departure from a settled practice resulting in prejudice for the staff member in the context of not granting retroactive effect to a promotion. Staff members promoted before new guidelines were issued had relied on the old practice. The ILOAT found that in view of the principles of good faith and of estoppel, the organisation was obliged to follow that practice. A careful examination of estoppel was made in the *JW* case (2010),[92] in the context of a non-assignment to a new post. Estoppel was rejected in this case, since it could not be shown that the organisation acted on some representation of the staff member (by his inactivity) or that there was an altering of position as a consequence of that representation.

E. Acquiescence

Silence and passivity may modify the set of rights and obligations applicable between the organisation and the staff member. In the old *Waghorn* case (1957), the ILOAT affirmed that a staff member who repeatedly without any protest had accepted certain generous payments made by the organisation could be considered to have abandoned any additional pretences.[93] In the *JW* case (2010),[94] the organisation argued that the lack of protest of the staff member against a non-assignment meant that he had acquiesced in that course (while raising a mainly estoppel argument). The Tribunal however recalled that the silence could only be

86 *Rothbarth* (1947) ILOAT, Judgment no 6, no paragraphs, "On the Substance".

87 *Perrasse* (1935) Administrative Tribunal of the League of Nations, Judgment no 14. See MB Akehurst, 'Le principe de l'estoppel en droit administratif international' (1966) *JDI* 93 297.

88 *Podniesinski* (1970) ILOAT, Judgment no 181, § 4.

89 *Luqman* (1985) UNAT, Judgment no 348, pp 407–08, § Vff.

90 *Pinto de Magelhaes (no 3)* (1992) ILOAT, Judgment no 1189, Letter C and § 5 of the Considerations.

91 *DD and others* (2009) ILOAT, Judgment no 2770, § 17.

92 *JW* (2010) ILOAT, Judgment no 2873, §§ 6–7.

93 *Waghorn* case (1957) ILOAT, Judgment no 28, last point of section B; also, in (1957) 24 *ILR* 752.

94 *JW* (2010) ILOAT, Judgment no 2873, § 6–7.

relevant if the circumstances required an answer on the part of the staff member. It then went on to examine the situation under the limb of the main argument, which was estoppel.

F. Subjective Good Faith

Subjective good faith is not absent from the case law of the administrative tribunals. Thus, in the *Fellhauer* case (1988),[95] the staff member could not establish his subjective good faith (ie excusable error) in the context of certain financial irregularities. Contrariwise, subjective good faith (ie excusable error) could be established in the *Ranaivoson* case (1989)[96] in the context of the reimbursement of certain expenses.

G. Objective Good Faith

There are some applications of the principle of good faith raising several relevant aspects and therefore not fitting in isolation into any of the previous headings. An example can be found in the *C (no 3)* case (2016) of the ILOAT. The debated issue occurred in the context of the correction of an error. The Tribunal stated the case thus:

> However, notwithstanding that a decision which is based on a purely factual error did not create any rights, it could be reversed only on certain considerations dictated by the principle of good faith. This principle requires, first, that the power to reverse a decision resting on a factual error must be exercised as soon as the competent authority notices the error in question and not at a later date chosen at its own convenience. Secondly, this principle requires that if the person who benefitted from the error has not contributed to it, she or he must not suffer any unfavourable consequences from the application of the decision in question during the period before it was reversed.[97]

We may notice in passing that the last sentence relies on the maxim 'nobody should profit from his own wrong': it implies that if the person benefiting from the error had contributed to its occurrence, he or she would have to suffer the unfavourable consequences that arose.

Overall, there is thus impressive case law on good faith and its related principles in the jurisprudence of the international administrative tribunals. The reader will in particular appreciate that this case law applies the whole spectrum of good faith-related principles in a capillary and reasoned manner. In particular, this case law is a rich playground for abuse of power, abuse of authority, abuse of process and abuse of rights-related arguments.

[95] *Fellhauer* (1988) ILOAT, Judgment no 937, § 14.
[96] *Ranaivoson* (1989) ILOAT, Judgment no 976, § 7.
[97] *C (no 3)* (2016) ILOAT, Judgment no 3693, § 18.

IV. Good Faith in International Commercial and WTO Law

Commercial law is heavily dependent on notions of legal certainty and confidence between the contracting parties. No one engages into investments and commerce without some guarantees on the foreseeability of action and on concomitant protection of his economic interests. Thus, well before the WTO was created, international commercial law and arbitration practice relied on the principle of good faith.[98] The importance of this principle in the branch of commercial international law has been emphasised in many awards, among which *Palbalk Ticaret v Norsolor* (1979).[99] The principle of good faith has founded in this subject area the various rules we have encountered elsewhere: (i) a series of awards apply the doctrine of legitimate expectations;[100] (ii) another series of awards apply the doctrine of abuse of rights;[101] (iii) pre-contractual duties were derived from good faith, in analogy to article 18 VCLT, 1969;[102] (iv) the duty to negotiate in good faith gave rise to similar concretisations as in general international law;[103] (v) good faith directs

[98] For these earlier times, see A Goldstajn, 'Bona fides in International Commercial Arbitration', in *Hague/Zagreb Colloquium on the Law of International Trade, Session 1978* (The Hague, 1980) 235ff; JDM Lew, 'Bona fides in International Commercial Arbitration' ibid, 244ff; P Lalive, 'Sur la bonne foi dans l'exécution des contrats', *Essays in Honor of R van der Elst*, vol I (Brussels, 1986) 425ff; P Kahn, 'Les principes généraux du droit devant les arbitres du commerce international' (1989) 116 *JDI* 305ff, 318ff; F Osman, *Les principes généraux de la lex mercatoria* (Paris, 1992) 18ff; N Nasser, 'The Development and Evolution of Rights and Obligations in Long-Term International Commercial Transactions' (PhD thesis, Geneva, 1993) 160ff; P Mayer, 'Le principe de bonne foi devant les arbitres du commerce international', *Essays in Honor of P Lalive* (Basle, 1993) 543ff; R Harrison, *Good Faith in Sales* (London, 1997; P Pinsolle, 'Distinction entre le principe de l'estoppel et le principe de bonne foi dans le droit du commerce international' (1998) 125 *JDI* 905ff. Some awards and a short comment can be found, in *Collection of ICC Arbitral Awards*, several volumes: 1986–90; 1991–95; 1996–2000; 2001–07; 2008–11(Kluwer Law).

[99] *Palbalk Ticaret v Norsolor* (1979) 29 *Revue de l'arbitrage* 530.

[100] *ICCo Award no 1434* (1976) 103 *JDI* 978; *ICCo Award no 3380* (1981) 108 *JDI* 928; *ICCo Award no 3460* (1981) 108 *JDI* 939. In *ICCo Award no 5904* (1989) 116 *JDI* 1107, it was held that in the case of a contract that was constantly renewed, there accrued a legitimate expectation of that continuity, having as a consequence that a period of notice of two months was considered too short.

[101] Thus, for example, the withdrawal from a contract in the face of minor delays in its execution and without other valid reason to terminate was considered to be abusive: *ICCo Award no 5904* (1989) 116 *JDI* 1107. Similarly, disproportionate claims of reparation with regard to the profits to be expected were rejected as being abusive: *ICCo Award no 4145* (1987) 12 *Yearbook of Commercial Arbitration* 109. The prohibition of abuse of rights had been applied also in the context of fundamental change of circumstances (*ICCo Award no 4761* (1986) 113 *JDI* 1137; *ICCo Award no 5953* (1990) 117 *JDI* 1056; *ICCo Award no 6219* (1990) 117 *JDI* 1047; *ICCo Award no 2508* (1977) 104 *JDI* 940–41) and of the piercing of the corporate veil (*ICCo Award no 5721* (1990) 117 *JDI* 1019). See also *ICCo Award no 12,456* (2004), in *Collection of ICC Arbitral Awards, 2008-2011* (Alphen a d Rijn, 2013) 821, 823.

[102] *ICCo Award no 2540* (1977) 104 *JDI* 943, *culpa in contrahendo*.

[103] *Aminoil* (1982) 21 *ILM* 1004; *ICCo Award no 5953* (1990) 117 *JDI* 1056ff, 1060. On duties to inform the other party, see eg *Atlantic Triton* (1988) 115 *JDI* 182; *Klöckner Industrie-Anlagen GmbH*, ICSID arbitration (1983) 114 *ILR* 153ff.

the interpretation and execution of contracts;[104] as well as the withdrawal from contracts;[105] (vi) there is a good faith duty to attempt to mitigate the amount of damage suffered through an unlawful act by taking reasonable measures;[106] (vii) estoppel was applied in a series of awards;[107] (viii) a party is not allowed to profit from its own wrong (*nemo auditur turpitudinem allegans*);[108] (ix) good faith founds some duties to cooperate to the administration of evidence in arbitral procedure;[109] (x) during the arbitral procedure, and on the basis of good faith, the parties shall not undertake acts that aggravate the dispute or prospectively hamper the execution of the final judgment.[110] These examples show that the principle of good faith had a rich and dense application in this branch of the law—and continues to have it.

A novelty of the last 20 years is the blossoming of an institutional mechanism of dispute settlement through the instrumentality of the WTO.[111] This system, unlike that of the International Chamber of Commerce, is centred on inter-state litigation. It grants the members states of the WTO the right to pursue their claims within a tightly moulded time-scheme through a system of panels in first instance and appellate review in a second phase. Moreover, there is multilateral control over implementation of the decisions taken. As a last resort, counter-measures against non-complying states can be allowed (this had occurred in roughly 20 cases at the time of writing).[112] In this institutionalised context, the principle of good faith has received a significant number of applications. In particular, a robust and original

[104] *ICCo Award no 2291* (1976) 103 *JDI* 989; *ICCo Award no 5904* (1989) 116 *JDI* 1109–11. This may encompass a duty to cooperate: *ICCo Award no 12,127* (2003), in *Collection of ICC Arbitral Awards, 2008–2011* (Alphen a d Rijn, 2013) 70: 'good faith performance implies a certain degree of spontaneous co-operation between the parties' especially with regard to the duty of information on non-confidential matters'.

[105] Especially through the requirement of action within reasonable time when the motive to terminate the contract has become known: *ICCo Award no 10,422* (2001), in *Collection of ICC Arbitral Awards, 2001–2007* (Alphen a d Rijn, 2009) 614.

[106] *ICCo Award no 2103* (1974) 101 *JDI* 902; *ICCo Award no 4761* (1987) 114 *JDI* 1017; *ICCo Award no 5910* (1988) 115 *JDI* 1215. See Y Derains, 'L'obligation de minimiser le dommage dans la jurisprudence arbitrale' (1987) 6 *Revue de droit des affaires internationales* 375ff. And compare in general international law: J Crawford, *State Responsibility* (Cambridge, 2013) 494–95.

[107] *Amco v Indonesia* (1983) 23 *ILM* 351; *Phillips Petroleum v Iran* (1989) 21 *Iran/US Claims Tribunal Reports* 155–56. See also *ICCo Award no 13,763* (2006), § 133ff, in *Collection of ICC Arbitral Awards, 2008–2011* (Alphen a d Rijn, 2013) 898ff; or *ICCo Award no 10,671* (2005), ibid, 736, with further references.

[108] *ICCo Award no 12,456* (2004), in *Collection of ICC Arbitral Awards, 2008–2011* (Alphen a d Rijn, 2013) 817–18, 827.

[109] *ICCo Award no 1434* (1976) 103 *JDI* 978. See S Jarvin, 'L'obligation de coopérer de bonne foi', in Chambre du commerce international (ed), *L'apport de la jurisprudence arbitrale: L'arbitrage commercial international* (Paris, 1986) 158ff and G Morin, 'Le devoir de coopération dans les contrats internationaux—Droit et pratique' (1980) 6 *Droit et pratique du commerce international* 9ff.

[110] *ICCo Award no 3896* (1983) 110 *JDI* 914.

[111] On the WTO, see the brief explanations and the literature in PT Stoll, 'World Trade Organization (WTO)', in R Wolfrum (ed), *The Max Planck Encyclopedia of Public International Law*, vol X (Oxford, 2012) 968ff.

[112] See PT Stoll, 'World Trade Organization, Dispute Settlement', in R Wolfrum (ed), *The Max Planck Encyclopedia of Public International Law*, vol X (Oxford, 2012) 990ff.

doctrine of legitimate expectations has been expounded.[113] The following lines will not engage into a detailed analysis of the many subtleties of WTO law. The aim is to provide a sense of the main functions the principle of good faith is called to play in this branch of the law and to compare it with the position under general international law.

The doctrine of 'protection of legitimate expectations' (PLE) is often said to be a GATT/WTO-specific doctrine of good faith.[114] This is both true and untrue. True insofar as this doctrine has received a considerable development in that branch of the law, more than in any other area of international law with the exception of international investment law. It has become a principle in itself of GATT/WTO, alongside its nourishing source, ie the principle of good faith. Untrue insofar as a doctrine of legitimate expectations has been elaborated in other branches of international law, such as international investment law, administrative international law, and also in general international law, albeit in a more haphazard way. Further, it has to be noted that the doctrine of PLE has been developed by the case law of the various adjudication panels, first in GATT later in WTO.[115] Lastly, it has to be emphasised

[113] See T Cottier and K Nadakavukaren Schefer, 'Good Faith and the Protection of Legitimate Expectations in the WTO', in M Bronckers and R Quick (eds), *New Directions in International Law, Essays in Honor of JH Jackson* (The Hague, 2000) 47ff; HE Zeitler, 'Good Faith in WTO Jurisprudence: Necessary Balancing Element or an Open Door to Judicial Activism?' (2005) 8 *Journal of International Economic Law* 721ff; M Panizzon, *Good Faith in the Jurisprudence of the WTO* (Oxford, 2006); AD Mitchell, 'Good Faith in WTO Dispute Settlement' (2006) 7 *Melbourne Journal of International Law* 339ff; G Cook, *A Digest of WTO Jurisprudence on Public International Law Concepts and Principles* (Cambridge, 2015) 5ff, 153ff; O Federico, 'Good Faith in the Jurisprudence of the WTO' to be published in *International Trade Law*, 2016. On the issue to what extent good faith could ease the problem of parallel remedies pursued *pari passu*, eg through arguments of abuse of process, estoppel, bad faith litigation, and so on, see T Voon, AD Mitchell and J Munro, 'Good Faith in Parallel Trade and Investment Disputes', in AD Mitchell, M Sornarajah and T Voon (eds), *Good Faith and International Economic Law* (Oxford, 2015) 60ff. I wish to thank my colleague, Prof G Marceau, for valuable bibliographic information.

[114] T Cottier and K Nadakavukaren Schefer, 'NVNI Complaints in WTO/GATT Dispute Settlement: Past, Present and Future', in EU Petersman (ed), *International Trade Law and the GATT/WTO Dispute Settlement* System (The Hague, 1997) 182. On this principle and its jurisprudential developments, the most elaborate presentation can be found in Panizzon, op cit, p 127ff. The doctrine has been applied mostly in the context of what are called 'non-violation, nullification and impairment' claims. A particular case is the so-called 'non-violation complaints' under WTO law (Art XXIII, 1, GATT, 1994). Some trade benefits for a state could here be nullified independently of any formal breach of an agreement. This may occur when competitive advantages were gained by unilateral measures contrary to reasonable expectations of the other party in view of some special relationship. In most cases, such non-violation complaints are brought alongside with complaints for classical breaches. Looking more closely to the matter, it can however be said that these so-called 'non-violation' complaints have created new legal obligations on the primary level, ie the obligation not to frustrate legitimate expectations in a certain set of circumstances. It is the breach of that distinct rule which triggers the nullification of the advantages through some compensation granted by the Dispute Settlement Body. We thus remain rooted in the context of a responsibility for 'breach', even if the specific nullification consequences are regulated under WTO law as *lex specialis*. On this issue, see Cottier and Nadakavukaren Schefer (op cit, 1997). It has to be added, however, that PLE could sometimes be applied also in the context of allegation of breach of the law: examples in Panizzon, op cit, p 160ff. As to arguments levied by scholars and states against the doctrine of PLE, see Panizzon, op cit, p 179ff: fragmentation of the law, impairment of flexibilities, going against rule-orientation, downplaying non-trade concerns, etc.

[115] Panizzon, op cit, p 129.

that the function of the PLE is one of equity and equality. The point is to protect legitimate expectations which led to the financial or commercial engagement of an actor and which it would be inequitable to ignore. Moreover, there is a dynamic equality aspect in the doctrine, namely the upholding of the reciprocal equilibrium reached in the context of a certain venture between the various actors. This equilibrium shall not be unilaterally upset after the fact, to the detriment of one party. The functions of the PLE can thus be defined here as in other branches of international law: legal certainty, foreseeability, non-unilateralism, equity and equality. The doctrine has been applied in various contexts: (i) the conditions of competition, eg the legitimate expectation that if a tariff concession is made, it will not be nullified or offset by other measures;[116] (ii) the frustration of expectations by violations of explicit treaty goals, such as the continued existence of a mandatory legislation that requires the rejection of product patent applications in respect of certain goods;[117] (iii) in an extended version, the PLE encompasses also the conditions necessary to assure predictability for planning of future trade, eg precisely in the context of patent legislation;[118] (iv) the assurances given during negotiations that competitive bidding opportunities would be given for the construction of an airport, and which were finally nullified by Governmental policies.[119] If a violation of PLE is found, the legal consequences are not the ordinary effects of state responsibility (since there is no classical 'breach of the primary law'), but special effects under WTO law follow. In particular, the aggrieved state obtains compensation, ie it is entitled to take measures to offset the disadvantages suffered or potentially suffered. In some cases, retaliatory measures can be granted to re-establish the broken equilibrium.

In addition to the doctrine of PLE, we find in the WTO law the main corollaries of good faith applicable also in general international law: (i) the duty to negotiate in good faith;[120] (ii) pre-conventional or implementation obligations analogous to article 18 VCLT, 1969 (preservation of the object and purpose of an agreement);[121] (iii) the duty to implement the treaty obligations in good faith;[122] (iv) the

[116] *EEC/Oilseeds I* (GATT, 1990), Panel Report, BISD 37S/86, § 148. On this issue of rendering concessions meaningless, see Panizzon, op cit, p 142ff.

[117] *India Patents* case (US, WTO, 1998), Panel Report, WT/DS79/R, § 7.34–7.35.

[118] ibid, § 7. 30ff.

[119] *Korea Government Procurement* case (US, WTO, 2000), Panel Report, WT/DS163/R, § 7.95ff.

[120] *US Shrimp* case (WTO, 1998), Panel Report, WT/DS58/R, § 7.56. See generally M Panizzon, *Good Faith in the Jurisprudence of the WTO* (Oxford, 2006) 72ff.

[121] *Peru Agricultural Products* case (WTO, 2014), Panel Report, WT/DS457/R, § 7.88ff, obligation not to defeat the object and purpose of a treaty prior to its entry into force; *Korea Procurement* case (WTO, 2000), Panel report, WT/DS163/R, § 7.93ff, duty not to deprive a treaty of its object and purpose and thus development of 'non-violation' remedies. See generally G Cook, *A Digest of WTO Jurisprudence on Public International Law Concepts and Principles* (Cambridge, 2015) 154ff, 159ff.

[122] *US Offset Act* case ('Byrd Amendment' WTO, 2003), Panel Report, WT/DS217/R and WT/DS234/R, § 7.63ff. The Panel had found that an US Act on dumping and subsidies had undermined the value of some treaty provisions for the trading partners of the US; *US Section 211* ('Havana Club' WTO, 2002) Appellate Body Report, WT/DS176/AB/R, § 233ff. The issue turned on a less favourable treatment of non-US nationals contrary to certain international obligations. See generally Panizzon, op cit, p 61ff, 84ff; G Cook, *A Digest of WTO Jurisprudence on Public International Law Concepts and Principles* (Cambridge, 2015) 162ff.

prohibition of abuse of rights;[123] (v) estoppel[124] and (vi) acquiescence;[125] and (vii) the presumption of (subjective) good faith;[126] as well as (viii) the duty of good faith in the dispute settlement procedures.[127] Good faith has served in other areas. Thus, it has been held that measures threatening prohibited conduct could in themselves give rise to a violation of the agreement. This finding was based on the principle of good faith.[128] Further, it has been suggested that good faith may compel a state to withdraw a measure if new evidence demonstrates that the critical determination it had made when introducing it was based on a factual error.[129] More importantly, good faith has also been used to underpin the law on

[123] *US Shrimp* case (WTO, 1998), Appellate Body Report, WT/DS58/AB, § 158. The US had used its turtle protection laws in a discriminatory and arbitrary manner. See also *Peru Agricultural Products* (WTO, 2014), Panel Report, WT/DS457/R, § 7.95. There are also examples for a balancing test under abuse of rights, as in the context of *sic utere tuo…*: see eg *US Hot Rolled Steel* case (WTO, 2001), Appellate Body Report, WT/DS184/AB/R, § 101. See generally Panizzon, op cit, p 88ff, and for the balancing test, pp 92–93; G Cook, *A Digest of WTO Jurisprudence on Public International Law Concepts and Principles* (Cambridge, 2015) 157ff.

[124] Some Panels have left open the applicability of estoppel (coming from general international law) to WTO issues, especially on points of admissibility of claims: see eg *EC Export Subsidies on Sugar* case (WTO, 2005), Panel Report, WT/DS265/R, § 7.63 and Appellate Body Report, WT/DS265 (and 266 and 283)/AB/R, § 312; *EC and certain member states Large Civil Aircraft* case (WTO, 2011), Panel Report, § 7.104. In other cases, the Panels simply found that the conditions for the application of estoppel were not fulfilled: see eg *EC Asbestos* case (WTO, 2001), Panel Report, WT/DS135/R, § 8.60; *Argentina Poultry Anti-Dumping Duties* (WTO, 2003), Panel Report, WT/DS241/R, § 7.39. There are also examples of a more relaxed estoppel applied to the procedure in the dispute settlement system (*allegans contraria…*). Thus, in the *China GOES* case (WTO, 2012), Appellate Body Report, WT/DS414/AB/R, § 195, the Appellate Body held that statements made in the context of the Panel procedure could not be simply substituted by a different position of appeal. See generally Panizzon, op cit, pp 106–07; and see G Cook, *A Digest of WTO Jurisprudence on Public International Law Concepts and Principles* (Cambridge, 2015) 8ff.

[125] *EEC Bananas I* (GATT, 1993), Panel Report, DS32/R, § 1.40–1.41, the complaining parties had not protested against banana import restrictions of the EEC for a prolonged time. The issue of the duty to protest is checked as it is under general international law. Thus, in the *EEC Pasta Subsidies* case (GATT, 1983), SCM/43, § 4.10, the Panel held: 'As contracting parties were under no legal obligation to challenge the legality of export subsidies of other contracting parties, the mere abstaining from such a legal challenge could not be relied upon as acquiescence to or construed as approval of the legality of such export subsidies'. Further, see the *Guatemala Cement II* case (WTO, 2000), Panel Report, WT/DS156/R, § 8.23. See Cook, op cit, p 5ff.

[126] See eg *EC Sardines* case (WTO, 2002), Appellate Body Report, WT/DS231/AB/R, § 278. See generally G Cook, *A Digest of WTO Jurisprudence on Public International Law Concepts and Principles* (Cambridge, 2015) 165ff.

[127] Thus, it has been held that a party to the procedure cannot for tactical reasons withhold arguments until the interim review stage. See the *US 1916 Act (EC)* case (WTO, 2000), Panel Report, WT/DS136/R, § 5.18: 'parties must engage in dispute settlement in good faith. This implies that they should not withhold until the interim review stage arguments that they could be legitimately expected to have raised at a much earlier stage of the proceedings'. The same is true for inappropriate maneuvers to avoid dispute settlement: *EC Fasteners (China)* case (WTO, 2011), Panel Report, WT/DS397/R, fn 205. See generally Cook, op cit, pp 170–71.

[128] *US Section 301 Trade Act* case (WTO, 2000), Panel Report, WT/DS152/R, § 7.64ff. See Cook, op cit, pp 168–69.

[129] *US Cotton Yarn* case (WTO, 2001), Appellate Body Report, WT/DS192/AB/R, § 81. See Cook, op cit, pp 169–70.

exceptions from trade liberalisation and facilitation under the extremely important article XX of the GATT Agreement (1947, revised in 1994). WTO organs have tried to ascertain whether a state has invoked an exception, eg for environmental standards, in good faith and not abusively, so as to determine whether the exception is justified.[130] Hence, good faith plays a pivotal role in the system.

Overall, these findings are hardly a surprise. The need for the main corollaries of good faith can be found in all breaches of the law, since they express fundamental legal ideas. This is all the more true in a very technical and detailed area of international law such as commerce, where standards of fairness, expectations and equity are of the essence in its very functioning. It therefore stands to be expected that the principle of good faith will continue to develop in that branch. It will however have to be squared with the need of respecting legal predictability as its flows from the application of 'black letter law'. There is certainly a concern that the doctrine of PLE should not lead to a whole body of parallel or excessively activist normative propositions, whose effect would be to overgrow and erase the law agreed upon by the parties. The case law as it stands does seem to be sufficiently sensitive to that issue. No principle of law can be pushed too far, lest equilibrium is lost and detrimental effects be felt in other parts of the legal system, and ultimately in the social order.

As to the content of the principle of good faith and its concretisations, no significant alterations can be found with respect to general international law. The functions and the working of abuse of rights (which is a multiple and flexible notion), of estoppel and acquiescence, or of obligations to protect the object and purpose of some transaction or process, are the same as in the general body of law. True, the doctrine of PLE has received in the trade context a significant refinement in the context of so-called 'non-violation complaints'. This goes beyond the quite rudimentary manner in which the protection of legitimate confidence is treated in the general body of law. However, the gist and spirit of the principle remain the same. At the same time, its concrete application to intricate, technical and partially numerical issues of trade and economic advantages, provides it a distinctive and teethed cloth of significantly greater capillarity.

The foregoing developments also show that WTO law is and remains a branch of public international law. The great debate on *lex specialis*, ie WTO law as being entirely or not entirely distinct from the main body of international law, a debate

[130] See eg *US Shrimp* case (WTO, 1998), Appellate Body Report, WT/DS58/AB, § 158: 'The chapeau of Article XX is, in fact, but one expression of the principle of good faith. This principle, at once a general principle of law and a general principle of international law, controls the exercise of rights by states. One application of this general principle, the application widely known as the doctrine of *abus de droit*, prohibits the abusive exercise of a state's rights and enjoins that whenever the assertion of a right "impinges on the field covered by [a] treaty obligation, it must be exercised bona fide, that is to say, reasonably". An abusive exercise by a Member of its own treaty right thus results in a breach of the treaty rights of other Members and, as well, a violation of the treaty obligation of the Member so acting.'

which rages in the circles of WTO lawyers,[131] is little more than unhelpful. *Lex specialis* is itself a principle of public international law and is applied in other contexts of international law. The true issue is thus one of the correct *interpretation* of the WTO-specific rules. Alongside these special rules, a series of rules and concepts of general international law remain applicable, as on issues of treaty interpretation or on good faith. In other words, the point is one as to the correct measure and scope of the respective rules in their proper interaction, which has to be sensitively calibrated in every single context. General statements on secession or full appurtenance conceal this real issue more than they contribute to clarifying it. It may certainly be regretted that the *lex specialis* approach creates such problems of adjustment and interpretation. But this state of affairs is inherent in the articulation of two branches of law, the general and the special one. After all, to say that there is a special law logically implies that there is behind it also a general one—lest the qualification 'special' and 'general' are themselves deprived of legal sense. If both exist, the question of their articulation cannot be suppressed by shorthand simplifications. It must be sorted out by careful and learned analysis.

[131] See J Pauwelyn, *Conflict of Norms in Public International Law: How WTO Law relates to other Rules of International Law* (Cambridge, 2003; J Pauwelyn, 'The Application of Non-WTO Rules of International Law in WTO Dispute Settlement', in P F Macrory (ed), *The World Trade Organization: Legal, Economic and Political Analysis* (New York, 2005) 1405ff. For a contrary perspective, considering the contribution of WTO law to general international law: DM McRae, 'The Contribution of International Trade Law to the Development of International Law' (1996) 260 *RCADI* 99ff.

8

Good Faith in the Law of International Responsibility

It has been claimed that the whole law of international responsibility is but a manifestion of the principle of good faith taken as an expression of *pacta sunt servanda* and *obligatio est servanda*.[1] This is an extremely broad statement. If followed, it could be said that the whole legal order based on agreements and practice is ultimately but an expression of the principle of good faith. *Hanc si tollis*... Such a statement is not wrong, but hardly helpful in dealing with concrete legal issues. In a rather more technical sense, the principle of good faith has only some partial functions in the neat, dense and equilibrated body of the law of state responsibility.[2] The most important of these functions may now be briefly reviewed. It must however be noted that this body of secondary rules is based mainly on a well-tailored set of precise rules, and less on the operation of broad principles, as are some areas of primary rules. 'Liquidation of the unlawful act' requires precise rules on attribution, preclusion of wrongfulness and compensation. Good faith operates in the context of the general rules of international law, eg with regard to the formulation of claims, where estoppel can operate some preclusion. But this operation is nothing but the application of the general rules of international law *on occasion* of responsibility issues. It is not law inherent in the responsibility limb. Summing up, it can be said that good faith is mainly linked with the primary rules of international law: the creation, modification and termination of rights and obligations. The secondary rules on the consequences of a breach are more technical and precise and less permeated by broad considerations of good faith. There are however some applications of the principle, to which we may now turn.

[1] II Lukashuk, 'Introduction', in M Bedjaoui (ed), *Droit international—Bilan et perspectives*, vol I (Paris, 1991) 320: 'Le principe de la responsabilité internationale de l'Etat découle de celui de l'exécution de bonne foi des obligations contractées en vertu du droit international'. On the principle of good faith in the context of the law of international responsibility, see: L Cavaré, 'La notion de bonne foi et quelques-unes de ses applications en droit international public', *Cours IHEI* (Paris, 1963/64) 51ff; E Zoller, *La bonne foi en droit international public* (Paris, 1977) 245ff; Kolb, *Bonne* 547ff.

[2] On the law of state responsibility, see J Crawford, *State Responsibility, The General Part* (Cambridge, 2013).

I. Good Faith and Ultra Vires Responsibility

The responsibility for ultra vires acts of states (acts in excess of authority) has progressively developed since the nineteenth century.[3] In ancient times, there was a doctrine making the matter dependent on the applicable municipal law: when the agent had acted in accordance with that law or with instructions, the state could not be held responsible. With the intensification of international relations and the development of equitable considerations, this conception, which tended to absolve the state of responsibility even in the case of internationally unlawful acts of some gravity, weakening the impact of international law and impairing legal security, could no longer be upheld. An autonomous rule of international responsibility for acts in excess of authority was thus shaped.[4] Since that rule of responsibility could be excessively strict in some cases, a new limitation to it was developed: that the agent must have acted in 'apparent (public) authority', i.e. that the organ must have acted in official capacity, *ex qualitate*, as it is sometimes said, 'in his quality as an official'.[5] In other words, the agent must have acted under the guise of his state functions or by usurping the means his official function put at his disposal. The issue is similar to the one of 'imperfect ratifications' under article 46 of the VCLT of 1969: in that context there must be a manifest violation

[3] C Fischer, 'La responsabilité internationale de l'Etat pour les comportements ultra vires de ses organes' (PhD thesis, Lausanne, 1993). See further T Meron, 'International Responsibility of States for Unauthorized Acts of their Officials' (1957) 33 *BYIL* 85ff; T Meron, 'Repudiation of *ultra vires* State Contracts and the International Responsibility of States' (1957) 6 *ICLQ* 273ff; JP Quéneudec, *La responsabilité internationale de l'Etat pour les fautes personnelles de ses agents* (Paris, 1966) 121ff; I Brownlie, *System of the Law of Nations, State Responsibility*, Pt I (Oxford, 1983) 145ff; F Przetacznik, 'The International Responsibility of States for *ultra vires* Acts of their Organs', 'The International Responsibility of States for the Unauthorized Acts of their Organs' (1989) 1 *Sri Lanka Journal of International Law* 151ff. In the older literature, see eg D Anzilotti, *Cours de droit international* (Paris, 1929) 470ff; H Accioly, 'Principes généraux de la responsabilité internationale d'après la doctrine et la jurisprudence' (1959-I) 96 *RCADI* 360ff; AV Freeman, 'Responsibility of States for Unlawful Acts of their Armed Forces' (1955-II) 88 *RCADI* 263ff, 290ff; C Eagleton, *The Responsibility of States in International Law* (New York, 1928) 54ff. And see mainly the extremely thorough report by R Ago for the ILC: Fourth Report (1972-II) 1 *YbILC* 71ff, § 1ff. For international practice, see the report of Ago quoted above, at § 20ff; or eg *Jones v Saudia Arabia* (2006) 129 *ILR* 718–19, House of Lords (Lord Bingham); and *Armed Activities on the Territory of the Congo* (*DRC v Uganda*) (2005) *ICJ Reports* 242, § 214 (for looting committed by members of the armed forces). The solution finally adopted by the ILC was promoted by a series of authors in the first part of the twentieth century, especially for reasons of legal security and protection of injured states: see eg M Bourquin, 'Règles générales du droit de la paix' (1931-I) 35 *RCADI* 215–16.

[4] See the *Youmans* case, (1926) IV *RIAA* 110ff; *Mallén* (1927) IV *RIAA* 173ff; and *Caire* (1929) V *RIAA* 516ff.

[5] This criterion was first developed by the US State Department for Foreign Affairs, various Secretaries of State having argued that the responsibility of the state is not engaged when the agents or organs have acted beyond their apparent authority. Thus, in the *American Bible Society* case (1885), a note of the Secretary of State dated 17 August 1885 stated that 'it is a rule of international law that sovereigns are not liable, in diplomatic procedure, for damages to a foreigner when arising from the misconduct of agents acting out of the range not only of their real but of their apparent authority'. On the later developments, see Kolb, *Bonne* 554.

of a fundamental rule of municipal law so as to allow a state to void a treaty concluded in violation of municipal law provisions on its conclusion, since in that case the treaty partner does not deserve protection for a legitimate expectation of regularity which it could not have had. In our context, analogously, the responsibility of the state cannot be sought when the injured party was manifestly confronted with somebody acting in a private capacity and not under the colour of his public functions. Roughly speaking, the issue becomes one of good faith as legitimate reliance on status or function (*apparence, apparenza, Anschein*). The state is responsible for the appearance that the conduct of its organs has created and on which the injured subject could legitimately rely.[6] In case of manifest action outside the sphere of capacity or manifest incompetence, the state is not responsible under this heading.[7] Other remedies, under private law, must be pursued.

Article 7 of the Articles on State Responsibility for Internationally Wrongful Acts of 2001 partly adopts this criterion of appearance. It reads as follows:

> The conduct of an organ of a state or of a person or entity empowered to exercise elements of the governmental authority shall be considered an act of the state under international law if the organ, person or entity *acts in that capacity*, even if it exceeds its authority or contravenes instructions (emphasis added).

But it can be noted that the rule enunciated does not exclude the responsibility in case of manifest incompetence—it is sufficient that the agent acted under the cover of official capacity. The responsibility has thus to some extent been tightened. Moreover, the criterion of 'apparent authority' is not sufficient for giving a satisfactory answer in all cases.[8] Other sources of responsibility may or indeed must exist: the abuse of particularly dangerous means (eg weapons) linked with due diligence duties for prevention; the fact that when a damage is done directly to a state and not to an individual, or when fundamental norms of international law are at stake, the responsibility could be stricter; etc. As has been rightly said, and even if the formula seems somewhat handy, 'much depends on the type of activity and the related consequences in the particular case'.[9] It must be added that the

[6] C Fischer, 'La responsabilité internationale de l'Etat pour les comportements ultra vires de ses organes' (PhD thesis, Lausanne, 1993) 170ff, 207ff; JP Quéneudec, *La responsabilité internationale de l'Etat pour les fautes personnelles de ses agents* (Paris, 1966) 121ff. See also the clear analysis of G Dahm, *Völkerrecht*, vol III (Stuttgart, 1961) 21ff, 182–83; E Jiménez de Aréchaga, 'International Law in the Past Third of a Century' (1978-I) 159 *RCADI* 277–78. The conception whereby the issue revolves on a criterion of subjective good faith (excusable error of apparent authority) must be rejected, since such a criterion would not serve the purpose of enhancing legal security: Fischer, op cit, 181–82.

[7] A criterion favoured by R Ago, Fourth Report (1972-II) 1 *YbILC* § 58–59.

[8] Apart from that, it may not always be evident in application: The issue becomes difficult in the grey area. If a policemen performs some action in uniform and with the service weapons he will be considered to have acted in apparent authority. If he acts without uniform but with the service weapon while he is travelling back home from his workplace, he may well be deemed to have still acted in apparent authority. If he acts with the service weapon but during a private trek, the link with the state becomes elusive and attribution is not any more probable or indeed warranted.

[9] I Brownlie, *System of the Law of Nations, State Responsibility*, Pt I (Oxford, 1983) 146.

criterion of apparent authority has also been applied to the law of international organisations.[10]

Overall, it can thus be said that the criterion of reliance on good faith influenced the solution finally adopted with regard to the criterion of action in 'capacity'. But the solution finally chosen is not based entirely upon that principle. Other aspects than simple apparent authority are taken into consideration for deciding whether an agent or organ acted in ostensible authority.

II. Good Faith and Exceptions to the Exhaustion of Local Remedies Rule

There is a rule of customary international law prescribing the exhaustion of local remedies by an individual claiming to have been injured by some act contrary to international law of a foreign state on whose territory he or she is resident or present, before his or her home state can take the matter up in diplomatic protection.[11] This rule is based on the following rationales. First, it expresses the principle of subsidiarity and of economy of means. Before a matter should be brought to the international scene and give rise to a dispute between states, the responsible state should be allowed to remedy the situation by its own internal means.[12] Second, the issue is one of sovereignty and equality. An alien should not be placed in a privileged condition with respect to the nationals of the territorial state, which have in any case to exhaust the remedies municipal law offers to them.[13]

The rule on exhaustion of remedies has however been constantly applied with a certain flexibility as a matter of equity. Thus, many exceptions to the duty to exhaust local remedies have been admitted in international practice. The rule has been said to be inapplicable in the following situations: when the municipal tribunals are not in a position to decide or else when the remedy cannot lead to any change in the initial decision;[14] for direct breaches of rights of states, including damage to diplomatic personnel or other persons covered by international immunities;[15] when the damage is caused outside the territory of the responsible

[10] Kolb, *Bonne* 558–61; and art 8 of the Articles on Responsibility of International Organizations (2011). See P Klein, *La responsabilité des organisations internationales* (Brussels, 1998) 388ff.

[11] *Interhandel* case, (1959) *ICJ Reports* 27; *Diallo (Preliminary Objections)* (2007-II) *ICJ Reports* 599, § 42.

[12] P Cahier, 'Cours général de droit international public: Changements et continuité du droit international' (1985-VI) 195 *RCADI* 323.

[13] See E Jiménez de Aréchaga, 'International Law in the Past Third of a Century' (1978-I) 159 *RCADI* 291.

[14] PCIJ, ser A/B, no 76, p 18.

[15] *Phosphates in Morocco* (1938) PCIJ, ser A/B, no 74, p 28. The interpretation and application of a treaty, even in the context of individual rights and obligations, is never subjected to the rule: *Switzerland v Germany* (1958) 25 *ILR* 42ff; *Aerial Services, France/US* (1978) 54 *ILR* 322ff; *Ireland v UK* (1978) 58 *ILR* (ECtHR).

state (since it would be inequitable to require from an alien to exhaust remedies in a foreign territory with which he or she has had no voluntary contact);[16] if the duty to exhaust local remedies is excluded by a treaty;[17] if the defendant renounces the benefit of the rule after the judicial organ has been seized[18] (renunciation may be implicit if there are clauses providing for the arbitration of a class of disputes); if there are no appropriate remedies for the dispute at stake,[19] in particular if the remedies are illusory or ineffective[20] by reason of objective circumstances (municipal judicial organisation,[21] state of municipal law,[22] nature of the competent organ,[23] excessive delays,[24] substantial risk to have the damage increasing,[25] etc) or by reason of subjective circumstances (the dependence of the tribunals on the executive, bad faith or notorious xenophobia of the judges,[26] etc); if the remedy is only one for the extraordinary revision of the judgment and not an ordinary appeal or cassation;[27] possibly also if the question is limited to points of law to the exclusion of any point of fact;[28] if an estoppel impeaches the plea that the remedies have not been exhausted;[29] if the exhaustion of local remedies

[16] E Jiménez de Aréchaga, 'International Law in the Past Third of a Century' (1978-I) 159 *RCADI* 296; I Brownlie, 'International Law at the Fiftieth Anniversary of the United Nations' (1995) 255 *RCADI* 112–13. This is however a controversial matter: see CF Amerasinghe, *Local Remedies in International Law* (Cambridge, 1990) 138ff. See eg *M/V Saiga (No 2), (Admissibility and Merits) St Vincent and Grenadines v Guinea* (1999) 120 *ILR* 183–84 (ITLOS); and the Seperate Opinion Wolfrum, ibid, 233.

[17] *Amoco* (1982) 1 *Iran/US Claims Tribunal Reports* 493. This is also the case under the ICSID system under the Washington Convention of 1965, art 26: (1965) 4 *ILM* 536. See also the *Uzielli* case, (1963) 40 *ILR* 149ff; *Gallardo* (1981) 67 *ILR* 578.

[18] *Müller v Austria* (1974), Communication no 5849/72, European Commission of Human Rights Report.

[19] *Altesor v Uruguay* (1982) 70 *ILR* 253; *Nielsen v Denmark* (1961), Communication no 343/57, European Commission of Human Rights Report; *Englert v FRG* (1987) Series A no 123, pp 51–53 (ECtHR); *Velasquez Rodriguez* (1988) 95 *ILR* 233ff, 270ff (Inter-American Court of Human Rights). See also the concluding observations of the Belgian Government in the *Barcelona Traction* case, *ICJ Memorials, Pleadings and Documents*, vol I, pt III, pp 218–19, and vol III, p 602.

[20] See CF Amerasinghe, *Local Remedies in International Law* (Cambridge, 1990) 166ff, 193ff. For a finding of lack of adequate or effective remedies, see eg *Salas v US* (1993) 123 *ILR* 135–38 (Inter-American Commission of Human Rights).

[21] This may occur, for example, if the supreme tribunal depends on the executive with regard to a particular question whose international legality is disputed: see the *Salvador Commercial Company* case, (1902) XV *RIAA* 476–77; *Valentine Petroleum* (1967) 44 *ILR* 91–92.

[22] Eg when the decision flows from a formal law for which the judge has no power of review: see the *Rhodope Forests* case, (1933) III *RIAA* 1405.

[23] Eg acts of government: *Finnish Shipowners* (1934) III *RIAA* 1490ff.

[24] *El Oro* (1931) V *RIAA* 191 (nine years); *Mike Campbell v Zimbabwe* (2008) 135 *ILR* 395 (Southern African Development Community Tribunal),; *Inter-State Petition 02 (Ecuador/Colombia) (Admissibility)* (2010) 150 *ILR* 503, § 160 (Inter-American Commission of Human Rights). See CF Amerasinghe, *Local Remedies in International Law* (Cambridge, 1990) 203ff.

[25] *De Sabla* (1934) 28 *AJIL* 607, implicitly.

[26] *Brown* (1923) VI *RIAA* 120ff, 129. See CF Amerasinghe, *Local Remedies in International Law* (Cambridge, 1990) 193ff.

[27] *Salem* (1932) II *RIAA* 1190.

[28] *Aerial Services, France/US* (1978) XVIII *RIAA* 469.

[29] *Awas Tingni v Nicaragua (Preliminary Objections)* (2000) 136 *ILR* p 95, § 50, p 97, § 57 (IACtHR). See also R Kolb, *La bonne foi en droit international public* (Paris, 2000) 565ff.

would have severe financial consequences;[30] etc. Moreover, the rule of exhaustion is satisfied even when the municipal procedures do not have exactly the same subject matter as the international procedures, provided that the substance of the demand has been presented on the internal level and that there has been maximum possible action in the light of internal procedures and laws.[31] We may notice that article 15 of the ILC Articles on Diplomatic Protection (2006) rationalises some of these exceptions, but the list is not exhaustive. Practice will possibly continue to shape further equitable exceptions. Article 15, in letters a–e, recognises five exceptions:

(a) there are no reasonably available local remedies or no real chance for redress of the tort;
(b) there is undue delay in the remedial process attributable to the state alleged to be responsible;
(c) there was no relevant connection between the injured person and the state alleged to be responsible at the date of the injury, eg when the injury occurred because of the shooting down of an airliner;
(d) the injured person is manifestly precluded from pursuing local remedies (which is a sort of equitable saving clause, eg for an estoppel or other reasons);
(e) the state alleged to be responsible has waived the requirement of exhaustion of local remedies.

The conjunction of all these exceptions, developed in the case law, has blunted the sharp edge of the main rule and brought it in line with equitable considerations. A German author proposed as long ago as the 1930s that the rule should be cast aside each time there are 'valid motives' to dispense the aggrieved party from its purview.[32]

Some of the above-mentioned exceptions are based on the principle of good faith. This is the case notably of the three following exceptions.

A. Inexistence or Lack of Effectiveness of the Local Remedies

This exception can be considered to be an application of the principle of preclusion. As has been graphically said: 'if a state lacks effective local remedies, this accounts to a breach of the minimum standard. This omission itself constitutes an international tort and, in good faith, precludes the tortfeasor from invoking the local remedies rule'.[33] The issue is plainly an instance whereby nobody can

[30] NAFTA arbitration, *Loewen v US* (2003) 128 *ILR* 400.
[31] *Elettronica Sicula (ELSI)* (1989) *ICJ Reports* 46, § 59.
[32] E Kaufmann, 'Règles générales du droit de la paix' (1935-IV) 54 *RCADI* 457. See also the analysis of the exceptions in R Ago, Sixth Report, § 95ff.
[33] G Schwarzenberger, *A Manual of International Law*, 5th edn (London, 1967) 177. See *Salvador Commercial Company* (1902) XV *RIAA* 476–77; *Brown* (1923) VI *RIAA* 124ff; *Velasquez Rodriguez* (1989) 28 *ILM* 304–09. See also *Bandes v Harlow* (1988) 92 *ILR* 477(US Court of Appeals): '[T]he

profit from his own wrong. The PCIJ expressed itself in the following terms in the *Chorzow Factory* case (1927):

> It is, moreover, a principle generally accepted in the jurisprudence of international arbitration, as well as by municipal courts, that one Party cannot avail himself of the fact that the other has not fulfilled some obligation or has not had recourse to some means of redress, if the former Party has, by some illegal act, prevented the latter from fulfilling the obligation in question, or from having recourse to the tribunal which would have been open, to him.[34]

This holding may be extended to situations where the initial act was not illegal but simply faulty.

B. Official Assurances on the Availability of Local Remedies

When agents of the state have made official statements on the absence of available local remedies, that state may be precluded from pleading to the contrary in the proceedings of an international tribunal. The requirements however are strict:

> there must be cogent evidence that the conduct was not only intended to lead the alien or individual to believe that local remedies need not be further exhausted ... but also that the latter could reasonably be expected to rely on that conduct, did rely on it and for that reason did not resort to the local remedies which were available.[35]

If the information emanated from a petty official or a manifestly incompetent organ, no legitimate expectation could arise. International practice is rather sparse on this point. The argument was presented by Switzerland and considered by the ICJ in the *Interhandel* case, where however the conditions for the application of a preclusion were apparently not fulfilled.[36]

C. Other Situations of Estoppel

An ongoing pattern of conduct by the defendant can be interpreted as an implicit waiver or as giving rise to a preclusion with regard to the argument that local remedies have not been exhausted.[37] Moreover, if a state has asserted that local

alleged remedies may well be deemed illusory ... We conclude that Decree No 10 belies the existence of a *bona fide* administrative remedy'. See generally CF Amerasinghe, *Local Remedies in International Law* (Cambridge, 1990) 193ff; and AA Cançado Trindade, *The Application of the Rule of Exhaustion of Local Remedies in International Law* (Cambridge, 1983) 71ff.

[34] *Chorzow Factory* (1927) PCIJ, ser A, no 9, p 31.

[35] CF Amerasinghe, *Local Remedies in International Law* (Cambridge, 1990) 273.

[36] *Interhandel* (1959) *ICJ Reports* 27 and Amerasinghe, op cit, 274.

[37] Amerasinghe, op cit, 255ff; AA Cançado Trindade, *The Application of the Rule of Exhaustion of Local Remedies in International Law* (Cambridge, 1983) 131ff.

remedies were exhausted, it cannot later plead the contrary.[38] By the same token, the European Court of Human Rights stated a long time ago that a defendant who had not raised the argument of non-exhaustion of local remedies at the European Commission of Human Rights could not invoke the same argument when the Court was seized.[39] The argument of estoppel in the context of the exhaustion of local remedies can also be found in the arbitral case law. An example is the *Heathrow Airport User Charges* arbitration (1992), where the tribunal held that the UK's words and conduct in 1988, which envisaged arbitration as resolving a dispute if all other means failed, estopped that state from claiming that local remedies should have been exhausted.[40]

As can be seen, the whole subject matter is permeated by the principle of preclusion/estoppel, which is an aspect of the principle of reliance on good faith or legitimate expectations. It can be added that the exceptions discussed also serve other legal purposes, for example the maxim of procedural economy.

III. Good Faith and the Clean Hands Doctrine

Some old arbitral awards stipulated a requirement for the admissibility of diplomatic protection of aliens, namely that the individual to be protected had not caused or amplified the damage suffered by his own unlawful or reprehensible conduct.[41] In the words of *Black's Law Dictionary* of 1979: 'Under clean hands

[38] See *Neira Alegria (Preliminary Objections)* (1991) *Inter-American Yearbook on Human Rights* 1188, § 29 (IACtHR): 'It follows from the above that on September 29, 1989, Peru contended that domestic remedies had not been exhausted, but that a year later, on September 24, 1990, it asserted the contrary to the Commission, as it does now to the Court. International practice indicates that when a party in a case adopts a position that is either beneficial to it or detrimental to the other party, the principle of estoppel prevents it from subsequently assuming the contrary position. Here the rule of *non concedit venire contra factum proprium* applies',.

[39] For the case law, see *ILR* vol 61, pp 301–02, or *ILR* vol 71, pp 380–82, 402–03.

[40] *Heathrow Airport User Charges* (1992) XXIV RIAA 281–88.

[41] On the clean hands doctrine, see mainly: EM Borchard, *The Diplomatic Protection of Citizens Abroad* (New York, 1927) 713ff; JC Witenberg, 'La recevabilité des réclamations devant les juridictions internationales' (1932-III) 41 *RCADI* 63ff; CC Hyde, *International Law—Chiefly as Interpreted and Applied by the United States*, 2nd edn, vol II (Boston, 1947) 891ff; L Garcia Arias, 'La doctrine des clean hands en droit international public' (1960) 30 *Annuaire des anciens auditeurs de l'Académie de droit international* 14ff; L Delbez, *Les principes généraux du contentieux international* (Paris, 1962) 195ff; J Salmon, 'Des mains propres comme condition de recevabilité des réclamations internationales', (1964) 10 *AFDI* 225ff; A Miaja de la Muela, 'Le rôle de la condition des mains propres de la personne lésée dans les réclamations devant les tribunaux internationaux', *Essays in Honor of J Andrassy* (The Hague, 1968) 189ff; B Bollecker-Stern, *Le préjudice dans la théorie de la responsabilité internationale* (Paris, 1973) 302ff; A Tommasi di Vignano, 'Clean Hands, protezione diplomatica della vittima di un illecito ed eccezioni preliminari nel processo dinanzi alla Corte internazionale di giustizia', *Essays in Honor of M Udina*, vol. I (Milan, 1975) 769ff; C Rousseau, *Droit international public*, vol V (Paris, 1983) 170ff; C Jiménez Piernas, *La conducta arriesgada y la responsabilidad internacional del Estado* (Alicante, 1988) 155ff, 249ff; S Schwebel, 'Clean Hands', in R Wolfrum (ed), *The Max Planck Encyclopedia of Public*

doctrine, equity will not grant relief to a party, who as actor, seeks to set judicial machinery in motion and obtain some remedy, if such party in its prior conduct has violated conscience or good faith or other equitable principle'.[42] The matter is plainly one of good faith: *ex dolo malo/delicto non oritur actio*; *nemo ex propria turpitudine commodum capare potest*; prohibition of abuse of rights; estoppel.

This doctrine of clean hands can be applied at three different stages: (i) the policy decision to grant or not to grant diplomatic protection, which is normally a discretionary act; (ii) the phase of admissibility of an international claim at some tribunal; and (iii) the fixing of the compensation due on the merits. For some authors,[43] the doctrine is applicable only at phase (i), ie in the decision to grant or not to grant diplomatic protection. Such protection ought not to be granted in such situations. Hence, in the *Gros* case (1876), the Mexico/US Mixed Arbitral Commission declared:

> The claimant entered of his own free will into the arrangements for supplying arms, munitions of war, and provisions ... Under these circumstances the umpire is of the opinion that the losses suffered by Camille Gros and for which he claims compensation were due to his own acts, committed in violation of the law of the United States and of international law, and he thinks that the United States ought not to support such a claim, and would not be justified in doing so.[44]

Can the doctrine moreover be applied in the admissibility or merits phase of judicial or arbitral proceedings? Precedents exist for both propositions.[45] In the sense of inadmissibility the famous *Good Return and Medea* case (1862) can be quoted;[46] and for an examination exclusively on the merits, the *O Redler & Cy* case (1903) can be mentioned.[47] It may be noted that in a recent case an arbitral tribunal doubted that the doctrine of clean hands is established in international law and was prepared to apply the relevant arguments only on the merits stage, if at all.[48] Legal doctrine is also split: for some the criterion is to be applied in the admissibility phase,[49] for others it can be applied both in admissibility and on

International Law, vol II (Oxford, 2012) 232ff. In the context of good faith in particular, see Zoller, *Bonne* 297ff; Kolb, *Bonne* 568ff; B Cheng, *General Principles of Law—As Applied by International Courts and Tribunals* (London, 1953) 155ff. For arbitral practice: V Coussirat-Coustère and PM Eisemann, *Repertory of International Arbitral Jurisprudence*, vol I (1794–1918) (Dordrecht, 1989) 381ff; ibid, vol II (1919–1945)) (Dordrecht, 1989) 643ff.

[42] *Black's Law Dictionary* (St Paul MN, 1979) 227.

[43] CC Hyde, *International Law—Chiefly as Interpreted and Applied by the United States*, 2nd edn, vol II (Boston MA, 1947) 891–93.

[44] V Coussirat-Coustère and PM Eisemann, *Repertory of International Arbitral Jurisprudence*, vol I (1794–1918) (Dordrecht, 1989) 383.

[45] See the thorough analysis in J Salmon, 'Des mains propres comme condition de recevabilité des réclamations internationales' (1964) 10 *AFDI* 232ff; and Kolb, *Bonne* 570–71.

[46] V Coussirat-Coustère and PM Eisemann, *Repertory of International Arbitral Jurisprudence*, vol I (1794–1918) (Dordrecht, 1989) 381–82.

[47] *O Redler & Cy* (1903) X *RIAA* 382–84.

[48] *Guyana/Suriname* arbitration (2007) 139 *ILR* 685ff, 688, §§ 421–22.

[49] See eg JC Witenberg, 'La recevabilité des réclamations devant les juridictions internationales' (1932-III) 41 *RCADI* 63–64.

the merits,[50] and for still others it is only a criterion for adjusting the damages on the merits.[51] The correct answer has to be sought in the function and equitable nature of the doctrine. There is no general rule on clean hands in the law of international responsibility. The reason is simply that a concurring fault by one person cannot absolve *de plano* another from his own torts or illegal conduct (*tu quoque*).[52] Moreover, in case of concurring faults, the inadmissibility of one claim would lead to an inequitable result: one party would be completely sanctioned for its fault while the other would suffer no consequences for his own fault; the better course is manifestly to adjust the faults on the merits, notably in the phase of the calculation of the indemnity.[53] However, clean hands may sometimes lead to an inadmissibility of a claim. This will be the case if the judge considers that the fault or illegality of the claimant is so considerable or overwhelming that the fault or illegality of the defendant is thereby rendered completely negligible and that procedural economy is better served if the judicial debate is closed from the very beginning. The same may be true if the two faults or roughly equivalent—but even in such a case, the merits approach is the better course if there is a counter-claim, since the judge will then be able to reject both claims with substantive *res judicata* effect.

Overall, the doctrine of clean hands has considerably declined in the modern case law. It is not a condition for the admissibility of diplomatic protection,[54] but it can lead to an adjustment of indemnities or in some extreme cases to an inadmissibility of a claim. The ICJ has for itself refused to apply this doctrine outside the context of diplomatic protection, for example when the US claimed that a case brought by Nicaragua and leading to two judgments of 1984 and 1986 should have been declared inadmissible on account of the 'dirty hands' or 'unclean hands' of Nicaragua.[55] It followed the same path in the *Oil Platforms* case (2003), when the US raised the argument against Iran. The Court held that the US did not frame that argument as a question of admissibility, but rather demanded that the claims

[50] See eg B Cheng, *General Principles of Law—As Applied by International Courts and Tribunals* (London, 1953) 158.

[51] See eg A Tommasi di Vignano, 'Clean Hands, protezione diplomatica della vittima di un illecito ed eccezioni preliminari nel processo dinanzi alla Corte internazionale di giustizia', *Essays in Honor of M Udina*, vol I (Milan, 1975) 782–83; G Perrin, 'Réflexions sur la protection diplomatique', *Essays in Honor of M Bridel* (Lausanne, 1968) 402.

[52] As has been rightly said: 'jamais la conduite irrégulière de la victime ne devrait dégager un Etat de l'obligation qu'il a de respecter un certain standard minimum de justice'. See P de Visscher, 'Cours général de droit international public' (1972-II) 136 *RCADI* 176–77. See also the clear statement of the ICJ in the *Barcelona Traction* case, (1970) *ICJ Reports* 51.

[53] An apportionment of the indemnities in view of the faults committed by each side was achieved in the *I'm Alone* case (1935) III *RIAA* 1609ff. See GG Fitzmaurice, 'The Case of the I'm Alone' (1936) 17 *BYIL* 82ff; CC Hyde, 'The Adjustment of the I'm Alone Case' (1935) 29 *AJIL* 296ff; W Friede, 'Der Fall I'm Alone' (1935) 5 *ZaöRV* 658ff.

[54] And was thus not inserted as a condition of admissibility in the 2006 ILC Draft Articles on Diplomatic Protection.

[55] As is known, Judge S Schwebel, of the US, took up and developed this argument in his Dissenting Opinion to *Military and Paramilitary Activities in and Against Nicaragua (Merits)* (1986) *ICJ Reports* 392ff.

of Iran be rejected on the merits.[56] This overall course is certainly correct. If at all, the issue is once more mainly one for the merits and for the calculus of the damages to be paid. Moreover, which state has entirely clean hands in international policies? It would not be proper that tribunals enter into such political minefields when judging on a concrete legal demand presented by a state.

IV. Good Faith and Subsidiary Responsibility within an International Organisation

An arbitral tribunal in 1984 considered that the member states of a small international organisation (composed of four member states) incurred subsidiary responsibility for debts of the organisation when the latter was in default, since the four states had not excluded that responsibility and thus third entities could rely in good faith on its existence.[57] There is no doubt that the small size of the organisation and the actual conduct of the states involved contributed to that finding.[58] It is however doubtful that such a legal rule on responsibility could be generalised. Be that as it may, this case shows that the principle of good faith can flexibly be called into action in order to justify a development of international law where there is a lack of more precise legal provisions. The question of subsidiary responsibility of members states of an international organisation is now regulated by article 62 of the ILC Articles on the Responsibility of International Organizations (2011).[59]

We may notice that according to article 62, § 1, letter b, Articles on the Responsibility of International Organizations (2011), when a member state of an international Organisation induces another state to rely on its assumption of responsibility for a conduct of that international organisation, it shall be responsible as it has represented to be.[60] This heading is an application of the principle of good faith, ie the protection of legitimate expectations freely created. Detrimental reliance must not be shown to have existed. The issue is not one of estoppel in the technical sense, but the presence of detrimental reliance reinforces the argument for an application of the good faith standard. Overall, the issue turns on the assessment of conduct in regard of the legitimate trust and expectation it could not

[56] *Oil Platforms (Iran v US)* (2003) *ICJ Reports* 176–78, § 27–30.

[57] *Westland Helicopters v Arab Organisation for Industrialisation* (1984) 23 *ILM* 1082–83, or (1984) 80 *ILR* 613.

[58] Thus, there was only a weak international legal personality of the organisation in that case, the four states being the true masters of the entity: (1984) 80 *ILR* 596, 602–03, 610ff.

[59] A state assumes residual responsibility by its acceptance of such responsibility or by its conduct leading other states to rely on its subsidiary responsibility.

[60] See also the Note of the Swiss International Law Directorate, Ministry of Foreign Affairs, 25 January 2010, (2012) 22 *RSDIE* 123–24.

fail to create. Could and should the state relying on the representation reasonably have understood the representation in that way? Did the other state possibly reap a benefit from that reliance of the injured state? Could it expect that benefit to accrue, and did it perhaps even intend it? These are relevant questions to be asked in concretising the applicable legal standard to the single case. There will hardly ever be much affirmative practice on this rather residual rule. According to § 2 of article 62 the responsibility of the member state is only subsidiary to that of the organisation.

9

Good Faith in the Law on the Peaceful Settlement of International Disputes

The law for the peaceful settlement of international disputes rests on two pillars: the principle of cooperation and the principle of consent. The principle of cooperation is concerned since the attempt at settlement gives rise to some extent to a common process, eg a judicial procedure, which can be a success only if there is a minimum of loyalty and coordinated effort; the principle of consent is relevant since all the means for settling international disputes rest ultimately on the acceptance of the states involved. In both contexts, the principle of good faith plays a major role: in the context of cooperation for the protection of the common finalities in the process; in the context of consent as a limitation on the true will of a subject in favour of considering the objective meaning of a certain conduct and what other subjects could and should have expected on the basis of such conduct. Thus, as has been said, the principle of good faith dominates the subject area of the pacific settlement of international disputes.[1]

I. Good Faith and Negotiation

The epithet 'in good faith' is often added to the word 'negotiation'. This leads to the concept of 'negotiations in good faith' or to some related formula.[2] It has

[1] L Delbez, *Les principes généraux du droit international public*, 3rd edn (Paris, 1964) 41.

[2] See eg s I, 1 5 of the Manila Declaration on the Peaceful Settlement of International Disputes, UNGA, Res 37/10 (1982). Many other instruments contain similar wording: see eg the Nuclear Non-Proliferation Treaty of 1968, art 6. On the issue, see: JP Cot, *La bonne foi en droit international public, Cours de l'IHEI* (Paris, 1968/69) 21ff; Zoller, *Bonne* 54ff; Kolb, *Bonne* 580ff; NE Ghozali, 'La négociation diplomatique dans la jurisprudence internationale' (1992) 25 *RBDI* 348–49; G White, 'The Principle of Good Faith', *Essays in Honor of M Akehurst* (London, 1994) 233–34. The concept of negotiation in good faith has been sometimes called 'mere rhetoric': R Baxter, 'International Law in Her Infinite Variety' (1980) 29 *ICLQ* 552, which is an exaggeration. The duty to behave in a constructive way during negotiations has been recognised for a long time. Thus, for example, R Piédelièvre, *Précis de droit international public*, vol II (Paris, 1895) 4 writes: 'il est inutile d'insister longuement sur l'esprit qui doit présider aux négociations. Il va sans dire qu'il faut trouver de part et d'autre la bonne foi et le désir sincère d'aboutir à un résultat équitable de la difficulté pendante…'.

been doubted that this concept has a true legal impact. International negotiations would in fact be characterised rather by unbridled competition and selfishness.[3] The case law of international tribunals, at least, does not support such a negative conclusion. A short overview of that jurisprudence may be given before attempting to systematise the legal rules implicit in it. It is indeed through the case law that the concept of 'negotiations in good faith' has been brought forth and that the epithet 'in good faith' has received some more concrete meaning. However, it has to be immediately emphasised that the conclusions to be drawn from this case law are to be carefully considered. A series of decisions were based on some particular law sources, namely agreements providing for some duty to negotiate or to conclude an agreement. The precise scene-setting of the issue is also of importance: it is not the same to negotiate in a bilateral relation on the apportionment of a common resource than to negotiate multilaterally about disarmament. It is not the same to negotiate about legal rights or about mere interests, since it might be easier to refuse compromise on a right versus an interests than between competing interests. The main point to be grasped here is that all these issues are fact- and circumstance-intensive and that the proper rules of law cannot be applied in isolation of such factors.

In the *North Sea Continental Shelf* cases (1969), the ICJ insisted on the fact that the negotiating parties have to behave in such a way that the process is not only a formal or artificial one but that there is a true intention to reach an agreement.[4] In the *Fisheries Jurisdiction* case (1974), the ICJ recalled that a party must reasonably take into account the positions and rights of the other party.[5] Otherwise a meaningful negotiation is impossible. In the *Interpretation of the Agreement of 25 March 1951 between the WHO and Egypt* advisory opinion (1980), the Court considered at length the duties the parties owe to each other in case of negotiations.[6] The Court insisted on obligations of cooperation and consultation when an international organisation has to be moved out of the former headquarter state. In the *Applicability of the Obligation to Arbitrate under Section 21 of the*

[3] E Zoller, 'La bonne foi en droit international public', in Travaux de l'Association H Capitant, *La bonne foi* (Paris, 1994) 575.

[4] *North Sea Continental Shelf* (1969) *ICJ Reports* 47: 'the parties are under an obligation to enter into negotiations with a view at arriving at an agreement, and not merely to go through a formal process ... they are under an obligation so to conduct themselves that the negotiations are meaningful, which will not be the case when either of them insists upon its own position without contemplating any modification of it'; the Chamber of the Court recalled this principle in the *Gulf of Maine* case, (1984) *ICJ Reports* 299. The principle can easily be applied to a situation such as the one at stake, ie a delimitation of maritime spaces, where the parties must compromise. Application of the principle to all other negotiations is not obvious, since a state may well refuse any compromise when it considers itself to have the law on its side.

[5] *Fisheries Jurisdiction* (1974) *ICJ Reports* 33, 202. This utterance was made again in a context which supposed some compromise, ie the apportionment of fishing resources. But the statement can be generalised, since it appears to express the minimum necessary for each type of meaningful negotiation.

[6] *Interpretation of the Agreement of 25 March 1951 between the WHO and Egypt* (1980) *ICJ Reports* 92ff.

United Nations Headquarters Agreement of 26 June 1947 advisory opinion (1988), the Court insisted on the fact that the negotiation must not have been long to fulfil the exigency of good faith. Even in the case of a short contact, when it appears that the other party opposes a clear *non possumus* or *non volumus*, the party attempting to break the ice has fulfilled its duties under good faith.[7] If there is an obligation to reach an agreement (*pactum de contrahendo*), the obligations under the principle of good faith are strengthened.[8] In the *Gabcíkovo-Nagymaros* case (1997), the ICJ stated that readiness to accept the assistance of a third party may be seen as compliance with the duty to negotiate in good faith.[9] In the *Application of the Interim Accord* case (*FYROM v Greece*, 2011), the ICJ was confronted with a treaty clause providing for negotiations between the parties and summed up its position on the notion of negotiations in good faith. It held that there must be an effort towards the conclusion of an agreement, so that the negotiations are meaningful; that the parties shall not insist on their position without contemplating any modification of it; that a party shall not interrupt communications or cause delays in an unjustified manner or disregarding the procedures agreed upon; that each party shall pay reasonable regard to the interests of the other.[10] In this case, the Court quoted extensively from its own and the arbitral jurisprudence. Lastly, it may be emphasised that an important case on that issue is pending at the ICJ, namely the *Obligation to Negotiate* case between Bolivia and Chile.

Arbitral jurisprudence is at least as dense. In the *Tacna Arica* case (1925), the arbitrator mentioned attempts at frustration of the object and purpose of the negotiation as being incompatible with good faith. The issue revolved around the holding of a meaningful plebiscite.[11] In the *Pertusola* case (1951), the conciliation commission emphasised that when one party to a bilateral negotiation became aware of a mistake of the counterparty on the proper meaning of a word, it had a duty under good faith either to signal that error or to modify the provision so as to accommodate the meaning attached to the word by the counterparty.[12] In the *Apportionment of Property of Local Authorities* case (1953), between France and Italy, the conciliation commission requested that during the negotiation the parties would agree to avoid measures producing disproportionate disadvantages to one party in regard to the little advantages to the other party.[13] In the *Lake Lanoux* case (1957), the tribunal insisted on the fact that each negotiating

[7] *Obligation to Arbitrate under Section 21 of the United Nations Headquarters Agreement of 26 June 1947 (advisory opinion)* (1988) *ICJ Reports* 33–34.

[8] *Nuclear Weapons (advisory opinion)* (1996-I) *ICJ Reports* 264.

[9] *Gabcíkovo-Nagymaros* (1997) *ICJ Reports* 79, § 143.

[10] *FYROM v Greece* (2010-II) *ICJ Reports* 685 § 132. In the context of the case at hand, the Court did not find evidence that the applicant had breached its good faith obligations in the context of negotiation: ibid, 686, § 138.

[11] *Tacna Arica* (1925) *RIAA* 929–30.

[12] *Pertusola* (1951) XIII *RIAA* 195. See also the *French Railway* case, (1953) XIII *RIAA* 562.

[13] *Apportionment of Property of Local Authorities* (1953) XIII *RIAA* 521, (1953) 20 *ILR* 75. The basis of this holding was a treaty between the two parties which obliged them to negotiate on a certain subject matter.

party has to take properly into account the diverging interests and to try to give to the other party(ies) all the satisfactions compatible with the pursuit of the own interest, ie to try to conciliate the interests.[14] This is manifestly incompatible with absolute intransigency.[15] It has to be stressed that this case concerned a common resource and a bilateral setting of negotiations. The tribunal also suggested that the parties considered to what extent the exercise of certain rights or positions could be suspended during the negotiations, so that their conduct would be eased.[16] Finally, the tribunal considered that these notions were justiciable and that a sanction could be applied in case of breach of the good faith obligations, for example in case of contempt for the procedures agreed upon or in case of systematic refusal to take into account the positions of the other party.[17] In the *German External Debts* case (1972), based on a *pactum de negotiando*, the tribunal expressed itself thus:

> The negotiations to be conducted must be guided by the following principles:
>
> (a) They should be meaningful and not merely consist of a formal process of negotiations. Meaningful negotiations could not be conducted if either party insisted upon its own position without contemplating any modification of it.
> (b) Both parties were under an obligation to act in such a way that the principles of the Agreement are applied in order to achieve a satisfactory and equitable result.[18]

This agreement to negotiate obliges the parties to adopt a closer level of cooperation:

> A *pactum de negotiando* is also not without legal consequences. It means that both sides would make an effort, in good faith, to bring about a mutually satisfactory solution by way of a compromise, even if that meant the relinquishment of strongly held positions taken earlier. It implies a willingness for the purpose of negotiations to abandon earlier positions and to meet the other side part way.[19]

A useful summary of good faith duties during negotiation can be found in the celebrated *Kuwait v AMINOIL* case (1982):

> [The general principle that ought to be observed in carrying out an obligation to negotiate] is good faith as properly to be understood; sustained upkeep of the negotiations

[14] *Lake Lanoux* (1957) XII *RIAA* 315, 308.

[15] ibid, 311.

[16] ibid, 310–11. See also *Pulp Mills* case (*Argentina v Uruguay*), (2010-I) *ICJ Reports* 66–67, § 143ff, § 143: 'The Court finds that Uruguay was not entitled, for the duration of the period of consultation and negotiation provided for in Articles 7 to 12 of the 1975 Statute, either to construct or to authorise the construction of the planned mills and the port terminal. It would be contrary to the object and purpose of the 1975 Statute…'. This duty to preserve the object and purpose of the proceedings applies also to judicial procedures: see eg *Loayza Tamayo v Peru (Merits)* (1997) 116 *ILR* 355, § 24, letter c (IACtHR): 'When there is an international complaint against a State for violation of rights guaranteed in the American Convention, that State has the obligation, in good faith, to refrain from needlessly adopting measures that may adversely affect the situation of the plaintiff'. Notice that the term 'may adversely affect' is extremely broad, but that the term 'needlessly' operates a significant restriction.

[17] ibid (*Lake Lanoux*), 307.

[18] *German External Debts* case (1972) 47 *ILR* 422, (1972) XIX *RIAA* 56–57.

[19] ibid. On this arbitration, see G Guyomar, 'Tribunal d'arbitrage de l'accord sur les dettes extérieures allemandes' (1973) 19 *AFDI* 527ff, esp 534–37.

> over a period appropriate to the circumstances; awareness of the interests of the other party; and a persevering quest for an acceptable compromise. The Tribunal here makes reference in particular to the well-known *dicta* in the North Sea Continental shelf and Lac de Lanoux cases.[20]

In the *Delimitation of the Maritime Boundary* case (*Guyana v Suriname*) (2007), the arbitral tribunal had to apply articles 74, § 3, and 83, § 3, of the Montego Bay Convention on the Law of the Sea (1982), which requests the parties, pending agreements for the delimitation of the exclusive economic zone and the continental shelf, to 'make every effort' to enter into provisional arrangements of practical nature and, during this transitional period, not to jeopardise or hamper the reaching of the final agreement. The Tribunal considered that these provisions embodied an obligation to negotiate in good faith, which meant to adopt a conciliatory approach, ie a stance prepared to make concessions; it also held that permanent physical changes in the disputed area should not occur, except on the basis of agreement of the concerned states. Analysing the concrete behaviour of the parties, the tribunal found several violations of these principles, eg through the failure to send delegations of negotiation, to respond to offers, to act otherwise than just by disavowing a memorandum of understanding, etc.[21]

Summing up, there are three main aspects of good faith during negotiations: (i) in analogy with pre-contractual obligations, the object and purpose of the negotiation must be preserved against various strains; (ii) the prohibition on abuse of rights rules out the use of negotiations for inappropriate aims; (iii) the protection of legitimate expectations imposes a minimum of fair dealing during the conduct of negotiations. Further, there are some other minor obligations. The above-mentioned categories are party overlapping.

A. Prohibition on Depriving the Negotiations of their Object and Purpose

To negotiate means to enter into a phase of common effort for the achievement of a certain aim. It would be preposterous to allow one or other of the parties to conduct itself in such a way as to render the whole process futile.[22] In such a case, the negotiations ought simply to be suspended or terminated. There are two objects of a negotiation: a general one and a special one. The first concerns all what is necessary to secure that negotiations *as such* remain meaningful;[23] the second concerns the *specific object* of one negotiation, such as the sharing of water resources of a given river. On the issue of the general object and purpose, good faith provides

[20] *Kuwait v AMINOIL* (1982) 66 *ILR* 578.

[21] RIAA, vol. XXX, p. 128ff, § 453ff.

[22] See the *Tacna Arica* case, (1925) II *RIAA* 929–30.

[23] It has rightly been said that to negotiate otherwise than in good faith is surely not to negotiate at all: H Thirlway, 'The Law and Procedure of the ICJ (1960–1989): General Principles and Sources of Law' (1989) 60 *BYIL* 25.

for a series of material obligations, as does the principle of interpretation and execution in good faith in the context of the *pacta sunt servanda* rule. The case law analysed above has nourished this category:

(i) the negotiations must conducted in a way that they are meaningful, ie with a true intention to progress and conclude—which is not the case if a party refuses to take duly into account the positions of the adverse party or rejects immediately all reasonable proposals;[24]
(ii) during negotiations, measures causing disproportionate harm to the other party(ies) and little advantage to one own should be avoided;[25]
(iii) the contempt for agreed procedures is contrary to good faith and possibly also to some legal engagement;[26]
(iv) the manifestly unjustified interruption of negotiations, for example in order not to be confronted with a reasonable proposal of the other party, is contrary to good faith (but it will be sanctionable only in extreme cases);[27]
(v) in some cases of a closer knit between the parties, for example some strong agreement to negotiate or to agree, good faith may imply an obligation to accept a reasonable compromise;[28]
(vi) there is a general duty not to aggravate the dispute by deliberate acts during the negotiation (again, only manifest abuses can lead to a breach).[29]

The special object of a negotiation is protected by rules analogous to the ones under article 18 of the VCLT of 1969.[30] The duties are mainly of abstention.[31] In

[24] *North Sea* cases, (1969) *ICJ Reports* 47; *Gulf of Maine* (1984) *ICJ Reports* 299; *Tacna Arica* (1925) II *RIAA* 929–30; *Lake Lanoux* (1957) XII *RIAA* 307–08, 311, 315; *German External Debts* (1972) XIX *RIAA* 57; Guyana v. Suriname (2007), XXX RIAA, 130;

[25] *Apportionment of Property of Local Authorities* (1953) XIII *RIAA* 521.

[26] *Lake Lanoux* (1957) XII *RIAA* 307.

[27] ibid.

[28] *German External Debts* (1972) XIX *RIAA* 56; *Lake Lanoux* (1957) XII *RIAA* 308, 311, 315; *AMINOIL* (1982) 66 *ILR* 578.

[29] *Aerial Services, France/US* (1978) 54 *ILR* 338–39: 'It is tempting to assert that when parties enter into negotiations, they are under a general duty not to aggravate the dispute, this general duty being a kind of emanation of the principle of good faith'. The tribunal however—rightly—refused to consider that this implies an obligation to abstain from all counter-measures in that phase: 'The Arbitral Tribunal does not believe that it is possible, in the present state of international relations, to lay down a rule prohibiting the use of counter-measures during negotiations, especially where such counter-measures are accompanied by an offer for a procedure affording the possibility of accelerating the solution of the dispute'. This is so especially when, as in the present case, the counter-measures are protective and were accompanied by offers to negotiate. In the case of manifest disproportion of interests, ie counter-measures inflicting severe damage on the one side and of little advantage to the other side, the principle of good faith may well prohibit such a course: see Dissenting Opinion Bedjaoui, *Delimitation of the Maritime Boundary (Guinea-Bissau v Senegal)* (1989) 83 *ILR* 83, § 72. On the issue, see LF Damrosch, 'Retaliation or Arbitration—Or Both? The US/France Aviation Dispute' (1980) 74 *AJIL* 797ff. As another example, it may be considered contrary to this limb of the principle of good faith to resort to propaganda and high-tuned accusations against the other party during the negotiations phase so as to try to manoeuvre the other party into a less favourable position. See on that point A Plantey, *La négociation internationale* (Paris, 1980) 118.

[30] See above, Ch 5, section I.

[31] JF O'Connor, 'L'accord anglo-irlandais de 1985' (1985) 31 *AFDI* 197; E Jiménez de Aréchaga, 'International Law in the Past of a Century—General Course on Public International Law' (1978-I) 159 *RCADI* 200.

the *Samoa* case (1902) the sole arbitrator considered that during the negotiation on the new constitutional regime in a place where more than one government had rights, the US could not unilaterally militarily intervene without consulting one other party, since the military intervention unilaterally modified the situation on which the negotiations bore.[32] In the *Fisheries Jurisdiction* case (*UK v Iceland*, 1974), the ICJ stated that negotiations in good faith on fish stocks presupposed that necessities of conservation of those stocks had to be taken into account during the negotiations[33]—which implied a limitation of the fishing practised by Iceland and the UK. Duties of good faith in this phase may imply keeping the discussions confidential or exceptionally to submit some document to the other party when it is essential and the other party has no access to it (at least if there are no important countervailing interests). Finally, we may recall the *Delimitation of the Maritime Boundary* (*Guyana v Suriname*) case of 2007, where the arbitral tribunal held, on the basis of special provisions of the Montego Bay Convention on the Law of the Sea (1982), that no permanent physical changes should be unilaterally operated in the area in dispute pending the final agreement on delimitation, since such changes would breach the obligation to negotiate in good faith and to preserve the specific object of the negotiation.[34]

B. Prohibition of Abuse of Rights

Good faith prohibits recourse to certain means during negotiation, such as fraud (hence also the possibility to void the treaty if concluded through fraud).[35] By the same token, if negotiations are not used to reach a solution on a certain point, but as a mere camouflage or sham to gain time, for example so as to prepare a military aggression, this would amount to a breach of good faith with regard to the negotiations. It stands to reason that in most cases such misuses are difficult to establish and to prove.

C. Protection of Legitimate Expectations

The engagement of the parties in a common process of negotiation, which may last for a long time, creates some needs of mutual confidence. These cannot be ignored by the law. Clearly, negotiations have to remain flexible. A strict legal straitjacket would be of no utility. On the other hand, a complete absence of rules protecting the legitimate mutual expectations would jeopardise the whole process.

[32] *Papers Relating to the Foreign Relations of the United States*, vol 43 (1902) (Washington DC, 1903) 446: 'Pending instruction from the three treaty powers … those powers were bound upon principles of international good faith to maintain the situation thereby created until by common accord they had otherwise decided'.

[33] *Fisheries Jurisdiction* case (*UK v Iceland*) (1974) *ICJ Reports* 202.

[34] (2007) XXX RIAA 133.

[35] Art 49 VCLT, 1969.

The extent of such good faith obligations depends much on the precise relations of the parties, the particular law applicable, the previous conduct into which they indulged, and so on. Representations or assurances made before or during negotiations may thus bind the state having uttered them. Moreover, the case law has made clear that mere proposals made during the negotiations cannot be produced in a later judicial procedure to somehow bind the party from which they emanated, unless these negotiations led to an agreement (in which case, the utterances during the negotiations can be used as *travaux préparatoires*).[36] A contrary course would indeed be unwise: it would hamper the negotiations, since the parties would become reluctant to propose any significant or important concessions; and it would also increase the resistance of states to accept a judicial settlement. But the rule applies only to formal negotiations, not for example to notes sent by the foreign ministry;[37] or even to statements made by a minister of foreign affairs during negotiations (having led to some informal agreement);[38] and possibly an estoppel is still applicable, especially if an agreement was concluded.[39]

As noted earlier, these obligations of good faith depend much on the precise type of relation between the parties. There are several factors which tend to increase the scope and intensity of the obligations as discussed above:

(i) the existence of agreements creating a situation of cooperation, eg mandates or trusteeships;[40]
(ii) the negotiation among members of an international organisation, where there are special duties of good faith owed one to the other, eg under article 2, § 2, of the UN Charter;[41]
(iii) the presence of an agreement to negotiate, to consult or to conclude an agreement, according to its precise terms and scope;[42]
(iv) the fact that the negotiations are about a shared resource, trans-boundary cooperation, environmental issues, etc;[43]
(v) the general relations between the parties, eg closely allied or friendly nations (eg Switzerland and Liechtenstein) or conversely hostile and ideologically alien states (eg the US and North Korea).

[36] See eg *Maritime Delimitation and Territorial Questions (Jurisdiction and Admissibility, Qatar/Bahrain)* (1994) *ICJ Reports* 125–26: 'In any event, there is a rule of customary international law in this domain, defined in 1927 by the Permanent Court of International Justice, namely that the Court cannot take account of declarations, admissions or proposals which the parties may have made in the course of direct negotiations when the negotiations in question have not led to an agreement between the parties'.

[37] *Nottebohm* case, (1953) *ICJ Reports* 71.

[38] The famous Ihlen declaration: see the *Eastern Greenland* case (1933) PCIJ ser A / B, no 53, p 71.

[39] *Elettronica Sicula (ELSI)* (1989) *ICJ Reports* 44. Further case law in Kolb, *Bonne* 595.

[40] See eg the Dissenting Opinion C de Visscher, *International Status of South West Africa (advisory opinion)* (1950) *ICJ Reports* 188.

[41] See eg the *Interpretation of the Agreement of 25 March 1951 between the WHO and Egypt (advisory opinion)* (1980) *ICJ Reports* 92ff.

[42] See eg *German External Debts* (1972) XIX *RIAA* 56.

[43] See eg *Lake Lanoux* (1957) XII *RIAA* 307ff. see also M Bernad y Alvarez de Eulate, 'La coopération transfrontalière régionale et locale' (1993-VI) 243 *RCADI* 305ff, 396ff.

All of these factors, difficult to ponder as they may be, influence the extent and intensity of the obligations of negotiation in good faith. It must finally be recalled that the duty to negotiate in good faith concerns only the process once it is agreed upon. Conversely, good faith does not oblige states to negotiate in the first place. How these states want to resolve (or not) their dispute is a matter for other norms of international law.[44]

We may finally note that the Arbitral Commission for the Former Yugoslavia (European Communities) held that a state can have recourse to counter-measures when another state breaches its legal duties of negotiation in good faith.[45] Whether that is a wise course to take is a matter of legal policy. To the extent, however, that the good faith duties during negotiation are true legal obligations, their breach leads to an internationally wrongful act for which counter-measures are a remedy. The good faith obligations in the context of negotiations are therefore no *lex imperfecta*. They can give rise to a legal sanction.

II. Good Faith and Provisional Measures

When a tribunal is seized of a case, the question arises as to what extent it will be necessary to protect the substantive rights of the applicant *pendente lite*, ie while the case is under way, until the tribunal's binding judgment finally governs the parties' rights and obligations. From the moment judgment is given, the respondent ceases to be in a position to do anything further contrary to the rights of the applicant as set out in the judgment and is under a positive obligation to execute the judgment. Inherent in that obligation, a fortiori, is the negative obligation not to alter or destroy the subject-matter of these rights. But, while the case is still pending, this positive obligation under a judgment does not yet exist, and therefore the inherent negative obligation is not provided for either.[46] But the defendant may be tempted to alter or even to destroy the object of the dispute. The purpose of provisional measures is both to enable the court to preserve the value

[44] On the issue, see eg DN Hutchinson, 'The Material Scope of the Obligation under the United Nations Charter to Take Action to Settle International Disputes' (1992) 14 *Australian YbIL* 1ff, 47ff; CF Murphy, 'The Obligation of States to Settle Disputes by Peaceful Means' (1973) 14 *Virginia JIL* 15ff. And see C Tomuschat, 'Article 2(3)', in B Simma, DE Khan, G Nolte and A Paulus (eds), *The Charter of the United Nations, A Commentary*, vol I, 3rd edn (Oxford, 2012) 181ff, for the peaceful settlement of disputes in general.

[45] Opinion no 12 (1992) 96 *ILR* 725, § 2.

[46] In Roman law proceedings, parties were obliged, after the *litis contestatio*, to provide guarantees (*satisdationes*) as to their conduct during the proceedings and after judgment. In some cases (action *in rem* in proper name), the defendant had to give three undertakings: 1) to execute the judgment (*de re iudicata*); 2) to perform all the duties of a defendant in this type of case (*de re defendenda*); 3) to abstain from doing any harm, which included the obligation not to do any irreparable prejudice to the subject-matter of the dispute (*de dolo malo*). *Cf* G Pugliese, *Istituzioni di diritto romano* (Padua, 1986) 348.

of its judicial functions and to 'preserve the respective rights of the parties, pending the decision of the Court'.[47] Corresponding to this dual function are the dual powers to indicate provisional measures *proprio motu*, and to do so in response to a party's request. The objective aspect turns essentially on the 'non-aggravation of the dispute' and the subjective one on the 'preservation of the parties' rights', especially those of the applicant. If the provisional measures are not binding upon the parties, these two core necessities of a judicial procedure are jeopardised.

The question early appeared as to what extent such provisional measures of protection are or can be declared to be binding upon the parties. For example, the Statute of the ICJ, under article 41, is less than clear on this point.[48] It can be noted that many modern tribunals have affirmed their power to indicate binding provisional measures as an inherent judicial attribution. The ICJ affirmed this power under article 41 (under a teleological interpretation) in the famous *LaGrand* case (2001);[49] and so did the European Court of Human Rights in the *Mamatkulov v Turkey* case (2003),[50] the United Nations Human Rights Committee under the Civil and Political Right Covenant (1966) in the *Piandiong et al v The Philippines* case[51] (which is all the more remarkable, since the Committee has no power to issue binding decisions on the merits), and a series of ICSID tribunals, starting with *Maffezini v Spain*[52] under article 47 ICSID Convention (which again

[47] *Denunciation of the Sino-Belgian Treaty of 2 November 1865*, PCIJ ser A, no 8, p 6.

[48] See K Oellers-Frahm, 'Article 41', in A Zimmermann, C Tomuschat, K Oellers-Frahm and CJ Tams (eds), *The Statute of the International Court of Justice, A Commentary*, 2nd edn (Oxford, 2012) 1062ff.

[49] *LaGrand* (2001) *ICJ Reports* 501ff, § 98ff. See for example J Kammerhofer, 'The Binding Nature of Provisional Measures of the International Court of Justice—The *LaGrand* Case' (2003) 16 *Leiden Journal of International Law* 67ff.

[50] At § 104ff. On this decision, see K Oellers-Frahm, 'Verbindlichkeit einstweiliger Massnahmen: Der EMGR vollzieht—endlich—die erforderliche Wende in seiner Rechtsprechung' (2003) 30 *EuGRZ* 689ff; GS Letsas, 'International Human Rights and the Binding Force of Provisional Measures' (2003) 5 *European Human Rights Law Review* 527ff; H Tigroudja, 'La force obligatoire des mesures provisoires indiquées par la Cour européenne des droits de l'homme' (2003) 107 *RGDIP* 601ff.

[51] *Piandiong et al v The Philippines*, Communication No 869/1999 (15 June 1999), UN Doc CCPR/C/70/D/869/1999, § 5.1ff.

[52] *Maffezini v Spain*, ICSID ARB/97/7, Procedural Order No 2, 28 October 1999, § 9; *Pey Casado and President Allende Foundation v Chile*, ICSID ARB/98/2, Provisional Measures, 25 September 2001, §§ 19–20; *Tokios Tokelės v Ukraine*, ICSID ARB/02/18, Procedural Order No 1, 1 July 2003, § 4; *Azurix v Argentina*, ICSID ARB/01/12, Provisional Measures, 6 August 2003, §§ 30–31; *Occidental v Ecuador*, ICSID ARB/06/11, Provisional Measures, 17 August 2007, § 58; *City Oriente Ltd v Ecuador and Empresa Estatal de Petróleos del Ecuador*, ICSID ARB/06/21, Provisional Measures, 19 November 2007, § 52; *Perenco Ecuador Ltd v Ecuador*, ICSID ARB/08/6, Provisional Measures, 8 May 2009, §§ 39–41; *Burlington Resources Inc v Ecuador*, ICSID ARB/08/5, Provisional Measures, 29 June 2009, § 62 ff; *Quiborax SA and Non-Metallic Minerals SA v Bolivia*, ICSID ARB/06/2, Provisional Measures, 26 February 2010, §§ 108–12; *Tethyan v Pakistan*, ICSID ARB/12/1, Provisional Measures, 13 December 2012, § 120; *RSM Production Corporation v Saint Lucia*, ICSID ARB/12/10, Request for Security for Costs, 13 August 2014, § 48; *PNG Sustainable Development Program Ltd v Papua New Guinea*, ICSID ARB/13/33, Provisional Measures, 15 January 2015, § 102; *Transglobal Green Energy, LLC and Transglobal Green Energy de Panama, SA v Panama*, ICSID ARB/13/28, Provisional Measures, 21 January 2016, § 25; *Hydro Srl and others v Albania*, ICSID ARB/15/28, Provisional Measures, 3 March 2016, §§ 3.7, 3.12, 3.41 and 5.1; etc.

is remarkable since the text of the mentioned provision speaks only of 'recommendations'). The issue is not here to discuss the well-founded character of this position on the binding nature of such measures, but to explore to what extent the principle of good faith can contribute to a strengthening of the provisional measures when these are *not* considered to be binding by some judicial or other body.

For a long time, the issue of the binding nature of ICJ provisional measures has been extremely controversial.[53] Thus, absent a clear binding force, legal doctrine developed some corollary effects of provisional measures, some of which flow from the principle of good faith. Their effect was to subject the parties to the procedure to some legal obligations with regard to those measures and to the object of the dispute. Arguments relating to good faith were then also presented to justify the legally binding force of provisional measures.

A. Corollary Effects, Some of which under Good Faith

Various such effects have been proposed, some of which were not truly corollary. Thus, it has been said that the measures are not binding, but that the Court can take into account a violation of its order indicating the provisional measures and mete out some procedural disadvantages or sanctions for the non-complying state.[54] Equally, it has been argued that a state violating the order exposes itself to counter-measures (or at least retorsions) by the aggrieved state.[55] Further, it has been said that the 'binding effect' is simply delayed in time: 'if the later judgment on the merits is rendered in favour of the Applicant State, the respondent State may be made responsible for any action taken in defiance of the provisional measures'.[56] These corollary effects in fact and law imply a binding force of the measures. Thus, for example, a counter-measure is possible only if the breach of the measures constitutes an internationally wrongful act; and similarly any type of sanction for non compliance goes a long way to create an obligation to comply. A legal sanction is not a condition for the existence of a legal norm; but the existence of a legal sanction turns a norm automatically into a legal one.[57] A true corollary effect is the suspension of the power to adopt certain counter-measures when a

[53] See R Kolb, *The International Court of Justice* (Oxford, Hart, 2013) 644–45.

[54] H Lauterpacht, *The Development of International Law by the International Court* (London, 1958) 253–54; MH Mendelson, 'Interim Measures of Protection and the Use of Force by States', in: A Cassese (ed), *The Current Legal Regulation of the Use of Force* (Dordrecht, 1986) 347; E Dumbauld, *Interim Measures of Protection in International Controversies* (The Hague, 1932) 173.

[55] J Sztucki, *Interim Measures in the Hague Court: An Attempt at a Scrutiny* (Deventer, 1983) 299ff; A Pütz, *Der Erlass von einstweiligen Verfügungen durch den Ständigen Internationalen Gerichtshof* (Mainz, 1939) 42.

[56] S Oda, 'The International Court of Justice Viewed from the Bench (1976-1993)' (1993-VII) 244 *RCADI* 75.

[57] See eg H Kelsen, *The Law of the United Nations* (London, 1951) 107.

tribunal seized of the dispute has indicated binding provisional measures (but here the measures are indeed binding).[58] This latter aspect was sometimes linked to the principle of good faith.[59]

B. Binding Force of Provisional Measures based on the Principle of Good Faith

Some arguments are stronger and seek to establish the binding character of the measures by arguments gravitating in the orbit of the principle of good faith. The main argument used is the one seeking to protect the object and purpose of the whole proceedings against frustration by unilateral action of one party, and also against *mala fide* acts. The chain of argument resembles the pre-conventional obligations under article 18 of the VCLT. The issue revolves around the need to preserve the final subject matter of the decision the Court has to take, and thus by extension to preserve the value of the entire proceedings. Provisional measures are, above all other considerations, designed to preserve the subject of the proceedings from 'irreparable prejudice'. If irreparable prejudice was not prevented by a prohibition to act contrary to the indicated measures, the whole proceedings become nugatory and senseless. This teleological argument was developed with finesse and precision by the United Kingdom representative at the Security Council, Sir Gladwyn Jebb. He was concerned about the consequences of Iran's failure to comply with the provisional measures indicated by the Court in the *Anglo-Iranian Oil Cy* case (1951):

> The whole object of Provisional Measures … is to preserve the respective rights of the parties pending the final decision; in other words, to prevent a situation from being created in which the final decision would be rendered inoperative or impossible of execution because of some step taken by one of the parties in the meantime with the object of frustrating that decision. Now it is established that a final judgment of the Court is binding on the parties; that, indeed, is expressly stated by Articles 59 and 60 of the Statute and Article 94, paragraph 1, of the Charter. But, clearly, there would be no point in making the final [judgment] binding if one of the parties could frustrate that decision in advance by actions which would render the final judgment nugatory. It is, therefore, a necessary consequence, we suggest, of the bindingness of the final decision that the Provisional Measures intended to preserve its efficacy should equally be binding.[60]

[58] *Aerial Services (France/US)* (1978) 54 *ILR* 340–41: 'To the extent that the tribunal has the necessary means to achieve the objectives justifying the counter-measures, it must be admitted that the right of the Parties to initiate such measures disappears. In other words, the power of a tribunal to decide on interim measures of protection … leads to the disappearance of the power to initiate counter-measures'. See also art 52, § 3, letter b and § 4 of the Articles on State Responsibility of 2001: J Crawford, *The ILC's Articles on State Responsibility* (Cambridge, 2002) 299–300.

[59] Crawford, op cit, 299.

[60] *Security Council, Official Records*, 6th Year, 559th Meeting (1951), p 20, § 94.

This line of argument has received a considerable body of support among leading commentators;[61] others, however, have challenged it.[62] As can be seen, this is a typical good faith-argument under the limb 'prevention of acts contrary to the object and purpose'. The rationale of this holding also shows that if provisional measures are not indicated with the aim of preventing irreparable harm but for other motives (eg to ease the proceedings), the strength of the argument diminishes. Measures indicated to ease the proceedings could not be considered to be binding under the chain of argument as presented. If a legal operator wants to use the good faith-argument explained above, he or she will thus have to carefully check the object and purpose of the measures indicated. Finally, we may recall that other arguments were presented to the same effect of rendering mandatory the provisional measures indicated by the ICJ.[63] But these arguments were not directly linked with the principle of good faith and need not be considered here.

As can be seen, the principle of good faith intervenes in order to strengthen the judicial or arbitral procedure against the strain of some excessive unilateral action, depriving the whole process of its usefulness. The cooperation between the parties is preserved, abuses are ruled out and the object of a legal institution is preserved. These are core functions of the principle of good faith. Conversely, when the binding force of provisional measures is affirmed on this or other grounds, the principle of good faith turns to the other side of the coin, namely the proper execution of the legally binding order. The issue is now that of *pacta sunt servanda* and of interpretation and execution in good faith.

III. Good Faith and Estoppel or Acquiescence Jurisdiction

Although the idea that jurisdiction is based on will and consent has been formulated in an absolute way, as an abstract principle, its application to particular cases has been remarkably flexible, at the ICJ and elsewhere. Consent reaches from express will to implicit will, to tacitly expressed will, presumed will, imputed or constructive will, even perhaps to no true will at all (acquiescence through passivity). For this reason it is sometimes possible to interpret the 'consent' in a way which goes beyond any genuine psychological reality. Indeed, more often than not, a will which is described as 'tacit' is simply the result of a judge's putting a

[61] L Daniele, *Misure cautelari nel processo dinanzi alla Corte internazionale di Giustizia* (Milan, 1993) 149ff; E Hambro, 'The Binding Character of the Provisional Measures of Protection Indicated by the ICJ', *Essays H Wehberg* (Frankfurt-am-Main, 1956) 167; MO Hudson, 'The Thirtieth Year of the World Court' (1952) 46 *AJIL* 22–23; Individual Opinion of Judge Weeramantry (1993) *ICJ Reports* 379.

[62] J Sztucki, *Interim Measures in the Hague Court: An Attempt at a Scrutiny* (Deventer, 1983) 263, 287.

[63] See R Kolb, *The International Court of Justice* (Oxford, Hart, 2013) 643–44.

reasonable interpretation on the facts of the particular case. This is why examples of *forum prorogatum*, even when they conform to consensualist theory of the high classical kind, can be interpreted at one and the same time both as flexible applications of the principle of the will to consent and as limitations to (or sometimes even derogations from) that same principle.[64]

Acquiescence and estoppel, as we discussed them, could furnish a basis for an exceptional jurisdiction, to be interpreted very narrowly if the important principle of consent is not to be circumvented. Clearly, there can be no doubt that the Court or other tribunal would not like to formulate its reasoning on the basis of an exception to the principle of consent. It would prefer to set out its rationale in the context of a flexible and non-formalistic application of that principle. It would thus assert that, by keeping silent in the face of a petition to the Court, a state had accepted the Court's jurisdiction (acquiescence); or that by giving rise to a legitimate expectation that it would submit to the Court's jurisdiction (estoppel), the state in question had implicitly consented to it. But if one looks to the substance, a kind of exceptional jurisdiction based on good faith could emerge.

Can the jurisdiction of the ICJ in a particular case be founded on estoppel or acquiescence resulting from the behaviour of one of the parties *prior* to the time the Court was seized or before any procedural step was taken (after the Court has been seized, the question merges into the *forum prorogatum*)? On rare occasions, most often in the context of arbitration, commentators have come to the conclusion that acquiescence or estoppel can give rise to jurisdiction. M Reisman has expressed this view: 'If a communication creates an expectation of arbitration, that, if not executed, will prejudice the position of the other party, jurisdiction is founded by creative as opposed to extinctive prescription.'[65] S Rosenne took the same view:

> If State A by its conduct induces in State B the belief, which is acted upon, that State A will accept, or will not contest, the jurisdiction if State B brings a certain issue before the Court for decision, then State A ought not to be permitted, subsequently, to contest the jurisdiction of the Court when that issue is brought before the Court for decision.[66]

It is important to distinguish the two roles that estoppel and acquiescence can play in this context. On the one hand, the specific conduct of one or more of the parties to a dispute can operate as an *autonomous basis of jurisdiction*. Here, the principles discussed above are playing a creative role, in that their function is positive or attributive. On the other hand, estoppel or acquiescence can *prevent a party from raising a preliminary objection* to jurisdiction or admissibility, where the jurisdiction is based on a distinct and pre-existing title. In this case their function is negative or deprivatory. The jurisprudence has been faced with both these situations.

[64] This ambiguity, and the unease it causes voluntarist commentators, can be gauged by considering B Winiarski, 'Quelques réflexions sur le soi-disant forum prorogatum en droit international', *Essays in Honor of J Spiropoulos* (Bonn, 1957) 452.

[65] WM Reisman, *Nullity and Revision* (New Haven CT, 1971) 394.

[66] S Rosenne, *The Law and Practice of the International Court*, 2nd edn (Dordrecht, 1985) 322.

A. Estoppel and Acquiescence as Autonomous Bases of Jurisdiction

The Court has never made a decision exclusively on the basis that its jurisdiction is established by virtue of conduct giving rise to a legitimate expectation. The practice of the ICJ nevertheless provides us with various useful indicators in this regard.

In the case on the *Temple of Preah Vihear (Preliminary Objections)* (1961),[67] the Court had to examine the validity of a new declaration accepting its jurisdiction under article 36, § 2 of the Statute, made by Thailand in 1950.[68] Thailand argued, after the event, that its former declaration in 1940, deposited with the PCIJ, had lapsed with the dissolution of that court on 19 April 1946. Consequently, it argued, article 36, § 5 of the Statute[69] did not operate so as to transfer jurisdiction from the PCIJ to the ICJ. In making a new declaration in 1950, Thailand simply misunderstood the legal position. It followed, according to the Thai argument, that the new declaration in 1950 was necessarily invalid and inoperative, since its very purpose had disappeared with the dissolution of the PCIJ.[70] The Court rejected this argument and declared that it had jurisdiction.[71] Its analysis relied on acquiescence to confirm an interpretation reached by other means. Acquiescence corroborated the agreement to jurisdiction based on the new optional declaration in 1950. The Court put it as follows:

> To sum up, when a country has evinced as clearly as Thailand did in 1950, *and indeed by its consistent attitude over many years*, an intention to submit itself to the compulsory jurisdiction of what constituted at the time the principal international tribunal, the Court could not accept the plea that this intention had been defeated and nullified by some defect not involving any flaw in the consent given' (emphasis added).[72]

The Court thus relied on 'intention'—apparently meaning, by that word, to refer primarily to the legal act of 1950, ie Thailand's voluntary declaration. The subsidiary argument, relating to Thailand's 'consistent attitude', is probably best interpreted as an independent element, concerned with the application of normative principles such as acquiescence in the face of silence and conduct. The Court's reasoning, connecting them formally to intention ('indeed by its consistent attitude … intention to submit itself') indicates the point made above, that the Court hesitated to expose itself to the criticism that it had admitted an extra-voluntary element into the context in which its jurisdiction was established.

[67] *Temple of Preah Vihear (Preliminary Objections)* (1961) *ICJ Reports* 17ff.

[68] ibid, 24ff.

[69] 'Declarations made under Article 36 of the Statute of the Permanent Court of International Justice and which are still in force shall be deemed, as between the parties to the present Statute, to be acceptances of the compulsory jurisdiction of the International Court of Justice for the period which they still have to run and in accordance with their terms'.

[70] ibid, 26.

[71] ibid, 27ff.

[72] ibid, 34.

Above all, however, it is the case of the *Military and Paramilitary Activities in and against Nicaragua (Jurisdiction and Admissibility)* (1984), still on the interpretation of article 36, § 5 of the Statute, that the question of jurisdiction by acquiescence received the most significant amount of attention.[73] The Court was faced with a declaration accepting the jurisdiction of the PCIJ under article 36, § 2 of the Statute. The history of that declaration was, to say the least, an unusual one. In 1935 the Senate of Nicaragua, and then the Chamber of Deputies, had approved the optional declaration proposed by their Government: this had been formulated as early as 1929. A telegram had been sent by the Nicaraguan Minister of Foreign Affairs to the League of Nations, notifying the League of Nicaragua's ratification of the declaration. The telegram stated that the instrument of ratification would be sent to Geneva, but in fact it never was received. It seems to have been sent by a sea-borne courier during the Second World War, and was probably lost in transit.[74] The question was whether the 1929 declaration, which unquestionably had not acquired full binding force, might nevertheless benefit, as an imperfected legal act, from the transfer from the PCIJ to the ICJ under article 36, § 5 of the Statute. If it did, the simple deposit of a Nicaraguan instrument of ratification might perfect the 1929 Declaration and establish the Court's jurisdiction over the present case.[75] The essential legal question was thus whether article 36, § 5 of the Statute presupposed an optional declaration that was formally perfected and in force, or whether an unperfected legal act could also benefit from the transference to the new Court and there be completed by means of the necessary formalities.

The Court took the view that article 36, § 5 should be given a wide interpretation. The essential concern of those who drafted the Statute was to maintain the greatest possible continuity between the PCIJ and the ICJ. The point was to avoid loss—of whatever nature—resulting from the transfer of judicial activity from the old court to the new.[76] The interpretation that was most consistent with this conception and with this objective was the one that preserved even the potential[77]

[73] *Military and Paramilitary Activities in and against Nicaragua (Jurisdiction and Admissibility)* (1984) *ICJ Reports* 412, § 46. See: PM Eisemann, 'L'arrêt de the Cour internationale de Justice du 26 novembre 1984 (compétence et recevabilité) dans l'affaire des Activités militaires et paramilitaires au Nicaragua et contre celui-ci' (1984) 30 *AFDI* 372ff, 376–78; HW Briggs, 'Nicaragua v United States: Jurisdiction and Admissibility' (1985) 79 *AJIL* 374; S Rosenne, *The Law and Practice of the International Court*, 2nd edn (Dordrecht, 1985) 322; ML Wagner, 'Jurisdiction by Estoppel in the ICJ' (1986) 74 *California Law Review* 1777ff; C Lang, *L'affaire Nicaragua/Etats-Unis devant la Cour internationale de Justice* (Paris, 1990) 72–87; DW Greig, 'Nicaragua and the United States: Confrontation Over the Jurisdiction of the International Court' (1991) 62 *BYIL* 158ff; S Oda, 'The International Court of Justice Viewed from the Bench (1976–1993)' (1993-VII) 244 *RCADI* 45–47. See also JG Merrills, 'The Optional Clause Revisited' (1993) 64 *BYIL* 199.

[74] (1984) *ICJ Reports* 399–400.

[75] On the other hand, if Nicaragua deposited a new declaration, without retroactive effect, the Court would not have had jurisdiction in the case, because the United States of America had in the meantime withdrawn its optional declaration.

[76] (1984) *ICJ Reports* 407–08. This interpretation is analysed minutely, and with approval, by DW Greig, 'Nicaragua and the United States: Confrontation Over the Jurisdiction of the International Court' (1991) 62 *BYIL* 123ff.

[77] (1984) *ICJ Reports* 404.

(or unperfected) effects of the 1929 declaration, ie its capacity to be subsequently perfected through the necessary formalities. On the basis of these considerations, the words 'still in force' and 'for the period which they still have to run', in article 36, § 5, ought to be interpreted in a restricted sense. Having reached this point, the Court sought confirmation for its conclusion. It was at this point that it brought in considerations concerning jurisdiction by acquiescence. This was another case in which the Court was not seeking to found its jurisdiction on an autonomous basis of this kind, but only to use it to buttress an interpretation reached by other means. In this regard, the judges noted that the first ICJ *Yearbook*, for 1946/47, showed Nicaragua in the list of states bound by optional declarations under article 36, § 5 of the Statute.[78] This had not been the case in the PCIJ's 16th (and final) report.[79] Only with the *Yearbook* for 1955/56, and thereafter, was the reference to Nicaragua accompanied by a footnote indicating that the instrument of ratification had never been received by the League of Nations. Nicaragua nevertheless continued to appear on the list of states bound by the optional clause.[80] The same went for numerous other documents which Nicaragua was considered to have submitted to the compulsory jurisdiction: namely, from 1968, the Court's *Annual Reports* to the UN General Assembly (which did not mention the failure to deliver the instrument of ratification);[81] and various publications that had come out under the responsibility of the UN Secretary-General.[82] This practice had continued for some 40 years, without any protest. What were the legal consequences? The Court's argument was in five stages.

First, the Court indicated that it did not intend to rely decisively on any of the various publications cited. They were all exclusively documents that were part of the Court's administrative activities, and, as indeed the documents themselves indicated, were not binding either on states or on the Court in its judicial activity. The Court's view of them was quite different:

> It is that the listing found appropriate for Nicaragua amounted over the years to a series of attestations which were entirely official and public, and extremely numerous, and ranged over a period of nearly 40 years; and that hence the States concerned—first and foremost, Nicaragua—had every opportunity of accepting or rejecting the thus-proclaimed application of Article 36, paragraph 5....[83]

Hence:

> Having regard to the public and unchanging nature of the official statements concerning Nicaragua's commitment under the Optional-Clause system, the silence of its Government can only be interpreted as an acceptance of the classification thus assigned to it.

[78] ibid, 401–02, 408–09.
[79] ibid, 401.
[80] ibid, 402.
[81] ibid, 402.
[82] ibid, 402–03. On these questions, see particularly DW Greig, 'Nicaragua and the United States: Confrontation Over the Jurisdiction of the International Court' (1991) 62 *BYIL* 125ff, 158ff; C Lang, *L'affaire Nicaragua/Etats-Unis devant la Cour internationale de Justice* (Paris, 1990) 72ff.
[83] (1984) *ICJ Reports* 409, § 38.

> It cannot be supposed that that Government could have believed that its silence could be tantamount to anything other than acquiescence.[84]

Certain judges and commentators have severely criticised this line of reasoning. First, it has been said that the Court was giving excessive weight to administrative texts which had no binding force.[85] That objection seems, however, to confuse binding force with probative value. The Court took great pains to indicate that the only value of these publications was as an element influencing the question of interpretation, for which purpose a document does not need any particular legal status, and a fortiori does not need to have any legally binding force. It was also said that the information provided in these publications as to Nicaragua's legal situation was unclear because of the footnotes relating to non-ratification.[86] But these footnotes were certainly not designed to nullify the sense of the principal text, and could not do so. They simply provided a point of information, without invalidating what was said in the body of the text.[87] Besides, it was not the *Yearbook* and other entries, as such, which were the subject of the acquiescence. It was more a certain interpretation of them, according to which the entries showed an *opinio juris* of being bound to the compulsory jurisdiction.

In addition, three other plausible arguments have been made against the Court's interpretation. However, whether to refute them or confirm them would involve us in an analysis for which we do not have space here. One was that Nicaragua's attitude was not clear and consistent, and that therefore it could not be interpreted as acquiescence.[88] This raises questions of fact. The interpretation of the Court however does not seem arbitrary. Then it was said that Nicaragua could and should have put an end to all misunderstandings about its position by delivering its instrument of ratification to the UN Secretary-General or alternatively by sending him a fresh declaration. According to this argument, the Court, in finding that there had been acquiescence, enabled Nicaragua to profit from its own wrong.[89]

[84] ibid, 410, § 39.

[85] Dissenting Opinions of: Judge Oda, ibid, 488; Judge Jennings, ibid, 540–41; Judge Schwebel, ibid, 594.

[86] Dissenting Opinions of: Judge Oda, ibid, 484ff; Judge Jennings, ibid, 541ff; Judge Schwebel, ibid, 588–92. See also PM Eisemann, 'L'arrêt de la Cour internationale de Justice du 26 novembre 1984 (compétence et recevabilité) dans l'affaire des Activités militaires et paramilitaires au Nicaragua et contre celui-ci' (1984) 30 *AFDI* 376. Professor Greig subjected the question to minute analysis and concluded that the footnoted caveats were part of the backwash from the *Norwegian loans* case of 1957: D W Greig, 'Nicaragua and the United States: Confrontation Over the Jurisdiction of the International Court' (1991) 62 *BYIL* 141 et seq. Another explanation is given in the Dissenting Opinion of Judge Jennings (1984) *ICJ Reports* 543 and the Dissenting Opinion of Judge Schwebel, ibid, 590–91.

[87] C Lang, *L'affaire Nicaragua/Etats-Unis devant la Cour internationale de Justice* (Paris, 1990) 76; DW Greig, 'Nicaragua and the United States: Confrontation Over the Jurisdiction of the International Court' (1991) 62 *BYIL* 144.

[88] PM Eisemann, 'L'arrêt de the Cour internationale de Justice du 26 novembre 1984 (compétence et recevabilité) dans l'affaire des Activités militaires et paramilitaires au Nicaragua et contre celui-ci' (1984) 30 *AFDI* 377–78; Separate Opinion of Judge Mosler (1984) *ICJ Reports* 464.

[89] Separate Opinion of Judge Mosler (1984) *ICJ Reports* 464. See also C Lang, *L'affaire Nicaragua/Etats-Unis devant la Cour internationale de Justice* (Paris, 1990) 81.

One may reasonably wonder whether the wrongdoing was sufficiently serious to justify debarment. It is doubtful whether Nicaragua should have been sanctioned for not taking steps it was under no obligation to take. Finally, it has been argued that the absence of any binding force in the publications mentioned meant that there was no parallel duty to protest. Nicaragua's silence would, in that case, not be the kind of silence required for acquiescence, since Nicaragua would have been under no legal obligation to react.[90] However this argument overlooks the fact that the duty to break one's silence does not depend exclusively on the legal value of the act one might protest about. It suffices that the legal interests of the state in question are affected. It follows that the Court's argument was not a priori defective.

Second, to buttress its conclusion on acquiescence, the Court relied on a reciprocity argument. It considered the hypothetical situation in which Nicaragua might have found itself in the position of the Respondent to a claim brought by another state which sought to establish the Court's jurisdiction on the basis of the 1929 declaration. The Court concluded that 'probably', if Nicaragua had disputed the Court's jurisdiction, its argument would have been rejected because of its long silence. But the Court's jurisdiction cannot depend on the position of a state in proceedings before it as Claimant or as Respondent. It followed that 'If the Court considers that it would have decided that Nicaragua would have been bound in a case in which it was the Respondent, it must conclude that its jurisdiction is identically established in a case where Nicaragua is the Applicant.'[91]

That argument was as strongly disputed as the preceding ones. Eisemann[92] considered it a circular argument. Indeed, it does not seem that the reciprocity in question can be considered to be without defects.[93] Acquiescence or estoppel can serve as the basis of jurisdiction only if one party can invoke the argument *against the other party* in a concrete case, either as the basis of the action (positive function), or as a ground for debarring an objection (negative function). They cannot be used to justify a defective title or basis of jurisdiction without regard to the attitude of the opposing party. That being so, the Court's argument cannot be considered entirely valueless. It is part of the logic of a hypothetical argument in favour of a given interpretation.

Third, the Court took account of the conduct of states other than Nicaragua. It concluded that none of them had ever challenged the interpretation evidenced by the UN publications.[94] It must, however, be admitted that the absence of such

[90] PM Eisemann, 'L'arrêt de the Cour internationale de Justice du 26 novembre 1984 (compétence et recevabilité) dans l'affaire des Activités militaires et paramilitaires au Nicaragua et contre celui-ci' (1984) 30 *AFDI* 377.

[91] (1984) *ICJ Reports* 410, § 39.

[92] PM Eisemann, 'L'arrêt de the Cour internationale de Justice du 26 novembre 1984 (compétence et recevabilité) dans l'affaire des Activités militaires et paramilitaires au Nicaragua et contre celui-ci' (1984) 30 *AFDI* 378, n 33.

[93] *cf* the reservations expressed by DW Greig, 'Nicaragua and the United States: Confrontation Over the Jurisdiction of the International Court' (1991) 62 *BYIL* 162–63.

[94] (1984) *ICJ Reports* 410, §§ 40, 41.

a reaction is of little probative value. It cannot reasonably be expected that third states not directly affected, and with no concrete connection to Nicaragua's particular situation, would have looked into the matter and reacted accordingly.

Fourth, the Court was getting further detached from the interpretation of article 36, § 5 of the Statute, with which all the preceding arguments were to a greater or lesser degree concerned. It was now getting closer to the heart of an argument to the effect that the conduct of the parties might, in itself, be a basis of jurisdiction.[95] According to Nicaragua's argument, indeed, its conduct 'over a period of 38 years unequivocally constitutes consent to be bound by the compulsory jurisdiction of the Court'.[96] The Court, in an obiter dictum, accepted this possibility, thus giving credit to the argument for jurisdiction by acquiescence. This, however, leads back to the 'consent' to which this category of passive attitudes is considered to give expression. In this way, the Court paid tribute to the judicial prudence highlighted above. It began by recognising the unusual nature of Nicaragua's situation.[97] It followed this by saying:

> [The Court] considers therefore that, having regard to the origin and generality of the statements to the effect that Nicaragua was bound by its 1929 Declaration, it is right to conclude that the constant acquiescence of that State in those affirmations constitutes a valid mode of manifestation of its intent to recognize the compulsory jurisdiction of the Court under Article 36, paragraph 2, of the Statute.[98]

Here, then, the Court is appealing explicitly to the 'intent'—the word being used without any qualification. However it did not attempt to prove the real wishes of Nicaragua. In reality, the Court interpreted the acts in question on the basis of appearances and of the legitimate expectations they inspired.

Two main objections have been raised to any kind of jurisdiction based on acquiescence or estoppel, seen as extra-voluntary legal phenomena. The first objection does not really seem to call for much comment. It has been argued that the Court's jurisdiction is exclusively consensual and that therefore estoppel and normative acquiescence, not the consequence of an act of will, cannot give the Court jurisdiction.[99] In the author's view, this merely begs the question. The second objection is a question of form. The United States,[100] and some authors too,[101] have argued that a declaration expressing a state's consent to the jurisdiction is an act which is necessarily linked to a certain form. It must be done by depositing a document

[95] ibid, 411, § 43, p 413, § 47.

[96] ibid, 411, § 43.

[97] ibid, 412, § 46.

[98] ibid, 413, § 47.

[99] ML Wagner, 'Jurisdiction by Estoppel in the ICJ' (1986) 74 *California Law Review* 1800–01.

[100] (1984) *ICJ Reports* 411–12, § 44.

[101] ML Wagner, 'Jurisdiction by Estoppel in the ICJ' (1986) 74 *California Law Review* 1800. *Cf* also the Dissenting Opinion of Judge Ruda, (1984) *ICJ Reports* 459; the Dissenting Opinion of Judge Ago, ibid, 527; the Dissenting Opinion of Judge Schwebel, ibid, 595. *Contra*: DW Greig, 'Nicaragua and the United States: Confrontation Over the Jurisdiction of the International Court' (1991) 62 *BYIL* 158ff. *Cf* also C Lang, *L'affaire Nicaragua/Etats-Unis devant la Cour internationale de Justice* (Paris, 1990) 81ff.

with the Secretary-General of the United Nations. Also, the manifestation of will must be clear. Consent interpreted from conduct or silence is insufficient for these purposes. This line of argument should be rejected. Consent need not be given in any particular form. The practice of the Court in relation to the lack of formalism, like its jurisprudence on the *forum prorogatum* show this clearly.

Fifth and finally, the Court rejected the United States' argument that an estoppel would prevent Nicaragua's arguing that it had acquiesced in the Court's jurisdiction.[102] The conditions for an estoppel were not, in the Court's view, satisfied.[103] That view does appear to have been justified.

In the *Nicaragua* case, the Court thus gave a certain credibility to the idea of jurisdiction by acquiescence or estoppel, without however actually going so far as to cross the conceptual line between the 'voluntarist' concept and concepts based on legitimate expectation. In our view, the 'good-faith/legitimate expectation' concept can, as a matter of law and via the intervention of an acquiescence or an estoppel, be a basis for the Court to have jurisdiction independently of any 'voluntarist' interpretation. However any such case would be extremely exceptional, and it is absolutely essential that this remain the position. In particular, it is essential to be vigilant to ensure that the strictest conditions required for acquiescence or estoppel are manifestly satisfied in such cases, before concluding that jurisdiction exists on this (at least partially involuntary) basis.

B. Estoppel and Acquiescence as Factors Nullifying the Plea of Want of Jurisdiction

Estoppel and acquiescence can also play a more limited role, by preventing a party from raising a preliminary objection to jurisdiction or admissibility. There is extensive jurisprudence on this point.

The first thing to say about this jurisprudence is that the rule has sometimes been stated, yet without actually being applied to the particular cases in question. So, in *Aerial Incident of 3 July 1988* (*Iran v United States of America*) (Order, 1989), the Court noted the Iranian argument put forward in a letter of 11 October 1989, that 'the United States was estopped and time-barred from raising jurisdictional questions'.[104] The case was thereupon struck out, on the basis that the parties had reached a direct agreement. This type of argument is not new in international practice. In the case on the *Pious Funds of California* (1902), an arbitration between Mexico and the United States, the latter claimed that Mexico had acted in such a way that, under the principle of estoppel, it no longer had any right to dispute

[102] (1984) *ICJ Reports* 413–15, § 48–51. *Cf* C Lang, *L'affaire Nicaragua/Etats-Unis devant la Cour internationale de Justice* (Paris, 1990) 85–87.

[103] (1984) *ICJ Reports* 415, § 51.

[104] *Aerial Incident of 3 July 1988* (*Iran v United States of America*) (*Order*) (1989) *ICJ Reports* 133.

the jurisdiction of the Mixed Arbitral Commission which had been established.[105] The terms of the agreement to arbitrate, and the questions put to the tribunal, enabled the latter not to decide the various arguments that were advanced on the estoppel issues.[106] In the case on the *Aegean Sea Continental Shelf* (1978), the Greek *ad hoc* Judge Stassinopoulos took the view that Turkey's prolonged silence as to the validity of the General Act on Arbitration of 1928— after the question had received heavy publicity thanks to the *Nuclear Tests* cases—prevented Turkey from pleading desuetude and thereby depriving the Court of a basis on which its jurisdiction could be founded.[107]

The rule has, however, sometimes been given concrete application. For example, in the case of *Loizidou v Turkey (Preliminary Objections)* (1995), the European Court of Human Rights took the view that the Turkish Government's allegation that the principal objective of the claim was to make political propaganda was not only unfounded, but could not be raised as a preliminary objection, by virtue of the principle of estoppel. The reason was that the objection had not been raised earlier, at the time of the proceedings before the Commission.[108] As far as the ICJ itself is concerned, an important case for present purposes was *Barcelona Traction* (*Preliminary Objections*, 1964). Belgium had made a fresh application to the Court, having previously discontinued earlier proceedings so that direct

[105] H Lauterpacht, *Private Law Sources and Analogies of International Law* (London, 1927) 248–49.

[106] ibid, 249.

[107] *Aegean Sea Continental Shelf* (1978) *ICJ Reports* 73, Dissenting Opinion of Judge Stassinopoulos.

[108] *Loizidou v Turkey (Preliminary Objections)* (1995) Series A no 310, p 19, § 42ff. Since 1970 the European Court of Human Rights has examined the principle of estoppel in light of state conduct which, in some hundreds of cases, had never raised a Preliminary Objection before the Commission or in a relevant Memorial. In a majority of cases, the ECHR has given effect to estoppel arguments, either completely so or at least as regards certain objections. See for example *De Wilde, Ooms et Versyp* (1971) Series A no 12, §§ 53ff, 57, 58; *Artico* (1980) Series A no 37, §§ 27–28; *Corigliano* (1983) Series A no 57, §§ 25–27, 28–29; *Foti and others* (1982) Series A no 56, §§ 42–43, 49; *De Jong, Baljet et Van den Brink* (1984) Series A no 77, §§ 35, 37, 38–40; *Bozano* (1986) Series A no 111, §§ 44-47; *Barberà, Messegué and Jabardo* (1988) Series A no 146, §§ 56, 58, 63; the *Ciulla* case (1989) Series A no 148, §§ 28-29, 33; the *Bricmont* case (1989) Series A no 158, §§ 72–73; *Granger* (1990) Series A no 174, §§ 37–41; *Obermeier* (1990) Series A no 179, §§ 65–66; *Isgrò* (1991) Series A no 194-A, §§ 28–29; *Pine Valley Development Ltd* (1991) Series A no 222, § 45; *Tomasi* (1992) Series A no 241-A, §§ 105–06; *Padovani* (1993) Series A no 257-B, §§ 19–20; *Papamichalopoulos* (1993) Series A no 260-B, §§ 35–36; *Schuler-Zgraggen* (1993) Series A no 263, §§ 54–55; *Greek Stan Refineries* (1994) Series A no 301-B, §§ 31–36; *Mansur* (1995) Series A no 319-B, §§ 45–46, 47–48; *Yagci and Sargin* (1995) Series A no 319-A, §§ 45–46; *Erdagöz* (1997-VI) *ICJ Reports* §§ 45–46; *Szücs* (1997-VII) *ICJ Reports* § 40; *Werner* (1997-VII) *ICJ Reports* § 42; *Zana* (1997-VII) *ICJ Reports* § 65; *Sakik and others* (1997-VII) *ICJ Reports* §§ 47–48, 55–56; *Kaya* (1998-I) *ICJ Reports* §§ 56-60; *Gautrin and others* (1998-III) *ICJ Reports* §§ 49–51; *Vasilescu* (1998-III) *ICJ Reports* §§ 33–34; *Güleç* (1998-IV) *ICJ Reports* §§ 60-62; *Ergi* (1998-IV) *ICJ Reports* §§ 60–62, 65–67; *Demir and others* (23.09.1998), §§ 32–35; etc. In these cases the Court never examined the question of prejudice, inherent in the objection which it was concerned with rejecting. In other cases, the Court has examined estoppel, but rejected it, either because an argument had already, in substance, been presented before the Commission, or because special circumstances prevented the State from invoking the objection at an earlier stage. *Cf* for example *Guzzardi* (1980) Series A no 39, §§ 68–70; *Deweer* (1980) Series A no 35, §§ 25–26; *Van Oosterwijck* (1980) Series A no 40, §§ 25–26; *Eckle* (1982) Series A no 51, § 65; *Campbell and Fell* (1984) Series A no 80, §§ 58–59; *Nölkenbockhoff* (1987) Series A no 123, § 32; *Pfeifer and Plankl* (1992) Series A no 227, §§ 31–35; etc.

negotiations could proceed. The basis Belgium invoked to establish the Court's jurisdiction was a Hispano-Belgian treaty of 1927, article 17, § 4 of which gave jurisdiction to the PCIJ. The Court therefore had to interpret article 37 of the Statute, transferring the PCIJ's jurisdiction to the ICJ. In support of its conclusion, it relied on acquiescence or estoppel:

> The Respondent Government, in the course of the diplomatic correspondence preceding the original proceedings before the Court … implicitly recognised the competence of the Court for the purposes of Article 17(4) of the 1927 Treaty, and challenged the right of the Applicant Government to resort to the Court only on grounds connected with the third and fourth Preliminary Objections in the present case. It did not demur when the Applicant stated that the International Court of Justice had been substituted for the Permanent Court in Article 17(4) of the Treaty.[109]

This passage shows that the principles of acquiescence and estoppel do apply to preliminary objection proceedings.

The principle we are concerned with here was applied in an interesting way, outside the field of jurisdiction, in the case of the *Land, Island and Maritime Dispute (El Salvador v Honduras, Nicaragua's request to intervene*, 1990). Nicaragua had requested to intervene under article 62 of the Statute, with a view to taking part in the proceedings between El Salvador and Honduras. Nicaragua thought it unnecessary to produce evidence to show that it had a 'legal interest' which would be in issue, as required by that article. In Nicaragua's view, El Salvador and Honduras had made assertions of fact and law which amounted to recognition of Nicaragua's legal interests, and were now prevented by equitable estoppel from disputing their existence.[110] In light of its view of the facts, the Chamber of the Court rejected this argument, on the basis that the conditions for an estoppel had not been established.[111] The Chamber thus seems, by implication, to have admitted that estoppels can apply in such situations. From a general perspective, however, this attitude does not seem altogether desirable. Estoppel can arise only from the legal relationships of parties, on an *inter partes* basis. It cannot in any circumstances prejudice the question whether an application to the Court complies with the objective requirements of its Statute, of which the only guardian is the Court itself. If there can be no derogation from the Statute even by agreement between the parties, a fortiori there can be no derogation by acquiescence or estoppel.

Overall, it can be said that to the extent that acquiescence and estoppel intervene in the establishment of the jurisdiction of an international organ—and in particular of a court or tribunal—the principle of good faith plays a distinctive role in that subject matter through two of its most powerful vassals.

[109] *Barcelona Traction (Preliminary Objections)* (1964) *ICJ Reports* 36.
[110] *Land, Island and Maritime Dispute (El Salvador v Honduras, Nicaragua's request to intervene)* (1990) *ICJ Reports* 118, § 63.
[111] ibid, 118–19, § 63.

IV. Good Faith and Abuse of Procedure

The prohibition of abuse of procedure is an application of the principle prohibiting the abuse of rights, which itself is a concretisation of the general principle of good faith. Abuse of procedure consists in the use of procedural instruments and entitlements with a fraudulent, malevolent, dilatory, vexatious or frivolous intent, with the aim to harm another or to secure an undue advantage to oneself, with the intent to deprive the proceedings (or some other related proceedings) of their proper object and purpose or outcome, or with the intent to use the proceedings for aims alien to the ones for which the procedural rights at stake have been granted (eg pure propaganda).[112] Abuse of procedure is not presumed. It must be clearly established, by evidence or by judicial action *proprio motu*. There are some situations, however, in which the degree of nuisance caused by a party to the tribunal is such that it can no longer be tolerated. The abuse of procedure will then be admitted.

Rules on abuse of procedure have developed with particular strength in certain branches of international law. Thus, in human rights law, petitions and communications are declared inadmissible when there is an abuse of procedure. This has been the case, for example, under the mandate system at the League of Nations and under the UN trusteeship system,[113] and later under former article 27, § 2 of the ECHR (now article 35, § 3 ECHR (1950)),[114] article 90, letter c of the Rules of

[112] On abuse of procedure in international law, see eg Zoller, *Bonne* 142ff; Kolb, *Bonne* 637ff; M Gestri, 'Considerazioni sulla teoria dell'abuso del diritto alla luce della prassi internazionale' (1994) 77 *RDI* 27ff, 43ff. As was said by the Australian High Court in *Csr Ltd v Cigna Insurance Australia Ltd* (1997) 118 *ILR* 409-410: 'The counterpart of a court's power to prevent its process being abused is its power to protect the integrity of those processes once set in motion'.

[113] E Schwelb, 'The Abuse of the Right of Petition' (1970) 3 *Revue des droits de l'homme* 313ff, 324–26.

[114] 'The Court shall declare inadmissible any individual application … which it considers … an abuse of the right of application'. See eg D Appanah, 'A la recherche posthume de l'intention du requérant: l'identification délicate de la requête abusive au sens de la Convention' (2015) 26 *Revue trimestrielle des droits de l'homme* 1053ff. K Jungwiert, 'Sur la requête abusive devant la Cour européenne des droits de l'homme', *Essays in Honor of J P Costa* (Paris, 2011) 329ff; JF Flauss, 'L'abus de droit dans le cadre de la Convention européenne des droits de l'homme' (1992) 4 *Revue universelle des droits de l'homme* 461ff; M Hottelier, 'La requête abusive au sens de l'article 27, 2 de la Convention européenne des droits de l'homme' (1991) 2 *Revue trimestrielle des droits de l'homme* 301ff; AD Spielmann, 'La notion d'abus des droits de l'homme à la lumière de la Convention européenne de sauvegarde des droits de l'homme et des libertés fondamentales', in Conseil de l'Europe (ed), *L'abus de droit et les concepts équivalents: Principe et applications actuelles* (Strasbourg, 1990) 60ff; GM Palmieri, 'L'abuso del diritto di ricorso individuale dinanzi alla Commissione europea dei diritti dell'uomo', *Essays in Honor of G Sperduti* (Milan, 1984) 623ff; F Monconduit, 'L'abus du droit de recours individuel devant la Commission européenne des droits de l'homme' (1971) 17 *AFDI* 347ff. The interpretation is restrictive: *Aydin v Turkey* (1997), § 59–61; *Andronicou and Constantinou v Cyprus* case (1997), § 163–65; *Assenov and Others v Bulgaria* (1998), § 87–89; *Buscarini and Others v San Marino* (1999), § 20–21. In the more recent case law, see: *Saba v Italy* (2014), § 49ff; *Flores Quiros v Spain* (2016), § 21; *Bagdonavicius v Russia* (2016), § 64; *Kanaginis v Greece* (2016), § 23–24.

Procedure of the Human Rights Committee under the CCPR (2001),[115] articles 56, § 3 of the African Charter on Human Rights (requests written in disparaging or insulting language) or article 22, § 2[116] of the Convention against Torture (1984).[117] There is manifestly a danger that private individuals will abuse human rights remedies for frivolous or quixotic causes; and hence there is the screening under this heading. We have already seen that international administrative law and the case law of the administrative tribunals is replete with references to misuse of authority, including on the procedural plane.[118] We will still see that the law on international investments makes significant reference to the notion of abuse of procedure.[119] Further, article 294 of the Montego Bay Convention on the Law of the Sea (1982) gives the tribunal chosen by the parties to decide their dispute the power to scrutinise whether the claimant's request related to the coastal state's exercise of its sovereign rights under article 297 constitutes an abuse of procedure and to declare it inadmissible *in limine litis.*[120] The fact that such disputes are subjected to adjudication is a satisfaction given to the states attached to the freedom of the seas. The power to declare inadmissible a certain demand for abuse of procedure is a satisfaction given to the coastal states exercising their sovereign rights over the exclusive economic zone and continental shelf. This compromise around the notion of abuse of procedure allowed the acceptance of the overall scheme for the settlement of disputes of such maritime disputes.

At the ICJ, issues of abuse of procedure have often been put to the fore. However, the Court has never concluded that a certain course of conduct constituted an abuse of its procedure. The threshold for such a finding is indeed high, especially in inter-state litigation. The Court will hesitate before accusing a state of abusing its procedure. It will more probably find some other way to declare a case inadmissible or to avoid treating a frivolous argument. But it cannot be excluded that one day the Court will be faced with a situation calling for a clear statement. For the time being, we are confronted with a series of precedents where the issue has been considered. It must be added that states and their counsel are often different from the individuals in municipal law cases. It is less usual for states to attempt to cheat

[115] M Gestri, 'Considerazioni sulla teoria dell'abuso del diritto alla luce della prassi internazionale' (1994) 77 *RDI* 31; A Cassese, 'The Admissibility of Communications to the United Nations on Human Rights Violations' (1972) 5 *Revue des droits de l'homme* 375ff. See *KL v Denmark* (1985) *Human Rights Committee, Selected Decisions under Optional Protocol* (CCPR/C/OP/I, p 26).

[116] Gestri, op cit, 32–33; GM Palmieri, 'Aperçu du règlement intérieur de la Commission africaine des droits de l'homme et des peuples', in: GM Palmieri (ed), *La Charte africaine des droits de l'homme et des peuples* (Padova, 1990) 128.

[117] Gestri, op cit, 33.

[118] See above, Ch 7 section III.

[119] See below, Ch 10.

[120] MH Nordquist (ed), *United Nations Convention on the Law of the Sea, 1982, A Commentary*, vol V (Dordrecht, 1989) 75ff. See also A Cannone, *Il tribunale internazionale del diritto del mare* (Bari, 1991) 134ff; S Rosenne, 'Settlement of Fisheries Disputes in the Exclusive Economic Zone' (1979) 73 *AJIL* 100ff; L Caflisch, 'Le règlement judiciaire et arbitral des différends dans le nouveau droit international de la mer', *Essays in Honor of R Bindschedler* (Berne, 1980) 355–56.

or abuse an eminent international tribunal, to whose jurisdiction they have consented. They will not wish to have their prestige damaged, or to find themselves discredited, in the course of such proceedings. Obviously states do use all available procedural arguments to challenge the Court's jurisdiction. It also often happened that they failed to comply with interim measures. However such attitudes are not the same as manifest abuses. The legal consequence of applying the rule on abuse of procedure would be that an argument could not be entertained, because of its inadmissibility, either *in limine litis* or at the merits stage, or else that the Court might impose a sanction of appropriate kind on the abusing state, for example by 'taking note' of its attitude in the subsequent course of the proceedings and when dealing with the merits, or by rejecting some claim.

The principle of abuse of procedure was invoked by one side or the other in each of the following ICJ cases, each time being rejected by the Court: *Ambatielos* (abuse of process by excessive delay prior to the presentation of the claim to the Court);[121] *Right of passage over Indian territory* (abuse of process by beginning proceedings too rapidly after lodging an optional declaration—a 'surprise attack');[122] *Barcelona Traction* (abuse of process by introducing a new case based on the same arguments as those used in preceding proceedings that had been discontinued);[123] *Military and Paramilitary Activities in and against Nicaragua* (abuse of process because of the futility of the proceedings and the intention to make political propaganda out of a request for the indication of interim measures);[124] *Border and Transborder Armed Actions* (abuse of process by recourse to the ICJ in parallel with the so-called 'Contadora' negotiating process; abuse of process because of the political motivation of the application and its artificial character);[125] *Arbitral Award of 31 July 1989* (abuse of process by invoking a declaration by the president of the tribunal to throw doubt on the validity of the award);[126] *Certain Phosphate Lands at Nauru* (abuse of process in that Nauru was asking of the Respondent an attitude that Nauru itself had not respected);[127] *Genocide* (abuse of process in making a request for interim measures motivated by political considerations and abusive repetition of the request for such measures);[128] *Aerial incident of 10 August 1999* (abuse of process by invoking a reservation to a declaration under the optional clause the content of which was allegedly directed solely against Pakistan and was thus said to be discriminatory);[129] and *Avena and others* (abuse of process by delaying the presentation of claims.[130]

[121] (1953) *ICJ Reports* 23.
[122] (1957) *ICJ Reports* 146–47.
[123] (1964)*ICJ Reports* 24–25.
[124] (1984) *ICJ Reports* 178–79, § 21–25.
[125] (1988) *ICJ Reports* 91–92, § 51ff and p 105–06, § 94.
[126] (1991) *ICJ Reports* 63, § 26–27.
[127] (1992) *ICJ Reports* 255, § 37–38. But see Dissenting Opinion Oda, ibid, 324, § 29.
[128] (1993) *ICJ Reports* 336, § 19; (1996-II) *ICJ Reports* 622, § 46.
[129] (2000) *ICJ Reports* 30, § 40.
[130] (2004-I) *ICJ Reports* 37–38, § 44.

It must be confessed that the abuse of procedure argument was in these cases invoked mostly as a sort of last and additional item. Thus, for example, it is not obvious why Nauru should treat its own mines in a certain way before being allowed to claim some compensation from other states for their conduct. The legal situation in both cases is not the same: Nauru has a discretionary power with regard to its own mines, but the administering powers had no such discretionary power with regard to the mines they were entrusted. Morcover, even assuming that the contrary argument holds true under some estoppel, it stands to reason that this issue should be considered on the merits and hardly lead to a general inadmissibility of the claim. The reasons are the same as for the clean hands doctrine: the inadmissibility operates *en bloc* and gives rise to a *tu quoque* fallacy. Rather, the apportionment, if any, should be done by taking account of all the circumstances on the merits. It is also quite frequently the case that abuse of process argument are rejected in the case law of international arbitral tribunals.[131] But conversely one tribunal was prepared to accept that under some circumstances serial proceedings both under arbitral clauses and under municipal law could constitute an abuse of process.[132]

Further abuses of process might include an avalanche of preliminary objections or procedural arguments designed to delay the proceedings from progressing in the ordinary way; the late invocation of titles of jurisdiction or other arguments in the hope of disrupting or prejudicing the opposing party;[133] etc. Very often such problems are resolved at an early stage by precise rules of procedure. This is the position, for example, as regards delay in presenting titles of jurisdiction or arguments on the merits.[134] The reason these rules exist is precisely to ensure an appreciable degree of legal certainty and equality between the parties in the procedure of the Court and, from a negative perspective, to avoid procedural abuses. These rules thus represent indirect sanctions in support of the principle of the

[131] See eg the *Southern Bluefin Tuna* case (2000) 119 *ILR* 554, § 65.

[132] *Waste Management v Mexico (no 2) (Preliminary Objections)* (2002) 126 *ILR* 175–76 (NAFTA arbitration tribunal).

[133] *Legality of the Use of Force* (1999-I) *ICJ Reports* 124ff and 542ff. See also the Separate and Dissenting Opinion of Ansari in *Cal-Maine Foods v Iran* (1984) 6 *Iran/US Claims Tribunal Reports* 70: 'The issue was first introduced in the Claimant's Memorial of 14 July 1983, and the raising of this new issue, which has totally altered the Claimant's grounds of action, cannot by any means be construed as constituting an amendment or supplement to the Statement of Claim ... This method of changing the grounds of action is unquestionably prejudicial to the rights of the Respondents ... (*Alternativa petitio non est audienda*)'. The judgment accepted the argument on the prohibition of alternative petition for an 'accounts claims' (ibid, 59–60) and rejected it for investment interests (ibid, 60), on the ground that the latter had not been objected to in the Memorial of the defendant and that the latter had in any even had enough time to prepare an adequate defence. Conversely, the pursuit pari passu of two different alternative remedies is not per se contrary to good faith or estoppel: *Spp(me) Ltd v Egypt (Jurisdiction)* (1985) 106 *ILR* 523 (ICSID arbitration). This is true all the more in the case of absence of fork-in-the-road clauses in the context of investment arbitration: *SGS v Pakistan* (Objections to Jurisdiction) (2003) 129 *ILR* 438, § 176–77 (ICSID arbitration). Neither is the unilateral invocation of an arbitral procedure an abuse of rights under article 300 of the Montego Bay Convention on the Law of the Sea (1982): *Barbados/Trinidad and Tobago* arbitration (2006) 139 *ILR* 516, § 208.

[134] See r 48ff Rules of Court.

prohibition against abuse of process. The more detailed, comprehensive and precise a tribunal's rules of procedure, the less the need for recourse to the underlying general principle. However there is always a possibility that a particular rule may be used in a malevolent and abusive way. Thus, the general principle against abuse of procedure is not consumed by the special rules.

Conversely, some positions have not been regarded as abuses of procedure, eg the precipitate invocation of a new title of jurisdiction leading to a 'surprise attack' on the defendant. The ICJ held that states parties to the optional clause system have accepted that new states can at any time join the system by depositing a declaration, and that this deposit has immediate legal effect creating a basis for jurisdiction.[135] The issue has often been discussed under the aspect of good faith.[136] When looked at under the lens of good faith-reliance, the so-called untimely invocation of the basis of jurisdiction does not breach an expectation that is legitimate to the opposite, ie that this basis of jurisdiction will not be used for a certain amount of time. On the contrary: states must factor in the expectation that a newcomer may use the Court immediately after the deposit of its optional declaration.

What happens if a state that has been ordered by the ICJ to do something in a final judgment seizes the political organs of the UN in an endeavour to escape from the obligation to give effect to the judgment, or at least to slow down the judgment's implementation? Political and jurisdictional procedures have different objectives. That is one reason why we have the principle of parallel jurisdiction of political and judicial organs. It would therefore be mistaken to conclude that there is necessarily a procedural abuse if a state seizes a political organ after the Court proceedings. There may indeed be valid reasons for seeking to obtain the assistance of a political body, especially if the dispute has important extra-legal elements. However if the political organ so seized were obliged to conclude, in light of the facts, that the state's objective in seizing it was essentially to slow down or avoid the execution of the judgment, in breach of that state's obligations under article 59 of the Statute and of the *pacta sunt servanda* rule, the political organ might conclude that the procedure was a sham and refuse to take cognisance of the request made to it *in limine litis*.[137]

As can be seen, there is a myriad of variegated situations to which the abuse of procedure argument may be applied. It remains a flexible tool for the elimination of toxic arguments made in the context of legal or political procedures.

[135] *Right of Passage over Indian Territory (Preliminary Objections)* (1957) *ICJ Reports* 145–47; *Land and Maritime Boundary (Cameroon v Nigeria) (Preliminary Objections)* (1998) *ICJ Reports* 290ff, § 21ff. There is no duty under good faith to inform another state of the intention to subscribe to the optional clause system: ibid (1998) 297, § 39.

[136] See eg Separate Opinion Ajibola, *Land and Maritime Boundary (Cameroon v Nigeria) (Provisional Measures)* (1996-I) *ICJ Reports* 43–44; and Dissenting Opinion Koroma, *Land and Maritime Boundary (Cameroon v Nigeria) (Preliminary Objections)* (1998) *ICJ Reports* 385–86.

[137] See G Salvioli, 'Les règles générales de la paix' (1933-IV) 46 *RCADI* 138–39. See also the more reserved position of D Ciobanu, *Preliminary Objections Related to the Jurisdiction of the United Nations Political Organs* (The Hague, 1975) 138–39. However, the pursuit *pari passu* of two different alternative remedies is not per se contrary to good faith or estoppel: *Spp(me) Ltd v Egypt (Jurisdiction)* (1985) 10 *ILR* 523 (ICSID arbitration).

V. Good Faith in the Law of Self-Judging Reservations

The characteristic feature of so-called self-judging or automatic reservations to a title of jurisdiction is that the state making the reservation gives to itself the decisive last word on whether the conditions for the reservation's application are satisfied.[138] The Court is merely left to giving effect to the state's determination, automatically and without any autonomous control over the decision the state has taken. This makes such reservations a prolongation (both conscious and unconscious) of the former reservations as to the parties 'honour', 'sovereignty', 'independence' and 'vital interests', which used to feature in old treaties on the settlement of disputes by arbitration.[139] In the regime of the optional clause, the example traditionally cited is the US declaration of 14 August 1946. The United States accepted the Court's jurisdiction, with the exception of 'disputes with regard to matters which are essentially within the domestic jurisdiction of the United States of America *as determined by the United States of America*'.[140] In optional

[138] On such reservations, see FO Wilcox, 'The United States Accepts Compulsory Jurisdiction' (1946) 40 *AJIL* 699ff; H Waldock, 'The Plea of Domestic Jurisdiction before International Legal Tribunals' (1954) 31 *BYIL* 96ff, 131–37; G Guerrero, 'La qualification unilatérale de la compétence nationale', *Essays in Honor of J Spiropoulos* (Bonn, 1957) 207ff; HW Briggs, 'Reservations to the Acceptance of Compulsory Jurisdiction of the International Court of Justice' (1958-I) 93 *RCADI* 328–63; K Holloway, *Les reserves dans les traités internationaux* (Paris, 1958) 317ff; RY Jennings, 'Recent Cases on "Automatic" Reservations to the Optional Clause' (1958) 7 *ICLQ* 349ff; WP Rogers, 'The United States "Automatic" Reservation to Optional Clause Jurisdiction of the International Court of Justice' (1958) 7 *ICLQ* 758ff; HW Briggs, 'The United States and the International Court of Justice: A Re-Examination' (1959) 53 *AJIL* 301ff; B Maus, 'Les réserves dans les déclarations d'acceptation de la juridiction obligatoire de la Cour internationale de Justice' (PhD thesis, Geneva, 1959) 149–63; P Guggenheim, 'Der sogenannte automatische Vorbehalt der inneren Angelegenheiten gegenüber der Anerkennung der obligatorischen Gerichtsbarkeit des Internationalen Gerichtshofes in seiner neuesten Gerichtspraxis', *Essays in Honor of A Verdross* (Vienna, 1960) 117ff; LFE Goldie, 'The Connally Reservation: A Shield for an Adversary' (1962) 9 *University of California Los Angeles Law Review* 277ff; Ch de Visscher, *Problèmes d'interprétation judiciaire en droit international public* (Paris, 1963) 209–13; G Döker, 'Das Connally Amendment und die obligatorische internationale Gerichtsbarkeit' (1963/64) 11 *AVR* 155ff; M Dubisson, *La Cour internationale de Justice* (Paris, 1964) 180ff, esp 185–89; IF Shihata, *The Power of the International Court to Determine its Own Jurisdiction, Compétence de la Compétence* (The Hague, 1965) 271ff, 284–97; K Holloway, *Modern Trends in Treaty Law* (London, 1967) 654ff, 683ff; DW Greig, *International Law* (London, 1970) 501–06; 2nd edn (London, 1976) 651–57; E Zoller, *La bonne foi en droit international public* (Paris, 1977) 131ff; J Crawford, 'The Legal Effect of Automatic Reservations to the Jurisdiction of the International Court' (1979) 50 *BYIL* 63ff; S Rosenne, *The Law and Practice of the International Court*, 2nd edn (Dordrecht, 1985) 395–99; DW Greig, 'Nicaragua and the United States: Confrontation over the Jurisdiction of the International Court' (1991) 62 *BYIL* 182–86, 206–07; R Szafarz, *The Compulsory Jurisdiction of the International Court of Justice* (Dordrecht, 1993) 52–55; SA Alexandrov, *Reservations in Unilateral Declarations Accepting the Compulsory Jurisdiction of the International Court of Justice*, (Dordrecht, 1995) 76–91. See also the Separate Opinion of Judge H Lauterpacht, in *Norwegian Loans* (1957) *ICJ Reports* 43ff and the Dissenting Opinion of Judge H Lauterpacht, in *Interhandel (Preliminary Objections)* (1959) *ICJ Reports* 97ff.

[139] As to this connection between the two phenomena, *cf* Guerrero, op cit, 210; Maus, op cit, 154; Crawford, op cit, 70; the Separate Opinion of Judge H Lauterpacht in *Norwegian Loans* (1957) *ICJ Reports* 61ff. *Cf* also JL Brierly, 'Vital Interests and the Law' (1944) 21 *BYIL* 51ff.

[140] (1950/51) *ICJ Yearbook*, italics added. For the US senatorial debates and the other *travaux préparatoires* leading up to this declaration, *cf* L Preuss, 'The ICJ, the Senate and Matters of Domestic

declarations, the automatic reservation has usually been grafted onto the 'reserved domain'—matters of an exclusively internal nature. In this way it gains a considerable scope. Conceptually, however, this type of reservation can accompany any kind of subject matter. Paragraph 5 of the United Kingdom's Declaration of 18 April 1957 thus included an automatic reservation in connection with 'national defence'.[141] In all cases, the essential element is to know who has the ultimate power to decide whether the conditions for the reservation's application are satisfied. If the ultimate power belongs to the court or tribunal, the reservation is an objective one; if the power remains the exclusive privilege of the declaring state, the reservation is a subjective or 'automatic' one. The distinction depends solely on the criterion *ratione personae* and not *ratione materiae*. Currently, there are five extant automatic reservations (all accompanying the 'reserved domain' exception), namely to the optional declarations of Liberia (1952), Malawi (1966), Mexico (1947), the Philippines (1972) and Sudan (1958).

There are several arguments considering such automatic reservations as invalid; and sometimes the conclusion is that the whole optional declaration or jurisdictional title is therefore invalid, since the reservation would not be severable from it.[142] The main argument in this regard holds that the reservation is incompatible with article 36, § 6 of the Statute and is therefore void.[143] The mentioned provision grants to the Court—and it alone—the competence to decide in the last resort over its jurisdiction. But the reservation seeks to curtail this competence by forcing the Court to defer to the plea of the defendant: if that state raises the argument that the reservation's elements are satisfied (self-judgingly, as it were), the Court would have no other choice than to draw the consequences therefrom and to decline jurisdiction. We may not pursue that important question here,[144] since it does not directly touch upon the principle of good faith. The only point to be added is that the case law of the Court on this issue is unclear. The Court always found a way to circumvent the issue of the validity of such reservations, sometimes with a significant deal of legal imagination.[145] The problem is mainly that if the reservation is declared void, it may be difficult to uphold the validity of

Jurisdiction' (1946) 40 *AJIL* 720ff; HW Briggs, 'Reservations to the Acceptance of Compulsory Jurisdiction of the ICJ' (1958-I) 93 *RCADI* 328ff; HW Briggs, 'The United States and the ICJ: A Re-Examination' (1959) 53 *AJIL* 306–07. See also M Whiteman, *Digest of International Law*, vol 12 (Washington DC, 1971) 1295ff, 1305ff.

141 (1957/58) *ICJ Yearbook* 211: 'or relating to any question which, in the opinion of the Government of the United Kingdom, affects the national security of the United Kingdom or of any of its dependent territories'.

142 See art 44, § 3 of the VCLT of 1969, applied by analogy.

143 See eg Individual Opinion of Judge H Lauterpacht, in *Norwegian Loans* (1957) *ICJ Reports* 43–44; Dissenting Opinions of Judges Guerrero, ibid, 68ff and Read, ibid, 94–95; Dissenting Opinion of Judge H Lauterpacht, *Interhandel* (1959) *ICJ Reports* 101, 103ff; Separate Opinion of Judge Spender, ibid, 56; Dissenting Opinion of Judge Klaestad, ibid, 76; Dissenting Opinion of Judge Armand-Ugon, ibid, 92–93.

144 For a fuller development, see R Kolb, *The International Court of Justice* (Oxford, Hart, 2013) 503ff; Kolb, *Bonne* 650ff.

145 Kolb, *International*, op cit, 508–09.

the whole optional declaration, since it is doubtful whether that state would have accepted the declaration without the shield of the reservations;[146] the conditions for severability of treaty clauses under article 44, § 3 of the VCLT of 1969, seem not to be fulfilled.[147] The nullity of the reservation would then trigger the nullity of the whole declaration. Hence the Court would not only not possess jurisdiction in the single case (in other words the reservation would have full effect), but in addition the jurisdictional title would be nullified also for the future—overall a quite masochistic operation.

One of the proposals for a way out of the quagmire has recourse to the principle of good faith. Under this view, the Court is allowed to review the subjective allegation made by a state under an automatic reservation in the narrow and limited light of the principle of good faith and the prohibition against the abuse of rights. Such a limited scrutiny would respect the essence of article 36, § 6 of the Statute, since the Court would have the last word; and a firm obligation (albeit reduced in scope) would thus have been undertaken in advance, instead of subjectivism unlimited. Moreover, a state could not be heard with the argument that it accepted the compulsory jurisdiction of the Court only under the condition to be allowed to openly abuse it. The idea to use the good faith and abuse of rights principles as stabilisers seems to have originated with Maurice Bourquin in the *Norwegian Loans* case (1957). Norway had argued, along these lines, as follows:

> Certainly, such a reservation must be interpreted in good faith, and a Government which hid behind it in order to deny the Court's jurisdiction in a case which was not manifestly one 'belonging essentially to the internal jurisdiction' would be committing an abuse of its rights, to which the Court would not yield [our translation].[148]

The final phrase suggests that the Court can at least consider whether the allegations made by virtue of the reservation are or are not manifestly abuses, which in the last resort is the key danger from which the Court should be safeguarding the system.

On the basis of this line of legal analysis, if and when a state involved in a case invokes the reservation in a valid way, the result will be to exclude the Court's jurisdiction without doing any real collateral harm. Of course it will still be regrettable that the Court's jurisdiction was accepted on so qualified a basis; but even a very limited acceptance is better than none at all, unless, that is, it allows states to behave in an arbitrary way. If, on the other hand, the reservation is invoked in an

[146] See Separate Opinion of Judge H Lauterpacht in *Norwegian loans* (1957) *ICJ Reports* 55–59; Dissenting Opinion of Judge H Lauterpacht in *Interhandel* (1959) *ICJ Reports* 116–17; Separate Opinion of Judge Spender, ibid, 55, 57; Dissenting Opinion of Judge Chagla, *Right of Passage (Preliminary Objections)* (1957) *ICJ Reports* 167.

[147] Art 44, § 3(b) of the 1969 Vienna Convention provides that invalid clauses can be separated from the remainder of the treaty only if 'it appears from the treaty or is otherwise established that acceptance of those clauses was not an essential basis of the consent of the other party or parties to be bound by the treaty as a whole'. On this provision, see the short explanations of ME Villiger, *Commentary on the 1969 Vienna Convention on the Law of Treaties* (Leiden, 2009) 556ff.

[148] *Preliminary Objections of Norway*, (1957) I *ICJ Pleadings* 131, § 26.

abusive manner, it will be possible to avoid the general invalidation of the entire optional declaration and the toxic effects resulting for the whole system of the optional clause. It is then only the concrete abusive *argument*, based on the reservation (and not the reservation itself, nor indeed the optional declaration) which can be set aside by the Court, leaving the declaration and the reservation intact. In this way the application of the principles of good faith and abuse of rights leads to the declaration and the reservation being separated only for the purposes of the particular case. It is difficult to see any disadvantages in this intellectual structure. There are no apparent disadvantages for the state itself, which remains in a position to rely on its reservation without having to face an argument that the reservation is null *ab initio*; and equally, none for the opposing party, which will not have to suffer the consequences of seeing the title of jurisdiction declared void. In addition, there are no apparent disadvantages for the Court itself, which is thereby enabled to avoid having to set excessive limits to its own judicial functioning. Given all these advantages, a school of thought amongst leading commentators has not shied away from the idea of applying the good faith principle in this manner and context.[149]

It is interesting to notice that a parallel effort had been made in the early twentieth century in relation to reservations in arbitration clauses excepting 'vital interests' or the 'honour of the state'. It was stressed that such determinations must be made in good faith.[150] In the context of a Treaty between Brazil and Switzerland, containing an automatic reservation with regard to 'constitutional principles', the Swiss Federal Council, in a message of 1924 to the Federal Assembly, said that:

> [The parties] will interpret a reservation of this importance not from the perspective of their own convenience, but in light of the principles of good faith, and the good faith that activates States carrying out their international obligations remains the best guarantee for the loyal application of a Treaty.[151]

In a message of the same type, dated 15 June 1931, the Federal Council said, in relation to a Treaty between Switzerland and the USA:

> Nevertheless, the fact that there is no legal possibility of disputing the legitimacy of a reservation does not in itself lead to the inference that the application of the agreement

[149] JB Elkind, *Non-Appearance before the International Court of Justice* (Dordrecht, 1984) 162–63: 'The odiousness or difficulty of the exercice ought not to prevent the Court from doing it'; JHW Verzijl, *The Jurisprudence of the World Court*, vol II (Leiden, 1966) 288; DW Greig, *International Law* (London, 1970) 504–06; DW Greig, 'Nicaragua and the United States: Confrontation over the Jurisdiction of the International Court' (1991) 62 *BYIL* 182ff, 206–07; Dissenting Opinion of Judge Basdevant, *Norwegian Loans* (1957) *ICJ Reports* 73.

[150] H Lammasch, *Die Lehre von der Schiedsgerichtsbarkeit in ihrem ganzen Umfange* (Berlin, 1914) 69 (exclusion of arbitrary and abusive behaviour, etc); L Renault, in *Actes et Documents de la Seconde Conférence de La Haye, 15 juin–18 octobre 1907*, vol II (The Hague, 1907) 67. *Cf* also H Lauterpacht, *The Function of Law in the International Community* (London, 1933) 191–92; art 30 of the Draft on arbitral procedure, obligation to execute in good faith the undertaking to arbitrate: (1952-II) *YbILC* 58, 60; (1953-II) *YbILC* 201, 208; (1958-II) *YbILC* 85.

[151] Message of 28 October 1924, P Guggenheim (ed), *Répertoire suisse de droit international public*, vol III (Berne, 1975) 1825.

> will depend on the good pleasure of the contracting States. International treaties are governed by the principle of good faith, and there is no reason to suppose that the contracting parties will fail in loyalty to this principle in interpreting their reservations to the arbitration treaty.[152]

Although these messages did have to conclude that there could be no control over the exercise of good faith,[153] that was because, if a party refused to submit to arbitration, there was no tribunal in existence that could decide whether the refusal constituted an abuse. More recently, in the *Framatome* case (1982), an arbitral tribunal constituted under the auspices of the International Chamber of Commerce held that:

> The Iranian Government, in entering into the inter-State agreements which were the context for the disputed Contract, in creating the AEOI [Atomic Energy Organisation of Iran] and in having it enter into the disputed Contract, containing the compromissory clause … thereby accepted, or caused to be accepted, an international obligation as regards arbitration, one which it certainly considered valid and binding (when even the subject of the contract, the installation of nuclear factories, was a matter of national sovereignty). It is impossible to suppose that the Iranian Government, or the AEOI, could have subscribed such an obligation to arbitrate without truly intending to be bound. Such an interpretation would, indeed, be incompatible with the principle of good faith.

Citing an award of 1971, the tribunal added:

> International public policy [*(ordre public)*] would be strongly opposed to the idea that a State organ, dealing with persons foreign to that State, could openly and deliberately agree to an arbitration clause in which the co-contracting party confides, and then, whether in the arbitration proceedings or in the execution proceedings, plead the nullity of its own given word.[154]

This reasoning is capable of application mutatis mutandis to automatic reservations in respect of the Court's jurisdiction.

On several occasions since 1957, arguments have been advanced in favour of applying the principles of good faith and non-abuse of rights to automatic reservations. In particular, one can cite the pleadings by P Guggenheim on behalf of Switzerland in the *Interhandel* case (1959).[155] The United States had initially pleaded the same argument in the case on the *Aerial incident of 27 July 1955* (1959), when Bulgaria relied on its automatic reservation. According to the United States, the Connally reservation 'does not permit the Government of the United States, or any other government seeking to rely on this reservation reciprocally, arbitrarily to characterize the subject matter of a suit as essentially within the domestic jurisdiction'; it 'does not permit the United States or any other State to make an arbitrary

[152] ibid, 1829.
[153] '… there is no legal possibility of disputing the legitimacy of a reservation' (ibid, our translation.).
[154] *Framatome* (1984) 111 *JDI* 78–79 (our translation).
[155] *Interhandel* (1959) *ICJ Pleadings* 579–80.

determination, in bad faith'.[156] However subsequently, in a sudden change of tactics, the US agent asked for the case to be withdrawn. He explained, in a letter of 13 May 1960, that a more detailed study of the *travaux préparatoires* leading to the United States' reservation had led to the conclusion that the premises on which the argument about the control of abuses was based were not correct: that there could be no controls of that kind; and that the automatic reservation was a purely subjective and unilateral barrier to the Court's jurisdiction.[157] In D Greig's view,[158] the Court should not give any considerable weight to such assertions, dictated as they are by the needs of the moment. Besides which, the interpretation of an international reservation could not depend solely on the *travaux préparatoires* of internal bodies within the United States.

A school of thought among leading commentators, and among the judges of the Court also, remains resistant to the idea of applying the principles of good faith and non-abuse of rights to automatic reservations.[159] Some of them, however, have displayed a relatively nuanced attitude. For example, Sir Hersch Lauterpacht, objecting to the idea of the Court having ultimate control on the basis of these principles, accepted nevertheless that, as a matter of law, the principles do apply.[160] Similarly, the Canadian Judge Read, although 'little inclined' to introduce the concepts of good faith and abuse of rights into this field of law of the Court, because he considered that they were purely subjective and somewhat infamous, immediately added, from the objective perspective: 'the Respondent State, in invoking the reservation, must establish that there is a genuine understanding ie that the circumstances are such that it would be *reasonably* possible to reach the understanding that the dispute was essentially national'.[161] The Canadian judge accepted that there could be judicial control provided it was seen from an objective angle. His rejection of good faith and abuse of rights reflected a certain misunderstanding of the sense of these concepts, derived as they are from the Roman law tradition.

Three main objections have been raised to the Court's reviewing and controlling the question as a function of the good faith principle.

[156] *Aerial incident of 27 July 1955* (1959) *ICJ Pleadings* 305 and 308; *cf* also ibid, 324. On this aspect, see DW Greig, 'Nicaragua and the United States: Confrontation over the Jurisdiction of the International Court' (1991) 62 *BYIL* 184–86.

[157] (1959) *ICJ Pleadings* 676–77.

[158] DW Greig, 'Nicaragua and the United States: Confrontation over the Jurisdiction of the International Court' (1991) 62 *BYIL* 185–86.

[159] Separate Opinion of Judge H Lauterpacht, *Norwegian Loans* (1957) *ICJ Reports* 52ff; Dissenting Opinion of Judge Read, ibid, 94; Separate Opinion of Judge Lauterpacht, *Interhandel* (1959) *ICJ Reports* 111ff; Separate Opinion of Judge Spender, ibid, 58–59.

[160] Dissenting Opinion of Judge Lauterpacht, *Interhandel* (1959) *ICJ Reports* 113. This eminent jurist had also defended the contrary view, accepting the Court's control of the good faith aspect, when he was the ILC's rapporteur on the law of treaties: (1953-II) *YbILC* 90; he accepted it in the *Norwegian Loans* case, (1957) *ICJ Reports* 52. Without committing himself on the Court's powers, E Hambro, 'The Jurisdiction of the ICJ' (1950-I) 76 *RCADI* 189, expressed the hope that states would not invoke the reservation except by way of reasonable interpretations made in good faith.

[161] Dissenting Opinion of Judge Read, *Norwegian Loans* (1957) *ICJ Reports* 94 (emphasis added) and ibid, 94–95.

A. No Power of Ultimate Review by the ICJ

First, it is said that the ultimate power of control has been deliberately refused to the Court. The reserving state has declared itself to have sole and exclusive jurisdiction to decide the scope of the reserved domain or some other excepted category. The Court's power to examine and control such allegations is excluded, even from the perspective of controlling the abuse of rights and good faith.[162] It is, however, difficult for a reserving state to be heard arguing before the Court that its participation in the system of the optional clause was based on the right to abuse its position at will. The power conferred on the Court to sanction abuses cannot be hypothetically supposed to radically alter the nature of the obligation undertaken, since that would mean simply accepting a state's claim to have the right to commit any abuse, which is inadmissible both as a matter of general law, and more particularly under the law of treaties.

B. Unlimited Concept of Reserved Domain

Next it has been argued that the concept of the 'reserved domain' of internal jurisdiction is already devoid of any objective legal limit, to the point of becoming a subjective catch-all. For this reason it is said to be impossible to impose controls over it from the abuse of rights perspective. There would be no objective criterion on the basis of which to categorise a decision as an abuse.[163] This could be a valid objection only in relation to a cloudy and politicised conception of the reserved domain, not in relation to the legal concept. There simply is no legal notion of an unlimited or totally subjective reserved domain, and if there were, it could not be truly legal. The conception of the reserved domain in the legal sense that today has the widest currency, defines the reserved domain in negative terms, as the field from which international obligations are absent.[164] In addition it may be possible to base an argument on the practice of the particular reserving state (or state invoking the reservation via the reciprocity rule) in relation to the material to be examined by the Court. This practice may show that the state in question traditionally considers a particular concrete question as an essentially internal matter. If that is the case, there is no abuse. If it is not the case, and if indeed it seems that the state is invoking the argument in a manner inconsistent with its own

[162] Separate Opinion of Judge H Lauterpacht, *Norwegian Loans* (1957) *ICJ Reports* 52–53; Dissenting Opinion of Judge H Lauterpacht, *Interhandel* (1959) *ICJ Reports* 112, 115; Separate Opinion of Judge Spender, ibid, 59.

[163] Separate Opinion of Judge H Lauterpacht, *Norwegian Loans* (1957) *ICJ Reports* 54–55; Dissenting Opinion of the same judge in *Interhandel* (1959) *ICJ Reports* 54–55. *Contra*: DW Greig, 'Nicaragua and the United States: Confrontation over the Jurisdiction of the International Court' (1991) 62 *BYIL* 206–07; JHW Verzijl, *The Jurisprudence of the World Court*, vol II (Leiden, 1966) 288.

[164] *Cf* for example B Cheng, 'La jurimétrie: Sens et mesure de la souveraineté juridique et de la compétence nationale' (1991) 118 *JDI* 579ff, 590ff, 596.

consistent practice, then unless there is some exceptional justification, it will be possible to conclude that the invocation of the reservation is indeed an abuse. Who, for example, can doubt that military operations in the territory of another state are not a question for the reserved domain? Who can doubt that, in such a case, the invocation of an automatic reservation as to the reserved domain would constitute an abuse?[165]

C. Injurious Nature of the Standard to be Applied

Third, it has been claimed that the application of the principles of good faith and non-abuse of rights would introduce a practice whereby the Court would have to form an appreciation, covering subjective considerations of an odious and injurious nature, as to the motives and intentions of the state invoking the reservation. In Holloway's view '[it would be] placing the judicial functions of the Court on dangerous, delicate, movable and unstable grounds … of highly subjective character'.[166] This line of argument is based on a conceptual equivocation, under which good faith is necessarily a subjective psychological notion. But what would really be applied would be the objective limb—as a principle of law—of good faith and the prohibition of abuse of rights. The judges would refer to the habitual practice of the state in question, or of other states, in a given field. The actual terminology used to describe this judicial course hardly matters—prohibition of abuse of rights, requirement of good faith, examination of reasonableness, etc.

What, then, should be our overall conclusion? First of all, there is no decisive objection to the judicial examination of arguments based on the automatic reservation carried out from the perspective of good faith and abuse of rights. We have seen the advantages of such a proceeding. If the reservation is not invoked at all, the Court is not deprived of its jurisdiction. If the reservation is invoked, the Court can examine the state's decision as to whether the exception applies. The Court can then either declare that there is a legitimate reason to say that it has no jurisdiction, or, in an exceptional case, where the state's decision constitutes an abuse, can reject the argument and proceed to hear the merits. In this way the Court's functioning would be virtually unaffected by the harmful features of this reservation. This dual line of argument also serves the general interests of the system of the optional clause. It avoids the situation in which the whole head of jurisdiction simply becomes a nullity.

But is the principle of good faith in fact applicable in this way? Is the view of things outlined above compatible with the Statute? If, objectively speaking,

[165] Such an argument on the part of the USA in the *Nicaragua* case would have amounted to an abuse of rights, if it had been put forward. The USA seemed to understand this: *cf* R Szafarz, *The Compulsory Jurisdiction of the International Court of Justice* (Dordrecht, 1993) 53.

[166] K Holloway, *Modern Trends in Treaty Law* (London, 1967) 688, footnote 21. Dissenting Opinion of Judge H Lauterpacht, *Interhandel* (1959) *ICJ Reports* 111–12. *Contra*: JB Elkind, *Non-Appearance before the International Court of Justice* (Dordrecht, 1984) 163.

the automatic reservation is incompatible with the imperative requirements of article 36, §§ 2 and 6 of the Statute, then, in principle, it will necessarily entail the nullity of the reservation, and so, given non-severability, of the entire declaration. This would be the price payable for protecting the integrity of the Statute, which is a 'public policy' issue. The Court cannot dispense with respect for the provisions of the Statute.[167] Seen from this perspective, the choice is an extremely difficult one. Either one accepts the nullity of the reservation, in which case the head of jurisdiction simply disappears, and in that case the parties are deprived of the benefits of a solution which in fact serves their interests and would enable the Court's activities to develop with the fewest obstacles being left in the way; or alternatively one accepts the dual approach via good faith (or some *forum prorogatum* which supersedes the optional clause engrafted with an automatic reservation in a concrete case), in which case the Court's head of jurisdiction is preserved and the system of the optional clause does not suffer a major reverse. However a certain amount of damage is nevertheless then done to the Court's 'public policy', ie to the general public interest of the Court's proper functioning and the integrity of the Statute. Perhaps, then, it is right to make the choice in favour of applying the good faith theory, given the advantages of doing so. After all, it has not been proved beyond doubt that the solution based on good faith and non-abuse of right is actually incompatible with the Statute, ie that the solution outlined above, on the basis of these principles, in some way truly does contradict the requirements of articles 36, §§ 2 and 6.

VI. Good Faith and the Withdrawal from Optional Declarations on Jurisdiction

Can a state withdraw from an optional declaration of jurisdiction at any moment? Are there some obligations of good faith in this regard? Must the object and purpose of judicial proceedings be protected against excessive unilateralism in the denunciation of optional declarations through some time limits?[168] If there were no limitations, any state could simply withdraw its undertaking at any time. It could comply with it for the time it finds an interest in compliance, and withdraw with immediate effect as soon as it ceased to see such an interest. Alternatively, it could try to unilaterally modify the optional declaration, for example by adding new reservations addressed to the cases which that states risks to be confronted with in the next future. In short terms, a state could play fast and loose with the optional clause system. The principle of good faith is there to impede such

[167] KR Simmonds, 'The Interhandel Case' (1961) 10 *ILCQ* 531.

[168] The principle of good faith is often mentioned as a check on unilateralism. Similarly, the ICJ considered that the procedural provisions of the VCLT of 1969 (articles 65, 67) are based on the obligation to act in cooperation and not unilaterally: *Gabcíkovo-Nagymaros* case (1997) *ICJ Reports* 66, § 109.

unilateralist and system-damaging attitudes. Good faith has the role of protecting the legitimate expectations of the parties in a functioning adjudication system and in the preservation of the proper object and purpose of the whole system. The main issue turns on the notice period for the withdrawal from an optional declaration. There are two situations to be considered: (i) clauses containing no specification of the required period of notice; and (ii) clauses stating that a declaration can be withdrawn at any time with immediate effect.

A. Clauses with No Notice Period

If a declaration is completely silent as to the circumstances in which it may be withdrawn, in particular as to when a notice to that purpose will take effect, the law provides for a 'reasonable time'. The ICJ gave a very clear answer in the *Military and Paramilitary Activities in and Against Nicaragua* case (1984):

> But the right of termination of declarations with indefinite duration is far from established. It appears from the requirements of good faith that they should be treated, by analogy, according to the law of treaties, which requires a reasonable time for withdrawal from or termination of treaties that contain no provision regarding the duration of their validity. … from 6 to 9 April would not amount to 'a reasonable time'.[169]

This careful, and in a sense contingent, reasoning by the Court in the first part of the decision is explained by the place this aspect occupied in the Court's overall reasoning. The point was not an autonomous one; it was part of the general argument about reciprocity. The US had based its reciprocity argument on the hypothesis that Nicaragua had the right to withdraw its declaration with immediate effect. The Court, however, had rejected that claim, on the basis of other considerations, and in the context of its decision merely added, on what was strictly speaking only an obiter basis, that the first of the US's hypotheses, which supposed that Nicaragua could withdraw its declaration with immediate effect, was not itself based on a solid foundation. The Court had no need, for the purposes of deciding the case, to dwell any further on this aspect of the problem. That being so, the Court expressed a clear preference for what one may interpret without exaggeration as an expression of the law in force.

[169] *Military and Paramilitary Activities in and Against Nicaragua* (1984) *ICJ Reports* 420, § 63. See C Lang, *L'affaire Nicaragua/Etats-Unis devant la Cour internationale de Justice* (Paris, 1990) 88ff; DW Greig, 'Nicaragua and the United States: Confrontation Over the Jurisdiction of the International Court', (1991) 62 *BYIL* 166ff, 176ff; S Oda, 'Reservations in the Declarations of Acceptance of the Optional Clause and the Period of Validity of Those Declarations: The Effect of the Schultz Letter' (1988) 59 *BYIL* 1ff; H Thirlway, 'The Law and Procedure of the International Court of Justice (1960–1989), Treaty Interpretation and Other Treaty Points' (1992) 63 *BYIL* 68–71; R Szafarz, *The Compulsory Jurisdiction of the International Court of Justice* (Dordrecht, 1993) 70–78; SA Alexandrov, *Reservations in Unilateral Declarations Accepting the Compulsory Jurisdiction of the International Court of Justice* (Dordrecht, 1995) 56–66. See also, in the older literature, IF Shihata, *The Power of the International Court to Determine its Own Jurisdiction (Compétence de la compétence)* (The Hague, 1965) 164–68.

What, then, is a 'reasonable period' of notice? The first thing to be said, albeit in a sense obvious, is that the concept is the opposite of an unreasonably short period, meaning any period which opens the way to abuses of rights or to manipulation of the system. In the *Nicaragua* case (1984), the Court confined itself to the dry statement that 'it need only be observed that from 6 to 9 April would not amount to "a reasonable time"'.[170] Unless and until the notice period is fixed by the Statute or the Rules, the Court has to assess what is reasonable on a case-by-case basis. In this respect it will be influenced by whatever appears to it to be unreasonable given the intentions of the withdrawing state, the abusive effects of that state's attitude, and the distortive effects on the system of the optional clause. If one took a high normative view of the question, one would have to make reference to the time limits applicable under treaty law, ie one year[171] (or at least six months). Otherwise, the way the standard of 'reasonable time' is to be applied might either vary according to the circumstances (abuse in a particular case) or alternatively might be more standardised (six months or a year). Perhaps even three months might be accepted as the minimum period.[172] That should be enough to prevent undesirable *ad hoc* manipulations, which are the essential reason for insisting on any notice period at all. A six-month period seems, however, to be more in conformity with the good administration of the system of optional declarations. It also mirrors current practice in the drafting of clauses that specifically state the notice period for withdrawal. It is also closer to the residual rule of the law of treaties, as enshrined in article 56, § 2 of the VCLT, 1969.

B. Clauses Stating that the Declaration can be Withdrawn with Immediate Effect

A series of optional declarations reserve to the declaring state the right to withdraw or modify its declaration in any sense whatsoever, doing so with effect 'from the date of notification' or 'upon receipt by the Secretary-General'. Many declarations contain such a clause, including those of: Botswana (1970), Canada (1994), Cyprus (1988), Germany (2008), Kenya (1965), Madagascar (1992), Malawi (1966), Malta (1966 and 1983), Mauritius (1968), Nigeria (1998), Peru (2003), Portugal (2005), Senegal (1985), Slovakia (2004), Somalia (1963), Swaziland (1969), Togo (1979) and the United Kingdom (1969).[173] A particularly disquieting aspect is that some of these declarations, for example those of Canada, Cyprus, Madagascar, Nigeria, Peru, Slovakia and Senegal, were delivered *after* the Court's decision in the *Nicaragua* case (1984) had specifically stated that a reasonable notice period is required.

[170] *Nicaragua* (1984) *ICJ Reports* 420, § 63.

[171] See art 56, § 2, of the VCLT, 1969.

[172] In this sense, see JJ Quintana, 'The Nicaragua Case and the Denunciation of Declarations of Acceptance of the Compulsory Jurisdiction of the International Court of Justice' (1998) 11 *Leiden Journal of International Law* 118.

[173] These declarations can be reviewed in the Yearbook of the ICJ.

In the *Nicaragua* case, some eminent judges argued that the practice of the parties with regard to the Statute had by this point come to enshrine, beyond any shadow of doubt, a right to the 'immediate' withdrawal of optional declarations that were of indeterminate duration.[174] However matters are not so clear. From a close reading of the opinions of Judges Oda, Jennings and Schwebel, it would seem that their analysis was primarily concerned with the right to withdraw one's declaration at any time (*dies a quo*), and not necessarily the moment from which the withdrawal will take effect (*dies ad quem*). The fact that this was their primary concern is borne out by their frequent mention of 'perpetual obligations', which declarations in the sense of article 36, § 2, of the Statute shall not be.[175] The possibility of withdrawing at any time (and in that sense immediately) does not support the quite different proposition that such a withdrawal will necessarily have an immediate legal effect on the Court's jurisdiction.[176] No conclusive practice is put forward as the basis for the latter proposition.

The doctrine of the 'immediate effect' is no more than a unilateral assertion which has never been tested in the crucible of contentious proceedings. It is perfectly true that the existence of such declarations bears testimony to a view that cannot be ignored. But the mere fact that a reservation is included in a declaration, even if this is done frequently, cannot *eo ipso* give it legal validity.[177] Its validity depends solely on whether it is compatible with the Statute. The problem is similar to that of the automatic reservation.[178] The not infrequent use of that reservation has never been a reason to believe that the question of its validity was, by virtue of that simple fact, resolved. On the contrary, the majority of leading commentators had in fact concluded that it is a nullity.

Considering the problem more closely, it is difficult to avoid the conclusion that the 'reasonable delay' criterion, as applied by the Court in the cases of declarations that make no mention of a notice period, ought to apply in this situation also. The search for a solution involves a consideration of the object and purpose of

[174] Separate Opinion of Judge Oda (1984) *ICJ Reports* 489ff; Separate Opinion of Judge Jennings, ibid, 550ff; Dissenting Opinion of Judge Schwebel, ibid, 620ff.

[175] Separate Opinion of Judge Jennings, ibid, 553; Dissenting Opinion of Judge Schwebel, ibid, 622–23.

[176] This confusion has its counterpart among leading commentators: M Dubisson, *La Cour internationale de Justice* (Paris, 1964) 173–74; HM Waldock, 'Decline of the Optional Clause' (1955/56) 32 *BYIL* 265ff.

[177] The stance adopted by C Tomuschat, 'Article 36', in A Zimmermann, C Tomuschat, K Oellers-Frahm and CJ Tams (eds), *The Statute of the International Court of Justice, A Commentary*, 2nd edn (Oxford, 2012) 678–80, to the effect that the Court must bow to this practice as the price to be paid for getting states to submit to its jurisdiction, seems a curious one. The eminent author himself accepts (ibid, 679) that the right to withdraw with immediate effect would deprive of all 'real meaning' a declaration silent as to the notice period for withdrawal; why would the position be otherwise, here? On the other hand, if it is true that a declaration that can be withdrawn immediately is, in essence, deprived of any real effect, the only possible conclusion is that it is incompatible with the Statute and must be prohibited. Indeed, it would be better to have fewer optional declarations if all those that were deposited did at least involve States in assuming a minimum level of real obligation, rather than a hypocritical pretence of it.

[178] HM Waldock, 'Decline of the Optional Clause' (1955/56) 32 *BYIL* 273.

the system of the optional clause, and of its capacity to function efficaciously and in conditions of legal equality between the parties. In other words, one has to go back to the general principles of procedure and take account of the effects that any particular interpretation would have on the Court's ability to guarantee efficacious and equal treatment of cases.[179] If one were to accept the concept of a right to withdraw with immediate effect, the object and purpose of the system of the optional clause would be entirely subverted. Such reservations are, in effect, equivalent to an automatic reservation which comes into play prior to the moment the Court is seized. If the immediate effect concept were accepted, the declaring state would retain sole control over which cases could be brought against it before the Court. It would suffice if, even on the eve of the very day proceedings began, it were to give notice of withdrawal or modification. Since states know generally quite well which other state is likely to bring a claim against it (eg through prior negotiations), it would remain open to it to withdraw at the most opportune time. Acceptance of withdrawal with immediate effect thus amounts to a transformation of the entire optional clause system into a general framework within which there may be informal agreements to give the Court jurisdiction of an *ad hoc* nature, on a *forum prorogatum* basis. The compulsory jurisdiction would have been turned into an optional one. If the state did not withdraw or modify its declaration, it would be agreeing to submit to the Court's jurisdiction; and vice versa. A specific attitude of that kind would be necessary every time a case was brought, as a condition of the Court's jurisdiction over it. In the same way as Judge H Lauterpacht emphasised in relation to automatic reservations,[180] no autonomous obligation to submit to the Court's jurisdiction would in fact exist. There would be a mere illusion of compulsory jurisdiction,[181] its illusory nature manifestly contravening the object and purpose of the system. No state is obliged to submit to the Court's compulsory jurisdiction, but states that decide to do so must respect a certain number of limits inherent in the proper functioning of the Court, especially those necessary for the due administration of justice. This aspect was highlighted by a Swedish objection to the alleged right to restrict the jurisdiction by means of a modification taking immediate effect:

> The Swedish Government is compelled to state that in its opinion the cited condition in reality signifies that Portugal has not bound itself to accept the jurisdiction of the Court with regard to any dispute or any category of disputes. The condition nullifies the obligation intended by the wording of Article 36, paragraph 2, of the Statute where it is said that the recognition of the jurisdiction Court shall be 'compulsory *ipso facto.* For the stated reason, the Swedish Government must consider the cited condition as

[179] The Court followed a similar line of reasoning in the *LaGrand* case (2001), with regard to the binding force of provisional measures of protection: (2001) *ICJ Reports* 501ff, § 98ff.

[180] *Norwegian Loans* (1957) *ICJ Reports* 48; *Interhandel* (1959) *ICJ Reports* 106–07.

[181] HM Waldock, 'The Plea of Domestic Jurisdiction before International Legal Tribunals' (1954) 31 *BYIL* 135, on the subject of automatic reservations.

> incompatible with a recognition of the 'Optional Clause' of the Statute of the International Court of Justice'.[182]

A withdrawal of the declaration after the Court has been seized would clearly have no effect on its jurisdiction. However, a withdrawal effected some days or hours before the application is lodged would deprive the Court of jurisdiction.

The theory of immediate effect is therefore open to every kind of abuse and manipulation. The withdrawal of one's declaration just before the lodging of an application against one is an example, as the *Nicaragua* case (1984) shows. All kinds of other abuses can be imagined. For example, it would be permissible for a state to instantly modify its declaration just before a case was begun, with a view to avoiding some trap of reciprocity if, in the circumstances, it would work in its opponent's favour. When the case was finally adjudicated upon (or even just when the preliminary objections phase came to an end), the state in question might then make a further modification, bringing back the original form of declaration. The same is true for the insertion of new reservations in order to bar the jurisdiction of the Court or the admissibility of some claims. In fact, all kinds of *ad hoc* manipulations would become possible, and every such manipulation would constitute a challenge to the judicial integrity of which the Court is the guardian.[183] The malign effects would be just as serious at the practical level. It is to be feared that in such circumstances states would keep their claims secret,[184] avoiding negotiation altogether and trying to bring their cases on suddenly, precipitately, and prematurely, before the title of jurisdiction could be restricted or manipulated away.[185] Obviously this would be harmful to the development of the practice of peaceful dispute settlement, in which steps that are political in nature (direct contacts, negotiation, mediation etc) are vital elements. It was no accident that, in the *Free Zones* case (Order, 1929), the Permanent Court said that judicial settlement was 'simply an alternative [the French word is stronger: *succédané*] to the direct and friendly settlement of [such] disputes between the Parties'.[186]

Judges Oda and Schwebel thought it right to support the theory of withdrawal with immediate effect, in the best interests of the functioning of the system. In this regard they took a different attitude to the one put forward above. Their arguments merit closer examination. A more flexible position on the withdrawal of optional declarations than the 'reasonable period of time' concept was, in their view, advisable in order to encourage the 'maintaining and widening the extent of adherences to the compulsory jurisdiction of the Court'.[187] In Judge Oda's view

[182] *Right of Passage over India Territory* (1957–1960), ICJ, *Pleadings Oral Arguments and Documents*, vol. I, p. 217.

[183] See the very decided statement of the Court in *Northern Cameroons* (1963) *ICJ Reports* 29.

[184] Of course international disputes often crystallise only slowly, and states are almost always aware of their opponents' claims from the moment they choose to seize the Court. A contrary example, however, is the 'surprise attack' by Portugal on India in the 1950s.

[185] HM Waldock, 'Decline of the Optional Clause' (1955/56) 32 *BYIL* 266.

[186] *Free Zones (Order)* (1929) PCIJ, ser A no 22, p 13.

[187] Dissenting Opinion of Judge Schwebel, *Nicaragua* (1984) *ICJ Reports* 628.

the Court's own interpretation even risked accelerating the decline of the optional clause system:

> I am sure that the interpretation of the Optional Clause given by the present Judgment will inevitably induce declarant States to terminate their declarations or at least drop from them any advance notice clause, so as to avoid having to answer any case unilaterally brought by other States, which themselves can take advantage of withdrawing at any time from their obligations under the Court's jurisdiction. This would vastly diminish the importance of the Optional Clause.[188]

In our view these opinions were not well founded. To want to save the system of compulsory jurisdiction by lightening it of every element of real obligation is to indulge in what, in logical terms, can only be called a self-defeating exercise. C Lang delivered a fairly lapidary judgment on this line of reasoning:

> In the name of safeguarding the optional clause, the reality is that one risks killing it off. What is the point of safeguarding the clause if States can withdraw their declarations just before an application is lodged against them? It is true that Faust, by selling his soul to the devil, did recover some semblance of his youth, but in doing so he lost himself irretrievably.[189]

Today, in 2017, we can see that the pessimistic prognostications as to the effects of the *Nicaragua* decision were not, in the event, to be realised. There has not in fact been a decline in optional declarations.

Clauses allowing withdrawal with immediate effect are thus equivalent to a 'let-out' from all obligation to accept the jurisdiction, and thus violate the letter and spirit of article 36, § 2 of the Statute. If the reservation is incompatible with the Statute, then it should be considered a nullity. And if the provision as to withdrawal with immediate effect is indeed a nullity, does that make the entire declaration likewise a nullity? This question turns on whether the reservation is severable from the rest of the declaration.[190] The essential criterion is whether the declaring state would have made the declaration even without the invalid provision, or whether the invalid provision was so essential to the state's attitude that, without it, it would not have proceeded with the rest of the declaration.

It ought to be accepted that the rest of the declaration can be severed from the provision as to withdrawal with immediate effect. The consequence will then be that the declaration cannot be withdrawn without reasonable notice. The substitution of this delay for the stipulation as to immediacy does not radically alter the scope of the undertakings subscribed by the state concerned. It would be wrong to conclude that a state would not have made its declaration (ie to conclude that the condition as to immediacy was a *sine qua non*) unless it at the same time acquired the right to manipulate its participation in the system in light of

[188] Separate Opinion of Judge Oda, ibid, 513.

[189] C Lang, *L'affaire Nicaragua/Etats-Unis devant la Cour internationale de Justice* (Paris, 1990) 95, our translation.

[190] See again art 44, § 3 of the 1969 Vienna Convention on the Law of Treaties.

ad hoc considerations, or, in other words, that the state would not have made its declaration if it had known that it was assuming a real jurisdictional obligation and not just the appearance of one. It would follow that an immediate withdrawal provision is void, but is detachable from the remainder of the declaration, which survives and subsists. Absent any valid provision as to the period of notice, general international law applies. The withdrawal then takes effect after a reasonable period of time. This situation is not to be compared with that relating to automatic reservations. In the latter case, the state may not wish to engage itself unless protected by the very aggressive contours of its reservatory shield. Here, by contrast, it is difficult to accept that a notification period of merely reasonable duration would have been a sufficient reason not to adhere to the system, unless of course there were, in a particular case, circumstantial evidence to show that it would in fact have been considered sufficient reason.

To sum up, the withdrawal of optional declarations with immediate effect is inadmissible except in very particular circumstances. The essential legal reason for this rule, and indeed for the possible exceptions to it, is simply the requirements of the rule and pre-eminence of law. The principle of the rule of law is weak in general international law, but it becomes much more important in the judicial law of the Court. The Court cannot allow unlimited manipulation of the bases of its jurisdiction, inducing an improper administration of justice. The principle of good faith is the legal vector allowing a balancing of the terms of the present equation.

VII. Good Faith and Prospective Overruling

A specific problem of the protection of legitimate expectations arises in municipal law from the legitimate reliance of the subjects of law on the constant jurisprudence of the tribunals. It may occur that a tribunal wishes to change its jurisprudence. The reasons can be manifold: a change of social conditions; a transformation of legal conceptions in society; a new appraisal of the correct interpretation of the norms at stake; the change in some related legal provisions; and so on. If the change of the case law is performed at once and with no preannouncement, a subject of the law can suffer injury by seeing his or her rights unexpectedly curtailed. This is a question of detrimental reliance. The problem is manifestly one of good faith as the protection of legitimate expectations. It stands to reason that a subject of law must constantly expect that a tribunal could change its practice. But at the same time a constant case law is precisely there to create legal certainty and to arouse 'legitimate' expectations. The question is now to what extent a tribunal is itself bound by a sort of estoppel. Its effect is not to prevent the change prospected but to avoid all or some detrimental effects on the subject of law who was first and unexpectedly confronted with that change.

There are municipal legal orders which either require in some cases that the tribunal announces its intent to change its jurisprudence on a given point, or at least announces its intent to reconsider its jurisprudence on that point ('prospective overruling'). Thus, in the Swiss legal order a change of jurisprudence which restricts a remedy must be announced before it is applied for the first time.[191] In other situations, the Federal Tribunal requires at least that the subject of the law does not face procedural costs arising from the change of jurisprudence and the ensuing rejection of its claims.[192] The basis for these holdings is the constitutional principle of good faith.[193] Does such a doctrine against detrimental effects of sudden jurisprudential change apply to international tribunals?

In international law, the issue of the 'prospective overruling' has not yet taken shape. It may be speculated that at some time this municipal law good faith requirement might be extended to international law. When that will occur is impossible to foresee. But it can be said with a high degree of probability that when that will happen the doctrine will be based on the principle of good faith as protection of legitimate expectations. For the time being, the judicial institution has remained somewhat underdeveloped in international law. It has blossomed late and remains relatively marginal to the full spectrum of international legal life. Thus, *ad hoc* arbitration tribunals have no change to announce. They do not have a constant jurisprudence since they exist only to solve one particular case and thereafter disappear. Institutionalised tribunals, be they arbitral or judicial, have more often to deal with cases based on particular international law or otherwise with fact-specific situations. The cases brought to such tribunals are often few and the whole stream of similar questions posed to the court remains haphazard and shaky. It may take 50 years before a question comes back to the ICJ—the *Jurisdictional Immunities of the State* case (*Germany v Italy*) (2012)[194] was the first where the ICJ squarely took position on the jurisdictional immunities of states! It is therefore understandable that neither the ICJ nor other tribunals of the same type have as yet proposed a doctrine of prospective overruling. The issue will present itself probably rather in some tribunal hearing a considerable mass of similar

[191] See eg *ATF*, vol 133, s I, p 270; *ATF*, vol 120, s I, p 19; *ATF*, vol 116, s II, p 493.

[192] *ATF*, vol 122, s V, p 320.

[193] Art 9 of the Federal Constitution (1999). On this principle of good faith in Swiss law in the context of overruling, see: B Weber-Dürler, *Vertrauensschutz im öffentlichen Recht* (Basle, 1983) 234ff; JP Müller, *Grundrechte in der Schweiz*, 3rd edn (Bern, 1999) 485ff; E Chiariello, 'Treu und Glauben als Grundrecht nach Artikel 9 der schweizerischen Bundesverfassung' (PhD thesis, Bern, 2004); C Rohner, 'Article 9', in B Ehrenzeller, B Schindler, RJ Schweizer and KA Vallender (eds), *Die schweizerische Bundesverfassung*, 3rd edn (Zurich, 2014) 257ff; P Mahon, *Droit constitutionnel*, 3rd edn, vol II (Basle, 2015) 276ff. On the issue, generally: T Probst, *Die Änderung der Rechtsprechung: eine rechtsvergleichende, methodologische Untersuchung zum Phänomen der höchstrichterlichen Rechtsprechungsänderung in der Schweiz (civil law) und den Vereinigten Staaten (common law)* (Basel, 1993); V Klappstein, *Die Rechtsprechungsänderung mit Wirkung für die Zukunft: eine rechtsmethodische und rechtsvergleichende Untersuchung im Zivilrecht* (Berlin, 2009); J Wall, 'Prospective Overruling: It's About Time' (2009) 12 *Otago Law Review* 131ff.

[194] *Jurisdictional Immunities of the State* (*Germany v Italy*) (2012-I) *ICJ Reports* 100ff.

cases, such as the Iran/US Claims Tribunal or the human rights bodies. For the time being, even there, for example at the European Court of Human Rights, with its myriads of cases, there is no 'prospective overruling' principle applying.

The versatility of international affairs seems to motivate the judges not to announce much and to keep their hands free for the necessary adaptations in the difficult environment in which they have to move.

VIII. Good Faith and the Execution of Arbitral and Judicial Awards

Judicial decisions and arbitral awards must be executed in good faith by the parties to the proceedings.[195] This obligation of 'good faith' is sometimes explicitly stated,[196] and other times implicit in the term 'execution'.[197] The substantive legal issues are not different from the ones encountered in the interpretation and execution of treaties in good faith. Thus, we may refer to those earlier developments.[198]

In procedural terms, there is however one important difference. In general international law, it is the duty of each party to interpret and implement its international obligations in good faith. This is done in an exercise of self-interpretation and self-execution. This rule applies to most treaties, which are precisely not subjected to an external control mechanism. With international judgments, the question lies differently. There is the possibility of recourse to a request formulated to the tribunal having rendered the judgment or to some other tribunal to clarify

[195] See for example E Hambro, 'L'exécution des sentences internationales' (PhD thesis, Geneva, 1936) 6–7; EK Nantwi, *The Enforcement of International Judicial Decisions and Arbitral Awards in Public International Law* (Leiden, 1966) 75–77; O Schachter, 'Enforcement of International Judicial Decisions', in L Gross (ed), *International Law in the Twentieth Century* (New York, 1969) 931; and also E Fukatsu, *The Enforcement of Decisions of International Courts and Tribunals* (Tokyo, 1970).

[196] See for instance art 13, § 4, of the League of Nations Covenant (1919): S Vité, 'Article 13', in R Kolb (ed), *Commentaire sur le Pacte de la Société des Nations* (Brussels, 2015) 582–85; JM Yepes and P da Silva, *Commentaire théorique et pratique du Pacte de la Société des Nations et des Statuts de l'Union panaméricaine*, vol II (Paris, 1935) 115; J Ray, *Commentaire du Pacte de la Société des Nations* (Paris, 1930) 427ff; W Schücking and H Wehberg, *Die Satzung des Völkerbundes*, 2nd edn (Berlin, 1924) 532–33; O Hoijer, *Le Pacte de la Société des Nations* (Paris, 1926) 227–88. On the drafting history, see DH Miller, *The Drafting of the Covenant* (New York, 1928), vol I, pp 9, 55, 78, 80–81, 212, 326, 412 and esp 194–95, 207–09; vol II, pp 3, 54, 63, 100, 306. See also C Goubran, 'Le problème des sanctions dans l'évolution de l'arbitrage international' (PhD thesis, Paris, 1923). In the context of arbitration, the Special Agreement most often sets out that obligation. See for example art XIV, § 2, of the Arbitration Agreement between Egypt and Israel for the Taba Boundary Markers of 1986: 'Both parties undertake to implement the award in accordance with the Treaty of Peace as quickly as possible and in good faith': *RIAA*, vol XX, p 13.

[197] See eg. arts 94, § 1, of the UN Charter and 59 of the Statute of the ICJ. The obligation of good faith did not need to be specifically mentioned in this context, since it was framed as a general obligation always applicable under art 2, § 2, of the UN Charter. On art 94 UN Charter, see K Oellers-Frahm, 'Article 94', in A Zimmermann, C Tomuschat, K Oellers-Frahm and CJ Tams (eds), *The Statute of the International Court of Justice, A Commentary*, 2nd edn (Oxford, 2012) 1957ff.

[198] Above, Ch 5, sections V and VI.

the uncertainties of meaning, if a problem arises in that context. At the ICJ, this remedy is contained in article 60 of the Statute.[199] Therefore, the reach of unilateralism and self-interpretation is here to some extent blunted. A state is not entitled to insist on its own view of the judgment. The other state is entitled to unilaterally seize the tribunal—if it is an institutional one—to clarify the true meaning of the judgment. If the tribunal was *ad hoc* and has disappeared in the meantime, and if the other state renders its reconstitution impossible, the aggrieved state can try to have recourse to another tribunal, for example the ICJ, according to the existing titles of jurisdiction. Once the meaning of the judgment is clarified, the issue becomes one of implementation in good faith. On this latter plane also, there are special rules for some international judgments. Thus, judgments of the ICJ (but not arbitral awards) can be channelled to the UN Security Council so that the latter gives advice or takes measures to secure their execution.[200] In case of arbitral awards, the issue can be brought to other international fora, such as the Assembly of states parties to the relevant treaty instituting the arbitration mechanisms, to the United Nations General Assembly, or elsewhere. In short terms, in the context of judicial and arbitral decisions, the applicable good faith rule is reinforced by a stronger institutional element than in the realm of general international law.

It may be added that the record of the implementation of international judgments is rather good.[201] States are not obliged to accept judicial settlement. When they accept it, they have in most cases already envisaged that they could lose the case and have accepted this eventuality. Non-compliance obviously occurs. However, in such cases the issue is as much one of good faith as of blunt non-respect of the binding force of judgments. In other words, the *pacta sunt servanda* rule and the good faith rule are both undermined in such situations. States then most frequently reject the judgment straightforwardly, for example on grounds of incompetence of the tribunal or excess of power. This is as much a rejection of the binding force of the decision as it is engaging in manipulative interpretations on competence and excess of power.

[199] See A Zimmermann and T Thienel, 'Article 60', in A Zimmermann, C Tomuschat, K Oellers-Frahm and CJ Tams (eds), *The Statute of the International Court of Justice, A Commentary*, 2nd edn (Oxford, 2012) 1468ff.

[200] Art 94, § 2 of the UN Charter: K Oellers-Frahm, 'Article 94', in A Zimmermann, C Tomuschat, K Oellers-Frahm and CJ Tams (eds), *The Statute of the International Court of Justice, A Commentary*, 2nd edn (Oxford, 2012) 1966ff.

[201] For the ICJ, see for example C Schulte, *Compliance with Decisions of the International Court of Justice* (Oxford, 2004); A Azar, *L'exécution des décisions de la Cour internationale de Justice* (Brussels, 2003).

10

Good Faith in the International Law of Investments: Legitimate Expectations and Prohibition of Abuse of Procedure under 'Fair and Equitable Treatment'

The international law of investments has developed considerably in the last 30 years. It is dominated by a dense web of arbitral practice, not always as accessible as might be wished for. A perusal of the numerous arbitral awards in this branch of the law, and a concomitant reading of the various investment treaties and contracts, shows that the principle of good faith has pride of place in this area, as in others.[1] Investment as much as trade depends on the cultivation and protection of expectations, as well as of legal certainty. No one invests huge amounts of money without some legal and factual guarantees of continuity and reasonable return. Trust and confidence are of the essence in commerce and investment. In particular, the doctrine of 'legitimate expectations' was called forth to provide a fertile soil upon which to develop and shape ripening fruits. As in international commercial law, we therefore find here a distinctive and powerful doctrine of protection of legitimate expectations (PLE).[2] It goes further than that under general international law in scope and refinement, and which also tends to encompass

[1] See in particular: S Dajic, 'Mapping the Good Faith Principle in International Investment Arbitration: Assessment of its Substantive and Procedural Value', http://scindeks-clanci.ceon.rs/data/pdf/0550-2179/2012/0550-21791203207D.pdf; E De Brabandère, '"Good Faith", "Abuse of Process" and the Initiation of Investment Treaty Claims' (2012) 3 *Journal of International Dispute Settlement* 609ff; M Potestà, 'Legitimate Expectations in Investment Treaty Law: Understanding the Roots and the Limits of a Controversial Concept' (2013) 28 *ICSID Review* 88ff; R Dolzer, 'Fair and Equitable Treatment: Today's Contours' (2013) 12 *Santa Clara Journal of International Law* 7ff. See also the short contribution of AFM Maniruzzaman, 'The Concept of Good Faith in International Investment Disputes—The Arbitrator's Dilemma' (2012) 89 *Amicus Curiae* 16–18. I wish to thank my colleague, Prof T Gazzini, for valuable bibliographic information. For the principle of good faith and its related concepts in the interpretation of investment treaties, see T Gazzini, *Interpretation of International Investment Treaties* (Oxford, Hart, 2016) 45–46, 60–63, 206–09, 293–95.

[2] On this aspect, see Dajic, op cit, 213ff; Potestà, op cit; Dolzer, op cit, 17ff.

legal tools like estoppel or acquiescence.[3] On the other hand, there is a strongly developed prohibition of abuse of rights and abuse of procedure (or process) in this branch of the law.[4] To some extent, this is part of the search for a balanced legal regime. The doctrine of PLE benefits the foreign investor and burdens states. It limits their power to unilaterally modify the applicable regulatory framework. The doctrine of abuse of rights reverses the situation. It protects the state against frivolous claims, but also against fictitious legal constructions, with the aim of bringing certain investments artificially under the umbrella of applicable arbitration clauses. Thus, by corporate restructuring or by change of corporate nationality (forum shopping), investments which are not covered by a bilateral investment treaty (BIT) arbitration clause can be formally brought within the four corners of such protection. The doctrine of abuse of rights has the function of 'piercing the veil' of such constructions and denying the investor the protection he artificially created, aloof from the contractual terms with the host state. Taken as a whole, the two branches of the principle of good faith achieve a peculiar equilibrium which is distinctive of international investment law. Apart from these main expressions of good faith, we find in this branch of the law all the other main manifestations of good faith, such as the protection of the object and purpose of transactions (including pre-contractual positions), estoppel/acquiescence, no one profiting from their own fault, good faith in the negotiation process, etc.[5] Here however we will concentrate on the two distinctive limbs of PLE and abuse of rights.

[3] See eg *Occidental Cy v Ecuador, arbitration* (2004) 138 *ILR* 85, § 196.

[4] As to which see E De Brabandère, '"Good Faith", "Abuse of Process" and the Initiation of Investment Treaty Claims' (2012) 3 *Journal of International Dispute Settlement* 609ff.

[5] As to estoppel, see eg the pursuit of alternative remedies: *Spp(me) Ltd v Egypt (Jurisdiction)*, ICSID award, (1985) 106 *ILR* 523 or *Feldman v Mexico*, NAFTA award, (2002) 126 *ILR* 42ff; or *SGS v Pakistan (Objections to Jurisdiction)*, ICSID award (2003) 129 *ILR* 416, § 122 and 438, § 176–77. As to acquiescence, see eg *Sandline International v Papua New Guinea (arbitration)* (1998) 117 *ILR* 562–63, § 11.1–11.2. As to the maxim that no one shall profit from his own fault, see eg *Klöckner Industrie-Anlagen GmbH v Cameroon*, ICSID award (1983) 114 *ILR* 179. As to duties of information during negotiations and other contacts between the investor and the host state, see eg *Plama v Bulgaria* (2008) ICSID/ARB/03/24, § 145: 'If a material change occurred in the investor's shareholding that could have an effect on the host State's approval, the investor was, by virtue of the principle of good faith, obliged to inform the host State of such a change. Intentional withholding of this information is therefore contrary to the principle of good faith'. As to the protection of the object and purpose of a transaction against frustration, see eg *Quiborax S., Non Metallic Minerals SA and Allan Fosk Kaplún v Bolivia* (2015) ICSID/ARB/06/2, § 592: 'The principle of good faith involves the duty not to perform any act that would defeat the object and purpose of the obligation that has been undertaken by the parties, even if the act itself is not expressly prohibited by the provisions of the treaty'; *Caratube International Oil Company LLP v Kazakhstan* (2009) ICSID/ARB/08/12, Provisional Measures, § 67: 'The Tribunal confirms that the Parties have an obligation to conduct the procedure in good faith and that this obligation includes a duty to avoid any unnecessary aggravation of the dispute and harassment of the other party'. On this issue of protecting the object and purpose, see also C Schreuer (with L Malintoppi, A Reinisch and A Sinclair, *The ICSID Convention, A Commentary*, 2nd edn (Cambridge, 2009) 797: 'To the extent that legal consequences arise form provisional measures …, all Contracting States are under a general obligation to ensure in good faith that the Convention's object and purpose are not frustrated'.

The principle of good faith is said to be a fundamental principle of international investment law.[6] As such, it is directly applicable, either as a principle of international law or as a general principle of law of the municipal legal orders transposed to the international stage. Moreover, good faith is also part and parcel of the so-called 'fair and equitable' treatment clauses (FET) contained in BITs or multilateral investment treaties,[7] and having become part of customary law in the context of investments.[8] The issue is one of the rule of law, fairness and justice in the context of investment. True, there are a series of black-letter standards in the context of investment agreements and law. But such detailed standards are not sufficient. There is the additional need for some sweeping and general standard of a catch-all nature, which will guarantee a degree of 'fair treatment' in the changing circumstances in which investments occur. As evolving case law has determined, FET covers mainly the following more concrete standards:[9] (i) good faith and PLE; (ii) consistency of conduct; (iii) transparency of rules; (iv) due process; (v) prohibition of harassment; (vi) a reasonable degree of stability and predictability of the regulatory system; (vii) the prohibition of arbitrariness and discrimination. This standard is therefore protective of the investor. But at the same time, fairness requires a fair balance of the interests. This means that the position of the host state has to be taken careful account of.

It has sometimes been held that the whole FET standard is but an expression of the principle of good faith, ie an 'expression and part of the bona fide principle recognised in international law'.[10] If that is the position, good faith would apply through the FET standard which flows from it and gives rise to further good faith legal positions (such as PLE). Good faith would possibly also apply directly, outside the FET standards, as a general principle of law. This would account for a legally multi-layered application of good faith-concretisations. Whatever the position taken, the role of good faith is truly fundamental. The case law developed in this branch of international law shows graphically that the approach of the ICJ to good faith is imprecise: good faith is not limited to the interpretation and

[6] See eg *Malicorp Ltd v Egypt* (2011) ICSID/ARB/08/18, § 116: 'It is indisputable ... that the safeguarding of good faith is one of the fundamental principles of international law and the law of investments'; *Inceysa SL v El Salvador (Jurisdiction)* (2006) ICSID/ARB/03/26, § 230: 'Good faith is a supreme principle, which governs legal relations in all of their aspects and content...'; *Sempra Energy Int v* Argentine (2007) ICSID/ARB/02/16, § 299.

[7] I Tudor, *Fair and Equitable Treatment Standard in the International Law of Foreign Investment* (Oxford, 2008) 15ff.

[8] On FET clauses, see N Angelet, 'Fair and Equitable Treatment', in R Wolfrum (ed), *The Max Planck Encyclopedia of Public International Law*, vol III (Oxford, 2012) 1094ff, with a bibliography (on the customary nature of the standard, see p 1095, no 7); I Tudor, *Fair and Equitable Treatment Standard in the International Law of Foreign Investment* (Oxford, 2008); R Dolzer, 'Fair and Equitable Treatment: Today's Contours' (2013) 12 *Santa Clara Journal of International Law* 7ff; M Jacob and SW Schill, 'Fair and Equitable Treatment: Content: Practice, Method', in M Bungenberg, J Griebel and S Hobe (eds), *International Investment Law* (Baden-Baden, 2015) 700ff, and U Kriebaum, 'Arbitrary/Unreasonable or Discriminatory Measures', ibid, 790ff.

[9] See Dolzer, op cit, 15.

[10] *Tecmed SA v Mexico* (2003) ICSID/ARB(AF)/00/2, § 153.

application of other rules of international law;[11] it is also a source of rights and obligations itself, either directly or through a series of manifestations. We may now turn to the two distinctive features of good faith in this area, namely the doctrine of PLE and the doctrine of abuse of rights or procedure.

I. Protection of Legitimate Expectations

As in the context of the international law of commerce, the doctrine of PLE is a jurisprudential development.[12] Its formal basis is the principle of good faith and the FET clause, or an analogy to common principles of municipal administrative laws.[13] The jurisprudence had numerous occasions to give some precision to the question of which expectations are 'legitimate'. This is one of the aspects in which the principle of PLE has received a greater refinement in this branch of the law than in general international law. It must finally also be noted that the doctrine of PLE is objective in nature. It has to do with the expectations a reasonable investor could and should have had in the circumstances, and not with the idiosyncratic and subjective expectations this or that concrete investor did in fact nourish.[14] The principle of PLE has been applied mainly in three contexts, as follows.[15]

A. *Contractual Arrangements*[16]

State contracts manifestly raise legitimate expectations in their continuity and in their respect. Their breach is not automatically a breach of international law, unless there is a stabilisation clause contained in them. This flows from the fact that such contracts are not per se sources of international law. There is thus the need of some additional element to bring the breach of contract under the umbrella of international law. Such an element can be, among others, the breach of the FET standards, ie the breach of good faith (PLE) as a principle of international or of international investment law. Thus, there are legitimate expectations against unilateral changes

[11] See above, Ch 3.

[12] M Potestà, 'Legitimate Expectations in Investment Treaty Law: Understanding the Roots and the Limits of a Controversial Concept' (2013) 28 *ICSID Review* 3. In the case law, see generally *Saduka v Czech Republic*, PCA, Partial Award of 2006, §§ 301–02. Or the *Thunderbird Gaming Corporation v Mexico*, NAFTA award, (2006) § 147.

[13] ibid (Potestà), 5, 7ff.

[14] R Dolzer, 'Fair and Equitable Treatment: Today's Contours' (2013) 12 *Santa Clara Journal of International Law* 16.

[15] M Potestà, 'Legitimate Expectations in Investment Treaty Law: Understanding the Roots and the Limits of a Controversial Concept' (2013) 28 *ICSID Review* 15ff. The following developments rely heavily on this article.

[16] ibid.

of the terms of agreement through state legislation,[17] or against the denial of certain permits under municipal law which are necessary for the implementation of the contract.[18] The case law has also emphasised the difference between mere hopes in stability and legitimate expectations deserving a legal protection.[19] When an actor engages in foreign investments, there are a series of imponderables to be mustered and uncertainties to be accepted. The rates of return are normally calculated so as to take account of these risks. Not all the risks can be eliminated or smoothened through a doctrine of PLE, lest the freezing-effect of the law becomes total and reform of municipal regulations is disallowed. This cannot be the role of the law on international investments. Thus, it is important to see that tribunals are not allowed to rewrite the black law terms of contract under some overly generous doctrine of PLE.[20]

B. Informal or Formal Representations[21]

The issue here is akin to the one of estoppel or the binding force of unilateral acts (promises). It occurs that some high-standing authorities of the state give some formal or informal assurances to the investor. These guarantees nourish legitimate expectations and make possible the investment in the first place. It would be unfair later not to honour such assurances, to the detriment of the investor. The main issue is here when the assurance is sufficiently specific to give rise to a 'legitimate' expectation. General policy statements are not enough; they may nourish simple hopes but not protected expectations.[22] Conversely, precise assurances to receive a municipal permit create legitimate expectations.[23] If state organs prospect the possibility to enter into negotiations on a certain point, this does not create a legitimate expectation, since the state merely prospected a possibility and did not concede more.[24] Reliance will also not be admitted where the investor does not disclose all relevant information before obtaining related advice and assurances by a state organ.[25] It cannot then profit from its own wrong. The issue is plainly one depending on the circumstances of the case.

[17] *Continental Casualty Cy v Argentina* (2008) ICSID/ARB/03/9, § 261.

[18] *MTD v Chile* (2004) ICSID/ARB/01/7, § 160ff.

[19] M Potestà, 'Legitimate Expectations in Investment Treaty Law: Understanding the Roots and the Limits of a Controversial Concept' (2013) 28 *ICSID Review* 17.

[20] See J Crawford, 'Treaty and Contract in Investment Arbitration' (2008) 24 *Arbitration International* 373.

[21] M Potestà, 'Legitimate Expectations in Investment Treaty Law: Understanding the Roots and the Limits of a Controversial Concept' (2013) 28 *ICSID Review* 19ff.

[22] ibid, 23.

[23] *Metalclad v Mexico* (2000) ICSID/ARB(AF)/97/1, § 89.

[24] *Frontier Petroleum v Czech Republic* (2010) PCA §§ 76, 455.

[25] *Thunderbird v Mexico*, NAFTA award, (2006) § 155.

C. General Regulatory Framework under Municipal Law[26]

If the expectations doctrine is strong in the context of contractual arrangements, it is much weaker in the context of the general regulatory framework. It stands to reason that the investor evaluates carefully the municipal legal order and builds expectations upon it when deciding on his investments. But it is also clear that he must know that such legislation cannot remain frozen. It will evolve according to the needs revealed by new circumstances, including political changes introduced through elections. There can thus be no guarantee against unilateral change in this context.[27] The investor knows that he takes that average risk. He may and will react to it by negotiating stabilisation clauses, by asking for assurances, or by adapting the rates of return for the amount of risk taken.[28] The average regulatory risk is thus already fed into the rates of return and it would be unfair to factor it in again through an overly robust doctrine of PLE, which excessively limits the sovereign choices of the municipal constituency. The same is true considering investments in so-called third world states or in unstable states: that there is a greater risk is known here, and the legitimate expectations cannot be such as if the investment had been performed in a Western state.[29] The additional risk is normally equilibrated once more by contractual clauses and return rates. The case law also emphasises the due diligence duties of the investor. He must enquire into the regulatory framework and take the necessary steps to ensure himself against excessive risks.[30] But this freedom of the state to unilaterally change the municipal legal framework cannot be absolute. Some limits have to be devised under a perspective of overall fairness. Thus, the case law considers that foreign investors protected under BITs or other international law regulation should at least be immunised against 'radical changes' (or 'unreasonable' or 'arbitrary' changes) of the municipal regulatory framework.[31] Thus, a legitimate expectation could at least be

[26] M Potestà, 'Legitimate Expectations in Investment Treaty Law: Understanding the Roots and the Limits of a Controversial Concept' (2013) 28 *ICSID Review* 26ff.

[27] *Saluka BV v Czech Republic, Partial Award* (2006) PCA §§ 305, 351.

[28] M Potestà, 'Legitimate Expectations in Investment Treaty Law: Understanding the Roots and the Limits of a Controversial Concept' (2013) 28 *ICSID Review* 30–31.

[29] ibid, 35ff. See *Duke v Ecuador* (2008) ICSID/ARB/04/19, § 340: 'The assessment of the reasonableness or legitimacy [of the investor's expectations] must take into account all circumstances, including not only the facts surrounding the investment, but also the political, socioeconomic, cultural and historical conditions prevailing in the host State'. See also *Bayindir v Pakistan* (2009) ICSID/ARB/03/29, § 195 or *Toto v Lebanon* (2012) ICSID/ARB/07/12, § 245. For a critical assessment, see R Dolzer, 'Fair and Equitable Treatment: Today's Contours' (2013) 12 *Santa Clara Journal of International Law* 27, considering that the object and purpose of investment agreements is to overcome such unfavourable conditions and that they should thus not be factored in the legitimacy of expectations. This seems too severe, considering that the investor can and will normally receive consideration for the greater risk taken.

[30] *MTD v* Chile (2004) ICSID/ARB/01/7, § 168ff, 242ff; *Metalpar v Argentina* (2008) ICSID/ARB/03/05, § 187.

[31] *El Paso v Argentina* (2011) ICSID/ARB/03/15, § 274: 'unless the alternation of the legal framework is total'; *Toto v Lebanon* (2012) ICSID/ARB/07/12, § 244: 'only in a case of a drastic or discriminatory change'. Possibly, a prior warning could be required, so that the change is not too abrupt (no 'sudden change'): see by analogy Case no 74/74 *CNTA SA v Commission*, (1975) 533 *Court Reports* §§ 42–44 (CJEU).

admitted as against changes of an excessive reach, rendering the investment nugatory or jeopardising it to an unfair degree. The issue is finally one of a proper balance under the fairness clause of FET.

II. Prohibition of Abuse of Procedure

There is a strong limb of case law on abuse of procedure so as to protect the state against arbitrary or unjustified arbitration.[32] These arguments on abuse of procedure can be framed and used flexibly, either as bars to jurisdiction or admissibility, or as arguments on the merits, as is also the case of the 'clean hands' argument in general international law.[33] Thus, a claim may be declared inadmissible if certain facts have been forged and falsified, since this is a breach of good faith (i.e. a sort of clean hands doctrine).[34] By the same token, if an investment was acquired in violation of municipal law or in bad faith, it is not a 'protected investment' and the arbitration clause may not be applied. This leads to a lack of jurisdiction of the arbitral tribunal.[35] The same occurs when no real investment was made at all; or if the investment was purchased with the sole aim of commencing arbitral procedures.[36] Further, the principle of abuse of procedure applies to the cases where the investor restructures his assets—eg by the creation of new corporations, by acquiring a new corporate nationality which allows the application of a BIT[37]—with the sole aim of getting access to arbitration. If a purportedly new claim is substantially the same as a previous one and is resubmitted under some circumventing legal constructions (eg transfer of the claim to another entity), it will be dismissed under abuse of procedure.[38] The rule on abuse of procedure plays further a residual role for a series of other situations, eg the plea that proceedings are misused solely for the purpose to put political pressure on the state so as to have it abandon some criminal proceedings.[39] Finally, estoppel can also

[32] E De Brabandère, '"Good Faith", "Abuse of Process" and the Initiation of Investment Treaty Claims', (2012) 3 *Journal of International Dispute Settlement* 609ff; S Dajic, 'Mapping the Good Faith Principle in International Investment Arbitration: Assessment of its Substantive and Procedural Value', http://scindeks-clanci.ceon.rs/data/pdf/0550-2179/2012/0550-21791203207D.pdf, p 216ff.

[33] As to the latter, see above Ch 8, section III.

[34] *Inceysa v El Salvador* (2006) ICSID/ARB/03/26, § 226ff.

[35] ibid, § 208.

[36] *Europe Cement v Turkey* (2009) ICSID/ARB(AF)/07/2, § 174 and *Cementownia v Turkey* (2009) ICSID/ARB(AF)/06/2, § 159. False statements were here also the issue.

[37] *Phoenix v Czech Republic* (2009) ICSID/ARB/06/6, § 106ff; *TSA Spectrum v Argentina* (2008) ICSID/ARB/05/5, § 134ff, with the piercing of the corporate veil; *Pac Rim Cayman LLC v El Salvador, Decision on the Respondent's Jurisdictional Objections* (2012) ICSID/ARB/09/12, § 2.99ff.

[38] *Waste Management v Mexico* (2000) ICSID/ARB(AF)/98/2, § 49–50. Here were also a series of proceedings against Grenada where this issue came to the fore: E De Brabandère, '"Good Faith", "Abuse of Process" and the Initiation of Investment Treaty Claims' (2012) 3 *Journal of International Dispute Settlement* 631.

[39] The plea was finally withdrawn during the pleadings: *Rompetrol v Romania, Decision on Respondent's Preliminary Objections on Jurisdiction and Admissibility* (2008) ICSID/ARB/06/3, § 111ff.

be a reason not to entertain a claim.[40] As can be seen, there is a richly articulated doctrine of abuse of process in the context of international investment law arbitration.

Overall, it can thus be said that in the law of international investments there is a multifaceted and highly articulated doctrine of good faith. The principle has an overarching application in the most varied contexts of this branch of the law. It is meant to complete the more concrete black-letter standards, in a very mobile and confidence-dependent general environment, where host state and investor have legitimate, albeit competing, demands of fairness to reconcile. The main vector for sorting them out is the principle of good faith and its partial powerful vassal, the FET clause.

[40] *Chevron Corporation and Texaco Petroleum Cy v Ecuador, Interim Award* (2008) PCA case no 34877, § 125ff.

11

Good Faith in the Law of Armed Conflicts: The Prohibition of Perfidy

The principle of good faith plays a significant role not only in the law of peace but also in the law of armed conflicts. In the latter context, it is the prohibition of perfidy that is the main manifestation of the principle.[1] In past centuries, the prohibition of treacherous acts was broader than it is today. Additional Protocol I of 1977 to the four Geneva Conventions of 1949 (AP I), the contemporary rule on perfidy, reflects the lower standards of the twentieth century, characterised by ideological hatred and the loss of common civilisational standards. The main provision on perfidy is today article 37 of AP I. It reads as follows:

1. It is prohibited to kill, injure or capture an adversary by resort to perfidy. Acts inviting the confidence of an adversary to lead him to believe that he is entitled to, or is obliged to accord, protection under the rules of international law applicable in armed conflict, with intent to betray that confidence, shall constitute perfidy. The following acts are examples of perfidy:
   (a) the feigning of an intent to negotiate under a flag of truce or of a surrender;
   (b) the feigning of an incapacitation by wounds or sickness;
   (c) the feigning of civilian, non-combatant status; and
   (d) the feigning of protected status by the use of signs, emblems or uniforms of the United Nations or of neutral or other States not Parties to the conflict.

[1] On the notion and the law relating to perfidy, see R Bourdoncle, *De l'influence des ruses sur l'évolution du droit de la guerre* (Paris, 1958); B Hecht, *Perfidy* (New York, 1961); F Krüger-Sprengel, 'Kriegslist und Perfidieverbot: Völkerrechtliche Regeln für das Verhalten zwischen Kombattanten' (1971) 13 *Neue Zeitschrift für Wehrrecht* 161–70; D Fleck, 'Kriegslisten und Perfidieverbot', in D Fleck (ed), *Beiträge zur Weiterentwicklung des humanitären Völkerrechts für bewaffnete Konflikte* (Hamburg, 1973) 105ff; D Fleck, 'Ruses of War and Prohibition of Perfidy' (1974) 13 *Revue de droit pénal militaire et de droit de la guerre* 269ff; P Bretton, 'Le problème des "méthodes et moyens de guerre ou de combat" dans les protocoles additionnels aux Conventions de Genève du 12 août 1949' (1978) 82 *RGDIP* 39ff, 71; W Voit, 'Humanitäre Aspekte der Regeln über Perfidie und Kriegslist' (1980) 22 *Neue Zeitschrift für Wehrrecht* 19ff; M Bothe, KJ Partsch and WA Solf, *New Rules for Victims of Armed Conflicts* (The Hague, 1982) 201ff; M Arrassen, *Conduite des hostilités, droit des conflits et désarmement* (Brussels, 1986) 79ff; J de Preux, 'Article 37' in Y Sandoz, C Swinarski and B Zimmermann (eds), *Commentary on the Additional Protocols of 8 June 1977 to the Geneva Conventions of 12 August 1949* (Geneva, 1986) 429ff; HP Furrer, *Perfidie in der Geschichte und im heutigen Kriegsvölkerrecht* (Zurich, 1988); MM Gimmerthal, *Kriegslist und Perfidieverbot im Zusatzprotokoll vom 10 Juni 1977 zu den vier Genfer Rotkreuz—Abkommen von 1949 (Zusatzprotokoll I)* (Bochum, 1990); S Adam, *Kriegslisten und Perfidieverbot in der Geschichte des Kriegsaktionenrechts vor Abschluss der Haager Landkriegsordnung von 1899* (Frankfurt a M, 1992); G Politakis, 'Stratagems and the Prohibition of Perfidy with special Reference

Under § 2 of that provision, ruses of war are not prohibited.[2] It must be added that articles 38 and 39 of AP I prohibit certain types of conduct,[3] which constitute special provisions on perfidy. The difference between article 37 on the one hand and articles 38–39 on the other hand lies in the fact that the general provision of perfidy supposes that the acts are directed to killing, injuring or capturing the adversary, while the acts listed in articles 38 and 39 are prohibited per se and in all circumstances, eg the misuse of the emblem of the Red Cross to conceal the transport of weapons.

The essential aspect of perfidy is that of a belligerent using obligations under the law of armed conflicts for specific hostile purposes, ie the attack on the bodily integrity of the adversary under article 37, or the misuse of emblems, uniforms or distinctive signs under articles 38 and 39. With perfidy, a belligerent betrays the adverse party about the law; with ruses of war, a belligerent betrays the adversary on a point of fact. A belligerent owes good faith to the enemy parties in the context of the applicable legal rules. It does not owe good faith to it in the context of mere facts. Thus, a belligerent may try to deceive the other party on the D-day, send false military messages in the hope that they will be intercepted, and so on. But this approach cannot be allowed with regard to the main legal obligations under the international law of armed conflict. If a belligerent must fear each time that it is obliged to do something under international humanitarian law that it will fall into

to the Laws of War at Sea' (1993) 45 *ÖZöRV* 253ff; JM Henckaerts and L Doswald-Beck, *Customary International Humanitarian Law*, vol. I (Cambridge, 2005) 203ff; S Oeter, 'Means and Methods of Combat', in D Fleck (ed), *The Handbook of International Humanitarian Law*, 2nd edn (Oxford, 2008) 227ff; V Rusinova, 'Perfidy', in R Wolfrum (ed), *The Max Planck Encyclopedia of Public International Law*, vol. VIII (Oxford, 2012) 245ff.

[2] 'Ruses of war are not prohibited. Such ruses are acts which are intended to mislead an adversary or to induce him to act recklessly but which infringe no rule of international law applicable in armed conflict and which are not perfidious because they do not invite the confidence of an adversary with respect to protection under that law. The following are examples of such ruses: the use of camouflage, decoys, mock operations and misinformation'.

[3] Art 38 reads as follows: '1. It is prohibited to make improper use of the distinctive emblem of the red cross, red crescent or red lion and sun or of other emblems, signs or signals provided for by the Conventions or by this Protocol. It is also prohibited to misuse deliberately in an armed conflict other internationally recognized protective emblems, signs or signals, including the flag of truce, and the protective emblem of cultural property. 2. It is prohibited to make use of the distinctive emblem of the United Nations, except as authorized by that Organization'. Finally, art 39 states: '1. It is prohibited to make use in an armed conflict of the flags or military emblems, insignia or uniforms of neutral or other States not Parties to the conflict. 2. It is prohibited to make use of the flags or military emblems, insignia or uniforms of adverse Parties while engaging in attacks or in order to shield, favour, protect or impede military operations. 3. Nothing in this Article or in Article 37, paragraph 1(d), shall affect the existing generally recognized rules of international law applicable to espionage or to the use of flags in the conduct of armed conflict at sea'. On the abuse of uniforms of peacekeepers in Bosnia-Herzegovina in the Bosnian War (1992–95), see M Sassoli, A Bouvier and A Quintin, *How Does Law Protect in War?*, 3rd edn, vol III (Geneva, 2011) 1735ff.

a trap of the enemy, eg that providing help to an apparently injured enemy soldier under Geneva Convention I of 1949 will lead to an ambush, that belligerent is likely to withhold humanitarian assistance in such situations. In other words, the whole edifice of the law of armed conflict will crumble, since each belligerent will have a good reason not to implement its duties, fearing abuse by the other side. That the law cannot allow such a course stands to reason.

The link with good faith becomes apparent. It is multiple. First, the issue is about saving the functionality, i.e. the object and purpose of the whole law of armed conflict. Within a legal order, this function is typically performed by the principle of good faith. Second, the issue is one of legitimate expectations.[4] A belligerent may legitimately expect that the rules of the law of armed conflict will be respected and not abused for hostile purposes. This is emphasised through the concept of 'confidence' contained in article 37 AP I. In the French version of the text, the expression is even more explicit: 'tromper la bonne foi de l'adversaire'. Third, the issue is manifestly one of prohibiting abuse of rights. Perfidy is nothing less than the use of certain legal provisions and related obligations for purposes for which they were never intended or granted. In other words, perfidy is a great *détournement de pouvoir* or misuse of authority. The rules are perverted to serve hostile purposes; and thereby they are rendered ineffective and spoiled. The British Military Manual of 1958 cautions:

> Good faith ... is essential in war, for without it hostilities could not be terminated with any degree of safety short of the total destruction of one of the contending parties. Should it be found impossible to rely on the good faith, thus conceived, of the adversary, there is a grave danger of war degenerating into excesses and indiscriminate violence, the prevention of which has been the aim of the modern laws of war.[5]

Fourth, there is also an aspect of subjective good faith: the adverse party is induced into an error about the application of the obligations under the law of armed conflict, and it therefore acts in good faith. But this latter issue is not legally relevant. The reason is that the acts in conformity with the law of armed conflict, made by the adverse party, are not to be cured by some legal principle because of excusable error. Indeed, they are already initially lawful.

[4] This aspect of creating a reliable expectation is often stressed: see eg M Bothe, KJ Partsch and WA Solf, *New Rules for Victims of Armed Conflicts* (The Hague, 1982) 204; M Arrassen, *Conduite des hostilités, droit des conflits et désarmement* (Brussels, 1986) 80–81: 'La bonne foi de l'adversaire, c'est la position qui doit normalement être la sienne au regard des règles connues et reconnues par lui, et l'intention, c'est de créer la surprise là où doit régner la sécurité, la confiance'; MM Gimmerthal, *Kriegslist und Perfidieverbot im Zusatzprotokoll vom 10 Juni 1977 zu den vier Genfer Rotkreuz—Abkommen von 1949 (Zusatzprotokoll I)* (Bochum, 1990) 75–77.

[5] *British Manual of Military Law, The Law of War on Land* (London, 1958) 101, nos 308–09.

In regard of what has been said, the prohibition of perfidy is rightly called a fundamental principle of the law of armed conflicts.[6] This indirectly means that the principle of good faith is fundamental in this area as it is in other ones. We may add that beyond the narrow regulation of article 37 AP I, which is limited *ad hominem* (ie only acts directed at killing, injuring and capturing qualify as article 37 perfidy), international customary law and the Martens Clause must be considered to determine whether acts betraying the confidence of the adverse party on the application of legal positions should be considered contrary to the law of armed conflicts.[7] These acts may then not be considered to be perfidy in the strict sense (and this is also relevant for criminal law purposes) but may be simply unlawful deceits. The rationale for prohibiting such acts would be the same as for the narrowly defined perfidy. Good faith has to play an essential role in this context too.

[6] '[I]t has remained a cardinal principle in modern times, because perfidious abuse of protections under the law of armed conflict tends strongly to degrade the protection and restraints developed in the mutual interest of all Parties, their combatants and civilians. Combatants, in practice, find it difficult to respect protected persons and objects if experience causes them to believe or suspect that their adversaries are abusing their claim to protection under the rules of international law applicable in armed conflict in order to achieve a military advantage': M Bothe, KJ Partsch and WA Solf, *New Rules for Victims of Armed Conflicts* (The Hague, 1982) 202.

[7] On the gaps left by art 37 AP I, see eg M Bothe, KJ Partsch and WA Solf, *New Rules for Victims of Armed Conflicts* (The Hague, 1982) 203–04; MM Gimmerthal, *Kriegslist und Perfidieverbot im Zusatzprotokoll vom 10 Juni 1977 zu den vier Genfer Rotkreuz—Abkommen von 1949 (Zusatzprotokoll I)* (Bochum, 1990) 77.

12

Conclusion

The time has come to conclude this journey with the flight back home. The first thing this journey has shown is that there are some powerful general principles of law spanning the whole edifice and fabric of law, indeed overarching the entire legal order. These principles instil a certain normative content into the various branches of the legal order and thus ensure a certain degree of axiological and operational unity within it. They also allow the adaptation of the international legal order in a phase where a customary norm is not yet shaped. The legal operator can found his or her reasoning on certain principles of law. The principle of good faith is one of the most powerful of these principles.

The second thing this enquiry has shown is that the legal order has its own, peculiar, concept of good faith. This concept cannot be equated with the popular use of the term, which is suggestive of a vague idea of good and altruistic behaviour. It is a fact of experience that states act to maximise their interests, that some of them are prone to power politics, and that policy not infrequently pushes leaders into stratagems involving lies, manoeuvring and manipulation. This sociological state of affairs does not detract from the existence and operation of a principle of good faith on the legal plane. There, reciprocity, rule-orientation and faithfulness to certain common aims cannot be just given up without destroying the legal order itself. However, the general sociological environment has its impact upon the legal principle of good faith. The operator must be sensitive to what happens in the real world when the duties of states are shaped under the principle of good faith. In particular, constructions that are too bold could be self-defeating by reason of remaining utterly unrealistic.

Lastly, this study has shown that the main functions of the principle of good faith are the following:

(i) protection of the legitimate expectations of the subjects of law and search for stability, legal certainty and foreseeability;
(ii) protection of the object and purpose of legal processes against excessive unilateral action jeopardising the common processes and interest;
(iii) in both mentioned regards, the principle is a sort of counterpart to the principle of (real) intention: real but hidden intention cannot be opposed to the subject which could rely on a certain conduct and its objective social meaning, as much as unilateral reasons and will cannot prevail over the

protection of common objects and purposes; thus, good faith is an antithesis or a limitation on voluntarism as much as it is to unilateralism;

(iv) the principle further prohibits abusive and arbitrary action, notably the use of legal entitlements for aims and purposes alien to their grant and harmful to others or to the collectivity at large;

(v) overall, the principle of good faith imposes a certain nuanced standard of correction. The issue of subjective good faith remains of subordinate importance in the international legal order. Thus, 'objective good faith' is incomparably more present and important than 'subjective good faith', ie excusable errors.

Can all the various legal aspects mentioned above find their way into a single principle, ie good faith? Is that purported unity not just a speculation or an abstraction? To this, one may respond that unity is always a matter of belief, while multiplicity is a matter of experience. The following text of an ancient thinker may illuminate the matter. It is sufficient for the reader to replace the word 'power' by the concept of 'good faith':

> A hand may very well control an entire mass, a long plank, or anything of that sort; the control is effective throughout and yet is not distributed, unit for unit, over the object of control: the power is felt to reach over the whole area, though the hand is only hand-long, not taking the extension of the mass it wields; lengthen the object and, provided that the total is within the strength, the power handles the new load with no need of distributing itself over the increased area. Now let us eliminate the corporeal mass of the hand, retaining the power it exerted: is not that power, the impartible, present integrally over the entire area of control?.[1]

[1] Plotinus, *Enneads*, VI, 4, 7.

BIBLIOGRAPHY

Books

CAVARÉ, L, *La notion de bonne foi et quelques-unes de ses applications en droit international public, Cours de l'Institut de Hautes Etudes Internationales* (Paris, 1963–64).

CHENG, B, *General Principles of Law—As Applied by International Courts and Tribunals* (London, 1953) 105–60.

COT, JP, *La bonne foi en droit international public, Cours de l'Institut de Hautes Etudes Internationales* (Paris, 1968–69).

KOLB, R, *La bonne foi en droit international public* (Paris, 2000).

MÜLLER, JP, *Vertrauensschutz im Völkerrecht* (Köln, 1971).

O'CONNOR, JF, *Good Faith in International Law* (Aldershot, 1991).

YAKEMTCHOUK, R, *La bonne foi dans la conduite internationale des Etats* (Paris, 2002).

ZOLLER, E, *La bonne foi en droit international public* (Paris, 1977).

Articles

COT, JP, 'La bonne foi et la conclusion des traités' (1968) 4 *Revue belge de droit international* 140–59.

D'AMATO, A, 'Good Faith' (1984) 7 *EPIL* 107–09.

DRAGHICI, M, 'Le respect des obligations internationales par le principe de bonne foi (*pacta sunt servanda*)' (1984) 33 *Annuaire de l'Université de Bucarest* 55–60.

FITZMAURICE, GG, 'The Law and Procedure of the International Court of Justice 1954–9, General Principles and Sources of International Law' (1959) 35 *BYIL* 207–16.

HASSAN, T, 'Good Faith in Treaty Formation' (1981) 21 *Virginia Journal of International Law* 443–81.

HEYDTE, F, Von der, 'Die *bona fides* und die einzelne Rechtsnorm' (1961) 11 *Österreichische Zeitschrift für öffentliches Recht* 364–74.

KOLB, R, 'La bonne foi en droit international public' (1998) 31 *Revue belge de droit international* 661–732.

—— 'Aperçus sur la bonne foi en droit international public' (2001) 54 *Revue hellénique de droit internationa* 1–42, 383–428.

—— 'Article 2, § 2' in B Simma, DE Khan, G Nolte and A Paulus (eds), *The Charter of the United Nations, A Commentary*, vol I, 3rd edn (Oxford, 2012) 166–80.

KOTZUR, M, 'Good Faith (Bona Fides)' in R Wolfrum (ed), *The Max Planck Encyclopedia of Public International Law*, vol II (Oxford, 2012) 508–15.

LACHS, M, 'Some Thoughts on the Role of Good Faith in International Relations' in RJ Akkerman, PJ van Krieken and CO Pannenborg (eds), *Declaration on Principles—A Quest for Universal Peace, Essays in Honor of BVA Röling* (Leiden, 1977) 47–55.

MARKOVIC, M, 'Fulfilment in Good Faith of Obligations Assumed in Accordance with the Charter' in M Sahovic (ed), *Principles of International Law Concerning Friendly Relations and Cooperation* (Belgrade, Institute of International Politics and Economics, 1972) 375–424.

MÖSSNER, JM, 'Vertrauen als Prinzip der Völkerrechtsordnung' (1979) 3 *Politik und Kultur* 56–66.

—— 'Vertrauen in der internationalen Politik, Völkerrechtliche Aspekte' in B Simma, E Blenk-Knocke (eds), *Zwischen Intervention und Zusammenarbeit*, (Berlin, 1979) 245–97.

PAUL, V, 'The Abuse of Rights and Bona Fides in International Law' (1977) 28 *Österreichische Zeitschrift für öffentliches Recht* 107–30.

SCHWARZENBERGER, G, 'The Fundamental Principles of International Law' (1955–I) 87 *Recueil des cours de l'Académie de droit international de La Haye* 290–326.

SPERDUTI, G, 'Il principio della buona fede e l'ammissione di nuovi membri nelle Nazioni Unite' (1952) 7 *Comunità internazionale* 42–62.

STUYT, A M, 'Good and Bad Faith' (1981) 28 *Netherlands International Law Journal* 54–58.

THIRLWAY, H, 'The Law and Procedure of the International Court of Justice (1960–1989): General Principles and Sources of Law' (1989) 60 *BYIL* 7–49.

VERDROSS, A, 'La bonne foi comme fondement du droit international public' (1952) 5 *Revue hellénique de droit international* 17–21.

—— 'Die bona fides als Grundlage des Völkerrechts' in DS Constantopoulos and H Wehberg (eds), *Gegenwartsprobleme des internationalen Rechtes und der Rechtsphilosophie, Essays in Honor of R Laun* (Hamburg, 1953) 29–33.

—— 'Bona Fides' in K Strupp and HJ Schlochauer (eds) *Wörterbuch des Völkerrechts*, vol I (Berlin, 1960) 223–24.

VIRALLY, M, 'Review Essay: Good Faith in Public International Law' (1983) 77 *AJIL* 130–34.

WHITE, G, 'The Principle of Good Faith' in V Lowe and C Warbrick (eds), *The United Nations and the Principles of International Law, Essays in Honor of M Akehurst* (London, 1994) 230–55.

ZOLLER, E, 'La bonne foi en droit international public' (1994) 43 *Travaux de l'Association H Capitant, La bonne foi* 569–82.

—— 'Article 2, paragraphe 2, de la Charte' in JP Cot, A Pellet and M Forteau (eds), *La Charte des Nations Unies—Commentaire article par article*, 3rd edn, vol I (Paris, 2005) 417–23.

INDEX

Ingram Content Group UK Ltd.
Milton Keynes UK
UKHW021155040423
419514UK00003B/113

9 781509 914098